Lecture Notes in Computer Science 7981

Commenced Publication in 1973
Founding and Former Series Editors:
Gerhard Goos, Juris Hartmanis, and Jan van Leeuwen

Emiliano De Cristofaro   Matthew Wright (Eds.)

Privacy Enhancing Technologies

13th International Symposium, PETS 2013
Bloomington, IN, USA, July 10-12, 2013
Proceedings

 Springer

Volume Editors

Emiliano De Cristofaro
Palo Alto Research Center (PARC)
3333 Coyote Hill Road, Palo Alto, CA 94034, USA
E-mail: me@emilianodc.com

Matthew Wright
University of Texas at Arlington
Department of Computer Science and Engineering
500 UTA Boulevard, Arlington, TX 76019, USA
E-mail: mwright@cse.uta.edu

ISSN 0302-9743   e-ISSN 1611-3349
ISBN 978-3-642-39076-0   e-ISBN 978-3-642-39077-7
DOI 10.1007/978-3-642-39077-7
Springer Heidelberg Dordrecht London New York

Library of Congress Control Number: 2013940937

CR Subject Classification (1998): K.6.5, D.4.6, C.2, E.3, H.3-4, J.1

LNCS Sublibrary: SL 4 – Security and Cryptology

Typesetting: Camera-ready by author, data conversion by Scientific Publishing Services, Chennai, India

Printed on acid-free paper

Springer is part of Springer Science+Business Media (www.springer.com)

Preface

As the amount and the sensitivity of information disseminated in the online world grow, so do related privacy concerns. Extensive surveillance and massive tracking of users on the Web are only some of the threats to individual privacy. In the big data era, information increasingly equals power and money, and organizations are thus motivated to collect and retain large quantities of personal and, increasingly, contextual information.

These concerns motivate the need for privacy-enhancing technologies, such as data protection, anonymity networks, decentralization, zero-knowledge, and secure computation, by which individuals can achieve privacy in the online world.

The 13th Privacy Enhancing Technologies Symposium (PETS 2013) brought together privacy and anonymity experts from around the world to discuss recent advances and new perspectives. It fostered novel research efforts toward designing and building systems for privacy and anonymity protection as well as analyzing challenges and threats.

There were 69 papers submitted to PETS 2013, and each received an average of 4.33 reviews from the 43 members of the Program Committee (PC). Following an intensive discussion among the reviewers and other PC members, 13 papers were accepted for presentation. Topics addressed by the papers published in these proceedings include data privacy, privacy-oriented cryptography, location privacy, performance of the Tor network, censorship evasion, traffic analysis, and user-related privacy perspectives.

Compared to recent PETS editions, the number of PC members was increased to accommodate a broader range of expertise, deliver a greater number of reviews, and involve a wider representation of both senior and junior researchers.

We maintained the tradition of dedicating one day of PETS to the Workshop on Hot Topics on Privacy Enhancing Technologies (HotPETs), at which participants discussed exciting–though possibly preliminary–ideas. HotPETs 2013 included a keynote talk by Helen Nissenbaum of New York University. As with the previous five HotPETs editions, there are no published proceedings for Hot-PETs, except on the dark side of the moon.

PETS 2013 also included a keynote talk by Lorrie Cranor of Carnegie Mellon University, a rump session with brief presentations on a variety of topics, and two panels.

We would like to thank all PETS and HotPETs authors, especially those who presented their work that was selected for the program, as well as keynote speakers, panelists, and rump session presenters. We are very grateful to the PC members and additional reviewers, who contributed to editorial decisions with thorough reviews and actively participated in the PC discussions, ensuring a high quality of all accepted papers. We owe special thanks to the following PC members and reviewers who volunteered to shepherd some of the accepted papers:

Damon McCoy, Michael Hay, Jim Graves, Eugene Vasserman, Roger Dingledine, Julien Freudiger, Srdjan Capkun, Elaine Shi, and Alexei Czeskis. We gratefully acknowledge the outstanding contributions of the PETS 2013 General Chair, XiaoFeng Wang, the members of the Local Arrangements Committee, Apu Kapadia, Raquel Hill, and Haixu Tang, as well as our webmaster of seven years, Jeremy Clark. Moreover, our gratitude goes to the HotPETs 2013 Chairs, Prateek Mittal and Reza Shokri, who put together an excellent program. Last but not least, we would like to thank our sponsors, the Indiana University School of Informatics and Computing and Center for Security Informatics, the Indiana University Center for Applied Cybersecurity Research, and the Indiana University Pervasive Technology Institute, for their generous support, as well as Microsoft for its continued sponsorship with travel stipends.

May 2013   Emiliano De Cristofaro
                                                           Matthew Wright

Organization

Program Committee

Alessandro Acquisti	Carnegie Mellon University, USA
Kevin Bauer	MIT Lincoln Laboratory, USA
Michael Brennan	SecondMuse, USA
Srdjan Capkun	ETH Zurich, Switzerland
Claude Castelluccia	INRIA, France
Alexei Czeskis	University of Washington, USA
George Danezis	Microsoft Research, UK
Emiliano De Cristofaro	PARC (a Xerox company), USA
Roger Dingledine	The Tor Project, USA
Simone Fischer-Hübner	Karlstad University, Sweden
Julien Freudiger	PARC (a Xerox company), USA
Xinwen Fu	University of Massachusetts Lowell, USA
Seda Gürses	K.U. Leuven, Belgium
Michael Hay	Colgate University, USA
Jean-Pierre Hubaux	EPFL, Switzerland
Aaron Johnson	U.S. Naval Research Laboratory, USA
Jaeyeon Jung	Microsoft Research, USA
Apu Kapadia	Indiana University, USA
Markulf Kohlweiss	Microsoft Research, UK
Balachander Krishnamurthy	AT&T Labs–Research, USA
Adam J. Lee	University of Pittsburgh, USA
Anja Lehmann	IBM Research - Zurich, Switzerland
Marc Liberatore	University of Massachusetts Amherst, USA
Janne Lindqvist	Rutgers University, USA
Benjamin Livshits	Microsoft Research, USA
Damon Mccoy	George Mason University, USA
Prateek Mittal	University of California, Berkeley, USA
Gregory Neven	IBM Research - Zurich, Switzerland
Claudio Orlandi	Aarhus University, Denmark
Siani Pearson	HP Labs, UK
Alessandra Sala	Alcatel Lucent Bell Labs, Ireland
Pierangela Samarati	Università degli Studi di Milano, Italy
Elaine Shi	University of Maryland, College Park, USA
Reza Shokri	EPFL, Switzerland

Radu Sion   Stony Brook University, USA
Jessica Staddon   Google
Carmela Troncoso   Gradiant, Belgium
Eugene Vasserman   Kansas State University, USA
Lingyu Wang   Concordia University, Canada
Matthew Wright   University of Texas at Arlington, USA
Ting Yu   North Carolina State University, USA
Nan Zhang   The George Washington University, USA
Melek Önen   Eurecom, France

Additional Reviewers

Acar, Gunes   Graves, Jim
Acs, Gergely   Grothoff, Christian
Adjerid, Idris   Herrmann, Michael
Afroz, Sadia   Houmansadr, Amir
Androulaki, Elli   Huguenin, Kévin
Angulo, Julio   Kaafar, Mohamed Ali
Au, Man Ho   Kate, Aniket
Aviv, Adam   Kerschbaum, Florian
Ayday, Erman   Knezevic, Nikola
Bajaj, Sumeet   Lauradoux, Cedric
Balasch, Josep   Lerner, Adam
Balsa, Ero   Ling, Zhen
Beato, Filipe   Liu, Wenming
Berthold, Stefan   Liu, Zhongli
Brandimarte, Laura   Luo, Daniel Xiapu
Catalano, Dario   Olumofin, Femi
Chaabane, Abdelberi   Oya, Simon
Chaintreau, Augustin   Polychroniadou, Antigoni
Chen, Yinjie   Reardon, Joel
Cunche, Mathieu   Roca, Vincent
De Capitani Di Vimercati, Sabrina   Rubinstein, Benjamin
Diaz, Claudia   Ruiz Vicente, Carmen
Elahi, Tariq   Samat, Sonam
Elkhiyaoui, Kaoutar   Soriente, Claudio
Faran, Nicholas   Stefanov, Emil
Foresti, Sara   Visconti, Ivan
Gambs, Sebastien   Wang, Qiyan
Garg, Vaibhav   Winter, Philipp
Garrison, William   Zikas, Vassilis
Gasti, Paolo

Table of Contents

Optimizing ORAM and Using It Efficiently for Secure Computation 1
  Craig Gentry, Kenny A. Goldman, Shai Halevi, Charanjit Julta,
  Mariana Raykova, and Daniel Wichs

Anonymity-Preserving Public-Key Encryption: A Constructive
Approach 19
  Markulf Kohlweiss, Ueli Maurer, Cristina Onete,
  Björn Tackmann, and Daniele Venturi

Efficient E-Cash in Practice: NFC-Based Payments for Public
Transportation Systems. 40
  Gesine Hinterwälder, Christian T. Zenger, Foteini Baldimtsi,
  Anna Lysyanskaya, Christof Paar, and Wayne P. Burleson

Efficient Privacy-Preserving Stream Aggregation in Mobile Sensing
with Low Aggregation Error 60
  Qinghua Li and Guohong Cao

Broadening the Scope of Differential Privacy Using Metrics. 82
  Konstantinos Chatzikokolakis, Miguel E. Andrés,
  Nicolás Emilio Bordenabe, and Catuscia Palamidessi

Turning Off GPS Is Not Enough: Cellular Location Leaks over the
Internet 103
  Hamed Soroush, Keen Sung, Erik Learned-Miller,
  Brian Neil Levine, and Marc Liberatore

How Others Compromise Your Location Privacy: The Case of Shared
Public IPs at Hotspots 123
  Nevena Vratonjic, Kévin Huguenin, Vincent Bindschaedler, and
  Jean-Pierre Hubaux

The Path Less Travelled: Overcoming Tor's Bottlenecks with Traffic
Splitting 143
  Mashael AlSabah, Kevin Bauer, Tariq Elahi, and Ian Goldberg

How Low Can You Go: Balancing Performance with Anonymity
in Tor 164
  John Geddes, Rob Jansen, and Nicholas Hopper

OSS: Using Online Scanning Services for Censorship Circumvention 185
  David Fifield, Gabi Nakibly, and Dan Boneh

The Need for Flow Fingerprints to Link Correlated Network Flows   205
  Amir Houmansadr and Nikita Borisov

How Much Is Too Much? Leveraging Ads Audience Estimation to
Evaluate Public Profile Uniqueness   225
  Terence Chen, Abdelberi Chaabane, Pierre Ugo Tournoux,
  Mohamed-Ali Kaafar, and Roksana Boreli

On the Acceptance of Privacy-Preserving Authentication Technology:
The Curious Case of National Identity Cards   245
  Marian Harbach, Sascha Fahl, Matthias Rieger, and Matthew Smith

Author Index   265

Optimizing ORAM and Using It Efficiently for Secure Computation

Craig Gentry[1], Kenny A. Goldman[1], Shai Halevi[1], Charanjit Julta[1],
Mariana Raykova[1], and Daniel Wichs[2,*]

[1] IBM Research
[2] Northeastern University

Abstract. Oblivious RAM (ORAM) allows a client to access her data
on a remote server while hiding the *access pattern* (which locations she
is accessing) from the server. Beyond its immediate utility in allowing
private computation over a client's outsourced data, ORAM also allows
mutually distrustful parties to run secure-computations over their joint
data with sublinear on-line complexity. In this work we revisit the tree-
based ORAM of Shi et al. [20] and show how to optimize its performance
as a stand-alone scheme, as well as its performance within higher level
constructions. More specifically, we make several contributions:

- We describe two optimizations to the tree-based ORAM protocol of
  Shi et al., one reducing the storage overhead of that protocol by an
  $O(k)$ multiplicative factor, and another reducing its time complexity
  by an $O(\log k)$ multiplicative factor, where k is the security parameter. Our scheme also enjoys a much simpler and tighter analysis than
  the original protocol.
- We describe a protocol for binary search over this ORAM construction, where the entire binary search operation is done in the same
  complexity as a single ORAM access (as opposed to $\log n$ accesses
  for the naive protocol). We then describe simple uses of this binary-
  search protocol for things like range queries and keyword search.
- We show how the ORAM protocol itself and our binary-search protocol can be implemented efficiently as secure computation, using
  somewhat-homomorphic encryption.

Since memory accesses by address (ORAM access) or by value (binary
search) are basic and prevalent operations, we believe that these optimizations can be used to significantly speed-up many higher-level protocols for secure computation.

1 Introduction

Oblivious RAM. Oblivious RAM (ORAM), introduced by Goldreich and Ostrovsky [9,16,11], allows a client to outsource her data to a remote server (e.g., "the
cloud") and access it efficiently and privately. In particular, the client can access

---

* Work done in part while in IBM Research.

E. De Cristofaro and M. Wright (Eds.): PETS 2013, LNCS 7981, pp. 1–18, 2013.

individual elements of her data without revealing to the server *which* elements she is accessing. The efficiency of the client and server on each such data access should be small and essentially independent of (polylogarithmic in) the size of the entire client data. Using ORAM, a client can privately execute arbitrary RAM computations over her remotely stored data, without having to download the data from the server in its entirety. In particular, the client/server computation and communication is essentially only proportional to the time-complexity of the RAM computation itself (with polylogarithmic overhead). Therefore ORAM offers tremendous savings when the client wants to execute simple computations (e.g., binary search) over huge amounts of data.

ORAM for Multiparty Computation. Another use of ORAM is to speed up *secure multi-party computation (MPC)* protocols (e.g., [21,10] etc.), where two or more parties want to execute some computation over their inputs without revealing the inputs to each other. When the total size of the input is large (e.g., one of the inputs is a large database), one may often want to compute functions whose running time on a RAM is sublinear in the total size of the input. However, secure computation protocols that use either Boolean or arithmetic circuits as a representation of the evaluated functionality, inherently incur computation complexity at least linear in the total size of the input for each secure evaluation. This is also the case for secure computation based on fully homomorphic encryption [6,5,4,3,7] that uses arithmetic circuits. Several works [17,14] have demonstrated that ORAM can be used to construct secure computation protocols whose (amortized) complexity can be sub-linear in the total size of the input. In particular, the efficiency of these protocols is proportional to the time-complexity of the underlying computation on a RAM (which may be sublinear in the input size), in contrast to traditional approaches whose efficiency is proportional to the circuit size of the underlying computation (which cannot be sublinear in the input size).

Efficiency of ORAM. Although there has been much recent progress in constructing progressively more efficient ORAM schemes [18,12,20,13], the concrete computation and storage overhead introduced by ORAM is usually significant in practice. Most ORAM schemes are based on a hierarchical structure of [11]. Despite their asymptotic efficiency, these schemes suffer in practice due to their reliance on fairly complex "sorting networks". (Some constructions also have large "spikes" of complexity, where every so often the client and server need run a maintenance procedure of complexity linear in the entire data set.) A recent solution of Shi et al. [20] (which we describe in Section 2) takes a very different approach over these other schemes. Despite having worse asymptotic performance, it is significantly simpler to implement (and understand conceptually), and is deemed to be more efficient in practice because it does not hide any large constant factors. It has been implemented and used in past projects [14]. The client/server computation and communication needed to perform each operation in this protocol is $O(k \log^2 N)$, and the server storage is $O(kN)$, where N is the size of the client data and k is the "security parameter." (Roughly in every operation we incur at most a 2^{-k}-probability of privacy loss. Clearly to support M operations we need $k \gg \log M$ where M is the number of operations; a typical setting may be $k \in [50, 80]$.)

1.1   Our Results

We propose some significant optimizations to the ORAM construction of Shi et al. [20] and its use in performing private RAM computation over outsourced data and secure multiparty computation. These optimizations improve both asymptotic and concrete efficiency of the scheme. We briefly describe each of these optimizations below.

Reduced Storage and Query Time. One of the main disadvantages of the Shi et al. scheme is the large $O(k)$ multiplicative storage overhead on the server. We show a very simple modification to the scheme that gets rid of this overhead; the server only needs to store $O(N)$ bits for N bits of client data (the hidden constant is no more than 4). Another modification improves the computation and communication complexity by a factor of $\log k$ from $O(k \log^2 N)$ to $O(k \log^2 N / \log k)$, and also greatly simplifies and tightens the analysis. Since we usually assume that $N = k^c$ for some small constant c, our improved time/communication complexity simply becomes $O(k \log N)$. These improvements only require relatively minor changes to the scheme of Shi et al., and do not introduce any hidden complexity to its implementation (in fact they may make it even easier to implement). Together, these changes yield a scheme whose asymptotic efficiency matches the best "hierarchal ORAM" construction, while being significantly simpler and with much better concrete efficiency.

Optimized Binary Search. One of the most commonly used sub-linear time operations over large data is *binary search*. This operation is performed whenever executing any query over an indexed database (or sorted data) and only accesses logarithmic number of elements in the database. A direct execution of binary search using ORAM requires a logarithmic number of ORAM queries. We propose a modification for the ORAM scheme of Shi et al. [20] (or our variant of it) that allows the execution of binary search with the efficiency of a single ORAM query.

Optimizations Using Homomorphic Encryption. Lastly, we show that it is possible to optimize the asymptotic communication complexity and the client's computation time using *homomorphic encryption* (HE) [6]. Moreover, by only relying on very limited low-complexity homomorphic operations, these optimizations can be made practically efficient using *somewhat* homomorphic encryption schemes. In particular, the client's computation and the communication complexity per data access is reduced from at least $O(k \log^2 N / \log k)$ to $O(k \log N)$. This may provide a constant-factor savings even for $N = k^c$, and the saving gets larger for larger value of N.

2   Tree ORAM Construction

In this section we summarize the oblivious RAM (ORAM) construction of Shi et al. [20]. Recall that an ORAM construction allows a client to request storage blocks from a server in a way that hides the access pattern. Roughly, the server should not be able to discern if an access query refers to the same storage block as a previous query, or to a new block that was not queried before. The original protocol of Shi et al. uses $O(k \cdot DN \log N)$ storage on the server to store a database of N elements, each of which is D-bits long, with security parameter k (i.e., with failure probability $\exp(-k)$). The client only needs $O(k \log n(D + \log D))$ memory,[1] and the time complexity of the protocol is $O(k \log^2 N(D + \log N))$ per access.

We note that most prior work assumed a computation model with D-bit word size, so the expressions above become $O(kN \log N)$ and $O(k \log^2 N)$, respectively, but here we stick to the more accurate notation that includes also the D factors. We also note that in [20] they use $k = O(\log N)$, but again here we follow the more standard convention of having a separate security parameter, unrelated to the database size.

2.1   Recursive Structure

At the heart of the construction of Shi et al. is the following recursive structure: Suppose that we have an underlying basic ORAM protocol, where the client stores a *table* of N "addresses" of size $\log N$ bits in order to implement oblivious access to a *database* of N elements of size $D > 2 \log N$ bits (and moreover, a single ORAM access to the database only requires a accessing a single address in the table). Since the client's table is at most half the size of the database, it suggests storing the table itself in the same ORAM structure recursively, reducing the client storage by a factor of two with every level of recursion.

In more detail, in level 0 of the recursion the client "outsources" a database consisting of $N_0 := N$ values of D bits each, using a client-stored table consisting of N_0 addresses of size $\log N_0$ bits each. In each future level, the client outsources the table of the previous level using the underlying scheme. In level $i + 1$ of the recursion, the client outsources a table with N_i entries of size $\log N_i$ bits, by thinking of it as a database of $N_{i+1} = \lceil N_i/2 \rceil$ elements, each of of size $2 \log N_i$ bits. This is done using the underlying basic ORAM construction, in which the client only needs to store a level $i + 1$ table of N_{i+1} entries of $\log N_{i+1}$ bits each. Repeating this for $\log N$ levels of recursion reduces the client table to only a constant number of entries.

To access the j'th entry of the level-i table, the client computes the address of that entry in the level-$(i + 1)$ database (with $N_{i+1} = \lceil N_i/2 \rceil$ elements), specifically that address is $j' = \lfloor j/2 \rfloor$. The client uses the level-$(i + 1)$ basic ORAM to fetch that element, and extracts from it the desired entry. For that instance of

---

[1] The client memory can be made as small as $O(k + D + \log N)$, but in the variant that we describe here the server's messages can be as long as $O(k \log N(D + \log N))$ so the client needs this much memory just to store them.

the basic ORAM protocol, the client needs to access a single entry of its level-$(i + 1)$ table, and this is done recursively using the level-$(i + 1)$ basic ORAM. Therefore, altogether, the recursive scheme uses at most $\log N$ accesses of the underlying ORAM.

Clearly, the same recursive structure can be applied with any integer factor $\tau \geq 2$ between the size of successive levels. Specifically, we store the i-level client table (with N_i entries) as a database of $N_{i+1} = \lceil N_i / \tau \rceil$ elements of size $\tau \log N_i$ bits, accessing the j'th entry of the level-i table is done by retrieving the element $j' = \lfloor j/\tau \rfloor$ in the corresponding database, and we use $\log_\tau(N)$ levels of recursion. The drawback of using a large value of τ is that the size of elements in the i-level database grows linearly with τ, which impacts the running time of the underlying basic ORAM protocol. Below we assume that τ is a small constant, e.g., $\tau = 4$.

2.2   The Underlying Basic ORAM

The underlying basic ORAM protocol from [20] has the server keeping an N-element database in a complete binary tree of depth $\log N$, where each node in the tree contains a bucket large enough to store k data elements (k is the security parameter). Of course, the content of all the buckets is encrypted under the client's key, in particular the server does not know how many elements are actually stored in each bucket.

Each database element with logical address $v \in [N]$ is associated with a random leaf L_v, and the client keeps an N-entry table of the mapping $v \mapsto L_v$. (I.e., entry v in the table contains the leaf number L_v.)

Denote by d_v the data corresponding to logical address v. Throughout the protocol we maintain the invariant that the triple (L_v, v, d_v) is stored in one of the buckets on the path from the root to the leaf L_v. (Initially it is stored at the leaf itself.) Access to logical address v consists of two subroutines, one for doing the actual access and another one to clean up after the first.

Access. To access the data associated with logical address v, the client looks up L_v in its table and asks the server for the entire path from the root to leaf L_v. Upon receiving all the buckets in this path, the client decrypts them, finds a triple of the form (L_v, v, d_v) in one of the buckets (for some d_v), and this value d_v is the requested data.

The client either leaves the data unchanged (if the operation is a read) or overwrites it with a new value (if it is a write), and we denote the resulting data by d'_v. In either case, it chooses a new random leaf $L'_v \in [N]$ and updates its table with the new L'_v value. The client then removes the triple (L_v, v, d_v) from the bucket where it was found, and instead puts the triple (L'_v, v, d'_v) in the root bucket. Finally it re-encrypts all the buckets and send them back to the server, who replaces all the buckets on the path to L_v by the new encrypted buckets.

Observe that since the new triple is placed at the root, then this operation does not violate the tree invariant that we maintain.

Eviction. To prevent the root bucket from overflowing, the client and server run a "maintenance" subroutine whose goal is to evict triples from their current buckets and push them to buckets lower down the tree. Specifically, the client chooses at random two nodes from every level of the tree except the leaves. For every chosen node, it asks the server for the buckets in that node and its two children. The client decrypts these buckets, and if the parent bucket contains any triples then it chooses one of them at random, which we denote by (L_v, v, d_v). The client removes that triple from the parent bucket, and pushes it to the bucket of one of the two children.

The child to which this triple is evicted is determined by L_v. Namely, the tree invariant tells us that this triple is currently found in some node on the path from the root to leaf number L_v, and the client just pushes it one level down on that path. Clearly, this operation maintains the tree invariant. The client then re-encrypts the buckets of the parent and its two children and send them back to the server, who stores the new buckets in place of the old ones.

Shi et al. proved in [20] that the probability of any bucket overflowing is small. Specifically, the probability of an overflow in m operations is bounded by $O(mN/\exp(k))$. They also proved that as long as no overflow occurs, the view of the server is computationally independent of the access pattern (assuming the security of the encryption scheme).

2.3   Putting It Together

In the complete construction of [20], the server keeps $\ell - 1 = \lceil \log_\tau(N) \rceil - 1$ complete binary trees, with the level-i tree having $\tau^{\ell-i}$ leaves (rounded up to a power of 2). Each node in every tree has a bucket large enough to store k "entries", each entry is assigned a (changing) random leaf of the tree, and we maintain the invariant that each entry can be found in one of the buckets on the path from the root to "its leaf."

In the largest tree ($i = 0$), each entry corresponds to one logical address $v \in \{0, \ldots, N-1\}$, and it contains the user data for that logical address. For the next tree ($i = 1$), each entry corresponds to a size-τ interval of logical addresses, and it contains the τ leaf-numbers in the largest tree that are currently assigned to the entries of those τ logical addresses. More generally, each entry in the tree at level $i + 1$ corresponds to the union of τ level-i intervals (which is itself a size-τ^{i+1} interval of logical addresses), and that entry contains τ leaf-numbers of the level-i tree, namely the leaves that are currently assigned to the entries of those τ level-i intervals. With each entry in every tree we store also the first logical address of the interval of that entry, as well as the leaf that is currently assigned to that entry. Thus each entry is of the form

$$\begin{array}{ll} \text{level-0}: & (\ L^*, v, \text{user-data} \quad\quad\quad) \\ \text{level} > 0: & (\ L^*, v, (L_1, L_2, \ldots, L_\tau)\ ) \end{array}$$

where L^* is the leaf currently assigned to that entry, $[v, v + \tau^i)$ is its interval, and $(L_1, L_2, \ldots, L_\tau)$ are the leafs in the next tree that are currently assigned to the τ sub-intervals

$$[v, v + \tau^{i-1}), \ [v + \tau^{i-1}, v + 2\tau^{i-1}), \ [v + 2\tau^{i-1}, v + 3\tau^{i-1}), \ \ldots$$

Of course, all of the buckets in all of the trees are encrypted under a key known to the client.

The "tree at the last level ℓ", which has a single node, is kept by the client. That tree has just a single entry, corresponding to the interval $[0, \tau^\ell)$, and containing τ leaf-numbers of the tree at level $\ell - 1$ that are currently assigned to the entries of the sub-intervals $[0, \tau^{\ell-1}), [\tau^{\ell-1}, 2\tau^{\ell-1}), \ldots$

ORAM Access Query. To access the logical address v, the client looks up in its level-ℓ "tree" for the list $(L_1^{(\ell-1)}, \ldots, L_\tau^{(\ell-1)})$, and determines the level-$(\ell - 1)$ sub-interval containing v, namely j such that $(j - 1)\tau^{\ell-1} \le v < j\tau^{\ell-1}$. The client sets $v_{\ell-1} = (j - 1)\tau^{\ell-1}$ and $L^{(\ell-1)} = L_j^{(\ell-1)}$, chooses at random a new leaf $\hat{L}^{(\ell-1)}$ and replaces $L_j^{(\ell-1)}$ by this new value in the list. Then the client proceeds iteratively for $i = \ell - 1$ down to 0:

1. Request from the server all the buckets on the path from the root of the level-i tree down to the leaf $L^{(i)}$. Decrypt them and find in them an entry of the form $(L^{(i)}, v_i, \mathsf{data})$.
2. If $i > 0$ do the following:

   (a) Parse $\mathsf{data} = (L_1^{(i-1)}, \ldots, L_\tau^{(i-1)})$, choose a new random leaf in the next tree, $\hat{L}^{(i-1)}$.
   (b) Determine the level-$(i-1)$ sub-interval containing v, namely j such that $v_i + (j - 1)\tau^{i-1} \le v < v_i + j\tau^{i-1}$. Set $v_{i-1} = v_i + (j - 1)\tau^{i-1}$ and $L^{(i-1)} = L_j^{(i-1)}$.
   (c) Replace $L_j^{(i-1)}$ by $\hat{L}^{(i-1)}$ inside data, denoting the result by data'.
   Else $(i = 0)$, if this is a write operation then set data' to be the new value. Otherwise (read), set $\mathsf{data}' = \mathsf{data}$.
3. Remove the entry $(L^{(i)}, v_i, \mathsf{data})$ from the bucket where is was found, and instead place in the root bucket the entry $(\hat{L}^{(i)}, v_i, \mathsf{data}')$. Re-encrypt all the buckets and send to the server.

Finally, the client and server run the Eviction subroutine for each of the trees $i = 0, 1, \ldots, \ell - 1$. If this was a read operation then the return value is the data value from the last level $i = 0$.

The complexity of this protocol is essentially linear in the amount of information sent between the client and server. This information consists of a constant number of buckets from every level in every tree. Since the $(\ell - i)$'th tree has depth $\log_2(\tau^i) = i \log_2 \tau$, then the number of buckets sent is

$$\log_2 \tau \cdot \sum_{i=0}^{\ell-1} i = O(\log \tau \cdot \ell^2) = O(\log \tau \cdot (\log N / \log \tau)^2) = O(\log^2 N / \log \tau)$$

(with $\log N$ buckets sent in the largest tree). Each bucket has size either $O(k(D + \log N))$ (for the largest tree) or $O(k\tau \log N)$ (for all the smaller trees), hence the total communication (and computation) complexity is

$$O(\log^2 N / \log \tau) \cdot O(k\tau \log N) + \log_2 N \cdot O(k(D + \log N)) = O(k \log^2 N(D + \tau \log N / \log \tau)).$$

Using a small constant for τ, we get the claimed complexity of $O(k \log^2 N(D + \log N))$.

3   Parameter Optimizations for the Tree ORAM Scheme

In this section we present two optimization for the underlying basic tree-based ORAM construction of Shi et al. [20]. First we describe in Section 3.1 a very simple optimization that saves a factor of $O(k)$ in the storage overhead of the protocol. Then in Section 3.2 we describe a somewhat more involved optimization that reduces the time complexity per access by a factor of $O(\log k)$, and also considerably simplifies and tightens the overflow-probability analysis.

3.1   Reducing the Height of the ORAM Tree

The construction from [20] uses an N-leaf tree to store an N-element database. We first observe that increasing just slightly the capacity of the buckets, one can achieve the same overflow probability for many more elements than leaves. Note that the buckets in [20] are large enough to keep $O(k)$ elements, but the expected number of elements in each bucket in only $O(1)$, which is the reason for the $O(k)$ overhead in storage. We observer, however, that we can increase the expected number of elements per bucket to any desired number m, while keeping the overflow probability at $\exp(-k)$, simply by making the bucket capacity $O(m+k)$, thus reducing the overhead to $O(m/k)$. Hence by setting $m = k$, we reduce the storage overhead to only $O(1)$.

Specifically, by making the capacity of each bucket be $2k$ (rather than k as in [20]), we can use a shallower tree with only n/k leaves to store n elements. We reduce the number of nodes by a factor of k while increasing the bucket size by only a factor of 2, thus getting a factor $k/2$ saving in storage.

For this new setting, it is enough to analyze the overflow probability only in the leaves, since all the internal nodes have the exact same behavior as in the original construction of [20]. For the leaves we have the following:

Lemma 1. *Fix one particular leaf (out of the n/k leaves in the tree) and one particular access operation. With the bucket of that leaf having size $2k$, the overflow probability for this leaf in that operation is at most $e^{-k/3}$.*

Proof. For any fixed access operation, we can model the content of the leaves as having n balls thrown randomly into n/k bins. The expected number of balls in a bin is k, and using Chernoff bound [1] we get that the probability that any particular bin has more than $2k$ balls is upper-bounded by $e^{-k/3} \approx 2^{-k/2}$.

(We remark that to improve the bound from $2^{-k/2}$ to 2^{-k}, it suffices to increase the size of each bucket from $2k$ to just under $2.6k$.)

3.2   Increasing the Degree of the Tree

Our next observation is that instead of using just binary trees as in [20], we can use higher-degree trees. Specifically, we propose increasing the branching factor of the trees to k, and decreasing their depth accordingly to $\log_k(n/k) = (\log n / \log k) - 1$. Clearly, this modification reduces the running time of the Access subroutine from Section 2.2 by a $\log k$ factor (simply because the tree is shallower, and hence the size of the paths that the server sends is decreased). However, this would increase the complexity of the Evict procedure by a factor of k, since each eviction operation now involves a parent and all of its d children (rather than just two children as in [20]). We therefore change the eviction algorithm so as to avoid the increased computation cost, as described next.

A New Eviction Procedure

Notations. Below we denote $[k] = \{0, 1, \ldots, k-1\}$, and use the standard notation where we name each node in a degree-d tree using the path from the root to that node, represented as a sequence of integers in $[k]$. For example the root is the empty sequence (), child number 3 of the root it (3), the child number 2 of that node is $(3, 2)$, etc. Formally, the nodes of a complete k-ary tree of height h are $[k]^{\leq h}$, where each internal node $v \in [k]^{<h}$ is the parent of all the nodes $\{(v, i) : i \in [k]\}$.

With these notations, the *least common ancestor* of two nodes u, v, denoted $LCA(u, v)$, is just the longest common prefix in the names of these two nodes.

We also use the notation $\mathsf{DigitReverse}_k(t)$ to denote the order-reversal of the base-k digits of the integer t, for example in decimal representation we have $\mathsf{DigitReverse}_{10}(1234) = (4, 3, 2, 1)$. Formally, if $t < k^h$, $t = \sum_{j=1}^h i_j k^{j-1}$ for unique $i_i < k$, then $\mathsf{DigitReverse}_k(t) = (i_h, \ldots, i_2, i_1) \in [k]^h$.

The push-to-leaf procedure. We replace the randomized eviction procedure of Shi et al. with a deterministic procedure that just picks one leaf L in every time step (in a specific order to be described shortly), and tries to push items down along the path to L as far as they can go. Namely, if somewhere on the path from the root to L we found an item that is assigned to leaf L', then we push that item down the path to the node $LCA(L, L')$, i.e., the least common ancestor where the paths to L and L' diverge.

For example, if we choose leaf $L = (1, 2, 0, 3)$, and in the root we found an item (L', v, data) that is assigned to leaf $L' = (1, 2, 3, 3)$, then we remove that item from the root and push it down to the internal node two levels below $LCA(L, L') = (1, 2)$. We do the same for all the items on the path from the root to L. Notice that during the entire procedure, we only access nodes along this one path.

We observe that if our tree satisfies the tree invariant before the push-to-L procedure (i.e., every item in the tree is found on the path from the root to its assigned node), then it still satisfies that invariant also after the procedure. Moreover no item is ever *pushed up* by that procedure, only down (or not at all). We also note that it is possible to implement the push-to-leaf procedure in time complexity linear in the size of a root-to-leaf path.

Ordering the leaves. The deterministic order in which we pick the leaves for eviction is just the *digit-reversed lexicographic order.* For example, with $k = 3, h = 2$, we use the order

$$(0,0), (1,0), (2,0), (0,1), (1,1), (2,1), (0,2), (1,2), (2,2), \quad (0,0), (1,0), \ldots$$

Specifically, for a degree-k, height-h tree, we pick at every step $t \in N$ the leaf whose name is $L = \mathsf{DigitReverse}_k(t \bmod k^h)$. The new eviction procedure, using this ordering of the leaves, is described in Figure 1. The main property of this ordering is that, at each level i of the tree, these paths *cycle* through the k^{i-1} nodes of that level periodically every k^{i-1} steps.

EVICT(tree $= [k]^{\leq h}$, step $t \in \mathbb{N}$):
1. Set $t' = t \bmod k^h$, and $L = \mathsf{DigitReverse}_k(t')$;   // L is a leaf
2. For every item $I = (L', v, \mathsf{data})$ in any bucket on the path to L, do: // push-to-L
3.   Remove I from its current bucket and push it to the bucket of node $LCA(L, L')$.

Fig. 1. Our new eviction procedure

Overflow Analysis. The overflow analysis for the leaves does not change from the previous section. For internal nodes, we now prove that if we set the bucket size in the internal nodes to $2k$, then with the eviction procedure from Figure 1 the overflow probability is exponentially small in k. Surprisingly, the analysis for our deterministic evacuation procedure turns out to be a rather easy, quite similar to the analysis for the leaves. In particular we do not need any of the "heavy" queuing-theory tools that were used in the analysis of the original protocol in [20].

Lemma 2. *Fix one particular internal node in the tree, $v \in [k]^{<h}$, and one particular access operation. With the bucket of v having size $2k$, the overflow probability for this node in that operation is at most $e^{-k/3}$.*

Proof. We think of the evolution of data items in internal nodes as a game, in which in every step we throw a ball in the root and associate to it a random leaf, and then perform our deterministic evacuation procedure. Assume that the node v in question is at level i in the tree, which means that there are exactly k^{i-1} nodes in that level (and exactly k^i nodes one level below).

Fix some step $t \geq k^i$, and denote by $S_t(v)$ the set of all balls in the system that satisfy (a) the path from the root to the leaves of these balls go through the internal node v, and (b) the balls are at level i or above at time t. We prove that $\Pr[|S_t(v)| > 2k] < e^{-k/3}$, which clearly implies the lemma (since $S_t(v)$ is a superset of the balls in v at time t).

The property of the digit-reversed lexicographic order that we need for the analysis, is that every consecutive interval of k^i steps covers each length-i prefix exactly once. This means in particular, that every node at the level $i+1$ was on exactly one eviction path during the sequence of k^i steps $[t - k^i + 1, \ldots, t-1, t]$.

Hence every ball that entered the system *before that interval* must have been evicted to level $i + 1$ or below, and therefore in not in $S_t(v)$.

It remains to consider only the last k^i balls. For each of these balls we assign an indicator random variable χ_j ($j \in [t - k^i + 1, \ldots, t]$), which is 1 if the path of that ball goes though v and 0 otherwise. Clearly the χ_j's are i.i.d. and $\Pr[\chi_j = 1] = k^{-i+1}$ for all j. Moreover only balls with $\chi_j = 1$ can belong to $S_t(v)$, hence $|S_t(v)| < \sum_{j=t-k^i+1}^{t} \chi_j$. Since the expected value of the sum is $E[\sum_j \chi_j] = k^i \cdot k^{-i+1} = k$, we can use Chernoff bound to conclude that

$$\Pr[|S_t(v)| > 2k] \leq \Pr\left[\left(\sum_{j=t-k^i+1}^{t} \chi_j\right) > 2k\right] < e^{-k/3}.$$

Complexity Analysis. It remains to analyze the complexity of our new variant. As usual, the time complexity is governed by the communication complexity of the protocol. To analyze the communication, we recall the different parameters in our system:

We have security parameter k, and an N-element database, each element of size D bits. The largest tree has $\lceil N/k \rceil$ leaves, and each subsequent tree is smaller than the previous one by a constant factor of τ, hence the i'th tree has $\lceil N/(k\tau^i) \rceil$ leaves and we have $\ell = \lceil \log_\tau(N/k) \rceil$ trees. The trees have branching degree k, thus the height of the i'th tree is $\log_k(\lceil N/(k\tau^i) \rceil) \approx (\log N - i \log \tau)/\log k$. Every node in the largest tree contains $2k$ entries, each of size $D + O(\log N)$, for a total size of $O(k(D + \log N))$. In the smaller trees, every node contains $2k$ entries, each of size $O(\tau \log N)$, for a total size of $O(k\tau \log N)$.

Recall that in our protocol, for each access request the parties send to each other two paths in every tree (one for the access itself and another one for eviction). Hence the total communication complexity per access in our protocol is

$$O(\log N/\log k) \cdot O(k(D + \log N)) + \sum_{i=1}^{\ell-1} O((\log N - i \log \tau)/\log k) \cdot O(k\tau \log N)$$

$$= \frac{k \log N}{\log k} \cdot O(D + \log N + \tau\ell \log N) = \frac{k \log N}{\log k} \cdot O(D + \log N + (\tau/\log \tau) \log^2 N)$$

$$= O(k \log N(D + \log^2 N)/\log k),$$

where in the first two equalities above we assumed that $N > k^2$ (say), so that $\log(N/k) = O(\log N)$, and in the last equality we used the fact that τ was a constant, hence $(\tau/\log \tau) = O(1)$. As noted above, in the word model where we can process a D-bit word in one operation (and $D \geq \log N$), the above bound can be replaced by $O(k \log^2 N/\log k)$.

4   Oblivious Binary Search

Oblivious RAM lets us retrieve a value from the database by specifying its logical address, but in some applications we may want to retrieve the data by its key (or tag) rather than address. In such applications, we may initially sort the elements by their tags, then use binary search to retrieve the tag that we want in $\log n$ steps. Implementing this procedure obliviously is similarly going to take $\log n$ ORAM accesses, which may be quite expensive. Here we present a modification of the tree ORAM protocol from before that lets us to implement a binary search query with only a single ORAM access. For a logical address v (in the actual database) denote by (t_v, d_v) the tag and data that are associated with that address, respectively.

Consider the recursive structure of the tree ORAM construction from [20]. In this structure, an entry in the tree at level $i+1$ contains a list of τ leaf numbers in the next tree at level i, and a client that fetches that entry chooses one of these leaves (based on the logical address that it wants to access) and then fetches that leaf (and the path to it) from the next tree. To enable efficient binary search, we need to add some information to let the client decide what leaf to fetch next, based on its tag rather than on its virtual address.

For an interval I of logical addresses, denote by $t_\downarrow(I), t^\uparrow(I)$ the smallest and largest of the tags associated with I, namely $t_\downarrow(I) = \min\{t_v : v \in I\}$ and $t^\uparrow(I) = \max\{t_v : v \in I\}$. Since the database is sorted by tags, we know that an address $v \in [N]$ belongs to I if and only if the corresponding tag t_v satisfies $t_\downarrow(I) \leq t_v \leq t^\uparrow(I)$.

Consider an entry in the tree at level $i+1$, let $[v, v + \tau^{i+1})$ be the interval of logical addresses corresponding to that entry, and also let $I_1, \ldots, I_\tau$ be the corresponding level-i sub-intervals, namely $I_j = [v+(j-1)\tau^i, v+j\tau^i)$. We modify the ORAM protocol by storing the tags $t_\downarrow(I_j)$ together with the leaf numbers L_j that are currently assigned to these sub-intervals. Namely, an entry in the tree has the form

Level-0 : $(L^*, v, (t_v, d_v)$ $)$
Level-$i > 0$: $(L^*, v, (\{L_1^{(i)}, t_\downarrow(I_1)\}, \{L_2^{(i)}, t_\downarrow(I_2)\}, \ldots, \{L_\tau^{(i)}, t_\downarrow(I_\tau)\}))$

When accessing some tag t, the client fetches some level-$(i+1)$ entry, compares the tag t against all the τ tags $t_\downarrow(I_j)$ in that entry, and based on that comparison decides which of the leaves L_j to get from the next tree. Specifically, we replace the Access subroutine from Section 2.3 by the following:

Binary Search. To access the data for tag t (if exists), the client looks up in its level-ℓ "tree" for the list $(\{L_1^{(\ell-1)}, t_\downarrow(I_1)\}, \ldots, \{L_\tau^{(\ell-1)}, t_\downarrow(I_\tau)\})$, and let j be the largest index such that $t_\downarrow(I_j) \leq t$. (Such an index must exist since $t_\downarrow(I_1)$ is the smallest tag in the database.) The client sets $v_{\ell-1} = (j-1)\tau^{\ell-1}$ and $L^{(\ell-1)} = L_j^{(\ell-1)}$, chooses at random a new leaf $\hat{L}^{(\ell-1)}$ and replaces $L_j^{(\ell-1)}$ by this new value in the list. Then the client proceeds iteratively for $i = \ell - 1$ down to 0:

1. Request from the server all the buckets on the path from the root of the level-i tree down to the leaf $L^{(i)}$. Decrypt them and find in them an entry of the form $(L^{(i)}, v_i, \mathsf{data})$.

2. If $i > 0$ do the following:
   (a) Parse data $= (\{L_1^{(i-1)}, t_1\}, \ldots, \{L_\tau^{(i-1)}, t_\tau\})$, choose a new random leaf $\hat{L}^{(i-1)}$.
   (b) Let j be the largest index such that $t_j \leq t$. (Such an index must exists since t_1 is equal to the $t_\downarrow(\cdot)$ value from the previous iteration.) Set $v_{i-1} = v_i + (j-1)\tau^{i-1}$ and $L^{(i-1)} = L_j^{(i-1)}$.
   (c) Replace $L_j^{(i-1)}$ by $\hat{L}^{(i-1)}$ inside data, denoting the result by data'.
   Else ($i = 0$), parse data $= (t_v, d_v)$. if $t_v = t$ and this is a write operation then set data' $= (t_v, d_v')$ where d_v' is the new value. Else set data' $=$ data.
3. Remove the entry $(L^{(i)}, v_i, \text{data})$ from the bucket where is was found, and instead place in the root bucket the entry $(\hat{L}^{(i)}, v_i, \text{data}')$. Re-encrypt all the buckets and send to the server.

As before, the client and server then run the Eviction subroutine for each of the trees. If this was a read operation then the return value is either d_v from level-0 (if $t_v = t$) or $\perp$ (if $t_v \neq t$).

Complexity. The binary-search algorithm above is nearly identical to the ORAM access from Section 2.3, except in the way that the next label is chosen from the current entry (i.e., the choice of j in Step 2(b)). While in the original ORAM tree the client can compute j directly from its logical address, in the binary search algorithm the client needs to compare its tag against all the tags in the entry to find the index j. Still, the complexity of this algorithm is linear in the size of the messages that the server sends, and if the tags are short (of size $O(\log n)$ bits) then that size is asymptotically the same as for the ORAM access. We also note that the same ORAM modification can also be used for regular queries that access logical address, for example if we want to handle a sparse set of addresses out of a large universe.

4.1   Applications

Range queries. Another type of query we can perform on sorted data is a range query. Given a sorted databased stored in an ORAM and an interval $[t_l, t_r]$, we can retrieve all database items with search tag in the interval $[t_l, t_r]$ with computational complexity proportional to the size of the result set times the cost of a single ORAM access. To do this we just run the binary-search algorithm from above on the tag t_l, and this returns both the first tag $t \geq t_l$ in the database as well as its logical address v. We then just access logical addresses $v+1, v+2, \ldots$ until we get the first tag $t > t_r$. (It is easy to avoid that last extra query by paying attention to the values $t_\downarrow(I)$ throughout the queries.)

Assuming that the client has enough memory to store the result set, we can modify the ORAM binary search algorithm to implement a range query with fewer communication rounds (namely, have the client accesses each tree only once). This is done by the client requesting not just one leaf from each level, but also all the leaves $L_j^{(i)}$ with larger tag values, as long as their t_j values satisfy

$t_j \leq t_r$. In addition to saving communication rounds, this approach also saves on the total number of leaves accessed (especially in the small trees), since we do not access the same leaf more than once.

Keyword search. The keyword search problem is to retrieve all the records from a database that contain a given keyword. One solution is to build an (inverted) index, namely a list of all the words in the database, and for each word w keep a list of addresses of all the documents $D_1^{(w)}, \ldots, D_i^{(w)}$ that contain w. Having this index reduces the problem of keyword search to finding the keyword in the list of the inverted index, which can be done in sublinear time using binary search. With this setup we can use our binary search algorithm for an efficient access hiding algorithm for keyword search.

5 Secure Computation Using HE-Over-ORAM

An exciting application of ORAM is secure computation with sublinear online complexity [17,14]. In this setting, we have two players who first engage in an "offline" setup protocol, at the end of which one of them is holding the server state of the oblivious RAM, while the client state is shared between them so that no single player knows it. Then, in the "online" phase, the players just carry out secure computation for the evolving finite state of the control (i.e., the client state), and implement any memory access that the computation needs using the underlying ORAM. Using this configuration, the online complexity of the protocol is related to the amount of data which is actually accessed during this computation, rather that to the overall amount of data held by the server. This configuration was first mentioned by Ostrovsky and Shoup [17], and recently an optimized version was described and implemented by Gordon et al. [14], working over the ORAM protocol of Shi et al. [20]. A crucial difference between the standard ORAM setting and this configuration of MPC-over-ORAM is that in the latter, the client is not allowed to know in the clear the logical addresses that are accessed or the values that are returned. Instead, that information is shared between the two parties, and is processed by the secure-computation protocol in this shared format.

In this section we show how to leverage homomorphic encryption to reduce the communication and interaction between the client and the server in the during our ORAM protocol (which itself may be embedded inside a larger secure computation protocol). A practical concern is that the complexity of contemporary HE schemes degrades quickly with the complexity of the functions that are computed (especially the multiplicative depth). We show how the functions used inside ORAM can be expressed as low-depth functions that can be evaluated by *somewhat homomorphic encryption* [6] schemes, which are weaker but much faster than fully homomorphic encryption schemes.

5.1   Our High-Level Approach to Sublinear Secure Computation

In our system, we have a client and a server. The server roughly plays the role of the ORAM-server and the client roughly plays the role of the ORAM-client, but the mapping is not quite one-to-one. Below we say "client" and "server" when referring to the two parties in our secure computation protocol, and "ORAM-client" and "ORAM-server" when referring to the roles in the underlying oblivious RAM construction.

Just as in the underlying ORAM construction, for our protocol the content of the database is stored at the server. In our optimized version, the content is encrypted using a HE scheme *to which the client holds the secret key*. Since we are implementing secure computation rather than just ORAM, the client in our case cannot hold in the clear the address-to-leaf mapping for the smallest tree (since this will leak to the client information about the logical addresses being accessed). Instead, this table is shared between the two players in a simple two-out-of-two fashion: if in the underlying construction the ORAM-client has a table with the i'th entry being some value l_i, in our protocol the server holds a random mask value m_i and the client holds $l_i \oplus m_i$.

When implementing the access protocol, the client and server cooperate to jointly compute the ORAM-client messages in the clear. Note that this does not leak any information due to the privacy property of oblivious RAM. In our case, each message of the ORAM-client consists of a single leaf address in one of the trees. In the underlying construction the server would reply by returning the full path to that leaf, but in our system the server will return much less than that. In some cases the server will compute the entire ORAM-client logic homomorphically, returning to the client in our protocol just the encrypted result (namely the leaf address in the next tree). In some cases we need to hide even this final result from the client (e.g., the actual data in the largest tree), so the server will blind it using a random mask, and send to the client this blinded value to be decrypted. This will again result in the server holding a random mask m and the client holding the value $v \oplus m$ (where v is the value that the ORAM-client was supposed to get).

Note that homomorphic encryption allows us to save considerably on bandwidth. Below, we describe in more detail the implementation of the various sub-protocols involved.

5.2   ORAM Access

In the ORAM scheme of [20], the data that is stored in each node in any of the trees consists of pairs (v_i, d_i), where d_i is either the data element corresponding to logical address v_i (if this is the largest tree), or leaf identifiers in the next tree (if this is an intermediate tree). In the underlying ORAM construction the ORAM-client holds an address v, it gets from the ORAM-server an entire path in the tree, and it decrypts all the nodes and search for an entry matching that logical address v that it holds.

In our case, the client holds a masked logical address $u = v \oplus m$ and the server holds the corresponding mask m. The client encrypts its values u and sends to the server, who uses (additive) homomorphism to add-in its mask, thus obtaining a HE ciphertext encrypting v.

The server next evaluates homomorphically the client logic that selects the one entry from all of the nodes that match the logical address v. Specifically, for every encrypted entry of the form (v_i, d_i), the server first compute a single "choice bit" c_i which is one if $v_i = v$ and zero otherwise. This can be done naively by comparing each bit of v_i to the corresponding bit of v, then taking an AND of all the resulting bits. The bit-wise comparison is just a NOT XOR operation (hence it is linear), and the big AND has depth logarithmic in the size of v. Note that current homomorphic encryption schemes [3,7,8,2] can evaluate arithmetic circuits of *polynomial depth* even without an expensive procedure called "bootstrapping", and that a scheme capable of evaluating *logarithmic depth* is realizable using comparatively small parameters. Alternatively, if the size of v is too large and one wants to lower the depth of the circuit further, one can use a low-degree approximation of the AND function, such as the approximation due to Ben-Or described, e.g., in Example 2.4 of [15]. (The example is a low-degree approximation of OR, but it is straightforward to convert it to a low-degree approximation of AND.) For a soundness parameter k, this low-degree approximation introduces an error probability of 2^{-k}, but it can be computed in depth only $\log k$. Once the server computes all the choice bits c_i, it then evaluates homomorphically the MUX function

$$\mathsf{out} = \sum_i c_i \cdot d_i$$

thus obtaining only the value d that matches the logical address v. (Note that the c_i's are individual bits, but the d_i's are bit-string. The operation $c_i \cdot d_i$ thus refers to multiplying by c_i each of the bits of d_i.) This last computation only adds one to the depth of the multiplication depth of the circuit.

The harder part of the access procedure is removing the entry (v_i, d_i) from its current intermediate node putting the corresponding (v_i, d_i') at the root of the tree. To enable this homomorphic procedure, we keep with each entry in every node also an encrypted "full-bit" which is 1 if that entry is full and zero if it is empty (and this full-bit is used also in the comparison calculation above). After computing the choice bits c_i, we just multiply the negation of each c_i back into the corresponding full-bit, thus "removing" the entry from its current node. Choosing a new leaf value for the next tree (as needed for the intermediate trees) is done by both the client and server choosing random values, and the new address being the XOR of the two strings (this can be computed using additive homomorphism).

To put it in the top node, we compute for each entry in the top node a bit signaling whether that entry is the first empty entry in the node. This can be done naively in depth equal to the logarithm of the bucket size, namely for each entry we AND the negation of its full-bit with all the full-bits of previous entries. Here again we can use the Ben-Or trick to compute these bits in only $\log k$ depth, with k the security parameter. Once we compute these "first available" bits (call them a_i), we compute for each entry of the form (v, d) in the top node another MUX function, setting the new value of that entry to

$$(v'', d'') = a_i \cdot (v_i, d_i') + (1 - a_i) \cdot (v, d)$$

We note that repeated accesses gradually increase the noisiness of the encryptions of the data stored in the tree, hence they need to be periodically refreshed, which can be done using bootstrapping [6]. Alternatively, we can use an interactive protocol where the server blinds the encrypted data using additive homomorphism, then send it to the client to be decrypted and freshly re-encrypted, and finally remove the blinding factors.

ORAM Evictions. If we use HE for encryption of the data in the ORAM, then the evictions can be done completely noninteractively by the server. Given a node chosen for eviction, the server homomorphically evaluates a function that pushes each of the items stored in the node to an available slot in the least-common-ancestor of the "current eviction leaf" and the leaf associated with that item. The operations involved with eviction are similar to those required on read, and in particular can be implemented using functions of depth $\log k + \log \log N$.

5.3   Binary Search

In our extension of the ORAM scheme for more efficient binary search, we need to check not for exact match but whether the required address is within a given interval. For this purpose we can define a function:

$$g_{\overline{v_1 \ldots v_k}}(x_1, \ldots, x_k) = (x_1 - v_1)x_1 + (x_1 - v_1 + 1)g_{\overline{v_2 \ldots v_k}}(x_2, \ldots, x_k), \quad (1)$$

where the bits of x and v are ordered most significant to least significant. The function $g_v(x)$ takes value 1, if $x > v$ and 0, otherwise. Now, in order to implement a selection condition that v is in the interval (v_l, v_r) we can set $f_v(x) = g_{v_l}(v) \cdot g_v(v_r)$ for the selection function in Equation 1.

Acknowledgments. This work was supported by the Intelligence Advanced Research Projects Activity (IARPA) via Department of Interior National Business Center (DoI/NBC) contract number D11PC20202. The U.S. Government is authorized to reproduce and distribute reprints for Governmental purposes notwithstanding any copyright annotation thereon. Disclaimer: The views and conclusions contained herein are those of the authors and should not be interpreted as necessarily representing the official policies or endorsements, either expressed or implied, of IARPA, DoI/NBC, or the U.S. Government.

References

1. Alon, N., Spencer, J.: The Probabilistic Method. John Wiley (1992)
2. Brakerski, Z.: Fully homomorphic encryption without modulus switching from classical gapsvp. In: Safavi-Naini, Canetti (eds.) [19], pp. 868–886

3. Brakerski, Z., Gentry, C., Vaikuntanathan, V.: (leveled) fully homomorphic encryption without bootstrapping. In: Goldwasser, S. (ed.) ITCS, pp. 309–325. ACM (2012)

4. Brakerski, Z., Vaikuntanathan, V.: Efficient fully fomomorphic encryption from (standard) lwe. In: Ostrovsky, R. (ed.) FOCS, pp. 97–106. IEEE (2011)

5. Brakerski, Z., Vaikuntanathan, V.: Fully homomorphic encryption from ring-lwe and security for key dependent messages. In: Rogaway, P. (ed.) CRYPTO 2011. LNCS, vol. 6841, pp. 505–524. Springer, Heidelberg (2011)

6. Gentry, C.: Fully homomorphic encryption using ideal lattices. In: STOC, pp. 169–178 (2009)

7. Gentry, C., Halevi, S., Smart, N.P.: Fully homomorphic encryption with polylog overhead. In: Pointcheval, D., Johansson, T. (eds.) EUROCRYPT 2012. LNCS, vol. 7237, pp. 465–482. Springer, Heidelberg (2012)

8. Gentry, C., Halevi, S., Smart, N.P.: Homomorphic evaluation of the aes circuit. In: Safavi-Naini, Canetti (eds.) [19], pp. 850–867

9. Goldreich, O.: Towards a theory of software protection and simulation by oblivious rams. In: Aho, A.V. (ed.) STOC, pp. 182–194. ACM (1987)

10. Goldreich, O., Micali, S., Wigderson, A.: How to play any mental game or a completeness theorem for protocols with honest majority. In: STOC, pp. 218–229 (1987)

11. Goldreich, O., Ostrovsky, R.: Software protection and simulation on oblivious rams. J. ACM 43(3), 431–473 (1996)

12. Goodrich, M.T., Mitzenmacher, M.: Privacy-Preserving Access of Outsourced Data via Oblivious RAM Simulation. In: Aceto, L., Henzinger, M., Sgall, J. (eds.) ICALP 2011, Part II. LNCS, vol. 6756, pp. 576–587. Springer, Heidelberg (2011)

13. Goodrich, M.T., Mitzenmacher, M., Ohrimenko, O., Tamassia, R.: Privacy-preserving group data access via stateless oblivious RAM simulation. In: Rabani, Y. (ed.) SODA, pp. 157–167. SIAM (2012)

14. Gordon, S.D., Katz, J., Kolesnikov, V., Krell, F., Malkin, T., Raykova, M., Vahlis, Y.: Secure two-party computation in sublinear (amortized) time. In: CCS (2012)

15. Ishai, Y., Kushilevitz, E.: Randomizing polynomials: A new representation with applications to round-efficient secure computation. In: FOCS, pp. 294–304. IEEE Computer Society (2000)

16. Ostrovsky, R.: Efficient computation on oblivious rams. In: Ortiz, H. (ed.) STOC, pp. 514–523. ACM (1990)

17. Ostrovsky, R., Shoup, V.: Private information storage. In: STOC (1997)

18. Pinkas, B., Reinman, T.: Oblivious RAM Revisited. In: Rabin, T. (ed.) CRYPTO 2010. LNCS, vol. 6223, pp. 502–519. Springer, Heidelberg (2010)

19. Safavi-Naini, R., Canetti, R. (eds.): CRYPTO 2012. LNCS, vol. 7417. Springer, Heidelberg (2012)

20. Shi, E., Chan, T.-H.H., Stefanov, E., Li, M.: Oblivious RAM with $O((\log N)^3)$ worst-case cost. In: Lee, D.H., Wang, X. (eds.) ASIACRYPT 2011. LNCS, vol. 7073, pp. 197–214. Springer, Heidelberg (2011)

21. Yao, A.C.-C.: Protocols for secure computations (extended abstract). In: FOCS, pp. 160–164 (1982)

Anonymity-Preserving Public-Key Encryption: A Constructive Approach

Markulf Kohlweiss[1], Ueli Maurer[2], Cristina Onete[3],
Björn Tackmann[2], and Daniele Venturi[4]

[1] Microsoft Research, Cambridge, England
[2] ETH Zürich, Switzerland
[3] Darmstadt University of Technology, CASED, Germany
[4] Aarhus University, Denmark

Abstract. A receiver-anonymous channel allows a sender to send a message to a receiver without an adversary learning for whom the message is intended. Wireless broadcast channels naturally provide receiver anonymity, as does multi-casting one message to a receiver population containing the intended receiver. While anonymity and confidentiality appear to be orthogonal properties, making anonymous communication confidential is more involved than one might expect, since the ciphertext might reveal which public key has been used to encrypt. To address this problem, public-key cryptosystems with enhanced security properties have been proposed.

We investigate constructions as well as limitations for preserving receiver anonymity when using public-key encryption (PKE). We use the constructive cryptography approach by Maurer and Renner and interpret cryptographic schemes as constructions of a certain ideal resource (e.g. a confidential anonymous channel) from given real resources (e.g. a broadcast channel). We define appropriate anonymous communication resources and show that a very natural resource can be constructed by using a PKE scheme which fulfills three properties that appear in cryptographic literature (IND-CCA, key-privacy, weak robustness). We also show that a desirable stronger variant, preventing the adversary from selective "trial-deliveries" of messages, is unfortunately unachievable by any PKE scheme, no matter how strong. The constructive approach makes the guarantees achieved by applying a cryptographic scheme explicit in the constructed (ideal) resource; this specifies the exact requirements for the applicability of a cryptographic scheme in a given context. It also allows to decide which of the existing security properties of such a cryptographic scheme are adequate for the considered scenario, and which are too weak or too strong. Here, we show that weak robustness is necessary but that so-called strong robustness is unnecessarily strong in that it does not construct a (natural) stronger resource.

Keywords: public-key encryption, key privacy, robust encryption, anonymity, constructive cryptography.

E. De Cristofaro and M. Wright (Eds.): PETS 2013, LNCS 7981, pp. 19–39, 2013.

1   Introduction

Protocols and other mechanisms for protecting privacy often use cryptographic schemes in non-standard ways, sometimes requiring such schemes to have cryptographic properties that go beyond data authenticity and confidentiality. It is important that new cryptographic schemes take these requirements into account and that designers of privacy protocols are aware which cryptographic properties are needed in which situation. Several types of cryptographic schemes have been investigated with a focus on anonymity. In "key-private" public-key encryption, the ciphertext does not reveal information about the intended receiver [5,2], in private key exchange [8,1] two parties can exchange a key without revealing their identities, and "anonymous" signatures protect the signer's identity at least as long as parts of the signed plaintext remain hidden [27]. In this paper, we focus on public-key encryption and receiver anonymity.

The cryptographic community traditionally defines security notions for cryptographic schemes such as encryption from a game-based perspective, i.e., one defines properties of schemes by means of theoretical experiments, usually referred to as games. Though often used, well-studied, and improved over the years, game-based definitions have two major shortcomings. First, the models simplify the use of a scheme to the interaction between an *adversary* and a *challenger* (both somewhat artificial); thus, it is not clear what level of security is attained when a provably secure scheme is used in a specific context. Second, if a larger protocol employs such a provably secure (encryption) scheme, the security of the larger protocol is proved explicitly by reductions: one shows that breaking the security of the protocol leads to breaking the security of the (underlying) scheme. The reduction must in principle be tailor-made for each protocol.

A fundamentally different approach to defining the security of cryptographic schemes was proposed in [18]. In their *constructive cryptography* paradigm, one models both the resources assumed by a protocol and the desired functionality explicitly; the goal of the protocol is to *construct* (in a well-defined sense) the desired resource from the assumed resources. For a public-key encryption scheme, for instance, this means that one assumes an authenticated communication channel from the receiver to the sender to transmit the public key, and an insecure channel from the sender to the receiver to transmit the ciphertext. The goal is to construct, from the assumed channels, a confidential communication channel (from sender to receiver, cf. [20]). The assumed channels can be either physically realized or constructed cryptographically; the resulting channel can be used directly in any application requiring such a channel. Furthermore, as the constructive approach explicitly states the guarantees of both the assumed and the constructed resources, it allows to capture the *exact* cryptographic assumptions required for security.

Anonymity in constructive cryptography. In constructive cryptography, a network is a resource that can be accessed by multiple (honest or dishonest) parties. The parties use interfaces provided by the resource (and specific to each party) to access it; the interfaces specify exactly how each party can access the resource. In this context, anonymity is an explicit guarantee of the resource (e.g., a network). Since adversarial interaction with the network is also modeled by an interface (the attacker is a dishonest party), the security (or privacy) guarantees of the underlying network are described by the (absence of) capabilities of the adversary.

For the case of receiver-anonymous communication, we model a network resource with multiple receiver interfaces. Whenever a sender inputs a message at its interface and chooses a receiver, the network may leak some information (the length of the message, even the entire plaintext) at the adversary's interface; however, the resource will *not* reveal the receiver. In this context, a PKE scheme aims to construct a resource that still hides the receiver, while leaking no information on the message contents apart from (potentially) the length.

We consider the case where PKE schemes are used for end-to-end encryption between senders and receivers; in this case anonymity cannot be created through a cryptographic primitive. In fact, a constructive approach shows that schemes can only *preserve* the anonymity guaranteed by the underlying network, but never *produce* it.[1] If Alice sends a message to Bob over the Internet using Bob's publicly known IP address, then no encryption scheme (or key exchange protocol) can hide the fact that Bob is the intended receiver of Alice's message. In fact, encrypting messages can make the problem worse: Even if the transmission of the ciphertext is itself anonymous, the ciphertext might still reveal under which public key it was encrypted.

Hence, in a constructive analysis of the end-to-end use of cryptographic schemes, we always consider the *preservation* of anonymity. If the underlying network (one of the initial resources) is insecure, but guarantees some anonymity, then an "anonymity-preserving" scheme will improve security while retaining as much anonymity as possible. The obtained guarantees are strong in that they hold *regardless of the context*, i.e., of any prior knowledge the adversary might have and of any protocols executed in parallel.

Our contributions. We give a treatment of receiver anonymity in the context of public-key encryption (PKE) schemes from the perspective of constructive cryptography. Concretely, we describe anonymity as a feature of a communication resource, and we prove which security properties of the underlying encryption scheme are necessary and/or sufficient to achieve a confidential receiver-anonymous communication resource from a non-confidential, but also receiver-anonymous one. (Schemes with these properties exist in the literature.) Specifically, we consider the following network resources, where our notations extend the •-notation of [20]. See Section 3.1 for details.

---

[1] This observation does not hold, however, for active or overlay networks that can implement their own multi-hop anonymous routing strategy (here, encryption is crucial). Buses [4] is an example of this, while TOR [10] is the most widely-used anonymization system based on this principle.

- The insecure broadcast network $\prec$, allowing a single sender to broadcast messages to multiple receivers. The adversary may learn the entire message and may remove, change, or inject messages;
- The confidential receiver-anonymous channel $\multimap\!\!\diamond\!\!\prec$, preserving both message confidentiality and receiver anonymity, leaking only the length of the message and allowing the adversary only to delete or honestly deliver messages, and to inject arbitrary messages to chosen recipients.

We show that $\multimap\!\!\diamond\!\!\prec$ can be constructed from $\prec$ and authenticated channels $\longleftrightarrow\!\!\bullet$ (in an initial step), by employing a secure (IND-CCA), key-private (IK-CCA), and weakly robust (WROB-CCA) PKE scheme. We prove that constructing $\multimap\!\!\diamond\!\!\prec$ does *not* require strong robustness (SROB-CCA, a stronger property for anonymous, secure encryption proposed in [2]). Of course, using SROB-CCA encryption also constructs $\multimap\!\!\diamond\!\!\prec$; however, this property is not *required*. Thus, the treatment in [2] relies on slightly too strong assumptions. Using SROB-CCA security, however, *does* yield a tighter security reduction.

We also show that one (the only natural) channel providing stronger anonymity than we achieve with IND-CCA, IK-CCA, and WROB-CCA encryption *cannot* be achieved by *any* PKE scheme at all (see Section 3.3). Thus, using e.g. the stronger SROB-CCA property does *not* construct this stronger channel. This does not mean that SROB-CCA is not useful in other scenarios; however, our results indicate that improving the properties of $\multimap\!\!\diamond\!\!\prec$ in a natural way cannot be done by using SROB-CCA, or any other type of encryption.

Related work. The first definition of key-private public-key encryption appears in [5]; the goal of the primitive was to attain receiver anonymity. Abdalla et al. [2] noted that also robustness is needed for the PKE scheme to achieve this property, since otherwise an honest receiver is unable to detect whether he is the intended recipient of a given ciphertext and could obtain a bogus decryption. We explicitly describe the guarantees achieved without robustness in the resource $\multimap\!\!\diamond\!\!\prec$ in Section 4.1. Mohassel [22] analyzed game-based security and anonymity notions for KEM-DEM encryption schemes, showing that, for this particular type of composition, weak robustness together with the key privacy of the KEM (key-encapsulation mechanism) and DEM (data-encapsulation mechanism) components is sufficient to obtain a key-private hybrid public-key encryption scheme. Our result implies that weak robustness is sufficient even for universal composition; a *constructive* formulation of KEM-DEM schemes is currently being developed. However, as shown recently by Farshim et al. [11] (even strong) robustness is insufficient in certain contexts, such as Sako's auction protocol. The same concept (i.e., that only the intended recipient must be able to decrypt a ciphertext to a meaningful plaintext) lies at the core of *incomparable public keys* in [26].

More general (game-based) frameworks that mix the analysis of cryptographic schemes and traffic-analysis resistance have been proposed in [14] and [24]. Independently, different cryptographic [7,3] and traffic-analysis models [12,13] have been developed for variants of onion routing. Whereas our work here does not consider traffic analysis explicitly, our in-depth results can be composed with meaningful models of traffic analysis. We discuss implications of our results for traffic analysis in Section 5.

An early treatment of anonymity in networks (including receiver anonymity) was given in [25]. They explicitly considered the idea of using public-key encryption towards realizing receiver-anonymous networks. However, our treatment in this paper gives a more thorough, formal assessment of receiver anonymity and investigates necessary and sufficient resources that are necessary to achieve different levels of it. Nagao et al. [23] describe a similar resource for two sender-anonymous channels and show that such channels can be related by reductions to other types of channels, such as secure channels and direction hiding channels. Ishai et al. [15] provide a broader investigation on how to bootstrap cryptographic functionalities using anonymity. The resource we construct here provides receiver, rather than sender anonymity, and we also require confidentiality for our ideal resource (which is not the case for [15]).

2   Preliminaries

Notation. We use the symbol $\Diamond$ to denote an "error" output of an algorithm. Moreover, for an integer $n \in \mathbb{N}$, we let $[n] := \{1, \ldots, n\}$. We generally use typewriter fonts such as enc or dec to denote algorithms.

2.1   Systems: Resources and Converters, Distinguishers, and Games

We model objects like resources and protocols in terms of systems. At the highest level of abstraction—following the hierarchy in [18]—systems are objects with interfaces by which they connect to (interfaces of) other systems. Each interface is labeled with an element of a given label set and connects to only a single other interface. This concept, which we refer to as *abstract systems*, captures the topological structures that result when multiple systems are connected in this manner. In the following, we describe the basic types of systems that appear in this work at this level (of abstraction), and we introduce a notation for describing the structure in which multiple such systems are composed.

The abstract systems concept however does not model the behavior of systems, i.e., *how* the systems interact via their interfaces. As statements about cryptographic protocols are statements about behavior, they are formalized at the next (lower) abstraction level. In this respect, all systems in this work are (probabilistic) discrete systems, similar to [17].

Resources and converters. A *resource* for a multi-party setting is a system that provides one interface for each party. In our setting, resources have one interface labeled A for the sender, n interfaces labeled $B_1, \ldots, B_n$ for the n receivers, and one interface labeled E associated with the attacker. Resources are usually denoted either by special symbols such as $\prec$ or by bold-face upper-case letters like $\mathbf{R}$ or $\mathbf{S}$. Protocols are formalized as tuples of so-called *converters*, one for each honest party; converters are systems that have two interfaces: one *inside* and one *outside* interface. Standard notations for converters are small Greek letters or special identifiers such as enc or dec; the set of all converters is denoted as Σ. A complete protocol (i.e., a tuple of converters) is denoted by a bold-face Greek letter, such as $\boldsymbol{\pi}$.

Converters can be attached to resources by connecting the inside interface of the converter to one interface of the resource. Notationally, if we attach the inside interface of the converter $\phi \in \Sigma$ to interface I of the resource $\mathbf{R}$, we write $\phi^I \mathbf{R}$. The resulting system $\phi^I \mathbf{R}$ is again a resource which provides all the interfaces of $\mathbf{R}$ (apart from I) as the respective interfaces, and the outside interface of the converter as the I-interface. If multiple parties use a protocol $\boldsymbol{\pi}$, then all converters that together form $\boldsymbol{\pi}$, one for each (honest) party, are attached to the resource in this manner. This is then denoted as $\boldsymbol{\pi}\mathbf{R}$.

Multiple resources $\mathbf{R}_1, \ldots, \mathbf{R}_m$ can be composed in parallel. This is denoted $[\mathbf{R}_1, \ldots, \mathbf{R}_m]$ and is again a resource, such that each interface $I \in \mathcal{I}$ of $[\mathbf{R}_1, \ldots, \mathbf{R}_m]$ allows to access the corresponding interfaces of $\mathbf{R}_1, \ldots, \mathbf{R}_m$.

Distinguishers. A *distinguisher* $\mathbf{D}$ is a special type of system that connects to all interfaces of a resource $\mathbf{U}$ and outputs a single bit at the end of its interaction with $\mathbf{U}$. We write this as the expression $\mathbf{DU}$, which defines a binary random variable. The *distinguishing advantage of a distinguisher* $\mathbf{D}$ *on two systems* $\mathbf{U}$ *and* $\mathbf{V}$ is defined as

$$\Delta^{\mathbf{D}}(\mathbf{U}, \mathbf{V}) \coloneqq |P(\mathbf{DU} = 1) - P(\mathbf{DV} = 1)|,$$

and we define $\Delta^{\mathcal{D}}(\mathbf{U}, \mathbf{V}) \coloneqq \sup_{\mathbf{D} \in \mathcal{D}} \Delta^{\mathbf{D}}(\mathbf{U}, \mathbf{V})$ as the advantage of a class $\mathcal{D}$ of distinguishers. The distinguishing advantage measures how much the output distribution of $\mathbf{D}$ differs when it is connected to either $\mathbf{U}$ or $\mathbf{V}$. Intuitively, if no distinguisher differentiates between $\mathbf{U}$ and $\mathbf{V}$, they can be used interchangeably in any environment (otherwise the environment can serve as a distinguisher).

The distinguishing advantage is a pseudo-metric. In particular, it satisfies the triangle inequality, i.e., $\Delta^{\mathbf{D}}(\mathbf{U}, \mathbf{W}) \leq \Delta^{\mathbf{D}}(\mathbf{U}, \mathbf{V}) + \Delta^{\mathbf{D}}(\mathbf{V}, \mathbf{W})$ for all resources $\mathbf{U}$, $\mathbf{V}$, and $\mathbf{W}$, and for all distinguishers $\mathbf{D}$. Two systems are *equivalent*, denoted by $\mathbf{U} \equiv \mathbf{V}$, if they have the same behavior, which is the same as requiring that $\Delta^{\mathbf{D}}(\mathbf{U}, \mathbf{V}) = 0$ for *all* distinguishers $\mathbf{D}$.

The notion of construction. The formalization of constructive security definitions follows the ideal-world/real-world paradigm. The "real world" corresponds to an execution of the protocol $\boldsymbol{\pi}$ in which all honest parties have their converter attached to the assumed resource $\mathbf{R}$; more formally, we consider the *real-world system* $\boldsymbol{\pi}\mathbf{R}$. The "ideal world" corresponds to the constructed resource $\mathbf{S}$ with a simulator σ connected to the E-interface of $\mathbf{S}$, written $\sigma^E \mathbf{S}$ and referred to as *ideal-world system*. The purpose of σ is to adapt the E-interface of $\mathbf{S}$ such that it resembles the corresponding interface of $\boldsymbol{\pi}\mathbf{R}$.[2] If the two systems $\boldsymbol{\pi}\mathbf{R}$ and $\sigma^E \mathbf{S}$

---

[2] Indeed, the adversary can emulate the behavior of any efficient simulator σ; thus, using $\sigma^E \mathbf{S}$ instead of $\mathbf{S}$ can only restrict the adversary's power, so using $\sigma^E \mathbf{S}$ and hence $\boldsymbol{\pi}\mathbf{R}$ instead of $\mathbf{S}$ is safe.

are indistinguishable, then this roughly means that "whatever an attacker can do in the real world, he can also do in the ideal world".

Apart from the *security* condition described above, we also require an *availability* condition,[3] which excludes trivial protocols: If no attacker is present, the protocol must implement the specified functionality. In the definition, we use the special converter "⊥" that, when attached to a certain interface of a system, blocks this interface for the distinguisher.[4]

Definition 1 (Construction). *The protocol π constructs* **S** *from the resource* **R** *within ε and with respect to the class $\mathcal{D}$ of distinguishers if*

$$\exists \sigma \in \Sigma: \ \Delta^{\mathcal{D}}(\pi \mathbf{R}, \sigma^E \mathbf{S}) \leq \varepsilon \qquad \text{and} \qquad \Delta^{\mathcal{D}}(\bot^E \pi \mathbf{R}, \bot^E \mathbf{S}) \leq \varepsilon.$$

An important property of Definition 1 is its composability. Intuitively, if a resource **S** is used in the construction of a larger system, then the composability implies that **S** can be replaced by a construction $\pi \mathbf{R}$ without requiring an explicit security reduction. For completeness, we include the composition theorem (which is adapted from [21]) in the full version of the paper [16].

Public-key encryption schemes. A public-key encryption (PKE) scheme with message space $\mathcal{M}$, ciphertext space $\mathcal{C}$, and public-key space $\mathcal{PK}$ is typically described as three algorithms PKE = (kgen, enc, dec). The key-generation algorithm kgen outputs a key pair (pk, sk), the (probabilistic) encryption algorithm enc takes a message $m \in \mathcal{M}$ and a public key pk and outputs a ciphertext $c = \mathsf{enc}(pk; m)$, and the decryption algorithm takes a ciphertext $c \in \mathcal{C}$ and a secret key sk and outputs a plaintext $m = \mathsf{dec}(sk; c)$. The decryption algorithm may also output the special symbol $\Diamond$ (for an invalid input c).

In constructive cryptography, using PKE in a setting with only one sender and one receiver can be described as deploying converters enc_1 (associated with the sender) and dec_1 (associated with the receiver) as follows. The receiver (within dec_1) initially runs the key-generation algorithm kgen to obtain a key pair (sk, pk), stores the private key sk locally, and sends the public key pk via an authenticated channel (denoted $\leftarrow\!\!\bullet$, the first assumed resource). Upon receiving a ciphertext $\tilde{c}$ at the inside interface (via an a priori insecure communication channel $\longrightarrow$, the second assumed resource), dec_1 computes $\tilde{m} = \mathsf{dec}(sk; \tilde{c})$ and outputs $\tilde{m}$. The encryption converter enc_1 initially obtains the public key pk (via $\leftarrow\!\!\bullet$) and, for each message m obtained at the outside interface, enc_1 computes $c = \mathsf{enc}(pk; m)$ and sends c over the insecure channel $\longrightarrow$. As pointed out already in [20], this constructs a confidential channel $\longrightarrow\!\!\bullet$.

In this paper, we consider PKE schemes deployed in a setting with one sender A and n receivers $B_1, \ldots, B_n$, corresponding to a tuple (enc, dec, ..., dec) of $n+1$ converters. Each converter dec is defined similarly to dec_1 above, but if the decryption algorithm dec outputs $\Diamond$, then the converter dec outputs nothing. The encryption converter enc connects at its inside interface to $n+1$ resources.

---

[3] This corresponds to the completeness or correctness properties in some contexts.
[4] The ⊥-converter also signals to the resource that no attacker is there.

By using the first n resources (here instantiated by $\longleftarrow\!\bullet^n$, i.e. for each receiver B_i there is one authenticated channel from B_i to A), enc expects to obtain public keys $pk_1, \ldots, pk_n$. Upon receiving $(m, i) \in \mathcal{M} \times [n]$ at the outside interface, enc computes $c = \mathsf{enc}(pk_i; m)$ and sends (c, i) via the $(n+1)$st resource (instantiated by an insecure broadcast network $\prec$) at the inside interface.

Games and security properties. Game-based definitions specify a property of a cryptographic scheme based on an interaction between two (hypothetical) entities: the game (or challenger) and the adversary. During the interaction, the adversary may issue "oracle queries" to the challenger, the responses of which model what information may be leaked to the adversary. The adversary's goal is specified by the game, and could be, e.g., forging a message or distinguishing encryptions of different messages. If this game cannot be won by any (efficient) adversary, then the scheme is secure against the considered type of attack.

We formalize the adversary and the game as systems that are connected by their interfaces. The game, often denoted as $\mathbf{G}$ with additional super- and subscripts, allows the adversary $\mathbf{A}$ to issue "oracle queries" via that interface. Whether or not the game is won is signaled by a special (monotone) output bit of $\mathbf{G}$ (this can be considered as an additional interface) that is initially 0 but switches to 1 as soon as the winning condition is fulfilled. This bit is denoted Output. For a game $\mathbf{G}$ and an adversary $\mathbf{A}$, we define the *game-winning probability* after q steps (queries) as

$$\Gamma_q^{\mathbf{A}}(\mathbf{G}) \coloneqq \mathsf{P}^{\mathbf{AG}}(\mathsf{Output}_q = 1).$$

For an adversary $\mathbf{A}$ that halts after (at most) q steps, we write $\Gamma^{\mathbf{A}}(\mathbf{G}) \coloneqq \Gamma_q^{\mathbf{A}}(\mathbf{G})$.

Many games considered in the context of encryption schemes, including most games considered here, are *bit-guessing games*. These games can often be described by a pair of systems $\mathbf{G}_0$ and $\mathbf{G}_1$; in the beginning of the game, a bit $B \in \{0, 1\}$ is chosen uniformly at random and the adversary is given access to $\mathbf{G}_B$. The goal is to find the bit B; thus, the adversary has a probability $\frac{1}{2}$ to simply guess this value. Hence, we measure the adversary's success in terms of his *advantage*, that is, the (absolute) difference between $\mathbf{A}$'s probability of winning $\mathbf{G}$ and the success probability for these "trivial" strategies, formally $\Phi^{\mathbf{A}}(\mathbf{G}) = 2 \cdot |\Gamma^{\mathbf{A}}(\mathbf{G}) - \frac{1}{2}|$. Note also that $\Phi^{\mathbf{A}}(\mathbf{G}) = \Delta^{\mathbf{A}}(\mathbf{G}_0, \mathbf{G}_1)$.

For a security property that is defined by means of $\mathbf{G}$, we say that the scheme is secure within ε and with respect to a class $\mathcal{A}$ of adversaries if the advantage $\mathbf{A} \in \mathcal{A}$ has in winning $\mathbf{G}$ is bounded by ε.

Asymptotics. To allow for asymptotic security definitions, cryptographic protocols are often equipped with a so-called *security parameter*. We formulate all statements in this paper in a non-asymptotic fashion, but asymptotic statements can be obtained by treating systems $\mathbf{S}$ as asymptotic families $\{\mathbf{S}_k\}_{k \in \mathbb{N}}$ and letting the distinguishing advantage be a real-valued function of k. Then, for a given notion of efficiency, one can consider security with respect to classes of efficient distinguishers and a suitable negligibility notion. All reductions in this work are efficient with respect to the standard polynomial-time notions.

2.2   Games for Key Privacy and Robustness

We describe the queries that an adversary can ask in a game formally as *procedures* that he can *call*; the specific game structure is enforced by the order in which they are called. This is not a technically new approach (see for instance [6]); however, it integrates smoothly with the security statements we aim for in this work. The most important properties for our work are IND-CCA-security, key privacy, and robustness.

Key privacy. In a key-private PKE scheme, the adversary, given two public keys pk_0 and pk_1, must be unable to tell which key was used to generate a given ciphertext [5]. This definition is similar in spirit to the standard "left-or-right" IND-CCA definition, where the adversary is given the public key, but does not know which of two messages is encrypted under it. In the key-privacy game the message is known, but not the public key. The standard notion of key privacy, i.e. key privacy for chosen ciphertext attacks (IK-CCA) is recalled in the full version [16] together with the two variants we use in our reductions.

Robustness. The notion of *robustness* in encryption was formalized by Abdalla et al. [2] in two flavors: *weak* and *strong* robustness. They consider both versions under both chosen plaintext and chosen ciphertext attacks. We focus here on weak, resp. strong robustness under chosen ciphertext attacks (WROB-CCA, resp. SROB-CCA), associated with the experiments in Figures 1, resp. 2, where the adversary may call the following oracles.

- On input an identifier ID, the oracle **GenUser**($\cdot$) generates a public and a private key for the user ID and returns the public key. A set U keeps track of the honestly generated key pairs and identifiers.
- On input a valid identifier $\text{ID} \in U$, the oracle **Corrupt**($\cdot$) returns the private key corresponding to user ID and adds the identifier to a set V.
- On input a valid identifier $\text{ID} \in U$ and a ciphertext c, the decryption oracle **Decrypt**($\cdot, \cdot$) outputs the corresponding plaintext m.

Init()	GenUser(ID)	Corrupt(ID)	Decrypt(ID,c)	GameOutput(m, ID$_0$, ID$_1$)
$U \leftarrow \emptyset$	$(sk_{\text{ID}}, pk_{\text{ID}}) \leftarrow \textbf{kgen}()$	if (ID; $\cdot$; $\cdot$) $\notin U$	if (ID; $\cdot$; $\cdot$) $\notin U$	if (ID$_0$ = ID$_1$) $\vee$ {ID$_0$, ID$_1$} $\cap V \neq \emptyset$
$V \leftarrow \emptyset$	$U \leftarrow U \cup \{(\text{ID}; sk_{\text{ID}}; pk_{\text{ID}})\}$	return $\Diamond$	return $\Diamond$	return $\Diamond$
Output $\leftarrow 0$	return pk_{ID}	end if.	end if.	end if. $c \leftarrow \textbf{enc}(pk_{\text{ID}_0}, m)$
end.	end.	$V \leftarrow V \cup \{\text{ID}\}$	return $\textbf{dec}(sk_{\text{ID}}, c)$	$m_1 \leftarrow \textbf{dec}(sk_{\text{ID}_1}, c)$
		return sk_{ID} from U	end.	Output $\leftarrow (m \neq \Diamond) \wedge (m_1 \neq \Diamond)$
		end.		end.

Fig. 1. The weak robustness game, $\mathbf{G}^{\text{w-rob}}$

In the WROB-CCA game, the adversary chooses a plaintext and two identities. The plaintext is encrypted by the challenger (without tampering) for the first identity. The adversary wins if this ciphertext decrypts to a valid plaintext for the second identity. By contrast, for strong robustness (SROB-CCA),

Init()	GenUser(ID)	Corrupt(ID)	Decrypt(ID, c)	GameOutput(c, ID$_0$, ID$_1$)
$U \leftarrow \emptyset$	$(sk_{\mathsf{ID}}, pk_{\mathsf{ID}}) \leftarrow \mathsf{kgen}()$	if $(\mathsf{ID}; \cdot; \cdot) \notin U$	if $(\mathsf{ID}; \cdot; \cdot) \notin U$	if $(\mathsf{ID}_0 = \mathsf{ID}_1) \vee \{\mathsf{ID}_0, \mathsf{ID}_1\} \cap V \neq \emptyset$
$V \leftarrow \emptyset$	$U \leftarrow U \cup \{(\mathsf{ID}; sk_{\mathsf{ID}}; pk_{\mathsf{ID}})\}$	return $\Diamond$	return $\Diamond$	return $\Diamond$
Output $\leftarrow 0$	return pk_{ID}	end if.	end if.	end if.
end.	end.	$V \leftarrow V \cup \{\mathsf{ID}\}$	return $\mathsf{dec}(sk_{\mathsf{ID}}, c)$	Output $\leftarrow (\mathsf{dec}(sk_{\mathsf{ID}_0}, c) \neq \Diamond) \wedge$
		return sk_{ID} from U	end.	$(\mathsf{dec}(sk_{\mathsf{ID}_1}, c) \neq \Diamond)$
		end.		end.

Fig. 2. The strong robustness game, $\mathbf{G}^{\text{s-rob}}$

the adversary can manipulate ciphertexts and wins if a chosen ciphertext decrypts to valid plaintexts for two different public keys.

3   Receiver-Anonymous Communication

The main goal of this work is to model and achieve confidential and receiver-anonymous communication. We first formalize a useful anonymity guarantee by describing in Section 3.1 the resource $\text{—}\Diamond\!\!\!\blacktriangleleft$, which *can* actually be constructed from a "broadcast" channel and several authenticated channels (to transmit the public keys). We then discuss in Section 3.2 in which (inefficient) way this construction can be achieved by vanilla public-key encryption, and, in Section 3.3, we argue that "much more" anonymity is impossible to achieve. Finally, in Section 3.4 we show how to achieve this construction more efficiently, by using a PKE scheme that is IND-CCA, IK-CCA [5], and WROB-CCA [2].

3.1   Resources for Receiver-Anonymous Communication

An n-receiver channel is a resource with an interface labeled A for the sender, interfaces labeled $B_1, \ldots, B_n$ for the receivers, and a third type of interface labeled E that captures potential adversarial access. The security properties of different n-receiver channels are described in the following; the symbolic notation for the channels extends that from [20].

The security statements in this work are parametrized by the number of messages that are transmitted over the channels. More precisely, for each of the following channels and each $q \in \mathbb{N}$, we define the q-*bounded channel* as the one that processes (only) the first q queries at the A-interface and the first q queries at the E-interface as described, and ignores all further queries at these interfaces. We then require from a protocol that it constructs, for all $q \in \mathbb{N}$, the q-bounded "ideal" channel from the q-bounded assumed channel.[5] Wherever the number q is significant, such as in the theorem statements, we denote the q-bounded versions of channels by writing the q on top of the channel symbol (e.g., $\overset{q}{\blacktriangleleft}$); we omit it in places that are of less formal nature.

---

[5] This condition is equivalent to considering an "unbounded" channel; the important feature is that *the protocol* is independent of the number q of messages.

Insecure broadcast communication. We base our constructions on a resource $\prec$, which allows the sender to broadcast a given message to all receivers $B_1, \ldots, B_n$. Such a channel can be implemented, for example, by multi-sending the same message individually to each receiver over an insecure network; the channel models also what is achieved by wireless broadcast. The resource $\prec$ leaks the complete message at the E-interface, and allows to delete, change, or inject messages destined for particular receivers via the E-interface. In more detail:

- If at the E-interface the $\perp$-converter is connected,[6] then on input the k-th message m_k at the A-interface, output m_k at B_j for all $j \in [n]$.
- Otherwise, on input the k-th message m_k at the A-interface, output m_k at the E-interface. Upon the query $(\texttt{inject}, j, \tilde{m})$ at the E-interface for $j \in [n]$ and $\tilde{m} \in \mathcal{M}$, deliver $\tilde{m}$ at interface B_j.

Confidential receiver-anonymous communication. The confidential receiver-anonymous channel $-\!\diamond\!\!\prec$ leaks neither the message contents nor the intended recipient to the adversary, just the message length. It allows, however, to "conditionally" deliver a message to a chosen user if and only if this chosen user was the originally intended recipient.

- If at the E-interface the $\perp$-converter is connected, then on the k-th input (m_k, i_k) at the A-interface, output m_k at B_{i_k}.
- Otherwise, on the k-th input (m_k, i_k) at the A-interface, output the message length $|m_k|$ at the E-interface. Furthermore, the E-interface allows the following queries:
  - $(\texttt{inject}, j, \tilde{m})$ for $j \in [n]$ and $\tilde{m} \in \mathcal{M}$: delivers $\tilde{m}$ at interface B_j;
  - $(\texttt{deliver}, j, \bar{k})$ for $j \in [n]$, $\bar{k} \in \mathbb{N}$: If at least $\bar{k}$ messages have been sent via A and $i_{\bar{k}} = j$, then it delivers the message $m_{\bar{k}}$ at B_j.

This is also depicted in Figure 3. In the application of a public-key cryptosystem to a broadcast network such as $-\!\diamond\!\!\prec$, the capabilities at the E-interface correspond to trial deliveries of intercepted messages and to adversarial encryptions.

Authenticated channel. Each receiver uses one authenticated channel $\longleftarrow\!\bullet$ to send its public key to the sender; we use n parallel authenticated channels, denoted $\longleftarrow\!\bullet^n$ (one for each receiver), as assumed resources in our constructions. Formally, a single authenticated channel $\longleftarrow\!\bullet$ with message space $\mathcal{M}$ is a three-party resource with interfaces A, B_i (for some i), and E. On input a message $m \in \mathcal{M}$ at interface B_i, the channel outputs m at the E-interface. The channel outputs m at the A-interface only upon receiving an acknowledgement from the E-interface (the adversary controls message delivery).

---

[6] Formally, there is a special input that provokes this behavior, and the converter $\perp$ provides this input.

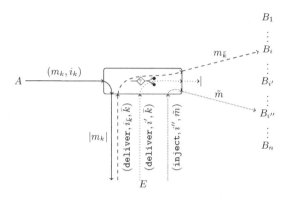

Fig. 3. The confidential receiver-anonymous channel

3.2 Generic Construction Using Public-Key Encryption

The channel $\multimap\!\!\diamond\!\!\prec$ can be constructed from $\prec$ and $\longleftarrow\!\!\bullet^n$ using any secure public-key scheme: Each receiver generates a key pair and sends the public key through its authenticated channel $\longleftarrow\!\!\bullet$ to the sender; the sender transmits a message to a specific receiver by concatenating (in a fixed predetermined order): an encryption of this message under the intended receiver's public key and a "garbage" message encrypted with the appropriate key for each additional potential receiver; this composite message is then sent via the broadcast channel. Each receiver decrypts only "its" part of the composite ciphertext and checks whether or not the message was "garbage." (Typically, the "garbage" message can be set to a constant message $\bar{m} \in \mathcal{M}$ not otherwise used.) If the broadcast channel is achieved by multi-sending the same message to each receiver, then one can also send only the corresponding part to each receiver.

Yet, this approach has two main disadvantages. First, the computation and communication complexity is linear in the (potentially large) number of possible receivers. Second, the sender must *know* the public keys of all potential receivers, not just of the one intended receiver.

3.3 "Upper Bounds" on Anonymity

Anonymity beyond the guarantees of $\multimap\!\!\diamond\!\!\prec$ seems unlikely to be achieved from the resources $\prec$ and $\longleftarrow\!\!\bullet^n$ which we assumed. Indeed, we show that a (minor and natural) extension of $\multimap\!\!\diamond\!\!\prec$ cannot be achieved from our assumed resources. The extension, denoted by ANON, removes the "conditional delivery" capability provided at the E-interface in resource $\multimap\!\!\diamond\!\!\prec$, and enables deliveries of the type (deliver, $\bar{k}$) for $\bar{k} \in \mathbb{N}$, where, if at least $\bar{k}$ messages have been sent via A, then the message $m_{\bar{k}}$ is delivered to $B_{i_{\bar{k}}}$. In particular, the distinguisher can use the E-interface of system $\prec$ to deliver the messages to, e.g., only one chosen receiver, which will output the message if and only if it is the intended recipient. We call this process a "trial delivery" and show that it allows the distinguisher to tell the real-world system apart from the ideal-world system with ANON, where trial deliveries are impossible by definition.

This result is formalized in in the full version [16]; the proof expands on the sketch we gave above. Note that the channel ANON is just one type of ideal resource providing stronger anonymity guarantees than $-\diamondsuit\!\!\!-\!\!\!\bullet$; however, our impossibility result extends easily to any resource without conditional deliveries.

3.4   Achieving Confidential Receiver-Anonymous Communication

A public-key encryption scheme constructs the resource $-\diamondsuit\!\!\!-\!\!\!\bullet$ from a broadcast channel if it has the properties IND-CCA, IK-CCA, and WROB-CCA. The property WROB-CCA (weak robustness) captures the guarantee that ciphertexts honestly generated for one user will not be successfully decrypted by another user. We show that weak robustness is sufficient for our construction. This may appear somewhat surprising since the adversary *can* inject arbitrary ciphertexts into the channel $\prec$, see [2]. The intuitive reason why WROB-CCA is sufficient is two-fold: First, preventing the adversary from generating a single "fresh" ciphertext that is accepted by two receivers is only helpful if injecting two different ciphertexts is impossible, or harder for the adversary than injecting a single one (cf. Section 4.3). Second, the non-malleability guarantees of IND-CCA exclude that the adversary can "maul" honestly generated ciphertexts such that unintended receivers decrypt "related" plaintexts (this is used in the reduction to IND-CCA in the proof of Theorem 1).

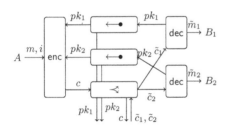 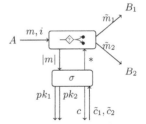

(a) Using public-key encryption over an (insecure) broadcast.

(b) The idealized setting, the value "$*$" depends on $\tilde{c}_1, \tilde{c}_2$.

Fig. 4. The security statement in a setting with two receivers

The security statement we prove below is depicted in Figure 4, where we show how the scheme is used together with the assumed resources: Each sender transmits its public key authentically to the sender, who then uses the broadcast channel to transmit the ciphertext to both receivers. Figure 4b shows the idealized setting, where the message is transmitted via the resource $-\diamondsuit\!\!\!-\!\!\!\bullet$ (which guarantees confidentiality). The value "$*$" is determined by the simulator and depends on the values $\tilde{c}_1$ and $\tilde{c}_2$ given by the adversary; the symbol may stand for a query to deliver the message m or to inject unrelated messages.

Theorem 1 shows that if the public-key encryption scheme has the three assumed properties, then the two settings in Figure 4 are indistinguishable. Intuitively, whenever such a scheme is used to protect messages transmitted via a broadcast channel like $\prec$, one obtains the guarantees explicitly described by the "idealized" network resource $\multimap\!\!\!\diamondsuit\!\!\prec$. The proof of the theorem shows that every distinguisher for the two settings can be transformed into an adversary against (at least) one of the three properties IND-CCA, IK-CCA, and WROB-CCA with loss qn for q messages and n receivers. The games $\mathbf{G}^{\text{ind-cca}}$ and $\mathbf{G}^{\text{ik-cca}}$ referred to in the theorem are defined in the full version [16].

Theorem 1. *Let* (kgen, enc, dec) *be a public-key encryption scheme that has the three properties* IND-CCA-, IK-CCA-, *and* WROB-CCA. *Then, the protocol* (enc, dec, . . . , dec) *defined as in Section 2.1 transforms* $\prec$ *and* $(\longleftarrow\!\!\bullet)^n$ *into* $\multimap\!\!\!\diamondsuit\!\!\prec$. *More formally, there are a simulator* σ *and for each* $q \in \mathbb{N}$ *four reductions* $\mathbf{A}_q(\cdot)$, $\mathbf{A}'_q(\cdot)$, $\mathbf{A}''_q(\cdot)$, $\mathbf{A}'''_q(\cdot)$ *such that*

$$\Delta^{\mathbf{D}}\left(\text{enc}^A\text{dec}^{B_1}\ldots\text{dec}^{B_n}\bot^E\left[\overset{q}{\prec},\longleftarrow\!\!\bullet^n\right],\bot^E\overset{q}{\multimap\!\!\!\diamondsuit\!\!\prec}\right)$$
$$\leq qn\cdot\Gamma^{\mathbf{A}_q(\mathbf{D})}\left(\mathbf{G}^{\text{w-rob}}\right),\quad(1)$$

and

$$\Delta^{\mathbf{D}}\left(\text{enc}^A\text{dec}^{B_1}\ldots\text{dec}^{B_n}\left[\overset{q}{\prec},\longleftarrow\!\!\bullet^n\right],\sigma^E\overset{q}{\multimap\!\!\!\diamondsuit\!\!\prec}\right)$$
$$\leq qn\cdot\Phi^{\mathbf{A}'_q(\mathbf{D})}\left(\mathbf{G}^{\text{ind-cca}}\right)+2qn\cdot\Phi^{\mathbf{A}''_q(\mathbf{D})}\left(\mathbf{G}^{\text{ik-cca}}\right)+qn\cdot\Gamma^{\mathbf{A}'''_q(\mathbf{D})}\left(\mathbf{G}^{\text{w-rob}}\right).\quad(2)$$

Proof (sketch). We sketch the proofs for conditions (1) and (2) independently.

Availability. We describe a reduction $\mathbf{A}_q(\cdot)$ that turns a distinguisher $\mathbf{D}$ between the real-world system $\text{enc}^A\text{dec}^{B_1}\ldots\text{dec}^{B_n}\bot^E[\prec,\longleftarrow\!\!\bullet^n]$ (which we denote $\mathbf{R}_\bot$) and the ideal-world system $\bot^E(\multimap\!\!\!\diamondsuit\!\!\prec)$ (denoted $\mathbf{S}_\bot$) into an adversary for the the WROB-CCA game. The idea of the proof is to construct a monotone event sequence (MES, see [17]), which becomes true once the distinguisher inputs a pair (m, i) at the A-interface such that a receiver B_j for some index $j \neq i$ outputs some plaintext $m_j \neq \Diamond$. If the encryption scheme has perfect correctness, the systems $\mathbf{R}_\bot$ and $\mathbf{S}_\bot$ are equivalent, conditioned on the MES remaining false (if the scheme is *not* perfectly correct, we alter the MES to take this into account). Yet, note that even isolating a query (m, i) that invokes the MES does not immediately imply that a new encryption of the same m and pk_i will yield another ciphertext (in the query of the WROB-CCA game) that decrypts to $m'_j \neq \Diamond$ by sk_j for the index $j \neq i$. Instead, for the reduction to be successful, the reduction $\mathbf{A}_q$ guesses the query and the receiver where this erroneous decryption will occur. Thus, the reduction loses a factor qn, as claimed.

Security. We first describe the simulator σ attached to the E-interface of the ideal resource. The role of σ is to simulate the interaction at the E-interface to a distinguisher. We then prove that σ is indeed a good simulator: in other words, we provide reductions that transform a given successful distinguisher into a successful adversary against one of the following games: IND-CCA, IK-CCA, or WROB-CCA. The simulator σ runs as follows:

- Generate n private-/public-key pairs (pk_i, sk_i) with $i \in [n]$ to simulate each pk_i that it is transmitted via the corresponding channel $\longleftarrow\bullet$. Furthermore, generate one auxiliary key pair $(\tilde{pk}, \tilde{sk})$.
- Upon the k-th message length ℓ_k from $-\diamondsuit\!\!\!\prec\!\!\!\bullet$, generate a new ciphertext $c_k = \mathsf{enc}(\tilde{pk}; 0^{\ell_k})$ and simulate c_k as a message on $\prec$.
- When $\mathbf{D}$ delivers a message $\tilde{c}$ to some user $j \in [n]$:
  - In case $\tilde{c} = c_{\bar{k}}$ for some $\bar{k} \in \mathbb{N}$, issue $(\mathsf{deliver}, j, \bar{k})$ to $-\diamondsuit\!\!\!\prec\!\!\!\bullet$.
  - In case $\tilde{c}$ is "fresh," compute $\tilde{m}_j := \mathsf{dec}(sk_j; \tilde{c})$, and, if $\tilde{m}_j \neq \Diamond$, issue $(\mathsf{inject}, j, \tilde{m}_j)$ to $-\diamondsuit\!\!\!\prec\!\!\!\bullet$.

Assume that there exists a distinguisher $\mathbf{D}$ that successfully distinguishes the real-world system $\mathsf{enc}^A \mathsf{dec}^{B_1} \ldots \mathsf{dec}^{B_n} [\prec, \longleftarrow\bullet^n]$ from the ideal-world system $\sigma^E -\diamondsuit\!\!\!\prec\!\!\!\bullet$. We sketch the security reductions to the underlying games.

WROB-CCA. As a first intermediate step, we introduce a hybrid resource $\mathbf{H}_1$. This resource behaves like $-\diamondsuit\!\!\!\prec\!\!\!\bullet$, except that it allows for the delivery of an arbitrary message to a party other than the intended recipient: namely, instead of the query $(\mathsf{deliver}, j, \bar{k})$, we allow to deliver a message $\tilde{m}$ to a user B_j for $j \neq i_{\bar{k}}$ (still $m_{\bar{k}}$ for $j = i_{\bar{k}}$) by means of $(\mathsf{deliver}, j, \bar{k}, \tilde{m})$. We use a modified simulator σ_1 that sends the decryption of the ciphertext simulated for message $\bar{k}$ under the key of user j. The systems $\sigma_1^E \mathbf{H}_1$ and $\sigma^E -\diamondsuit\!\!\!\prec\!\!\!\bullet$ are equivalent unless, for some query, there is a user B_j, not the intended recipient of some ciphertext, that outputs a message upon receiving the ciphertext. A distinguisher that provokes this situation (i.e., it causes some unintended recipient to output a message from a ciphertext) can be used to win the WROB-CCA game. The reduction $\mathbf{A}_q'''(\cdot)$ obtains n generated keys from the WROB-CCA game, which correspond to the users, and an additional key, used to simulate ciphertexts. As in the availability proof, $\mathbf{A}_q'''$ has to guess on which query $(\tilde{m}_l, i_l)$ and with respect to which other index j the erroneous decryption will occur, for sending the appropriate $\tilde{m}_l$, i_l, and j as its challenge in the weak robustness game. In order to properly simulate the eavesdropper to the environment, we use a slightly tweaked version of weak robustness (equivalent to the original one) where we also obtain the generated ciphertext when running the **GameOutput** oracle.

IND-CCA. We introduce a second hybrid $\mathbf{H}_2$ that behaves as $\mathbf{H}_1$ but additionally leaks the receiver's identity (no anonymity). The suitable simulator σ_2 always encrypts the all-zero string of appropriate length for the respective user, and decrypts as needed. Two things must be shown: first, that $\sigma_2^E \mathbf{H}_2$ is indistinguishable from the real-world system; and second, that $\sigma_1^E \mathbf{H}_1$ and $\sigma_2^E \mathbf{H}_2$ are indistinguishable. We start with the former one, where the reduction $\mathbf{A}_q'(\cdot)$ uses a hybrid argument to employ a distinguisher for $\sigma_2^E \mathbf{H}_2$ and $\mathsf{enc}^A \mathsf{dec}^{B_1} \ldots \mathsf{dec}^{B_n} [\prec, \longleftarrow\bullet^n]$ to win the IND-CCA game. Technically, one defines a sequence of hybrid systems, where the i-th hybrid simulates "ideal" encryptions for the first $i - 1$

receivers, uses the game to simulate for the i-th receiver, and "real" encryptions for the remaining receivers. The reduction $\mathbf{A}_q'(\cdot)$ then chooses $i \in [n]$ uniformly at random. Overall, the first hybrid with no simulated encryptions is equivalent to $\mathsf{enc}^A \mathsf{dec}^{B_1} \ldots \mathsf{dec}^{B_n} [\prec, \longleftarrow\!\!\bullet^n]$, while the hybrid with only simulated encryptions is equivalent to the hybrid $\sigma_2 \mathbf{H}_2$. As the IND-CCA game offers only a single challenge query, another hybrid argument must be employed to account for the number of encryptions; this adds a factor of q.

IK-CCA. The last step is to show a reduction $\mathbf{A}_q''(\cdot)$ that turns a distinguisher between $\sigma_1 \mathbf{H}_1$ and $\sigma_2 \mathbf{H}_2$ corresponding, respectively, to the first and second hybrid introduced in the proof, into an IK-CCA-adversary. Recall that $\mathbf{H}_2$ behaves just like $\mathbf{H}_1$ except that it does not grant anonymity. We again use a hybrid argument with qn "intermediate" systems between $\sigma_1^E \mathbf{H}_1$ and $\sigma_2^E \mathbf{H}_2$, similarly to the IND-CCA case, such that each intermediate system embeds the challenge at a different position (as above). All other keys, encryptions, or decryptions are either simulated as "real" or as "ideal," depending on their position. The system where only the queries are "real" is equivalent to $\sigma_2 \mathbf{H}_2$, and the system where only $\widetilde{pk}$ was used (all queries are "ideal") is equivalent to $\sigma_1 \mathbf{H}_1$. $\square$

4   Relation to Notions of Robustness

While the confidential receiver-anonymous channel can be achieved using an encryption scheme that fulfills IND-CCA, IK-CCA, and WROB-CCA, anonymity without robustness is not sufficient. This was already noted by Abdalla et al. [2], who point out that if one receiver obtains a ciphertext that was intended for a different receiver, the decryption should yield this information—by producing an error symbol—instead of an arbitrary, but well-formed plaintext, because this undetected, but unintended plaintext message might "upset" higher level protocols. This "robustness," however, is not guaranteed by IND-CCA or IK-CCA.

This section formalizes and proves statements related to robustness. In Section 4.1 we describe the type of channel one obtains if the PKE scheme is only IND-CCA- and IK-CCA-secure; this confirms the intuition given in [2]. We then show in Section 4.2 that WROB-CCA is indeed formally *necessary* to construct the channel $-\!\!\diamondsuit\!\!\prec$: Every (IND-RCCA and IK-RCCA-secure) scheme that achieves the constructive notion *must* be weakly robust. Finally, in Section 4.3 we show that a strongly robust scheme will also *only* construct the resource $-\!\!\diamondsuit\!\!\prec$, though with a tighter reduction. We also explain why a strongly robust scheme does *not* help to construct a "qualitatively better" resource.

4.1   Anonymity with Erroneous Transmission

The channel one obtains from applying an IND-CCA and IK-CCA-secure scheme to $\prec$ and $\longleftarrow\!\!\bullet^n$ is the resource $-\!\!\diamondsuit\!\!\prec$ which is parametrized by a family of distributions $\left(\mathsf{P}_{Y_1 \ldots Y_n}^\ell\right)_{\ell \in \mathbb{N}}$ and differs from $-\!\!\diamondsuit\!\!\prec$ only in the cases where honestly generated messages are transmitted to receivers other than the intended one (either during an honest transmission or because the adversary forwards an honestly sent message to such a receiver). Without weak robustness, the unintended receiver will output a message according to the (scheme-specific) distribution. A formal description of —◈—⚡ follows.

- If at the E-interface the $\perp$-converter is connected, then for the k-th input (m_k, i_k) at the A-interface, choose $m'_{k,1}, \ldots, m'_{k,n}$ according to $\mathsf{P}^{|m_k|}_{Y_1 \ldots Y_n}$, output m_k at B_{i_k} and $m'_{k,j}$ at B_j for $j \neq i_k$ (if $m'_{k,j} \neq \Diamond$, else nothing).
- Otherwise, on the k-th input (m_k, i_k) at the A-interface, output only the message length $|m_k|$ at the E-interface. Furthermore, the E-interface allows the following queries:
  - (inject, $j, \tilde{m}$) for $j \in \{1, \ldots, n\}$ and $\tilde{m} \in \mathcal{M}$: Delivers $\tilde{m}$ at B_j,
  - (deliver, $j, \bar{k}, \tilde{m}$) for $j \in \{1, \ldots, n\}$, $\bar{k} \in \mathbb{N}$, and $m \in \mathcal{M}$: If at least $\bar{k}$ messages have been sent via A, then delivers message $m_{\bar{k}}$ at B_j if $i_{\bar{k}} = j$, and delivers $\tilde{m}$ at B_j otherwise.

In the full version [16] we show that the channel —◈—⚡ is constructed from —◁ and n authenticated channels ◀—● if the encryption scheme is IND-CCA- and IK-CCA-secure. In the proof, we instantiate the channel —◈—⚡ with a distribution $\mathsf{P}^\ell_{Y_1 \ldots Y_n}$ that we define by honestly choosing keys for the receivers and, whenever a message is sent to a party B_i, decrypting a "random ciphertext" of the correct length with respect to the keys of all parties B_j with $j \neq i$.

4.2 "Equivalence" with Weak Robustness

In Section 3.4 we showed that IND-CCA, IK-CCA, and WROB-CCA security are *sufficient* to construct —◈—⚡. Indeed, (slightly weaker variants of) these properties are also *necessary*: If a PKE scheme is sufficient for the construction, then it must also be weakly robust, IND-RCCA, and IK-RCCA. Note that "CCA"-notions are sufficient, but not necessary, as they also prohibit that a scheme allows for "trivial" modifications of the ciphertext, which do not have an impact on the actual security [9,19]. We explicitly describe the IND-RCCA-game and the IK-RCCA-game in the full version. These notions, compared to the original ones, have more "elaborate" decryption oracles that prevent decryptions of "trivially modified" ciphertexts.

The formal statement and the proof are deferred to the full version [16]. The basic idea is that for each of the three games for weak robustness, IND-RCCA, and IK-RCCA, we show that a successful adversary will also serve as a good distinguisher in the constructive security statement.

4.3 Anonymity with Strong Robustness

Strong robustness (SROB-CCA, [2]) is strictly stronger than weak robustness. Intuitively, whereas weak robustness states that honestly generated ciphertexts are not decryptable by two distinct receivers, strong robustness requires this even for adversarially generated ciphertexts. A strongly robust scheme will of course also be sufficient to achieve $-\!\!\diamondsuit\!\!\prec$, in the full version we show that we even achieve better bounds in the reduction. Intuitively, due to the exact definition of the oracles in the games, the reduction to SROB-CCA can exploit *every* inconsistency in an emulated interaction with the distinguisher, whereas the reduction to WROB-CCA has to guess *when* the inconsistency will occur.

Somewhat surprisingly, strong robustness does not provide a "qualitatively" better security guarantee than weak robustness. ("Qualitative" refers to the properties of the resources, in contrast to the "quantitative" reduction tightness.) This is particularly relevant since obtaining a WROB-CCA secure scheme from a non-robust one is easier than obtaining an SROB-CCA one [2].

To some extent, the fact that the "qualitative" guarantees of weak and strong robustness coincide stems from the assumed resource $\prec$. Since $\prec$ allows the adversary to inject arbitrary ciphertexts to arbitrary receivers, there is no incentive to send *the same* (faked) ciphertext to two or more different users; the adversary could also send different ciphertexts. Technically, from a network that allows the adversary to inject one message to multiple receivers more "easily" than it allows him to inject different messages, a strongly robust scheme indeed achieves a "better" resource than a weakly robust one; in the weakly robust case the adversary can inject messages to *several* receivers "easily," in the strongly robust case *only to one*. We think, however, that such a network guarantee (injecting several different messages is more difficult) would have to be justified by a particular application and should not be the focus of a general-purpose discussion as ours.

Theorem 2. *An encryption scheme that is* IND-CCA-, 1-sided-IK-CCA-, *and* SROB-CCA-*secure will transform* $\prec$ *and* $(\leftarrow\!\bullet)^n$ *into* $-\!\!\diamondsuit\!\!\prec$. *More formally, there exist a simulator* σ' *and reductions* $\mathbf{A}_{nq}(\cdot), \mathbf{A}'_q(\cdot), \mathbf{A}''_q(\cdot), \mathbf{A}'''_{nq}(\cdot)$ *such that*

$$\Delta^{\mathbf{D}}\left(\mathsf{enc}^A\mathsf{dec}^{B_1}\ldots\mathsf{dec}^{B_n}\bot^E\left[\overset{q}{\prec},\overset{}{\leftarrow\!\bullet}^n\right],\bot^E(\overset{q}{-\!\!\diamondsuit\!\!\prec})\right)\leq\Gamma^{\mathbf{A}_{nq}(\mathbf{D})}\left(\mathbf{G}^{\text{s-rob}}\right),\quad(3)$$

and

$$\Delta^{\mathbf{D}}\left(\mathsf{enc}^A\mathsf{dec}^{B_1}\ldots\mathsf{dec}^{B_n}\left[\overset{q}{\prec},\overset{}{\leftarrow\!\bullet}^n\right],\sigma'^E(\overset{q}{-\!\!\diamondsuit\!\!\prec})\right)$$

$$\leq qn\cdot\Phi^{\mathbf{A}'_q(\mathbf{D})}\left(\mathbf{G}^{\text{ind-cca}}\right)+qn\cdot\Phi^{\mathbf{A}''_q(\mathbf{D})}\left(\mathbf{G}^{\text{1-sided-ik-cca}}\right)+\Gamma^{\mathbf{A}'''_{nq}(\mathbf{D})}\left(\mathbf{G}^{\text{s-rob}}\right).\quad(4)$$

5   Conclusion and Possible Extensions

We analyzed the problem of achieving confidentiality for a receiver-anonymous channel; our results are the constructive counterpart of the notions discussed in [5,2]. In particular, we showed that confidentiality, key privacy, and weak robustness are indeed sufficient for such a scheme to be useful, and that (slightly relaxed versions of) these are indeed necessary. We have also discussed why strong robustness is not necessary in this context. Our results do not only support the trust in existing schemes and constructions; they also show that the simpler and more efficient weakly robust schemes (see [2]) can be used safely.

Our constructive statements help explore the boundary between cryptography and traffic analysis. For example, an (active) instance of the latter, conditional delivery, cannot be prevented by end-to-end encryption (even if it has all the properties we suggest); indeed countermeasures against such attacks at the application level are critical to provide any meaningful traffic analysis resistance. Our ideal resource, thus, does not yet correspond directly to the black-box system models used by traffic analysis research, but is a component upon which such a model could be based. In contrast to our model here, traffic analysis frameworks usually consider restricted attackers that observe only parts of the system and a probabilistic model for sender and receiver behavior.[7]

Protocols in which encrypted messages are processed by multiple parties can, to some extent, prevent conditional deliveries. In a MIX-network, for instance, the attacker cannot direct a multi-layered ciphertext at a particular recipient, as he will be unable to remove the outer ciphertext layers. Thus receiver-anonymous communication using onions, threshold decryption, or verifiable re-randomization bypasses our impossibility result, instead requiring additional (distributed) trust in third parties.

Our study of anonymity properties of end-to-end encryption is only a first step in the constructive modeling of resources with useful anonymity properties and constructions thereof. The general paradigm of examining the security of anonymity-preserving cryptographic schemes in a constructive manner can (and should) be applied to other schemes as well, including topics such as anonymous signature schemes and key-exchange protocols.

Acknowledgments. Ueli Maurer and Björn Tackmann were supported by the Swiss National Science Foundation (SNF), project no. 200020-132794. Daniele Venturi acknowledges support from the Danish National Research Foundation, the National Science Foundation of China (under the grant 61061130540), the Danish Council for Independent Research (under the DFF Starting Grant 10-081612) and also from the CFEM research center within which part of this work was performed.

References

1. Abadi, M., Fournet, C.: Private authentication. Theor. Comput. Sci. 322(3), 427–476 (2004)
2. Abdalla, M., Bellare, M., Neven, G.: Robust encryption. In: Micciancio, D. (ed.) TCC 2010. LNCS, vol. 5978, pp. 480–497. Springer, Heidelberg (2010)
3. Backes, M., Goldberg, I., Kate, A., Mohammadi, E.: Provably secure and practical onion routing. In: Chong, S. (ed.) CSF, pp. 369–385. IEEE (2012)

---

[7] In this aspect, our analysis plays a role similar to the cryptographic analysis of an onion routing protocol in [3], which provides a formal foundation for the traffic analysis of onion routing in [13]. Our analysis targets a cryptographic primitive and not a protocol, and can thus be more detailed.

4. Beimel, A., Dolev, S.: Buses for anonymous message delivery. Journal of Cryptology 16(1), 25–39 (2003)
5. Bellare, M., Boldyreva, A., Desai, A., Pointcheval, D.: Key-privacy in public-key encryption. In: Boyd, C. (ed.) ASIACRYPT 2001. LNCS, vol. 2248, pp. 566–582. Springer, Heidelberg (2001)
6. Bellare, M., Rogaway, P.: The security of triple encryption and a framework for code-based game-playing proofs. In: Vaudenay, S. (ed.) EUROCRYPT 2006. LNCS, vol. 4004, pp. 409–426. Springer, Heidelberg (2006)
7. Camenisch, J., Lysyanskaya, A.: A formal treatment of onion routing. In: Shoup, V. (ed.) CRYPTO 2005. LNCS, vol. 3621, pp. 169–187. Springer, Heidelberg (2005)
8. Canetti, R., Krawczyk, H.: Security analysis of IKE's signature-based key-exchange protocol. In: Yung, M. (ed.) CRYPTO 2002. LNCS, vol. 2442, pp. 143–161. Springer, Heidelberg (2002)
9. Canetti, R., Krawczyk, H., Nielsen, J.B.: Relaxing chosen-ciphertext security. In: Boneh, D. (ed.) CRYPTO 2003. LNCS, vol. 2729, pp. 565–582. Springer, Heidelberg (2003)
10. Dingledine, R., Mathewson, N., Syverson, P.: Tor: The second-generation onion router. In: Proceedings of the 13th USENIX Security Symposium (August 2004)
11. Farshim, P., Libert, B., Paterson, K.G., Quaglia, E.A.: Robust encryption, revisited. In: Kurosawa, K., Hanaoka, G. (eds.) PKC 2013. LNCS, vol. 7778, pp. 352–368. Springer, Heidelberg (2013)
12. Feigenbaum, J., Johnson, A., Syverson, P.F.: A model of onion routing with provable anonymity. In: Dietrich, S., Dhamija, R. (eds.) FC 2007 and USEC 2007. LNCS, vol. 4886, pp. 57–71. Springer, Heidelberg (2007)
13. Feigenbaum, J., Johnson, A., Syverson, P.F.: Probabilistic analysis of onion routing in a black-box model. ACM Trans. Inf. Syst. Secur. 15(3), 14 (2012)
14. Hevia, A., Micciancio, D.: An indistinguishability-based characterization of anonymous channels. In: Borisov, N., Goldberg, I. (eds.) PETS 2008. LNCS, vol. 5134, pp. 24–43. Springer, Heidelberg (2008)
15. Ishai, Y., Kushilevitz, E., Ostrovsky, R., Sahai, A.: Cryptography from anonymity. In: FOCS, pp. 239–248. IEEE Computer Society (2006)
16. Kohlweiss, M., Maurer, U., Onete, C., Tackmann, B., Venturi, D.: Anonymity-preserving public-key encryption: A constructive approach. Cryptology ePrint Archive, Report 2013/238, http://eprint.iacr.org/
17. Maurer, U.: Indistinguishability of random systems. In: Knudsen, L.R. (ed.) EUROCRYPT 2002. LNCS, vol. 2332, pp. 110–132. Springer, Heidelberg (2002)
18. Maurer, U., Renner, R.: Abstract cryptography. In: Innovations in Computer Science. Tsinghua University Press (2011)
19. Maurer, U., Rüedlinger, A., Tackmann, B.: Confidentiality and integrity: A constructive perspective. In: Cramer, R. (ed.) TCC 2012. LNCS, vol. 7194, pp. 209–229. Springer, Heidelberg (2012)
20. Maurer, U., Schmid, P.: A calculus for security bootstrapping in distributed systems. Journal of Computer Security 4(1), 55–80 (1996)
21. Maurer, U., Tackmann, B.: On the soundness of Authenticate-then-Encrypt: Formalizing the malleability of symmetric encryption. In: ACM CCS. ACM (2010)
22. Mohassel, P.: A closer look at anonymity and robustness in encryption schemes. In: Abe, M. (ed.) ASIACRYPT 2010. LNCS, vol. 6477, pp. 501–518. Springer, Heidelberg (2010)
23. Nagao, W., Manabe, Y., Okamoto, T.: Relationship of three cryptographic channels in the UC framework. In: Baek, J., Bao, F., Chen, K., Lai, X. (eds.) ProvSec 2008. LNCS, vol. 5324, pp. 268–282. Springer, Heidelberg (2008)

24. Onete, C., Venturi, D.: Security & indistinguishability in the presence of traffic analysis. Cryptology ePrint Archive, Report 2011/260 (2011)
25. Pfitzmann, A., Waidner, M.: Networks without user observability – design options. In: Pichler, F. (ed.) EUROCRYPT 1985. LNCS, vol. 219, pp. 245–253. Springer, Heidelberg (1986)
26. Waters, B.R., Felten, E.W., Sahai, A.: Receiver anonymity via incomparable public keys. In: ACM CCS, pp. 112–121 (2003)
27. Yang, G., Wong, D.S., Deng, X., Wang, H.: Anonymous signature schemes. In: Yung, M., Dodis, Y., Kiayias, A., Malkin, T. (eds.) PKC 2006. LNCS, vol. 3958, pp. 347–363. Springer, Heidelberg (2006)

Efficient E-Cash in Practice: NFC-Based Payments for Public Transportation Systems*

Gesine Hinterwälder[1], Christian T. Zenger[1,2], Foteini Baldimtsi[3],
Anna Lysyanskaya[3], Christof Paar[1,2], and Wayne P. Burleson[1]

[1] Department of Electrical and Computer Engineering, University of Massachusetts Amherst
{hinterwalder,burleson}@ecs.umass.edu
[2] Horst Görtz Institute for IT Security, Ruhr-University Bochum, Germany
{christian.zenger,christof.paar}@rub.de
[3] Computer Science Department, Brown University
{foteini,anna}@cs.brown.edu

Abstract. Near field communication (NFC) is a recent popular technology that will facilitate many aspects of payments with mobile tokens. In the domain of public transportation payment systems electronic payments have many benefits, including improved throughput, new capabilities (congestion-based pricing etc.) and user convenience. A common concern when using electronic payments is that a user's privacy is sacrificed. However, cryptographic e-cash schemes provide provable guarantees for both security and user privacy. Even though e-cash protocols have been proposed three decades ago, there are relatively few actual implementations, since their computation complexity makes an execution on lightweight devices rather difficult. This paper presents an efficient implementation of Brands [11] and ACL [4] e-cash schemes on an NFC smartphone: the BlackBerry Bold 9900. Due to their efficiency during the spending phase, when compared to other schemes, and the fact that payments can be verified offline, these schemes are especially suited for, but not limited to, use in public transport. Additionally, the encoding of validated attributes (e.g. a user's age range, zip code etc.) is possible in the coins being withdrawn, which allows for additional features such as variable pricing (e.g. reduced fare for senior customers) and privacy-preserving data collection. We present a subtle technique to make use of the ECDHKeyAgreement class that is available in the BlackBerry API (and in the API of other systems) and show how the schemes can be implemented efficiently to satisfy the tight timing imposed by the transportation setting.

1 Introduction

In the year 2011 about 52% of the world population lived in urban areas. It is anticipated that the urbanization trend is going to continue, leading to an expected 67% of the population living in urban areas by the year 2050 [35]. This trend calls for well functioning public transportation systems, to ensure the mobility of people and limit air pollution in cities [32].

---

* This work is supported by the NSF under CNS-0964641 and CNS-0964379. Any opinions, findings, and conclusions or recommendations expressed in this material are those of the authors and do not necessarily reflect the views of the NSF.

E. De Cristofaro and M. Wright (Eds.): PETS 2013, LNCS 7981, pp. 40–59, 2013.

Use-based fees and payments allow the costs of transportation systems to be fairly passed on to their users, facilitating revenue generation and user incentives. But, the payment process for trips should not impact the smooth operation of a transportation system. Hence, a payment needs to be executed quickly. This favors the use of electronic payment systems, which can lead to a better throughput and greater user convenience while at the same time allowing for congestion-based pricing. For the transportation authority a further advantage of electronic payments is that they enable the collection of meaningful data about customer behavior which helps to maintain and improve the system. However, currently employed electronic public transportation payment systems have suffered security attacks [20,3], and they do not incorporate means to protect the user's (locational) privacy. For example it is reported that "in the period from August 2004 to March 2006 alone, the Oyster system was queried 409 times"[31], which shows that location data about customers is collected and stored and later used by other agencies. "Anonymous" cards are offered in some systems, but even with those cards user privacy can be sacrificed. The reason is that there is a unique identifier assigned in each card which makes payments made using the same card linkable. So a natural question is how to get the best of both worlds: all the benefits of electronic payments in public transportation systems but without sacrificing user privacy?

Cryptographic techniques make this possible. Electronic cash (e-cash) schemes allow secure and private electronic payments by providing similar security and anonymity as physical cash. The general e-cash concept describes the interaction between three types of entities: the bank, users, and shops. Monetary value is represented by electronic coins, which are pieces of data blindly signed by the bank. The bank is the only entity able to generate coins. It issues coins to a user, who utilizes them to pay at a shop. In an electronic coin its serial number as well as the identity of its possessing user is encoded in a blinded fashion. During spending this serial number and the user's identity are not revealed. At a later point in time the shop deposits the coins that he received from users to his bank account. During or after the deposit process the bank checks, whether a deposited coin had been deposited before. If so the bank can also check, whether a shop deposited the same coin twice, or whether a user double-spent a coin, in which case his identity will be revealed. An important property of certain e-cash schemes is that they support the encoding of users' attributes into coins (i.e. user's age or zip code). This is very convenient for two reasons: (1) it allows the collection of meaningful user data in order to analyze and improve the system in a privacy preserving way (2) it allows to implement additional features in the system such as variable pricing (e.g. reduced fares for senior customers).

This paper presents an implementation of several e-cash schemes that suit the transportation setting on a smartphone which can be used as a potential payment device. To satisfy the tight timing requirements imposed by the transportation setting, we choose a payment device that can communicate with an access point in a contactless fashion. A standard for contactless communication integrated in modern smartphones is Near Field Communication (NFC) [1]. It allows a smartphone to communicate with other NFC-enabled devices within a range of a few centimeters. While the throughput is moderate, the benefit of this type of communication is its simple and hence fast establishment, as electronic devices can be connected with a simple touch. There are predictions that in the long run NFC devices will replace the multitude of smart cards that many users carry around currently. For transportation authorities the advantage of relying on users' NFC-enabled smartphones, is that no additional (electronic) tokens will have to be handed out. Instead only a software-app has to be provided that the user can download to his phone. This contributes to decreasing the revenue collection cost, and further allows the payment system to be updated easily. If a change to the system is made, the transportation authority only needs to provide a software update, rather than a hardware rollout.

Several attacks on NFC enabled mobile phones have been shown, yet most of them target the use of passive tags [36,28], while we make use of the card emulation mode whose security greatly depends on its implementation (in our case the Blackberry Java API). The main threats introduced by the NFC communication link include: eavesdropping, data corruption/modification or insertion, as well as denial-of-service attacks [22]. Eavesdropping is not so harmful for our system as intercepted data is of no use to an attacker. This is because (1) no user information is sent, apart from user attributes, which are assumed not to reveal private information and (2) if an attacker knew the representation of a user's coin, he could not use it to pay for a trip, as knowing the user's secret key is required during the spending phase. An attacker could harm a user, by corrupting or modifying sent data, and hence not letting him execute the payment. Preventing these denial-of-service attacks is very hard as known from other contactless communication links. Relay attacks are also considered a threat for NFC [36]. However, in the transportation domain it is hard to realize them in practice since it would require an attacker to bring one device in close proximity to the payment machine and another one in close proximity to the user device, while additionally having access to the e-cash application on the user device. The user interface and the NFC properties can prevent this attack easily by deactivating the NFC functionality, which is a further benefit of relying on an NFC smartphone rather than on contactless smart cards.

1.1 Related Work

E-Cash. In 1982, Chaum [15] was the first to propose the idea of an e-cash system that allows anonymous, unlikable payments, which are secure against double spending in the offline setting. Following Chaum's paradigm many schemes were proposed [11,16,7,12,14]. The one due to Brands [11] is known for its efficiency during spending, however, a formal proof of security has never been given for it and it has been recently shown that it cannot be proven secure in the Random Oracle model using currently known techniques [5]. In 2001 Masayuki Abe proposed a three-move blind signature scheme [2] that can be extended to e-cash, is only slightly less efficient compared to Brands' and has a proof of security in the RO model for concurrent composition. However, he later found together with Ohkubo that his proof suffered some restrictions, since it was only valid for an adversary with overwhelming success probability, and they gave a new proof in the generic model [29]. Very recently, Baldimtsi and Lysyanskaya proposed Anonymous Credentials Light (ACL) [4], which extends Abe's scheme to allow the encoding of attributes into coins while preserving its efficiency. In contrast to Abe's proof, their proof of security goes through since they limit their attention to sequential composition only.

Privacy-Preserving Payment Schemes. Sadeghi et al. [33] and Blass et al. [9] proposed RFID-based, privacy-preserving e-ticket schemes for transit applications which are limited to only protect the users' privacy against outsiders and not against the transportation authority. Pirker et al. described how to make use of certain hardware capabilities of some mobile phones to build a secure, NFC-based, privacy-preserving, prepaid payment system [30], but the system requires the devices accepting a payment to be online at all times. Heydt-Benjamin et al. [23] proposed the use of recent advances in anonymous credentials and e-cash to design offline privacy-preserving public transportation payment systems. They consider a hybrid system with two kinds of tickets: passive RFID transponders and embedded systems such as cell phones.

E-Cash Implementations. Implementations of anonymous credentials on Java cards have been presented in [8] and [6]. Hinterwälder et al. presented an implementation of Brands' e-cash scheme for a computational RFID tag [24]. It is shown that it is feasible to execute the spending part efficiently on the tag, while the execution of the withdrawal part is still problematic. Derler et al. [19] implemented an NFC-based mobile ticketing system, which is based on Brands' private credential scheme. Execution times of several seconds are achieved, which can be a limiting factor in some application settings. Similarly, [18] presented a PDA implementation of an offline e-cash scheme that is based on Brands', which achieves an execution time of several seconds for the withdrawal phase.

1.2   Contributions

The work at hand presents a detailed description of how to encode attributes in Brands' e-cash scheme [11] and how to use ACL [4] for e-cash. Although the construction of Brands' e-cash was given in detail, it was never explicitly described how to use it combined with attributes. We also explain how ACL [4] can be used as an e-cash scheme, although it is pretty straightforward. The main contribution of this paper is that we present NFC-smartphone implementations of: Brands' scheme (with and without attributes), Abe's e-cash scheme (which does not support the encoding of attributes) and ACL and we compare and evaluate the performance of those four different schemes (Section 5). Our results are very promising: first of all we have fully realized the *first efficient and practical implementation of e-cash in smartphones*, and moreover, we show that a provable secure e-cash scheme like ACL is actually practical and has running time comparable to those of schemes without rigorous security proofs.

   Our implementation is based on Elliptic Curve Cryptography (ECC), which is the most efficient established public-key primitive. The device used is the BlackBerry Bold 9900, featuring a Qualcomm Snapdragon MSM8655 processor running at 1.2 GHz. It is equipped with the operating system BlackBerry OS 7 and is programmed using Java SDK API 7.1.0 provided by Research in Motion (RIM). We have developed a subtle technique that enables us to use the *ECDHKeyAgreement* class for calculating the scalar multiplication on an elliptic curve, which is present in this and other Java APIs. While developed and shown for this device, the use of this technique is not limited to the BlackBerry Bold 9900. It can be applied to devices that support efficient implementations of ECC, but only allow access to most commonly used results, as ECDH key agreement or ECDSA (as for example some Java smart cards). While the ECDH key agreement essentially executes a scalar multiplication, the APIs often only give access to the x-coordinate of the resulting point, since only the x-coordinate is needed for the ECDH key agreement. Our technique shows, how to efficiently recover the y-coordinate for those cases. Using these techniques, we achieve execution times that meet real-world requirements. Interestingly, our results show, that the computation necessary to execute the different schemes can easily be handled by a device as the BlackBerry Bold, whereas the component limiting the execution time is the NFC communication link.

Yet, this work is not limited to demonstrating and evaluating implementation results of a theoretical concept. We also present several ideas of why e-cash fulfills the unique requirements of transportation payment systems, and hence show how to make use of efficient e-cash in practice.

2   Payment System Requirements of the Transportation Setting

Several features of the considered e-cash schemes are especially useful for the design of a payment system that fulfills the requirements of transportation payments.

Verifying a Payment Offline. We envision a scenario that is based on currently employed transportation payment systems, where a user buys fares at a vending machine and pays at an entrance point of the transportation system. For example in the case of buses it cannot be assumed that the device granting access to users is permanently connected to the back-end system of the transportation authority. Yet, we assume temporary connection to transfer the data of collected payments. Consequently, *verifying a payment needs to be possible in an offline fashion*. This holds for the chosen schemes, where a verification of the payment does not require access to the database. However, in this case fraud cannot be detected at the time of the payment, as it requires comparing the received data with the database. Alternatively the chosen e-cash schemes reveal a crime after the fact, and allow a user to be penalized, when misusing the system.

Modular Payment System. In case of multiple transportation authorities the e-cash concept offers great convenience advantages for users, as it allows for multiple banks and shops. A user does not need multiple payment devices to use different transportation systems. Rather he can withdraw coins at one transportation authority TA_1 and use them to pay for a trip in the transportation system of TA_2. Thus, TA_1 would act as the bank and TA_2 as a shop. TA_2 can later deposit the received coins to its account at TA_1. This is achieved, as no trust between shops and banks is assumed in the e-cash concept.

Different Denominations. A transportation authority needs to offer different fare prices. This can be accomplished by assigning a low monetary value to coins and letting the user spend many coins to pay for a fare. Yet, spending many coins increases the execution time of a payment which should remain low. In the e-cash sending we can conveniently allow for different denominations of coins and thus reduce the number of coins that need to be spent. One way to accomplish this is to have the bank possess multiple public keys, one key for each possible denomination of coins.

Encoding Attributes. The collection of user data is important to analyze and improve the system in order to adapt it to customer needs[1]. However, the collection of data

---

[1] For example the number of elevators that should be provided at a station could be planned better, when knowing, how many people require wheelchair accessibility.

should be done in a way that wouldn't sacrifice a user's privacy. With the use of e-cash this can be achieved by encoding attributes into coins. Those attributes allow the user to reveal some information, as for example his zip code, while keeping further information hidden, and hence hiding his identity. Apart from private data collection, encoding attributes into coins allows for private variable pricing. The system could require the users to encode specific information like their age and then, when the coin is spent, compute the right fare according to the presented attributes.

3   E-Cash with Attributes

In this section we describe how e-cash with attributes works and we provide instantiations based on Brands' e-cash scheme [11] and ACL [4]. The descriptions are tailored to match the transportation setting but can be easily adopted for other settings as well. To our knowledge this is the first time that an explicit description of how Brands and ACL schemes can be used as e-cash schemes with attributes is given. Although at the end we will compare the implementation results of Brands with attributes, Brands without attributes, ACL and Abe's e-cash (which is essentially ACL without attributes), here we will only provide the detailed construction of the attribute supporting schemes. In our descriptions we will point out the differences between the attribute and the corresponding non-attribute version.

A transportation payment system based on e-cash is described as an interaction between three kinds of players: the transportation authority TA (with vending machines that are connected to its database), the users of the system U and the payment machines M that are placed at the entrance points and, after receiving a valid payment, grant a user access to the transportation system.

Setup. During the setup phase the transportation authority (or another trusted authority) generates the public parameters for the system together with the TA's secret key.

Account Opening. Initially, users need to register with the TA and open an account. To do so, a user U, would have to present some form of identification (e.g. a passport) to the TA and provide a cryptographic commitment C for a set of attributes $(L_1, \ldots, L_n)$ that are required for the system and for his public key $pk_U = g^{sk_U}$. The attribute types and their order are determined by the TA during the setup of the system. A possible setting is to use attribute L_1 for the user's secret key ($sk_U = L_1$), L_2 for his age, L_3 for his zip code etc. For the transportation setting we assume that revealing attributes in clear is good enough and does not violate user's privacy [2].

Withdrawal. Whenever U wants to withdraw coins from a vending machine, he first needs to prove ownership of his account and then he runs the withdrawal protocol. In order to prove ownership of his account, we require U to form a digital signature (i.e. a Schnorr signature [34]) on a message that describes the number of coins he wishes to withdraw and include some kind of timestamp. This is useful for two reasons: (1) the TA

---

[2] If there is need for extra privacy we could require for all attributes that are revealed during the spending phase to be binary attributes i.e. L_2 equals 0 if the user is more than 18 and less than 65 years old and 1 otherwise (used for age discounts). This way we avoid *range proofs* which are rather costly. Besides, for the transportation setting binary attributes would work rather well, given that we need the attributes mainly for variable pricing or private data collection.

can easily identify the user by checking whether the signature is valid under the user's public key and (2) it provides an extra level of security against a man-in-the-middle who may intercept the communication and try to withdraw more coins. Note that depending on the protocol the adversary may not be able to actually spend these coins (since he needs the user's secret key to execute the payment protocol). However, he can still hurt U by reducing his account balance. Alternatively, we could require the execution of the identification phase for every single coin withdrawn but this is obviously less efficient than identifying U once for all the coins he wishes to withdraw.

Spending. In order for a user U to spend a coin at a payment machine, U runs the spending protocol as described in the corresponding e-cash system. Moreover, he might be asked (by the system) to reveal some of his attributes. When a User reveals an attribute L_j he can either send the attribute value in clear or provide a proof of knowledge of that attribute. Note that in both cases he needs to prove that the attribute he reveals is the same one he committed to during the account opening phase.

Deposit. The payment machines present the spending transcript to the TA. Here, an extra mechanism, called *double spending detection*, is required to protect the TA against cheating users. The double spending detection is executed off-line in order to detect and penalize users, who spent the same coin more than once. In order for double spending detection to be possible, the TA needs to preserve a special database where all the deposited coins are stored. Obviously we cannot assume that all the coins are stored there forever, thus, we need to introduce some kind of *coin expiration date* after which the coin will be deleted from the database. This could be done either by having the expiration date encoded as an attribute in the coins (so the user would have to prove that the coin is still valid during spending) or by changing the TA's public key (i.e. once a year) and setting older coins invalid.

3.1   Brands' E-Cash with Attributes

We describe how Brands' e-cash scheme [11] can be modified to support the encoding of users' attributes. The main differences between the attribute and the non-attribute version can be found in the account opening and the spending phases (when attributes are revealed). The actual withdrawal protocol is essentially the same.

Setup. The TA (or another trusted authority) picks a group G of prime order q, generators $h, g, g_1, \ldots, g_n$, where n is the maximum number of attributes needed for the system, and a hash function $\mathcal{H} : \{0,1\}^* \to \mathbb{Z}_q^*$. The public key of the TA is $y = g^x$, where $x \in \mathbb{Z}_q$ is its secret key.

Account Opening. The account opening procedure of Brands with attributes is presented in Table 1. When a user U wants to open an account with the TA, he first presents an identification document to the TA and then encodes his attributes ($L_1, L_2, \ldots, L_n \in \mathbb{Z}_q$) into a commitment I^3. The value L_1 (which is not revealed to the TA) serves as the user's secret key. His public key is $pk_U = g_1^{L_1}$. Then, U provides a proof of

---

[3] Obtaining these attributes can be done similar to a credential system. A user would either have to reveal his attributes to the TA when committing to them or obtain them from some other trusted authority and then prove knowledge of them to the TA.

knowledge π that he knows the opening of the commitment I and that the same value L_1 has been used to generate I and pk_U. The proof π can be computed as a standard Schnorr *AND proof* of knowledge of several discrete logarithms [34,25]. Upon receiving π, I, pk_U, the TA checks the validity of the proof, stores the user's information and computes $z = (Ih)^x$ which is send to U. The corresponding protocol for Brands without attributes only requires the user to prove knowledge of his secret key.

Table 1. Brands' with Attributes Account Opening Protocol

TA($y = g^x$)		U($pk_U = g_1^{L_1}$)
		$I = g_1^{L_1} \dots g_n^{L_n}$
		$\pi = PK\{(\Lambda_1, \dots, \Lambda_n):$
		$I/pk_U = g_2^{\Lambda_2} \dots g_n^{\Lambda_n} \wedge pk_U = g_1^{\Lambda_1}\}$
Verify π	$\xleftarrow{\quad I, pk_U, \pi \quad}$	If $Ih \neq 1$
Store identifying information		
of U together with I		
$z = (Ih)^x$	$\xrightarrow{\quad z \quad}$	Store z

Withdrawal. To withdraw k coins, U first has to identify himself to the TA by proving knowledge of his secret key and then claiming how many coins he wants to withdraw. These two actions can be achieved simultaneously by computing a Schnorr signature [34] $\sigma(m)$ on a message m of the form: $m =$ "# of coins + time/date". The TA will authorize the user to perform the withdrawal, if the signature validates under the user's public key and there are sufficient funds in his account. Then the user runs the withdrawal protocol k times, once for each coin he withdraws (Table 2).

Table 2. Brands' with Attributes Withdrawal Protocol

TA($y = g^x$)		U($pk_U = g_1^{L_1}$)
$w \in_{\mathcal{R}} \mathbb{Z}_q, a = g^w, b = (Ih)^w$	$\xrightarrow{\quad a,b \quad}$	$s \in_{\mathcal{R}} \mathbb{Z}_q^*, A = (Ih)^s, z' = z^s$
		$x_0, x_1, \dots, x_n, u, v \in_{\mathcal{R}} \mathbb{Z}_q$
		$B = A^{x_0} g_1^{x_1} \dots g_n^{x_n}$
		$a' = a^u g^v, \ b' = b^{su} A^v$
		$c' = \mathcal{H}(A, B, z', a', b')$
	$\xleftarrow{\quad c \quad}$	$c = c'/u \mod q$
$r = cx + w \mod q$	$\xrightarrow{\quad r \quad}$	$g^r \stackrel{?}{=} y^c a, (Ih)^r \stackrel{?}{=} z^c b$
		$r' = ru + v \mod q$

For each coin, U needs to store the values: $A, B, \mathrm{sign}(A, B) \hat{=} A, B, z', a', b', r'$ together with s and the values $x_0, x_1, \dots, x_n$, where $\mathrm{sign}(A, b)$ is essentially a blind Chaum-Pedersen signature [17]. In order to verify the signature one needs to check whether: $g^{r'} = y^{c'} a'$ and $A^{r'} = z'^{c'} b'$. Note that the basic difference of Brands withdrawal when using attributes is found in the computation of B since you need to pick as many random values x_i as the number of attributes in the scheme and compute $B = A^{x_0} g_1^{x_1} \dots g_n^{x_n}$. Those random values x_i will be used later, during the spending phase in order for the user to prove knowledge of his attributes. For Brands withdrawal without attributes the value B is computed as $B = g_1^{x_1} g_2^{x_2}$: only two random values x_1 and x_2 are required and it will be used for proving knowledge of user's secret key in the spending phase.

Spending. When U spends a coin to M (with identifying information I_M) the spending protocol is executed. In Table 3 we present Brands spending protocol when supporting the encoding of but not revealing any attributes. During this phase the user presents the coin: $A, B, \text{sign}(A, B)$ to M and also proves knowledge of the representation of A (i.e. U proves knowledge of his attributes). After the transaction and if the signature verifies (i.e. the coin is valid), M saves the payment transcript consisting of $A, B, \text{sign}(A, B)$, $(R, r_1, \ldots, r_n)$ and the time stamp date/time.

This protocol is significantly less efficient compared to Brands e-cash without attributes, since the user needs to prove knowledge of the representation of A, which now includes $n + 1$ exponents. For Brands without attributes the user only needs to compute r_1 and r_2 to prove knowledge of his secret key.

Table 3. Brands' with Attributes Spending Protocol when not Revealing Attributes

$U(pk_U = g_1^{L_1})$		M
	$\xrightarrow{A, B, \text{sign}(A, B)}$	$A \overset{?}{\neq} 1$
$r_1 = -dL_1 + x_1 \mod q$	$\xleftarrow{\quad d \quad}$	$d = \mathcal{H}_0(A, B, I_M, \text{date/time})$
$\ldots$		
$r_n = -dL_n + x_n \mod q$		
$R = d/s + x_0 \mod q$	$\xrightarrow{(R, r_1, \ldots, r_n)}$	$g_1^{r_1} \ldots g_n^{r_n} h^{-d} \overset{?}{=} A^{-R} B$
		Verify $\text{sign}(A, B)$

What if U additionally wants to reveal an attribute, say L_j, during the spending protocol (remember that we assume that attributes are revealed in clear)? In order to reveal L_j, U does not need to compute r_j, when receiving the value d from M. Instead, he sends the attribute value L_j together with its blinding value x_j in his response to M, which is shown in Table 4. Thus, revealing a larger number of attributes reduces the user-side's computation, but increases the amount of data that U sends to the payment machine M.

Deposit. In order to deposit a coin, M submits the payment transcript to the TA. The TA first checks the validity of the coin (i.e. it verifies $\text{sign}(A, B)$ and checks whether $g_1^{r_1} \ldots g_n^{r_n} h^{-d} \overset{?}{=} A^{-R} B$) and then queries the database, where all deposited coins are recorded, to check whether this coin had been deposited before. This double spending check does not need to happen during the deposit phase. The TA could run it at specific time intervals for all the coins in the database. If the deposited coin had not been recorded in the database before, the TA will store $(A, d, R, r_1, \ldots, r_n)$ in her database. However, if the coin had been recorded, it means that it was spent twice by U (we assume that the payment machines in our system are trusted and will not try to submit the same coin twice: yet, this could easily be checked by storing the payment machine's identification I_M together with each coin that is stored). If a coin had been double spent the identity of the cheating user can be revealed by computing:

Table 4. Brands' with Attributes Spending Protocol when Revealing the Attribute L_j

$U(pk_U = g_1^{L_1})$	M
	$\xrightarrow{A,B,\text{sign}(A,B)}$ $\quad$ $A \overset{?}{\neq} 1$
$r_1 = -dL_1 + x_1 \mod q$	$\xleftarrow{\quad d \quad}$ $\quad$ $d = \mathcal{H}_0(A, B, I_M, \text{date/time})$
$\ldots$	
$r_{j-1} = -dL_{j-1} + x_{j-1} \mod q$	
$r_{j+1} = -dL_{j+1} + x_{j+1} \mod q$	
$\ldots$	
$r_n = -dL_n + x_n \mod q$	$\xrightarrow{(R,r_1,\ldots r_{j-1},r_{j+1},\ldots,r_n)(L_j,x_j)}$ $\quad$ $g_1^{r_1} \ldots g_j^{-dL_j + x_j} \ldots g_n^{r_n} h^{-d}$
$R = d/s + x_0 \mod q$	$\overset{?}{=} A^{-R} B$
	Verify sign(A, B)

$I = g_1^{(r_1 - r_1')/(R - R')} \ldots g_n^{(r_n - r_n')/(R - R')}$ which was stored together with some identifying information of U during the account registration phase.

3.2 ACL E-Cash with Attributes

The ACL scheme [4] is a recent, very efficient "linkable" [4] anonymous credential system, which was constructed on top of Abe's blind signature scheme [2]. It is straightforward to use a "linkable" anonymous credential scheme in order to describe e-cash with attributes since coins are essentially "single-use" credentials. In this section we explicitly describe how the ACL scheme can be used as e-cash with attributes. Note that Abe's blind signature scheme itself is immediately an e-cash scheme (without attributes though) and has been described in the past [2]. Thus, as mentioned above, we will not provide a detailed description of Abe's scheme; instead we will just point out the differences while describing ACL.

Setup. The setup phase of ACL e-cash is similar to the original ACL scheme. The TA chooses a group G of order q, a generator g and a hash function $\mathcal{H} : \{0, 1\}^* \to \mathbb{Z}_q$. It also picks $z, h, h_0, h_1, h_2, \ldots h_n \in_R G$, where n is the maximum number of attributes. The secret key of the transportation authority is $x \in_R \mathbb{Z}_q$, the public key is: $y = g^x$ and z is the "tag public key".

Account Opening. When a user U with attributes $(L_2, \ldots, L_n)$, secret key $L_1 \in_R \mathbb{Z}_q$ and public key $pk_U = h_1^{L_1}$ wants to open an account at the TA he presents a valid identification document and commits to his attributes and public key, as shown in Table 5. For each User the TA stores: $pk_U, C/pk_U$ and a copy of his identification document. U also needs to store the randomness R that corresponds to his commitment C.

Withdrawal. To withdraw k coins from his account U first identifies himself to the transportation authority (similar to Section 3.1). Then U runs the ACL blind signature protocol k times (Table 6) once for every coin.

---

[4] In a "linkable" anonymous credential system a user can only use a credential once if he does not want his transactions to be linkable.

Table 5. ACL with Attributes Account Opening Protocol

$\mathsf{TA}(y = g^x, z)$	$\mathsf{U}(pk_U = h_1^{L_1})$
	$R \in_{\mathcal{R}} \mathbb{Z}_q, C = h_0^R h_1^{L_1} \prod_{i=2}^n h_i^{L_i}$
	$\pi = PK\{(P, \Lambda_1, \ldots, \Lambda_n):$
Check π $\xleftarrow{\quad C/pk_U, pk_U, \pi \quad}$	$C/pk_U = h_0^P h_2^{\Lambda_2} \ldots h_n^{\Lambda_n} \wedge pk_U = h_1^{\Lambda_1}\}$
Store identifying information	
of U together with C	

Table 6. ACL with Attributes Withdrawal Protocol

$\mathsf{TA}(y = g^x, z)$	$\mathsf{U}(pk_U = h_1^{L_1})$
$rnd \in_{\mathcal{R}} \mathbb{Z}_q, z_1 = C g^{rnd}, z_2 = z/z_1$	
$u, c', r_1', r_2' \in_{\mathcal{R}} \mathbb{Z}_q$	
$a = g^u, a_1' = g^{r_1'} z_1^{c'}, a_2' = h^{r_2'} z_2^{c'}$ $\xrightarrow{\quad rnd, a, a_1', a_2' \quad}$	$z_1 = C g^{rnd}, \gamma \in_{\mathcal{R}} \mathbb{Z}_q^*$
	$\zeta = z^\gamma, \zeta_1 = z_1^\gamma, \zeta_2 = \zeta/\zeta_1$
	$\tau \in_{\mathcal{R}} \mathbb{Z}_q, \eta = z^\tau$
	Check whether $a, a_1', a_2' \in G$
	$t_1, t_2, t_3, t_4, t_5 \in_{\mathcal{R}} \mathbb{Z}_q$
	$\alpha = a g^{t_1} y^{t_2}, \alpha_1' = a_1'^\gamma g^{t_3} \zeta_1^{t_4}$
	$\alpha_2' = a_2'^\gamma h^{t_5} \zeta_2^{t_4}$
	$\varepsilon = \mathcal{H}(\zeta, \zeta_1, \alpha, \alpha_1', \alpha_2', \eta)$
$c = e - c' \mod q$ $\xleftarrow{\quad e \quad}$	$e = (\varepsilon - t_2 - t_4) \mod q$
$r = u - cx \mod q$ $\xrightarrow{\quad c, r, c', r_1', r_2' \quad}$	$\rho = r + t_1 \mod q$
	$\omega = c + t_2 \mod q$
	$\rho_1' = \gamma r_1' + t_3 \mod q$
	$\rho_2' = \gamma r_2' + t_5 \mod q$
	$\omega' = c' + t_4 \mod q$

After each execution of the withdrawal protocol, U obtains a $coin = (\zeta, \zeta_1, \rho, \omega, \rho_1', \rho_2', \omega')$, which he stores together with rnd, τ and γ. Note that he omits to compute and store the value μ of the original ACL scheme. Instead, during the spending phase (Table 7), he computes μ_p to "bind" the coin to a specific transaction. For each withdrawn coin, the TA stores z_1 together with the public key of U that this coin corresponds to (z_1 is going to be used to reveal the identity of the user in case of double-spending). The withdrawal of Abe's e-cash is essentially the same.

Spending. U releases the coin to the merchant together with ϵ_p and μ_p. The spending protocol for ACL e-cash and Abe's e-cash is identical and presented in Table 7.

In order for a user U to also reveal an attribute L_j during spending, he will have to execute the Revealing Attribute L_j protocol (Table 8) additionally to the Spending protocol. In this protocol he needs to prove that the attributes on his initial commitment correspond to the attributes encoded in the withdrawn coin (i.e. in value ζ_1). In other words, the user needs to provide a proof of equality of committed values under different commitment keys and bases [25], for a new commitment C' that the user computes for the attribute L_j and ζ_1 in which the attributes are encoded.

Table 7. ACL with Attributes Spending Protocol

$U(pk_U = h_1^{L_1})$	M
$\epsilon_p = \mathcal{H}(z^\tau, \text{coin}, \text{desc}) \xleftarrow{\quad \text{desc} \quad} desc = \mathcal{H}(I_M, \text{date/time})$	
$\mu_p = \tau - \epsilon_p\gamma \mod q \xrightarrow{\quad \epsilon_p, \mu_p, \text{coin} \quad} \zeta \overset{?}{\neq} 1$	
	$\epsilon_p \overset{?}{=} \mathcal{H}_4(z^{\mu_p}\zeta^{\epsilon_p}, \text{coin}, \text{desc}) \mod q$
	$\omega + \omega'$
	$\overset{?}{=} \mathcal{H}(\zeta, \zeta_1, g^\rho y^\omega, g^{\rho'_1}\zeta_1^{\omega'}, h^{\rho'_2}\zeta_2^{\omega'}, z^{\mu_p}\zeta^{\epsilon_p}) \mod q$

Table 8. ACL with Attributes Revealing the Attribute L_j Protocol

$U(pk_U = h_1^{L_1})$	M
recall $\zeta_1 = h_0^{R\gamma}h_1^{L_1\gamma}\ldots h_n^{L_n\gamma}g^{rnd\gamma}$	
$rnd' \in_R \mathbb{Z}_q$	
$C' = h_j^{L_j\gamma}g^{rnd'\gamma}$	
$\quad = h_j^{L_j\gamma}1^{R\gamma}1^{L_1\gamma}\ldots1^{L_{j-1}\gamma}1^{L_{j+1}\gamma}\ldots1^{L_n\gamma}g^{rnd'\gamma}$	
$r, r', r_0, \ldots, r_n \in_R \mathbb{Z}_q$	
$\widetilde{\zeta}_1 = h_0^{r_0}\ldots h_n^{r_n}g^r$	
$\widetilde{C'} = 1^{r_0}1^{r_1}\ldots h_j^{r_j}\ldots1^{r_n}g^{r'}$	
$c = \mathcal{H}(\zeta_1, \widetilde{\zeta}_1, C', \widetilde{C'}, \text{date/time})$	
$s_0 = r_0 + cR\gamma$	
$s_1 = r_1 + cL_1\gamma$	
$\ldots$	
$s_n = r_n + cL_n\gamma$	
$s = r + c\, rnd\, \gamma$	
$s' = r' + c\, rnd'\, \gamma \xrightarrow{\quad L_j, \zeta_1, \widetilde{\zeta}_1, C', \widetilde{C'}, s_0, \ldots, s_n, s, s' \quad}$	$c = \mathcal{H}(\zeta_1, \widetilde{\zeta}_1, C', \widetilde{C'}, \text{date/time})$
	$\widetilde{\zeta}_1\zeta_1^c \overset{?}{=} h_0^{s_0}\ldots h_n^{s_n}g^s$
	$\widetilde{C'}C'^c \overset{?}{=} 1^{s_0}1^{s_1}\ldots h_j^{s_j}\ldots1^{s_n}g^{s'}$

From a theoretical point of view the user side of the spending protocol of ACL (Table 7), when supporting the encoding but not revealing attributes, is more efficient than the one of Brands' scheme (Table 3), since, following the trick that was first suggested by Abe [2], the user only needs to compute the updated μ_p value for the coin verification instead of proving knowledge of all his attributes. In practice this depends on the relative cost for executing modular arithmetic in $\mathbb{Z}_q$ compared to the hash function and the communication cost.

Deposit. During deposit, the payment machine M sends the coin as well as $\varepsilon_p, \mu_p, desc$ and the date and time of the transaction to the TA which verifies that both the coin is valid and $desc$ correctly encodes date/time and I_M. Double spending can be checked later in an off-line fashion. In order to do that the TA needs to check whether a coin has been deposited with two different $desc$ and $desc'$. In this case we will have (ε_p, μ_p) and (ε'_p, μ'_p) and the TA can calculate: $\gamma = (\mu'_p - \mu_p)/(\epsilon_p - \epsilon'_p)$ and $z_1 = \zeta_1^{1/\gamma}$, the TA can find the user to whom z_1 was given and "punish" him. A useful observation is that in the ACL scheme, when a user is found cheating, his identity can be revealed without the TA learning his secret key and attribute values. From a privacy point of view this is much better, since the user does not need to form a new secret key and commit to his attributes all over again, after getting "punished" by the TA .

4   Framework Implementation

We will now describe important aspects of our implementation. In our measurement setup the terminal, which represents the vending as well as the payment machines, is composed of a personal computer and an OMNIKEY smart card reader from HID Global that is connected to the computer via USB. The user's payment device is represented by a BlackBerry Bold 9900, featuring NFC-capabilities. The BlackBerry Bold 9900 is programmed using the BlackBerry Java SDK API 7.1.0[5] provided by RIM.

4.1   Near Field Communication (NFC) Framework

All aspects of NFC are specified in ISO/IEC standards. We use the card-emulation mode provided by the BlackBerry API, in which the NFC-smartphone emulates a standard-conform smart card. Building the payment system on standard appliances, makes it conform to already installed payment infrastructure and hence facilitates deployment. The underlying standard of the card emulation mode is ISO/IEC 14443-A. This standard describes the communication signal interface of contactless smart cards, operating at 13.56 MHz with a bandwidth of 106 kbit/s. Both the Java SDK API 7.1.0 of the BlackBerry device, and the JRE 6 System Library of the terminal support this standard.

Data is exchanged between the terminal and the smart card using so called Application Protocol Data Units (APDUs). The reader initializes the communication by sending a command APDU to the smart card. The smart card executes this command and replies with a response APDU. This communication procedure is specified in standard ISO/IEC 7816-4. Note that the size of an APDU is limited to 256 bytes, which impacts the execution time of the protocols, as will be discussed further in Section 5.

4.2   Cryptographic Framework

We base the schemes on Elliptic Curve Cryptography, and deduce from [10] that a 160-bit elliptic curve presents sufficient security for a micro-payment system. We chose the standardized curve *secp160r1* from [13]. The underlying prime field of this curve $\mathbb{Z}_p$ is based on a generalized Mersenne prime $p = 2^{160} - 2^{31} - 1$, which allows for an efficient implementation of the curve arithmetic. On the terminal side we use the Bouncy Castle Crypto Library version 1.5[6]. This library provides a general elliptic curve framework supporting the use of many different curves. A dedicated implementation of the elliptic curve functionality for the terminal's hardware could lead to a better performance of the

---

[5] http://www.blackberry.com/developers/docs/7.1.0api/
[6] http://www.bouncycastle.org/

execution of the payment schemes and is realistic in the transportation setting. However, our investigations focus on the execution of the protocols on the user device and the communication of the protocols, which is why we chose to use a standard library for the terminal side's implementation.

The representation of finite field elements differs in the CryptoInteger class on the BlackBerry and the BigInteger class that the Bouncy Castle library on the terminal is based on. While BigInteger is a signed variable CryptoInteger is unsigned, which has to be regarded during the conversion between those two types. The data is sent as byte arrays over the NFC communication link, where an element in $\mathbb{Z}_p$ is represented as an array of 20 bytes. Since the size of the byte-array representation of the integer values can be shorter than the designated 20 bytes, we pad with leading 0x00, when receiving an element.

The BlackBerry API 7.1.0. supports the curve *secp160r1*. As such, an implementation of the ECDH key agreement based on this curve is provided by the API. Yet, the BlackBerry API does not implement all functionality necessary for the implementation of the proposed e-cash schemes, and hence had to be extended. Point addition and doubling were implemented in Java making use of the modular arithmetic functionality provided in the BlackBerry API. The implementation method to execute the scalar multiplication efficiently is described in detail in the following. Note, the implementation is customized for the curve *secp160r1*, but could easily be adapted to all other curves supported by BlackBerry API since version 3.6.0, which range from 160- to 571-bit curves[5].

Efficient Execution of EC Scalar Multiplication Using the ECDH Key Agreement. An implementation of the scalar multiplication $Q_k = k \cdot P$ in Java, making use of the modular arithmetic functionality provided in the BlackBerry API, leads to an execution time for the scalar multiplication of about 141 ms. Fortunately, the API contains the ECDHKeyAgreement class. This class offers the method *generateSharedSecret*, which executes a scalar multiplication of the input point $P = (x_P, y_P)$ with the input scalar k. This method executes in 1 ms, but only returns the x-coordinate x_{Q_k} of the resulting point Q_k. In the protocols of the considered payment schemes multiple point multiplications have to be executed. Hence, knowledge of the y-coordinate y_{Q_k} of Q_k is essential for further computations.

This drawback can be overcome. Going from the short Weierstrass equation ($y^2 = x^3 + ax + b$), on which the chosen elliptic curve is based, the magnitude of y_{Q_k} can be calculated as $y_{Q_k} = \sqrt{x_{Q_k}^3 + ax_{Q_k} + b} \mod p$.[7] This results in two options for the resulting point Q_k:

$$Q_k = (x_{Q_k}, \pm y_{Q_k}) \begin{cases} Q_k^{(+)} = (x_{Q_k}, +y_{Q_k}) \\ Q_k^{(-)} = (x_{Q_k}, -y_{Q_k}) \end{cases} \tag{1}$$

To choose the correct option ($Q_k^{(+)}$ or $Q_k^{(-)}$) for Q_k we verify y_{Q_k} over the coherence $Q_{k+1} = Q_k + P = (k+1) \cdot P$. We pick the positive result $+y_{Q_k}$ and calculate the

---

[7] Algorithm 3.36 in [27] describes how to calculate the square root in $\mathbb{Z}_p$, if $p \equiv 3 \mod 4$, which holds for the chosen curve.

x-coordinate of $Q_{k+1}^{(+)}$ by adding $Q_k^{(+)}$ and P, using the group law for point addition on an elliptic curve [21]

$$x_{Q_{k+1}}^{(+)} = \left(\frac{+y_{Q_k} - y_P}{x_{Q_k} - x_P}\right)^2 - x_P - x_{Q_k} \bmod p. \qquad (2)$$

Then we check whether the result is equal to the x-coordinate of Q_{k+1} returned when executing the *generateSharedSecret* function on $(k+1)$ and P. While this algorithm, which is summarized as Algorithm 4.1, executes the generateSharedSecret method twice and calculates a square root in the prime field $\mathbb{Z}_p$, it still achieves a major speed-up in execution time, when compared to the Java implementation based on the arithmetic functionality that is provided in the BlackBerry API, i.e. yields an execution time of around 4 ms.

Algorithm 4.1. Recovering the y-coordinate, when using the ECDH key agreement class for point multiplication

---

Data: input point P, input scalar k
Result: x- coordinate and y-coordinate of resulting point $Q = (x_Q, y_Q)$

1 **begin**
2      $x_{Q_k} \leftarrow$ generateSharedSecret(k, P)
3      $x_{Q_{k+1}} \leftarrow$ generateSharedSecret$((k+1), P)$
4      $\pm y_{Q_k} = \sqrt{x_{Q_k}^3 + a \cdot x_{Q_k} + b} \bmod p$
5      $x_{Q_{k+1}}^{(+)} = \left(\frac{+y_{Q_k} - y_P}{x_{Q_k} - x_P}\right)^2 - x_P - x_{Q_k} \bmod p$
6   **if** $x_{Q_{k+1}} == x_{Q_{k+1}}^{(+)}$ **then**
7   **return** $(x_{Q_k}, +y_{Q_k})$;
8   **else**
9   **return** $(x_{Q_k}, -y_{Q_k})$;

---

5 Implementation Results and Evaluation

The time critical phases of the e-cash schemes are the withdrawal and especially the spending phase, as those have to be executed frequently, whereas the account opening only happens once for each user (or once per year, when creating new public keys of the system each year). We limit the discussion of our results to those time critical parts.

The results for the execution of the withdrawal and the spending phase for all schemes are presented in the Tables 9 and 10 respectively. We present two cases: I) Brands' e-cash scheme, when not allowing, and Abe's scheme, which does not allow, the encoding of attributes, and II) Brands' scheme and ACL when allowing the encoding of two attributes and revealing both of them. Note that the private key of the user is not counted as an attribute, i.e. he encodes two attributes L_2 and L_3 additionally to his private key L_1. Of course, our implementation could support a bigger number of attributes if the transportation system requires so, but keep in mind that there is a trade-off between the number of attributes and the spending time.

Table 9. Execution time of withdrawal per coin for I) Brands and Abe not supporting attributes and II) Brands and ACL supporting the encoding of and revealing 2 attributes

Scheme		Execution time in milliseconds			
		Terminal	Communication	Smartphone	Total
I) Without attributes	Brands	66.1	45.1	123.8	235
	Abe	93.6	69.6	137.5	301
II) With attributes	Brands	73.2	44.1	128.7	246
	ACL	93.6	69.9	137.5	301

Table 10. Execution time of spending per coin for I) Brands and Abe not supporting attributes and II) Brands and ACL supporting the encoding of and revealing 2 attributes

Scheme		Execution time in milliseconds			
		Terminal	Communication	Smartphone	Total
I) Without attributes	Brands	58.8	96.8	1.4	157
	Abe	79.3	81.0	10.7	171
II) With attributes	Brands	87.3	114.8	2.0	204
	ACL	151.2	221.4	11.4	384

Figure 1 illustrates those results, where the execution times of the different protocols have been summarized to: *Terminal* all computation executed on the terminal side, *Communication* execution time of the entire communication, and *Smartphone* all computation executed on the BlackBerry smartphone. In our implementation all steps are executed serially, i.e. while waiting for the terminal the execution on the smartphone is suspended. This resembles the execution on a standard smart card. Due to the extended capabilities of the smartphone, computations on the smartphone and the terminal could be parallelized, which would lower the total execution time. For example could the TA in the withdrawal protocol of ACL send the number rnd to the user right after generating it. Then while the TA calculates a, a'_1 and a'_2 the user could at the same time calculate z_1, ζ, ζ_1 and ζ_2.

An advantage of the ACL scheme is that for the revealing attributes phase (Table 8) the values $C', \widetilde{\zeta_1}, \widetilde{C'}$ can be precomputed, which has been realized for the implementation at hand. The computation time for those precomputed values is 39 ms and is not included in the results. By doing so the total execution time for spending a coin of all schemes does not exceed 400 ms, which is close to the acceptance threshold for spendings in the transportation domain, which is 300 ms[31]. Hence, the implementation shows that it is feasible to spend a coin meeting the extreme time constraints of the transportation setting. Spending several coins serially exceeds those time constraints. Yet, the execution time could be further reduced by batching the executions that are required for spending several coins.

While the terminal side is represented by a powerful computer the execution of a scalar multiplication on the terminal takes longer than on the BlackBerry device; on the BlackBerry an execution of the point multiplication takes 4 ms, whereas on the computer it takes 6 ms. As mentioned in Section 4 we focus on the execution time on the payment device and of the communication. The implementation results could be

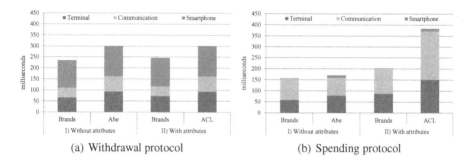

Fig. 1. Execution times of the (a) withdrawal and (b) spending protocols for the cases I) not supporting attributes and II) supporting the encoding and revealing 2 attributes

improved when not relying on a Java implementation for the terminal side, which is a realistic scenario, since the TA has full control over those devices.

Surprisingly, a limiting factor for the execution of the different protocols is the card emulation mode supported by the BlackBerry device. The communication bandwidth is limited to 106 kbits/sec, while the maximum bandwidth supported by the NFC standard is 424 kbits/sec. An additional deceleration limits the practical bandwidth on the application layer to 62.5 kbit/s. Since the communication plays an integral part in the execution of the spending protocol, a faster communication could significantly improve the execution timings (Figure 1). Moreover, the length of an APDU is limited to 256 bytes. For some protocol steps data had to be sent using two APDUs. Hence, the overall execution time could be improved when allowing longer APDUs.

A further observation is that the computational complexity of Brands' spending protocol, when allowing attributes, decreases the more of them are revealed. Yet, at the same time the data to be communicated increases. For our implementation the increase in data that needs to be communicated, dominates the change in execution time. This could be different for other platforms, where the communication plays a less important role in the overall execution time of the protocol.

Table 11 shows the coin size for each of the schemes, i.e. the data that needs to be stored on the user device for each coin. Since for the ACL scheme $C', \tilde{\zeta}_1, \widehat{C'}$ have been precomputed, they need to be stored together with rnd' on the device as part of the coin. If storage space would be more critical in comparison to the execution time, those values could be computed on-the-fly when spending a coin, which would lead to the same storage amount for a coin as in Abe's scheme, but longer execution times.

In the following we will estimate the database requirements for our e-cash based transportation payment system. We base our estimations on the Massachusetts Bay Transportation Authority (MBTA) system. The MBTA reports an average ridership of 1.28 million trips per day for February 2013 [26]. In the case of Brands' e-cash with attributes scheme the TA needs to store the values $A, d, (R, r_1, \ldots, r_n)$ for each coin in the database, in order to detect double-spending at a later point in time. Assuming the encoding of two attributes, this results in 146 bytes per coin or average 178 MB per day that need to be stored in the database. In the case of ACL the TA has to have two databases. One stores the values z_1 together with the public key pk_U of a user for

Table 11. Coin size (per coin data stored on user device) for the cases I) Brands and Abe not supporting attributes and II) Brands and ACL supporting 2 attributes

Scheme		Coin Elements	Coin Size in bytes
I) Without attributes	Brands	$A, B, z', a', b', r', s, x_1, x_2$	289
	Abe	$\zeta, \zeta_1, \rho, \omega, \rho'_1, \rho'_2, \omega', \tau, \gamma$	229
II) With attributes	Brands	$A, B, z', a', b', r', s, x_0, x_1, x_2, x_3$	331
	ACL	$\zeta, \zeta_1, \rho, \omega, \rho'_1, \rho'_2, \omega', \tau, \gamma, rnd, rnd', C', \widetilde{\zeta_1}, \widetilde{C'}$	394

each withdrawn coin and another one that stores $\zeta_1, desc, \varepsilon_p$ and μ_p for each spent coin (186 bytes per coin or 227 MB per day). Managing large databases does not primarily depend on the number of data records and the size of the related storage. It greatly depends on the complexity of the *search-and-join* algorithm. In our case the database just has to operate with primary-key related search requests – in the case of Brands' scheme it is the 21 byte value A. Executing the *search-and-join* algorithm to add a set of 1.28 million data records to a database that has 1 billion entries should be executable within a couple of minutes.

6 Conclusion

Brands' [11], Abe's [2] and ACL [4] e-cash are all suitable payment schemes for use in public transport, due to their efficiency during the spending phase. While the ACL scheme is a little less efficient than Brands' with attributes, it is the only practical e-cash with attributes that comes with a formal proof of security. This paper presented an explicit description of e-cash with attributes for both Brands' [11] and ACL [4] schemes. Further it presented a full implementation of Brands' with and without attributes, Abe's and ACL on a BlackBerry Bold 9900. We proposed a method that allows the use of the ECDHKeyAgreement class of the BlackBerry API to calculate the point multiplication, by recovering the y-coordinate of the resulting point, which led to transaction times that meet real-world requirements of transportation payment systems for all considered schemes. Surprisingly, a limiting factor of the transaction is the NFC communication bandwidth. Phones equipped with Android release, 4.0 (Ice Cream Sandwich, ICS) or higher can easily be extended with Spongy Castle, the repackage of Bouncy Castle for Android. It does support EC key generation, ECDH key exchange and ECDSA signatures. Yet, when using this class the execution of the generateSharedSecret function on the Samsung Galaxy S3 is much slower than the presented results on the BlackBerry Bold 9900. As part of future work use of the Android NDK can be investigated to reach the timing requirements of the transportation setting.

Acknowledgements. We would like to express our gratitude towards Research in Motion for providing us with a BlackBerry Bold 9900, Srdjan Capkun for shepherding this paper, and the anonymous reviewers for their helpful comments.

References

1. Near Field Communication Forum (2008), http://www.nfc-forum.org/
2. Abe, M.: A Secure Three-Move Blind Signature Scheme for Polynomially Many Signatures. In: Pfitzmann, B. (ed.) EUROCRYPT 2001. LNCS, vol. 2045, pp. 136–151. Springer, Heidelberg (2001)
3. Anderson, Z., Ryan, R., Chiesa, A.: The Anatomy of a Subway Hack: Breaking Crypto RFID's and Magstripes of Ticketing Systems (2008)
4. Baldimtsi, F., Lysyanskaya, A.: Anonymous Credentials Light. IACR Cryptology ePrint Archive, 2012:298 (2012)
5. Baldimtsi, F., Lysyanskaya, A.: On The Security of One-Witness Blind Signature Schemes. IACR Cryptology ePrint Archive, 2012:197 (2012)
6. Batina, L., Hoepman, J.-H., Jacobs, B., Mostowski, W., Vullers, P.: Developing Efficient Blinded Attribute Certificates on Smart Cards via Pairings. In: Gollmann, D., Lanet, J.-L., Iguchi-Cartigny, J. (eds.) CARDIS 2010. LNCS, vol. 6035, pp. 209–222. Springer, Heidelberg (2010)
7. Belenkiy, M., Chase, M., Kohlweiss, M., Lysyanskaya, A.: Compact E-Cash and Simulatable VRFs Revisited. In: Shacham, H., Waters, B. (eds.) Pairing 2009. LNCS, vol. 5671, pp. 114–131. Springer, Heidelberg (2009)
8. Bichsel, P., Camenisch, J., Groß, T., Shoup, V.: Anonymous credentials on a standard java card. In: Al-Shaer, E., Jha, S., Keromytis, A.D. (eds.) ACM Conference on Computer and Communications Security, pp. 600–610. ACM (2009)
9. Blass, E.-O., Kurmus, A., Molva, R., Strufe, T.: PSP: private and secure payment with RFID. In: Al-Shaer, E., Paraboschi, S. (eds.) WPES, pp. 51–60. ACM (2009)
10. Bos, J.W., Kaihara, M.E., Kleinjung, T., Lenstra, A.K., Montgomery, P.L.: On the security of 1024-bit rsa and 160-bit elliptic curve cryptography. IACR Cryptology ePrint Archive, 2009:389 (2009)
11. Brands, S.: Untraceable Off-line Cash in Wallets with Observers (Extended Abstract). In: Stinson, D.R. (ed.) CRYPTO 1993. LNCS, vol. 773, pp. 302–318. Springer, Heidelberg (1994)
12. Camenisch, J., Hohenberger, S., Lysyanskaya, A.: Compact E-Cash. In: Cramer, R. (ed.) EUROCRYPT 2005. LNCS, vol. 3494, pp. 302–321. Springer, Heidelberg (2005)
13. Certicom Research. Standads for Efficient Cryptography (SEC) 2: Recommended Elliptic Curve Domain Parameters, version 1.0 edition (2000)
14. Chan, A.H., Frankel, Y., Tsiounis, Y.: Easy Come - Easy Go Divisible Cash. In: Nyberg, K. (ed.) EUROCRYPT 1998. LNCS, vol. 1403, pp. 561–575. Springer, Heidelberg (1998)
15. Chaum, D.: Blind Signatures for Untraceable Payments. In: Chaum, D., Rivest, R.L., Sherman, A.T. (eds.) CRYPTO, pp. 199–203. Plenum Press, New York (1982)
16. Chaum, D., Fiat, A., Naor, M.: Untraceable Electronic Cash. In: Goldwasser, S. (ed.) CRYPTO 1988. LNCS, vol. 403, pp. 319–327. Springer, Heidelberg (1990)
17. Chaum, D., Pedersen, T.P.: Wallet databases with observers. In: Brickell, E.F. (ed.) CRYPTO 1992. LNCS, vol. 740, pp. 89–105. Springer, Heidelberg (1993)
18. Clemente-Cuervo, E., Rodríguez-Henríquez, F., Arroyo, D.O., Ertaul, L.: A PDA Implementation of an Off-line e-Cash Protocol. In: Aissi, S., Arabnia, H.R. (eds.) Security and Management, pp. 452–458. CSREA Press (2007)
19. Derler, D., Potzmader, K., Winter, J., Dietrich, K.: Anonymous Ticketing for NFC-Enabled Mobile Phones. In: Chen, L., Yung, M., Zhu, L. (eds.) INTRUST 2011. LNCS, vol. 7222, pp. 66–83. Springer, Heidelberg (2012)
20. Garcia, F.D., de Koning Gans, G., Muijrers, R., van Rossum, P., Verdult, R., Schreur, R.W., Jacobs, B.: Dismantling MIFARE Classic. In: Jajodia, S., Lopez, J. (eds.) ESORICS 2008. LNCS, vol. 5283, pp. 97–114. Springer, Heidelberg (2008)

21. Hankerson, D., Menezes, A.J., Vanstone, S.: Guide to Elliptic Curve Cryptography. Springer-Verlag New York, Inc., Secaucus (2003)
22. Haselsteiner, E., Breitfuß, K.: Security in Near Field Communication (NFC) - Strengths and Weaknesses (2006),
    http://events.iaik.tugraz.at/RFIDSec06/Program/papers/002
23. Heydt-Benjamin, T.S., Chae, H.-J., Defend, B., Fu, K.: Privacy for Public Transportation. In: Danezis, G., Golle, P. (eds.) PET 2006. LNCS, vol. 4258, pp. 1–19. Springer, Heidelberg (2006)
24. Hinterwälder, G., Paar, C., Burleson, W.P.: Privacy preserving payments on computational RFID devices with application in intelligent transportation systems. In: Hoepman, J.-H., Verbauwhede, I. (eds.) RFIDSec 2012. LNCS, vol. 7739, pp. 109–122. Springer, Heidelberg (2013)
25. Lysyanskaya, A.: Signature schemes and applications to cryptographic protocol design. PhD Thesis. Massachusetts Institute of Technology, AAI0804606 (2002)
26. M. B. T. A. (MBTA). MBTA ScoreCard (March 2013) [February 2013 Data], http://www.mbta.com/uploadedfiles/About_the_T/Score_Card/ScoreCard2013
27. Menezes, A., van Oorschot, P.C., Vanstone, S.A.: Handbook of Applied Cryptography. CRC Press (1996)
28. Mulliner, C.: Vulnerability analysis and attacks on nfc-enabled mobile phones. In: ARES, pp. 695–700. IEEE Computer Society (2009)
29. Ohkubo, M., Abe, M.: Security of three-move blind signature schemes reconsidered. In: SCIS 2003, Symposium on Cryptography and Information Security, Japan (2003)
30. Pirker, M., Slamanig, D.: A Framework for Privacy-Preserving Mobile Payment on Security Enhanced ARM TrustZone Platforms. In: Min, G., Wu, Y., Liu, L.C., Jin, X., Jarvis, S.A., Al-Dubai, A.Y. (eds.) TrustCom, pp. 1155–1160. IEEE Computer Society (2012)
31. Rankl, W., Effing, W.: Smart Cards in Transportation Systems, pp. 869–891. John Wiley & Sons, Ltd. (2010)
32. Ribeiro, S.K., Kobayashi, S., Beuthe, M., Gasca, J., Greene, D., Lee, D.S., Muromachi, Y., Newton, P.J., Plotkin, S., Sperling, D., Wit, R., Zhou, P.J.: Transport and its infrastructure. Climate Change 2007: Mitigation. Contribution of Working Group III to the Fourth Assessment Report of the Intergovernmental Panel on Climate Change (2007)
33. Sadeghi, A.-R., Visconti, I., Wachsmann, C.: User Privacy in Transport Systems Based on RFID E-Tickets. In: Bettini, C., Jajodia, S., Samarati, P., Wang, X.S. (eds.) PiLBA. CEUR Workshop Proceedings, vol. 397. CEUR-WS.org (2008)
34. Schnorr, C.-P.: Efficient Identification and Signatures for Smart Cards. In: Brassard, G. (ed.) CRYPTO 1989. LNCS, vol. 435, pp. 239–252. Springer, Heidelberg (1990)
35. United Nations New York. World Urbanization Prospects - The 2011 Revision (2012)
36. Verdult, R., Kooman, F.: Practical attacks on nfc enabled cell phones. In: 2011 3rd International Workshop on Near Field Communication (NFC), pp. 77–82 (2011)

Efficient Privacy-Preserving Stream Aggregation in Mobile Sensing with Low Aggregation Error

Qinghua Li and Guohong Cao

Department of Computer Science and Engineering
The Pennsylvania State University
{qxl118,gcao}@cse.psu.edu

Abstract. Aggregate statistics computed from time-series data contributed by individual mobile nodes can be very useful for many mobile sensing applications. Since the data from individual node may be privacy-sensitive, the aggregator should only learn the desired statistics without compromising the privacy of each node. To provide strong privacy guarantee, existing approaches add noise to each node's data and allow the aggregator to get a noisy sum aggregate. However, these approaches either have high computation cost, high communication overhead when nodes join and leave, or accumulate a large noise in the sum aggregate which means high aggregation error. In this paper, we propose a scheme for privacy-preserving aggregation of time-series data in presence of untrusted aggregator, which provides differential privacy for the sum aggregate. It leverages a novel ring-based interleaved grouping technique to efficiently deal with dynamic joins and leaves and achieve low aggregation error. Specifically, when a node joins or leaves, only a small number of nodes need to update their cryptographic keys. Also, the nodes only collectively add a small noise to the sum to ensure differential privacy, which is $O(1)$ with respect to the number of nodes. Based on symmetric-key cryptography, our scheme is very efficient in computation.

1 Introduction

Mobile devices such as smart phones are ubiquitous today with an ever-increasing popularity. These devices are equipped with various sensors such as camera, accelerometer, GPS, etc. Mobile sensing exploits the data contributed by mobile users (via the mobile devices they carry) to infer rich information about people (e.g., health, activity, and social event) and their surrounding (e.g., pollution and weather). Applications of mobile sensing include traffic monitoring [1], environmental monitoring [2], healthcare [3], etc.

In many scenarios, stream data from the mobile users over time can be collected, aggregated, and mined for obtaining or identifying useful patterns or statistics over a population [4]. In applications such as CarTel [5] and N-SMARTS [6], participants generate time-series data such as their location, speed, the pollution density and noise level in their surroundings, etc. These data can be aggregated to obtain the traffic pattern and pollution map. For another example, the average amount of exercise (which can be measured by motion sensors on smartphones [3]) that people do in every day can be used to infer public health conditions.

The above examples suggest that aggregate statistics computed from time-series data contributed by individual users can be very useful in mobile sensing. However, in many cases, the data from individual users may be privacy-sensitive, and the users do not trust

E. De Cristofaro and M. Wright (Eds.): PETS 2013, LNCS 7981, pp. 60–81, 2013.

any single third party to see their data in cleartext. A user's data, if directly collected, can be used to infer the user's daily activities and health conditions. For instance, to monitor the propagation of a new flu, the aggregator will collect information on the number of patients infected by this flu. However, a patient may not want to directly tell the aggregator that she is infected. Thus, a challenge is to allow an untrusted aggregator to obtain the useful aggregate while preserving individual users' privacy.

Table 1. Comparison between existing schemes and our scheme

Scheme	Total comm. per interval	Comm. model	Aggregation error	Dynamic join & leave	Comm. per join & leave	Cryptography
[7]	$O(n)$	N ↔ A	$O(1)$	No	-	Public-key
Basic [8]	$O(n)$	N → A	$O(1)$	No	$O(n)$	Public-key
Binary [9]	$O(n \log n)$	N → A	$\tilde{O}((\log n)^{\frac{3}{2}})$	Yes	$O(1)$	Public-key
[10]	$O(n)$	N → A	$O(1)$	Yes	$O(1)$	Public-key
Our scheme	$O(n)$	N → A	$O(1)$	Yes	$O(d)$	Symmetric-key

$N \to A$: node-to-aggregator uni-directional. $N \leftrightarrow A$: interactive between node and aggregator. n: number of nodes. d: a parameter of our scheme (smaller than 100 in most practical settings).

The problem of privacy-preserving aggregation of time-series data in presence of untrusted aggregator has been studied in [7] and [8]. They combine differential privacy [11, 12] and cryptography techniques to provide distributed differential privacy, such that only negligible information about the node can be leaked even if the aggregator has arbitrary auxiliary information. In these schemes, each node independently adds appropriate noise to her data before aggregation, and the aggregator gets a noisy sum instead of the accurate sum. A large enough noise is accumulated in the aggregate to achieve differential privacy. These schemes also rely on a special encryption technique where each node encrypts its noisy data with a key, sends the encrypted data to the aggregator which can decrypt the sum of the nodes' noisy data without learning anything else.

In these schemes, all nodes *collectively* add a sufficient amount of noise (required for differential privacy) to the sum aggregate, and there is only $O(1)$ aggregation error (i.e., the difference between the noisy sum and the accurate sum). However, these schemes cannot efficiently support dynamic joins and leaves. For example, in [8], when a node joins or leaves, the encryption keys of all nodes are updated, which means high communication overhead in a large system. Thus, these schemes are not suitable for applications with many nodes and high churn rate. Chan *et al.* [9] propose a binary interval tree technique which can reduce the communication cost for joins and leaves, but their scheme has high aggregation error which means poor utility of the aggregate. A recent scheme [10] can efficiently support dynamic joins and leaves, but it has high computation overhead due to the use of public-key cryptography, and thus may not be appropriate for mobile sensing scenarios with resource-constrained devices, short aggregation periods, and many aggregate statistics collected simultaneously.

In this paper, we propose a new scheme which can efficiently deal with dynamic joins and leaves and achieve low aggregation error (see Table 1). Specifically, when a node joins or leaves, only a small number of nodes need to update their encryption keys, which is in the order of tens in most practical settings irrespective of the total number of nodes. Also, the nodes collectively add $O(1)$ noise to the aggregate for differential privacy. Our main contribution is a new technique – interleaved grouping. We propose a novel ring-based interleaved grouping construction, which divides nodes into groups of smaller size such that (1) at most three (four) groups of nodes need to be updated for each join (leave) and (2) the aggregator can only learn the sum of all nodes' data but nothing else. The scheme is very efficient in computation since it is based on HMAC. Implementation-based measurements show that our scheme is two orders of magnitude faster than existing schemes in encryption and/or decryption.

The remainder of this paper is organized as follows. Section 2 discusses related work. Section 3 presents the system overview and models. Section 4 and 5 describe the basic idea of interleaved grouping and a ring-based construction. Section 6 presents an aggregation protocol based on ring-based interleaved grouping. Section 7 presents evaluation results. Section 8 discusses extensions. The last section concludes this paper.

2   Related Work

Security and privacy in mobile sensing systems have been addressed by many works (e.g., [13–16]), but they do not consider aggregation of data. There are many existing works (e.g., [17]) on privacy-preserving data aggregation, but most of them assume a trusted aggregator. Shi et al. [18] proposed an aggregation scheme for mobile sensing, but the scheme does not consider time-series data. The two constructions [19,20] based on additive homomorphic encryption [17] do not guarantee differential privacy.

Recent works [7–9] address differentially private aggregation of time-series data. Rastogi and Nath [7] designed an encryption scheme based on threshold Paillier cryptosystem, but their construction requires an extra round of interaction between the aggregator and the nodes in every aggregation period. Shi et al. [8] proposed a Diffie-Hellman-based encryption scheme, where no communication is required from the aggregator to the nodes. However, their scheme redistributes encryption keys to all nodes when a node joins or leaves, inducing high communication cost. To deal with dynamic joins and leaves and provide fault tolerance, Chan et al. [9] extend the construction in [8] with a binary interval tree technique which reduces expensive rekeying operations. However, in their scheme, since each node's data is aggregated into multiple sums, a large noise is added to each node's data to provide differential privacy, which leads to high aggregation error. Recent designs [21] employ an honest-but-curious proxy server to tolerate the churn of a small fraction of nodes, but it is unknown how they work when many nodes leave. Jawurek et al. [10] proposed a fault-tolerant aggregation scheme, but it employs Paillier cryptosystem which is expensive in computation.

Grouping has been recently used for differentially-private publication of graph topologies [22,23]. These solutions divide a dataset into *disjoint* groups, which is different from our *interleaved* grouping technique.

3   Overview

3.1   Problem Definition

Our system model is shown in Figure 1. An aggregator wants to get the sum aggregate of n mobile nodes periodically. Let $x_i^{(t)}$ ($x_i^{(t)} \in \{0, 1, ..., \Delta\}$) denote the data of node

i in aggregation period t ($t = 1, 2, 3, ...$). Then the sum aggregate for time period t is $\sum_{i=1}^{n} x_i^{(t)}$. Since the accurate sum may leak node privacy in presence of side information [11, 12], the aggregator is only allowed to obtain a noisy sum (i.e., the accurate sum plus some noise). In each time period t, each node i adds noise $r_i^{(t)}$ to her data $x_i^{(t)}$, encrypts the noisy data $\hat{x}_i^{(t)} = x_i^{(t)} + r_i^{(t)}$ with her key $k_i^{(t)}$ and sends the ciphertext to the aggregator. The aggregator uses the capability $k_0^{(t)}$ to decrypt the noisy sum $\sum_{i=1}^{n}(x_i^{(t)} + r_i^{(t)})$. Here, $k_i^{(t)}$ and $k_0^{(t)}$ change in every time period. In the following, when we describe our solution, we usually focus on the aggregation scheme in one time period. For simplicity, we omit the superscript t and write x_i, r_i, k_i and k_0 instead.

Each mobile node communicates with the aggregator via 3G, WiFi, or other available access networks. Source anonymity [24] is not necessary since data content is protected. Peer-to-peer communication among the nodes is not required, because nodes may not know each other for privacy reasons and such communication is nontrivial due to the mobility of nodes in mobile sensing. We assume that time is synchronized among nodes. In mobile sensing, mobile devices (e.g., smartphones) usually have embedded GPS receivers, which can easily synchronize time without communications among them.

There are three requirements regarding privacy. First, the aggregator only learns the noisy sum but nothing else (e.g., intermediate results). Second, a party without the aggregator capability learns nothing. This is *aggregator obliviousness* [8]. The third requirement is *differential privacy*. Intuitively, the sum obtained by the aggregator is roughly the same no matter if a specific node is in the system or not.

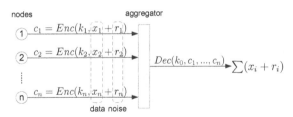

Fig. 1. An overview of our system

3.2 Trust Model

The aggregator is untrusted. A number of nodes may collude with the aggregator and reveal their data and noise values. We refer to these nodes as *compromised nodes* and refer to others as *good nodes*. We assume that the fraction of compromised nodes that collude is at most γ, and nodes are equally likely to collude. Similar to [8], we assume that the system has an a priori estimate over the upper bound of γ, and uses it in our protocol. The aggregator may eavesdrop all messages sent to/from every node. Also, all entities are computationally bounded.

We also assume a key dealer which issues keys to the nodes and the aggregator via a secure channel. For now, we assume that the key dealer is trusted, and we relax this assumption in Section 8. Malicious nodes may perform data pollution attacks in which they lie about their data values in order to change the aggregate. Data pollution attacks are outside the scope of this paper, and their influence can be bounded if each node uses a non-interactive zero-knowledge proof to prove that its data is in a valid range.

3.3   Basic Scheme

Let us first look at a simple basic scheme, which is a variant of the scheme proposed in [8]. Basically, it uses the same data perturbation algorithm as in [8]. However, since the encryption method of [8] is not efficient in computation (especially for the aggregator to get the sum), it replaces the encryption method with the construction in [20] which also achieves aggregator obliviousness but has much less computation overhead.

Encryption Method. *Setup*: The key dealer generates a set S of nc random secrets s_1, ..., s_{nc}. It divides them into n random disjoint subsets S_1, ..., S_n, with c secrets in each subset. Clearly, $S = \bigcup_{i=1}^{n} S_i$. The key dealer randomly selects a subset $\hat{S}$ of q secrets and assigns them to the aggregator. It then evenly divides $S - \hat{S}$ into n random disjoint subsets $\bar{S}_1$, ..., $\bar{S}_n$. Clearly, $S = (\bigcup_{i=1}^{n} \bar{S}_i) \bigcup \hat{S}$. It assigns S_i and $\bar{S}_i$ to node i.
Encryption: In time period $t \in \mathbb{N}$, node i generates key $k_i = (\sum_{s' \in S_i} h(f_{s'}(t)) - \sum_{s' \in \bar{S}_i} h(f_{s'}(t)))$ mod M, where $M = 2^{\lceil \log_2 (n\Delta) \rceil}$. Here, $f_{s'}$ is a member of the pseudorandom function (PRF) family $\mathbb{F}_\lambda = \{f_{s'} : \{0,1\}^\lambda \rightarrow \{0,1\}^\lambda\}_{s' \in \{0,1\}^\lambda}$ indexed by s'. As suggested in [17,20], it can be implemented with HMAC, where $f_{s'}(t)$ is the HMAC of t with s' as the key. Function h maps the output of $f_{s'}$ to a uniform random value in $[0, M - 1]$. A simple construction for h is to truncate the output of $f_{s'}$ into shorter bit strings of length $\log_2 M$ and use the exclusive-OR of all these strings as the output. Node i encrypts its noisy data $\hat{x}_i$ by computing $c_i = (k_i + \hat{x}_i)$ mod M.
Decryption: In time period $t \in \mathbb{N}$, the aggregator generates key $k_0 = (\sum_{s' \in \hat{S}} h(f_{s'}(t)))$ mod M and decrypts the noisy sum $\hat{S} = \sum_{i=1}^{n} \hat{x}_i$ by computing $\hat{S} = (\sum_{i=1}^{n} c_i - k_0)$ mod M. It is easy to verify that $k_0 = (\sum_{i=1}^{n} k_i)$ mod M. Hence, the aggregator can get the correct noisy sum. Also, since only the trusted key dealer and the aggregator know the secrets used by the aggregator, no other party can learn the sum.

By assigning a large-enough number of secrets to each node and the aggregator (i.e., c and q are large enough), this method ensures that it is computationally infeasible for the adversary to guess the secrets assigned to a particular node or the aggregator. More formally, for l-bit security, the probability of a successful guess is smaller than 2^{-l}. Table 2 shows the values of c and q for 80-bit security when $\gamma = 0.2$.

Table 2. The values of c and q for 80-bit security [20]

n	10^3	10^4	10^5	10^6
c	5	4	3	3
q	8	6	5	4

As a common practice of security, the secret used to calculate HMAC cannot be repeatedly used forever and should be updated after being used for a certain length of time (e.g., one year). The proper length of time can be determined following the guidelines discussed in [25]. After this period of time (which is usually long), the key dealer needs to rerun the setup phase and update the secrets.

The basic scheme is very efficient in computation due to the use of HMAC. We note that our interleaved grouping technique (see later) can also be applied upon other aggregator oblivious encryption schemes (e.g., [8,19]) with different tradeoffs.

Data Perturbation. Shi et al [8] show that differential privacy can be achieved by adding a noise that follows diluted geometric distribution to each node's data.

Definition 1. *Geometric Distribution. Let $\alpha > 1$. $Geom(\alpha)$ denotes the symmetric geometric distribution with parameter α. Its probability mass function at k ($k = 0, \pm 1, \pm 2, ...$) is $\frac{\alpha-1}{\alpha+1} \cdot \alpha^{-|k|}$.*

Definition 2. *Diluted Geometric Distribution. Let $\alpha > 1$ and $0 < \beta \le 1$. A random variable follows β-diluted Geometric distribution $Geom^\beta(\alpha)$ if it is sampled from $Geom(\alpha)$ with probability β, and is set to 0 with probability $1 - \beta$.*

In time period t, node i generates a noise r_i from $Geom^\beta(\alpha)$ and computes $\hat{x}_i = x_i + r_i$. Parameters α and β are set as $\alpha = e^{\frac{\epsilon}{\Delta}}$ and $\beta = \min(\frac{1}{(1-\gamma)n} \ln \frac{1}{\delta}, 1)$, where ϵ and δ are privacy parameters. Given that the encryption method is aggregator oblivious (i.e., the aggregator only learns the noisy sum but nothing else), the data perturbation procedure achieves (ϵ, δ)-differential privacy [8]:

Theorem 1. *Let $0 < \delta < 1$, $\epsilon > 0$, $\alpha = e^{\frac{\epsilon}{\Delta}}$ and $\beta = \min(\frac{1}{(1-\gamma)n} \ln \frac{1}{\delta}, 1)$, where γ is the maximum fraction of nodes compromised. If each node adds noise $Geom^\beta(\alpha)$, the above perturbation procedure achieves (ϵ, δ)-distributed differential privacy[1].*

With this data perturbation method, roughly one copy of geometric noise $Geom(\alpha)$ is added to the sum, which is required to ensure ϵ-differential privacy [26]. Strictly speaking, the basic scheme achieves differential privacy against polynomial-time adversaries, since the encryption method is secure against polynomial-time adversaries.

Problem with the basic scheme. In the basic encryption method [20], when a node joins or leaves, the key dealer must issue a new set of secrets to every node and the aggregator to ensure security. This induces high communication overhead and makes it impractical for large-scale mobile sensing applications with high churn rate. Thus, efficient techniques should be proposed to deal with dynamic joins and leaves.

3.4 Naive Grouping

Intuitively, we can apply grouping on top of the basic scheme to reduce the communication cost of dynamic joins and leaves.

Naive Grouping. The n nodes are divided into g *disjoint groups* of equal size, and the basic scheme is applied to each group independently. The aggregator has the capability to decrypt the sum of each group. To provide differential privacy, one copy of geometric noise is added to the sum of each group. As some positive and negative noises cancel out, the accumulated noise in the final aggregate is $O(\sqrt{g})$ with high probability. When a node joins or leaves a group, only the $\frac{n}{g}$ nodes in this group are redistributed secrets.

The problem with Naive Grouping is that it cannot achieve both low communication cost for dynamic joins and leaves and low aggregation error, since these two goals require the parameter g to be tuned in reverse directions. Thus, it is nontrivial to use grouping to achieve both churn resilience and low aggregation error.

Table 3 summarizes the notations used in this paper.

---

[1] If each node is compromised independently with probability γ, the data perturbation procedure is proved to achieve (ϵ, δ)-computational differential privacy [9].

Table 3. Notations

n	Num. of nodes	g	Num. of groups in Naive Grouping/our scheme
γ	Max. fraction of compromised nodes	α, β	Paras. used to generate noise
x_i	Data of node i	d, x	Parameters of our proposed scheme
r_i	The noise that node i adds to her data	k_0	The capability used by the aggregator to decrypt
$\hat{x}_i$	Noisy data of node i, $\hat{x}_i = x_i + r_i$		noisy sum
Δ	Each node's data is from $\{0, 1, ..., \Delta\}$	k_i	The encryption key used by node i
ϵ, δ	Parameters of differential privacy	l	The required security level is l-bit, e.g., $l = 80$

4   Interleaved Grouping

Although grouping can be used to reduce the communication overhead of dynamic joins and leaves, the naive grouping scheme has high aggregation error since it adds one independent copy of geometric noise to each group. To address this problem, we propose to use a new technique called *interleaved grouping*.

4.1   Basic Idea

The basic idea is to divide the nodes into *interleaved groups*, where each group shares some nodes with other groups. In the setup phase, an independent set of secrets are assigned to each group of nodes and the aggregator similarly as that in the basic scheme. For each group, the aggregator does not know the secrets assigned to each member of the group. A node that belongs to multiple groups will receive secrets from each group it belongs to. Each node (the aggregator) uses the union of the secrets that it receives to derive its encryption key (decryption capability). The encryption (decryption) process is the same as the basic scheme. Clearly the aggregator can decrypt the sum.

Interleaved grouping guarantees that *the aggregator cannot learn the sum of any individual group or the sum of any subset of (not all) nodes* (see the example below), and thus the nodes can collectively add just one copy of geometric noise to the aggregate, minimizing the aggregation error. When a node joins or leaves a group, the key dealer runs the setup phase again for this group only. Thus the communication cost is low.

We use the example in Figure 2 to show how interleaved grouping provides that guarantee. Seven nodes are divided into three interleaved groups, where group $\mathcal{G}_1$ shares

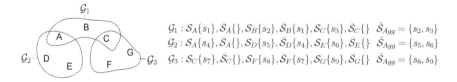

$\mathcal{G}_1 : \mathcal{S}_A\{s_1\}, \bar{\mathcal{S}}_A\{\}, \mathcal{S}_B\{s_2\}, \bar{\mathcal{S}}_B\{s_1\}, \mathcal{S}_C\{s_3\}, \bar{\mathcal{S}}_C\{\}$ $\hat{\mathcal{S}}_{Agg} = \{s_2, s_3\}$
$\mathcal{G}_2 : \mathcal{S}_A\{s_4\}, \bar{\mathcal{S}}_A\{\}, \mathcal{S}_D\{s_5\}, \bar{\mathcal{S}}_D\{s_4\}, \mathcal{S}_E\{s_6\}, \bar{\mathcal{S}}_E\{\}$ $\hat{\mathcal{S}}_{Agg} = \{s_5, s_6\}$
$\mathcal{G}_3 : \mathcal{S}_C\{s_7\}, \bar{\mathcal{S}}_C\{\}, \mathcal{S}_F\{s_8\}, \bar{\mathcal{S}}_F\{s_7\}, \mathcal{S}_G\{s_9\}, \bar{\mathcal{S}}_G\{\}$ $\hat{\mathcal{S}}_{Agg} = \{s_8, s_9\}$

Fig. 2. The basic idea of interleaved grouping. In this example, A is assigned secrets from both $\mathcal{G}_1$ and $\mathcal{G}_2$. A sets $k_A = h(f_{s_1}(t)) + h(f_{s_4}(t))$. B only receives secrets from group $\mathcal{G}_1$, and it sets $k_B = h(f_{s_2}(t)) - h(f_{s_1}(t))$. Other nodes set their keys similarly. The aggregator sets $k_0 = \sum_{i=\{2,3,5,6,8,9\}} h(f_{s_i}(t))$. The aggregator can only get the sum of *all nodes*.

node A with $\mathcal{G}_2$ and shares C with $\mathcal{G}_3$. The secrets assigned to each node and the aggregator are shown in the figure. Suppose the aggregator tries to get the sum of group $\mathcal{G}_2$, i.e., $\hat{x}_A + \hat{x}_D + \hat{x}_E$. From A's, D's and E's ciphertexts $\hat{x}_A + h(f_{s_1}(t)) + h(f_{s_4}(t))$, $\hat{x}_D + h(f_{s_5}(t)) - h(f_{s_4}(t))$ and $\hat{x}_E + h(f_{s_6}(t))$, it sums them and gets $(\hat{x}_A + \hat{x}_D + \hat{x}_E) + h(f_{s_1}(t)) + h(f_{s_5}(t)) + h(f_{s_6}(t))$. Although it knows $\hat{S}_{Agg} = \{s_5, s_6\}$ and can get $h(f_{s_5}(t)) + h(f_{s_6}(t))$, it does not know s_1 (i.e., the secrets assigned to A in group $\mathcal{G}_1$) and hence cannot get the sum of $\mathcal{G}_2$. Similarly, it cannot get the sum of $\mathcal{G}_1$, $\mathcal{G}_3$ or any other strict and non-empty subset of nodes.

4.2 Security Condition

When nodes may be compromised, the following security condition should be satisfied.

Condition 1: *Let $\mathbb{S}$ denote an arbitrary strict and non-empty subset of groups. There exists a good node N, group $\mathcal{G} \in \mathbb{S}$ and group $\mathcal{G}' \notin \mathbb{S}$, such that $N \in \mathcal{G}$ and $N \in \mathcal{G}'$.*

The following theorem (see proof in the technical report [27]) explains why Condition 1 is needed.

Theorem 2. *In interleaved grouping, the aggregator cannot obtain the sum of any strict and nonempty subset of good nodes if and only if Condition 1 is satisfied.*

According to Theorem 2, any specific interleaved grouping scheme needs to and only needs to satisfy Condition 1. Thus, Condition 1 can be used to guide the construction of interleaved grouping schemes. In the next section, we present such a scheme based on a ring structure.

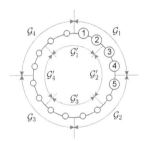

Fig. 3. Ring-based interleaved grouping. In this example, the nodes form eight groups, four disjoint groups in the outer ring ($\mathcal{G}_1$–$\mathcal{G}_4$) and four disjoint groups in the inner ring ($\mathcal{G}'_1$–$\mathcal{G}'_4$). Groups on different rings may overlap. Group $\mathcal{G}_1$ and $\mathcal{G}'_1$ overlap, and they share node 1 and 2.

5 Ring-Based Interleaved Grouping

For interleaved grouping, it is nontrivial to satisfy Condition 1. With a total of g groups, there are about 2^g possible subsets of groups. Unless g is very small, it is infeasible to adjust each possible subset to satisfy the condition. In this section, we present a novel interleaved grouping construction which addresses this challenge with a ring structure.

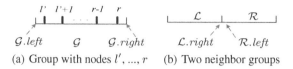

(a) Group with nodes $l', ..., r$ (b) Two neighbor groups

Fig. 4. Segment representation of groups

5.1 Ring-Based Group Structure

As shown in Figure 3, the nodes are arranged into a *node ring*, which is mirrored to two virtual rings, the *outer ring* and *inner ring*. Each virtual ring is partitioned into segments, and the nodes in a segment form a group. Each node belongs to two groups, one in each virtual ring. Groups in the same virtual ring are disjoint, but groups in different virtual rings may overlap (i.e., they share at least one node). A group in the inner (outer) ring will overlap with one or more groups in the outer (inner) ring.

The Basic Structure. Since the node ring and the two virtual rings are identical, we use "the ring" to refer to the structure when the context is clear. Suppose there are n ($n \geq 2d$) nodes in the ring indexed from 0 to $n - 1$ in the clockwise order. For convenience, we use a directed segment to represent a group, say $\mathcal{G}$ (see Fig. 4(a)). The direction from left to right corresponds to the clockwise order in the ring. Let l' and r denote the indexes of the leftmost and rightmost node in $\mathcal{G}$. Then the left and right boundary of $\mathcal{G}$ are defined as $\mathcal{G}.left = l' - 0.5$ and $\mathcal{G}.right = r + 0.5$, respectively. Let $|\mathcal{G}|$ denote the number of nodes in $\mathcal{G}$. We have $|\mathcal{G}| = (\mathcal{G}.right - \mathcal{G}.left) \mod n$.

Suppose $\mathcal{L}$ and $\mathcal{R}$ are two neighbor groups in the same virtual ring, and $\mathcal{L}.right = \mathcal{R}.left$ (see Fig. 4(b)). $\mathcal{L}.right$ (or $\mathcal{R}.left$) is the border between $\mathcal{L}$ and $\mathcal{R}$. Term "move $\mathcal{L}.right$ to the right by y" means that $\mathcal{L}.right$ and $\mathcal{R}.left$ are increased by $y \mod n$, i.e., the leftmost y nodes of $\mathcal{R}$ are moved to $\mathcal{L}$. Term "move $\mathcal{R}.left$ to the left by y" is interpreted similarly.

Overlap Patterns. Two groups in different virtual rings can overlap in two patterns (see Figure 5). In *Pattern I*, one group is a strict subset of the other group. In *Pattern II*, the two groups have nodes in common, but each group also has some nodes that the other group does not have.

5.2 Properties

To satisfy Condition 1 and reduce the communication cost of dealing with dynamic joins and leaves, the ring-based group structure has the following properties:

Overlap Property: Any two groups that overlap share at least x nodes. x is large enough to make it infeasible (i.e., with probability smaller than 2^{-l}) that none of the shared nodes is good (see later).

Interleave Property: If two neighboring nodes in the ring belong to two neighboring groups in one virtual ring, they belong to the same group in the other virtual ring.

Group Size Property: Each group has d ($d > 2x$) to $2d - 1$ nodes.

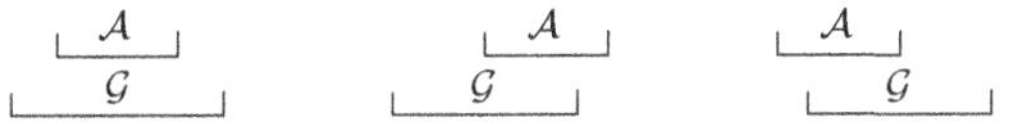

(a) Pattern I   (b) Pattern II   (c) Pattern II

Fig. 5. The two patterns that two groups $\mathcal{G}$ and $\mathcal{A}$ may overlap where $|\mathcal{G}| \geq |\mathcal{A}|$. $\mathcal{G}$ and $\mathcal{A}$ are in different virtual rings. In (b) and (c), $\mathcal{G}$ overlaps with the left and right part of $\mathcal{A}$, respectively.

An example of the interleave property is shown in Figure 3. Two neighboring nodes 4 and 5 belong to neighboring groups $\mathcal{G}_1$ and $\mathcal{G}_2$ in the outer ring, and they are in the same group $\mathcal{G}'_2$ in the inner ring. The group size property is required by our group adjustment algorithms.

Theorem 3. *In ring-based interleaved grouping, the overlap and interleave property ensure that Condition 1 is satisfied.*

Proof. See the technical report [27].

Comments: Due to Theorem 2 and 3, *the ring-based construction guarantees that the aggregator cannot obtain the sum of any strict and nonempty subset of good nodes.* For convenience, we say the ring-based grouping is *secure* if the overlap, interleave and group size property hold.

Practical Considerations. In practice, the value of x should be sufficiently large such that for any two groups that overlap, with a high probability (denoted by p_s) at least one of their shared nodes is good. Since each node can be compromised with the same probability, with standard combinatorial techniques, we can derive that $p_s = 1 - \binom{\gamma n}{x}/\binom{n}{x}$. When n is large, $p_s \gtrsim 1 - \gamma^x$. Parameter x can be set as the minimum value that satisfies $p_s > 1 - 2^{-l}$:

$$x = \lceil -l \log_\gamma 2 \rceil. \tag{1}$$

To minimize the communication cost of dynamic joins and leaves (see later), parameter d can be set as the minimum value that satisfies $d > 2x$, i.e., $d = 2x + 1$. Table 4 shows the values of x and d for 80-bit security.

Table 4. The values of x and d for 80-bit security

γ	0	0.01	0.05	0.1	0.15	0.2
x	1	13	19	25	30	35
d	3	27	39	51	61	71

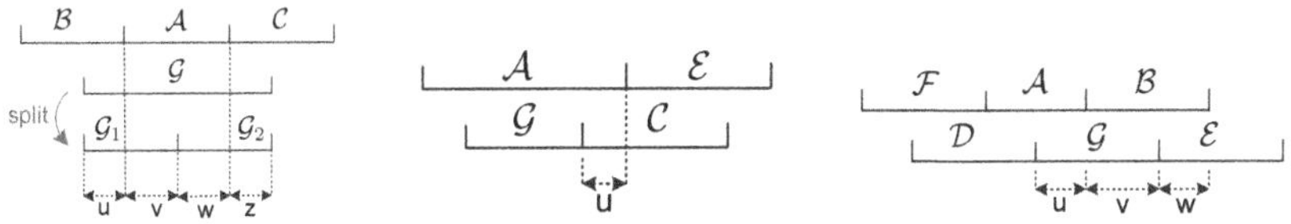

(a) Regrouping in Alg. 2   (b) Regrouping in Alg. 4   (c) Regrouping in Alg. 5

Fig. 6. The regrouping in Alg. 2, 4 and 5

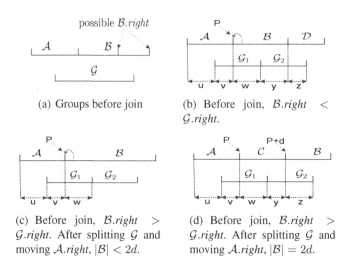

(a) Groups before join

(b) Before join, $\mathcal{B}.right < \mathcal{G}.right$.

(c) Before join, $\mathcal{B}.right > \mathcal{G}.right$. After splitting $\mathcal{G}$ and moving $\mathcal{A}.right$, $|\mathcal{B}| < 2d$.

(d) Before join, $\mathcal{B}.right > \mathcal{G}.right$. After splitting $\mathcal{G}$ and moving $\mathcal{A}.right$, $|\mathcal{B}| = 2d$.

Fig. 7. The regrouping (in Alg. 3) when a node joins $\mathcal{G}$ and $\mathcal{A}$ which overlap in Pattern II.

5.3 Group Management

Suppose initially there are n nodes. Algorithm 1 initializes them into $\frac{2n}{d}$ groups. Figure 3 shows an instance of initialized groups for $n = 16$ and $d = 4$. Clearly, each group overlaps with two other groups and shares $\frac{d}{2}$ nodes with each overlapping group. It is easy to verify that the grouping is secure.

Algorithm 1. initGroup(): Group initialization.

Require: Nodes $0,...,n-1$. Without loss of generality, n is divisible by d.
Ensure: $\frac{2n}{d}$ groups $\mathcal{G}_1, ..., \mathcal{G}_{\frac{n}{d}}, \mathcal{G}'_1, ..., \mathcal{G}'_{\frac{n}{d}}$, each of size d.
1: **for** i from 1 to $\frac{n}{d}$ **do**
2:   Add nodes $(i-1)\frac{n}{d}, (i-1)\frac{n}{d}+1, ..., (i-1)\frac{n}{d}+d-1$ to group $\mathcal{G}_i$
3:   Add nodes $(i-1)\frac{n}{d}+\frac{d}{2} \mod n, (i-1)\frac{n}{d}+\frac{d}{2}+1 \mod n, ..., (i-1)\frac{n}{d}+\frac{d}{2}+d-1 \mod n$ to group $\mathcal{G}'_i$

When a new node joins, it is inserted to a random location in the ring, and added to the two groups that cover the location of insertion. The two changed groups may violate the group size property (i.e., having more than $2d - 1$ nodes). Similarly, when a node leaves, it is removed from the ring and from the two groups it belonged to, which may violate the group size property and overlap property. In these cases, the nodes should be regrouped so that the three properties still hold.

Algorithm 2-5 show the group adjustment algorithms. Suppose the grouping is secure before the node joins or leaves. Lemma 1-4 show that these algorithms make the grouping secure. Their proofs can be found in the technical report [27].

Algorithm 2. adjust(JOIN, I): Re-grouping after a node joins two groups which overlap in pattern I (see Fig. 6(a)).

Require: $\mathcal{G}, \mathcal{A}$: The two groups that the node joins, $|\mathcal{G}| > |\mathcal{A}|$.

1: **if** $|\mathcal{G}| < 2d$ **then return**;
2: **else** Split $\mathcal{G}$ in the middle into two groups, each of size d;

Algorithm 3. adjust(JOIN, II): Re-grouping after a node joins two groups which overlap in pattern II (see Fig. 7(a)).

Require: $\mathcal{G}, \mathcal{A}$: the two groups that the node joins, $|\mathcal{G}| \geq |\mathcal{A}|$.
Require: $\mathcal{B}$: $\mathcal{A}$'s neighbor group which also overlaps with $\mathcal{G}$.
Require: Without loss of generality, $\mathcal{G}$ overlaps with the right part of $\mathcal{A}$, i.e., $\mathcal{G}.left > \mathcal{A}.left$ and $\mathcal{G}.right > \mathcal{A}.right$. In this case, $\mathcal{B}$ is the right neighbor of $\mathcal{A}$. See Figure 7(a).

1: **if** $|\mathcal{G}| < 2d$ **then**
2:    **return**;
3: **else**
4:    Split $\mathcal{G}$ in the middle into two groups, each of size d;
5:    Move $\mathcal{A}.right$ to the position $P = max\{\mathcal{G}.left + x, \mathcal{A}.left + d\}$;
6:    **if** $|\mathcal{B}| < 2d$ **then**
7:       **return**;
8:    **else**
9:       Create a group $\mathcal{C}$, with $\mathcal{C}.left = \mathcal{A}.right$ and $\mathcal{C}.right = \mathcal{C}.left + d$;
10:      $\mathcal{B}.left \leftarrow \mathcal{C}.right$;

Algorithm 4. adjust(LEAVE, I): Re-grouping after a node leaves two groups which overlap in pattern I (see Fig. 6(b)).

Require: $\mathcal{G}, \mathcal{A}$: the two groups that the node leaves, with $|\mathcal{G}| < |\mathcal{A}|$.
Require: $\mathcal{C}, \mathcal{E}$: the right neighbor of $\mathcal{G}$ and $\mathcal{A}$, respectively. See Figure 6(b).

1: **if** $|\mathcal{G}| \geq d$ **then**
2:    **return**;
3: **else if** $|\mathcal{C}| = d$ **then**
4:    Merge $\mathcal{G}$ and $\mathcal{C}$;
5: **else**
6:    $u \leftarrow |\mathcal{C} \bigcap \mathcal{A}|$;
7:    **if** $u \geq x + 1$ **then** Move $\mathcal{G}.right$ to the right by 1;
8:    **else if** $u = x$ **and** $|\mathcal{C}| \geq d + 2x$ **then** Move $\mathcal{G}.right$ to the right by $2x$;
9:    **else if** $u = x$ **and** $|\mathcal{C}| < d + 2x$ **then** Move both $\mathcal{G}.right$ and $\mathcal{A}.right$ to the right by 1;

Algorithm 5. adjust(LEAVE, II): Re-grouping after a node leaves two groups which overlap in pattern II (see Fig. 6(c)).

Require: $\mathcal{G}, \mathcal{A}$: the two groups that the node leaves.
Require: $\mathcal{D}, \mathcal{E}$: $\mathcal{G}$'s neighbors. $\mathcal{D}$ overlaps with $\mathcal{A}$; $\mathcal{E}$ does not.
Require: $\mathcal{B}, \mathcal{F}$: $\mathcal{A}$'s neighbors. $\mathcal{B}$ overlaps with $\mathcal{G}$; $\mathcal{F}$ does not.
Require: Without loss of generality, suppose $\mathcal{G}.left > \mathcal{A}.left$ and $\mathcal{G}.right > \mathcal{A}.right$.
  1: **if** $|\mathcal{G} \cap \mathcal{A}| \geq x$ **then**
  2:     **if** $|\mathcal{G}| \geq d$ **and** $|\mathcal{A}| \geq d$ **then**
  3:         return;
  4:     **if** $|\mathcal{G}| = d - 1$ **then**
  5:         **if** $|\mathcal{E}| = d$ **then** Merge $\mathcal{G}$ and $\mathcal{E}$;
  6:         **else** Move $\mathcal{G}.right$ to the right by 1;
  7:     **if** $|\mathcal{A}| = d - 1$ **then**
  8:         **if** $|\mathcal{F}| = d$ **then** Merge $\mathcal{A}$ and $\mathcal{F}$;
  9:         **else** Move $\mathcal{A}.left$ to the left by 1;
 10: **else**
 11:     **if** $|\mathcal{G}| \geq d$ **and** $|\mathcal{A}| \geq d$ **then**
 12:         **if** $|\mathcal{B}| \geq d + 1$ **then** Move $\mathcal{A}.right$ to the right by 1;
 13:         **else if** $|\mathcal{D}| \geq d + 1$ **then** Move $\mathcal{G}.left$ to the left by 1;
 14:         **else** Move $\mathcal{D}.right$ to the right by $2x - 1$;
 15:     **if** $|\mathcal{G}| = d - 1$ **then**
 16:         **if** $|\mathcal{D}| = d$ **then** Merge $\mathcal{G}$ and $\mathcal{D}$;
 17:         **else** Move $\mathcal{G}.left$ to the left by 1;
 18:     **if** $|\mathcal{A}| = d - 1$ **then**
 19:         **if** $|\mathcal{B}| = d$ **then** Merge $\mathcal{A}$ and $\mathcal{B}$;
 20:         **else** Move $\mathcal{A}.right$ to the right by 1;

Lemma 1(2): *Suppose a node joins two groups which overlap in Pattern I (II). After Algorithm 2 (3) is run, the grouping is secure.*

Lemma 3(4): *Suppose a node leaves two groups which overlap in Pattern I (II). After Algorithm 4 (5) is run, the grouping is secure.*

5.4   Communication Cost Analysis

We measure the communication cost of dynamic joins and leaves by the number of nodes that the key dealer should reissue secrets to (*number of updated nodes* for short). The communication cost of ring-based interleaved grouping is given in the following theorem (see proof in the technical report [27]).

Theorem 4. *In ring-based interleaved grouping, when a node joins (leaves), at most three (four) existing groups are updated and the number of updated nodes has an upper bound 4d (6d).*

This theorem indicates that the communication cost of ring-based interleaved grouping depends on parameter d, which in turn depends on parameter γ (see Table 4), the maximum fraction of compromised nodes. According to Table 4, the value of d is not large when γ is not too high. Thus, the communication cost is low. Note that the cost does not change with the number of nodes in the system.

6 Applying Ring-Based Interleaved Grouping to Data Aggregation

In this section, we propose a scheme to demonstrate how to apply the ring-based interleaved grouping technique to privacy-preserving data aggregation to achieve both churn resilience and low aggregation error.

6.1 Encryption Scheme

Setup: The key dealer divides the nodes into groups using Alg. 1, and independently assigns secrets for each group as done in the basic scheme. Each node i gets secrets from the two groups that it is in. Let $\mathcal{S}_{i1}$ and $\bar{\mathcal{S}}_{i1}$ denote the sets of secrets received from one group, and $\mathcal{S}_{i2}$ and $\bar{\mathcal{S}}_{i2}$ denote the sets of secrets received from the other group. The node merges the secrets as follows: $\mathcal{S}_i = \mathcal{S}_{i1} \bigcup \mathcal{S}_{i2}$ and $\bar{\mathcal{S}}_i = \bar{\mathcal{S}}_{i1} \bigcup \bar{\mathcal{S}}_{i2}$. Let g denote the number of groups generated by Alg. 1. The aggregator obtains $\hat{\mathcal{S}}_1, ..., \hat{\mathcal{S}}_g$, where each $\hat{\mathcal{S}}_j$ is the decryption capability of one group. It sets the overall decryption capability as $\hat{\mathcal{S}} = \bigcup_{i=j}^{g} \hat{\mathcal{S}}_j$.
Encryption: The same as in the basic scheme.
Decryption: The same as in the basic scheme.

Due to the guarantee provided by ring-based interleaved grouping, the aggregator can only decrypt the noisy sum but nothing else.

6.2 Data Perturbation

The perturbation algorithm is the same as that in the basic scheme, except that parameter β is set differently (see below).

6.3 Dealing with Dynamic Joins and Leaves

When a node joins or leaves, the key dealer runs Algorithm 2-5 to adjust grouping. For each adjusted group, it reruns the setup phase to distribute a new set of secrets to the nodes of the group and to the aggregator. In this process, it only communicates with the nodes in the adjusted groups, which constitute only a small portion of all nodes.

In the data perturbation part of the basic scheme, each node uses the number of nodes n to set parameter β (i.e., $\beta = \min(\frac{1}{(1-\gamma)n} \ln \frac{1}{\delta}, 1)$), such that all nodes collectively add just one copy of geometric noise to the aggregate. However, it requires communications with all nodes upon every join and leave to send the exact value of n to them. Obviously, it nullifies the benefits of grouping in reducing the communication cost. To address this issue, we relax the accuracy requirement on the value of n such that n does not have to be updated to every node upon every join and leave. As a tradeoff, a little more noise is added compared to the basic scheme.

Algorithm 6. Procedures run by the key dealer to manage the values of u for nodes.

Require: n: the real number of nodes
Require: u_i: the number of nodes that node i uses to set parameter β
1: **Initialization:**
2: **if** n is even **then** $u_1, u_2, ..., u_n \leftarrow \lfloor \frac{n}{2} \rfloor + 1, \lfloor \frac{n}{2} \rfloor + 1, \lfloor \frac{n}{2} \rfloor + 2, \lfloor \frac{n}{2} \rfloor + 2, ..., n, n$;
3: **else** $u_1, u_2, ..., u_n \leftarrow \lfloor \frac{n}{2} \rfloor + 1, \lfloor \frac{n}{2} \rfloor + 2, \lfloor \frac{n}{2} \rfloor + 2, ..., n, n$;
4:
5: **Join:**
6: **if** Node i joins **then**
7:     $n \leftarrow n + 1$;
8:     $u_i \leftarrow n$;
9:     Find a node j with $u_j = \min\{u_1, u_2, ..., u_n\}$;
10:    $u_j \leftarrow n$;
11:
12: **Leave:**
13: **if** Node i leaves **then**
14:    $n \leftarrow n - 1$;
15:    Find a node j with $u_j = \max\{u_1, u_2, ..., u_n\}$;
16:    **if** There exists another node m with $u_m = u_j$ **then** $u_m \leftarrow u_i$;
17:    $u_j \leftarrow \lfloor \frac{n}{2} \rfloor + 1$;

Specifically, each node records the value of n according to its knowledge. Let u denote the value recorded by the node. u may not always reflect n, which is the real number of nodes. Each node uses u to set parameter β for data perturbation, i.e., $\beta = \min(\frac{1}{(1-\gamma)u} \ln \frac{1}{\delta}, 1)$. The smaller u is, the more noise is added. u should not be larger than n to ensure that at least one copy of geometric noise is added to provide differential privacy, but u cannot be too small to avoid too much aggregation error. Thus, the values of u at the nodes should be updated appropriately upon dynamic joins or leaves. The challenge is how to update u without incurring too much communication cost.

We propose Alg. 6 to address this challenge. Table 5 shows a running example of it.

Table 5. An example of Algorithm 6

step	operation	u_1	u_2	u_3	u_4	u_5	u_6	n
0	initialize	3	3	4	4	-	-	4
1	Node 5 joins	3	5	4	4	5	-	5
2	Node 6 joins	6	5	4	4	5	6	6
3	Node 2 leaves	5	-	4	4	5	3	5
4	Node 1 leaves	-	-	4	4	3	3	4

Aggregation Error. We have a theorem (see proof in the technical report [27]).

Theorem 5. *Algorithm 6 guarantees that $\forall i$, $u_i \in (\frac{n}{2}, n]$.*

Comments: Since $u \leq n$, at least one copy of geometric noise is added to the sum aggregate to provide differential privacy; since $u > \frac{n}{2}$, at most one more copy of geometric noise is added. Thus, *the average aggregation error is roughly within twice of the geometric noise required for differential privacy.*

Communication Cost. Alg. 6 only incurs very small communication cost. When a node joins, the joining node and another node with the minimum u are updated; when a node leaves, (at most) two remaining nodes with the maximum u are updated. Thus, the u of at most two nodes are updated for each join or leave. Considering this property and Theorem 4, the overall communication cost is as follows.

Corollary 1. *When a node joins (leaves), our scheme communicates with at most $4d+2$ ($6d + 2$) nodes to update their secret keys and their values of u.*

7 Evaluations

This section evaluates the communication cost (measured by the number of updated nodes per join or leave) and the aggregation error of our solution through simulations, and evaluates the computation cost via implementation-based measurements. We compare our solution against four other schemes: the scheme proposed in [8] (denoted by *SCRCS*), the *Binary* scheme [9], the scheme proposed in [10] (denoted by *JK*), and the *Naive Grouping* scheme presented in Section 3.4.

7.1 Communication Cost of Ring-Based Interleaved Grouping

The communication cost of ring-based interleaved grouping is affected by parameter γ (i.e., the maximum fraction of nodes compromised). We first evaluate the effect of γ. We set x and d according to Table 4. To measure the communication cost of join (leave), we first generate a random initial grouping structure that includes 2000 (102,000) nodes, and then simulate 10^5 joins (leaves) over it, resulting in 102,000 (2000) nodes in the end. We compute the mean and standard deviation over the 10^5 measurements.

Figure 8 shows the simulation results as well as the analytical upper bound (see Theorem 4). As γ increases, the communication cost increases. This is because x is larger (see Eq. 1) and the group size is larger. However, only 170 nodes are updated even when 20% of nodes are compromised. Also, we found that the communication cost of our scheme is roughly half of the analytical upper bound.

7.2 Comparisons of Communication Cost

We compare our solution against the other four schemes in communication cost. In Naive Grouping, parameter g is set such that our scheme and Naive Grouping have the same average aggregation error. In our scheme, $\gamma = 0.05$. We vary the number of nodes n. For each value of n, we compute the mean and standard deviation over 10000 runs.

Figure 9 shows the results. Clearly, the communication cost of our scheme is much smaller than SCRCS and Naive Grouping, and is close to Binary and JK. This is because the ring-based interleaved grouping can effectively reduce the number of nodes that should be updated for dynamic joins and leaves. Also, the communication cost of our scheme does not change with parameter n, and hence it can scale to large systems. Interestingly, our scheme has much smaller communication cost than Naive Grouping with the same aggregation error, which demonstrates that interleaved grouping achieves a better balance between communication cost and aggregation error.

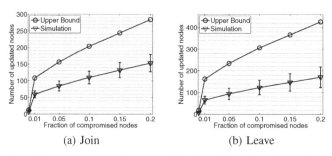

Fig. 8. The communication cost of ring-based interleaved grouping

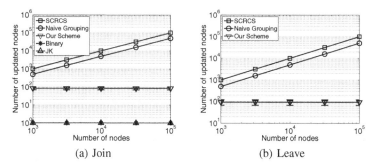

Fig. 9. Comparisons between our scheme and other schemes in the communication cost of dynamic joins and leaves (log-log scale). For dynamic leaves, the communication cost of Binary and JK is zero and thus not shown in the log-log plot.

7.3 Comparisons of Aggregation Errors

We compare our scheme with the other four schemes on aggregation error. In Naive Grouping, the parameter g is set such that Naive Grouping and our scheme have the same average communication cost for leave. In the simulation, we assume each node's data is either 0 or 1 (i.e., $\Delta = 1$). We vary parameters n, ϵ and δ. For each parameter, we measure the mean and standard deviation of aggregation error over 10000 runs.

Table 6 shows the mean and standard deviation of aggregation error. As the number of node increases, the aggregation error of Binary and Naive Grouping also increases quickly. However, the aggregation error of Our scheme, SCRCS and JK does not change too much, because on average they add a constant number of copies of geometric noise to the aggregate. As privacy parameter ϵ (δ, resp.) decreases, which means a stricter requirement for differential privacy, all schemes have a higher aggregation error, since each node needs to add more noise to meet the stronger privacy requirement. In nearly all cases, the aggregation error in our scheme is one order of magnitude smaller than Binary and Naive Grouping, and it is within 1.5 (2.5) times of the aggregation error SCRCS (JK). Thus, our scheme has low aggregation error.

7.4 Implementation and Comparisons in Running Time

We implemented a prototype system in Java. The prototype has two components which are used as the mobile node and the aggregator respectively. The mobile node

Table 6. The mean and standard deviation of aggregation error

	$n = 10^3$	3162	10^4	31623	10^5
Binary	247/211	300/260	360/308	386/333	439/381
Naive Grp.	63/48	112/85	199/152	358/269	631/479
Our Sch.	26/23	27/22	26/23	26/22	26/22
SCRCS	18/17	18/17	18/17	18/17	18/17
JK	9.9/9.8	10.2/10.1	10/9.9	10.1/10	10/9.9

	$\epsilon = 0.05$	0.1	0.2	0.3	0.4
Binary	704/609	363/307	178/153	121/103	88/75
Naive Grp.	398/301	199/152	100/75	66/51	50/38
Our Sch.	52/44	26/22	13/11	9/7	6/5
SCRCS	36/34	18/17	8.7/8.5	5.8/5.6	4.6/4.3
JK	19.9/19.8	10/9.9	5.1/5	3.3/3.2	2.5/2.4

	$\delta = 0.01$	0.05	0.1	0.15	
Binary	409/341	363/307	328/285	315/281	
Naive Grp.	248/189	199/152	174/132	159/120	
Our Sch.	33/27	26/22	23/20	20/19	
SCRCS	23/20	18/17	16/15	15/13	
JK	10.2/10.1	10/9.9	10/9.8	9.9/9.9	

The number on the left (right) of "/" is mean (standard deviation).
By default, $n = 10000$, $\gamma = 0.05$, $\epsilon = 0.1$ and $\delta = 0.05$.

component is implemented on a Android Nexus S Phone, which has 1GHz CPU and 512MB RAM, and runs Android 4.0.4 OS. The aggregator component is implemented on a Windows Laptop with 2.6GHz CPU, 4GB RAM and 64-bit Windows 7 OS. By running experiments over the prototype, we measured the time needed for the phone to encrypt a data value and the time needed for the laptop to decrypt the sum aggregate. For comparison, we also implemented SCRCS, JK and Binary and measured their running time. As to the JK scheme, the data consumer and the key manager (see [10]) are implemented together as the aggregator.

Table 7. The analytical computation cost of different schemes

	Mobile Node	Aggregator
Our Scheme	$4c$ PRFs	$\frac{2nq}{d}$ PRFs
JK	2 Paillier encryptions & 1 signature generation	2 Paillier decryptions & $2n$ mod. multiplications & n sig. verifications
SCRCS	2 mod. exp.	$\sqrt{n\Delta}$ mod. exp.
Binary	$2(\lfloor \log_2 n \rfloor + 1)$ mod. exp.	$\sqrt{n\Delta}$ mod. exp.

Table 7 shows the computation overhead of these schemes (see [8–10, 20] for details). In the implementation, HMAC-SHA256 is used as the PRF of our scheme. For JK, the Paillier cryptosystem uses a 1024-bit modulus, and RSA (1024-bit) is used as the digital signature algorithm. For SCRCS and Binary, the high-speed elliptic curve "curve25519" is used for modular exponentiation.

Table 8 shows the running time of these schemes. Compared with JK, our scheme is two orders of magnitude faster in both encryption and decryption. This is because JK uses the Paillier cryptosystem which is very expensive in computation, but our scheme is based on HMAC which is very efficient. Compared with SCRCS (Binary), our scheme is one (two) order(s) of magnitude faster in encryption, and two or three orders of magnitude faster in decryption when the plaintext space is 1000 or larger. SCRCS and Binary are very slow in decryption because they need to traverse the possible plaintext space to decrypt sum, computing one modular exponentiation for each possible value. Thus, our scheme is the most efficient in computation.

Comments. Our scheme's high efficiency in computation makes it a better choice for large-scale mobile sensing applications with large plaintext spaces, high aggregation loads (e.g., many parallel aggregation tasks per node or per aggregator, short aggregation period), resource-constraint mobile devices (e.g., personal healthcare devices besides smartphones) and rich statistics.

Table 8. The running time of different schemes

	Enc.	Decryption			
	-	$n = 10^3$	10^4	10^5	10^6
Our Scheme	3.4ms	1.2ms	12ms	0.12s	1.2s
JK	236ms	175ms	1.5s	15s	150s
SCRCS ($\Delta = 10^3$)	45ms	5.6s	18s	56s	177s
SCRCS ($\Delta = 10^4$)	45ms	18s	56s	177s	560s
SCRCS ($\Delta = 10^5$)	45ms	56s	177s	560s	1770s
Binary ($\Delta = 10^3$)	0.5~0.9s	5.6s	18s	56s	177s
Binary ($\Delta = 10^4$)	0.5~0.9s	18s	56s	177s	560s
Binary ($\Delta = 10^5$)	0.5~0.9s	56s	177s	560s	1770s

The encryption time of Binary depends on n, and range $[0.5, 0.9]$ is obtained for $n \in [10^3, 10^6]$. In our scheme, $\gamma = 0.2$.

8   Extensions and Discussions

Relaxing the Trusted Key Dealer Assumption. The assumption of trusted key dealer can be relaxed. Instead, we can assume an honest-but-curious key dealer that does not collude with the aggregator. It follows our protocol as specified, but may attempt to infer the data value of nodes from the the protocol transcript and from eavesdropping all communications. Under this semi-honest model, the only adaptation that should be made to our protocol is adding one more encryption/decryption to the data that each node submits to the aggregator. Specifically, each node first encrypts its noisy data as previously specified with the secrets received from the key dealer, deriving an intermediate result c, and then encrypts c using a pre-shared key shared with the aggregator. It sends the final ciphertext to the aggregator. The aggregator first decrypts each node's intermediate result c using the pre-shared key, and then decrypts the noisy sum as previously specified. So long as the key dealer does not collude with the aggregator, it cannot get any node's intermediate result c, and thus cannot get the node's data value. In future work, we will explore how to completely remove the key dealer.

Dealing with Node Failures. Fault tolerance is not the major focus of this paper, but our solution can be adapted in the following way such that, when some nodes fail, the aggregator can still obtain the aggregate over the remaining nodes.

Since the key dealer knows the secrets assigned to every node, if some nodes fail to submit data, the aggregator asks the dealer to submit data on behalf of those failed nodes. The dealer sets the data value as zero, adds a large-enough (see below) noise r to it, encrypts the noisy data with the secrets of all those failed nodes, and submits the obtained ciphertext to the aggregator. The aggregator can decrypt the sum over the functioning nodes' data. This method incurs a round trip communication between the key dealer and the aggregator. The overall communication cost is still $O(n)$.

Even if all nodes are functioning, the aggregator may dishonestly claim the failure of a subset $\tilde{\mathbb{S}}$ of nodes. (It can only claim one subset per aggregation period.) Then it can obtain two independent noisy sums, $S = \sum_i (x_i + r_i)$ and $S' = \sum_{i \notin \tilde{\mathbb{S}}} (x_i + r_i) + r$. It is easy to see that each node is included in at most two sums. Roughly speaking, to provide differential privacy, it suffices to add two copies of geometric noise to each sum. Thus, all nodes collectively add two copies of geometric noise to S and the key dealer itself adds two copies of geometric noise to S'. Considering that Alg. 6 may at most double the noise added to S, the final aggregation error is less than six copies of geometric noise when there is node failure, and less than four copies without node failure. Obviously, this method maintains $O(1)$ aggregation error.

If a node has failed for a long time, it can be removed from the system as a "leave". The recovery of a failed node can be processed as a "join".

In this method, the key dealer needs to be online, but it only makes online communications when there is node failure. In future work, we will study other solutions for fault tolerance, e.g., by exploring the direction pointed out in [9].

9   Conclusions

This paper proposed a novel ring-based interleaved grouping technique and applied it to privacy-preserving aggregation of time-series data in mobile sensing applications. Our solution achieves O(1) aggregation error irrespective of the number of nodes in the system. More importantly, it has very low communication overhead for dynamic joins and leaves. Simulation results show that only less than 170 nodes need to be updated for each join or leave when on average 20% of nodes are compromised, irrespective of the system scale. Our solution is very efficient in computation.

Acknowledgment. We would like to thank Elaine Shi for her insightful comments and suggestions. We would also like to thank the anonymous reviewers for their helpful suggestions.

References

1. Thiagarajan, A., Ravindranath, L., LaCurts, K., Madden, S., Balakrishnan, H., Toledo, S., Eriksson, J.: Vtrack: accurate, energy-aware road traffic delay estimation using mobile phones. In: Proc. SenSys, pp. 85–98 (2009)

2. Mun, M., Reddy, S., Shilton, K., Yau, N., Burke, J., Estrin, D., Hansen, M., Howard, E., West, R., Boda, P.: Peir, the personal environmental impact report, as a platform for participatory sensing systems research. In: Proc. ACM MobiSys, pp. 55–68 (2009)

3. Lane, N.D., Mohammod, M., Lin, M., Yang, X., Lu, H., Ali, S., Doryab, A., Berke, E., Choudhury, T., Campbell, A.: Bewell: A smartphone application to monitor, model and promote wellbeing. In: Intl. ICST Conf. on Pervasive Computing Technologies for Healthcare (2011)

4. Hicks, J., Ramanathan, N., Kim, D., Monibi, M., Selsky, J., Hansen, M., Estrin, D.: Andwellness: an open mobile system for activity and experience sampling. In: Proc. Wireless Health, pp. 34–43 (2010)

5. Hull, B., Bychkovsky, V., Zhang, Y., Chen, K., Goraczko, M., Miu, A., Shih, E., Balakrishnan, H., Madden, S.: Cartel: a distributed mobile sensor computing system. In: SenSys (2006)

6. Honicky, R., Brewer, E.A., Paulos, E., White, R.: N-smarts: networked suite of mobile atmospheric real-time sensors. In: NSDR (2008)

7. Rastogi, V., Nath, S.: Differentially private aggregation of distributed time-series with transformation and encryption. In: ACM SIGMOD (2010)

8. Shi, E., Chan, T.-H.H., Rieffel, E., Chow, R., Song, D.: Privacy-preserving aggregation of time-series data. In: Network and Distributed System Security Symposium, NDSS (2011)

9. Chan, T.-H.H., Shi, E., Song, D.: Privacy-preserving stream aggregation with fault tolerance. In: Keromytis, A.D. (ed.) FC 2012. LNCS, vol. 7397, pp. 200–214. Springer, Heidelberg (2012)

10. Jawurek, M., Kerschbaum, F.: Fault-tolerant privacy-preserving statistics. In: Fischer-Hübner, S., Wright, M. (eds.) PETS 2012. LNCS, vol. 7384, pp. 221–238. Springer, Heidelberg (2012)

11. Dwork, C.: Differential privacy. Invited talk at ICALP (2006)

12. Dwork, C., McSherry, F., Nissim, K., Smith, A.: Calibrating noise to sensitivity in private data analysis. In: Halevi, S., Rabin, T. (eds.) TCC 2006. LNCS, vol. 3876, pp. 265–284. Springer, Heidelberg (2006)

13. Li, Q., Cao, G.: Providing privacy-aware incentives for mobile sensing. In: Proc. IEEE PerCom (2013)

14. Zhu, Z., Cao, G.: Applaus: A privacy-preserving location proof updating system for location-based services. In: Proc. IEEE INFOCOM (2011)

15. Cristofaro, E.D., Soriente, C.: Short paper: Pepsi—privacy-enhanced participatory sensing infrastructure. In: Proc. ACM WiSec, pp. 23–28 (2011)

16. Li, Q., Cao, G.: Mitigating routing misbehavior in disruption tolerant networks. IEEE Transactions on Information Forensics and Security 7(2), 664–675 (2012)

17. Castelluccia, C., Chan, A.C.-F., Mykletun, E., Tsudik, G.: Efficient and provably secure aggregation of encrypted data in wireless sensor networks. ACM Transactions on Sensor Networks (TOSN) 5(3), 20:1–20:36 (2009)

18. Shi, J., Zhang, R., Liu, Y., Zhang, Y.: Prisense: privacy-preserving data aggregation in people-centric urban sensing systems. In: Proc. IEEE INFOCOM, pp. 758–766 (2010)

19. Rieffel, E.G., Biehl, J., van Melle, W., Lee, A.J.: Secured histories: computing group statistics on encrypted data while preserving individual privacy (2010) (submission)

20. Li, Q., Cao, G.: Efficient and privacy-preserving data aggregation in mobile sensing. In: Proc. IEEE ICNP (2012)

21. Chen, R., Reznichenko, A., Francis, P., Gehrke, J.: Towards statistical queries over distributed private user data. In: Proc. of NSDI (2012)

22. Proserpio, D., Goldberg, S., McSherry, F.: A workflow for differentially-private graph synthesis. In: Proc. ACM Workshop on Online Social Networks, WOSN, pp. 13–18 (2012)

23. Sala, A., Zhao, X., Wilson, C., Zheng, H., Zhao, B.Y.: Sharing graphs using differentially private graph models. In: Proc. ACM IMC, pp. 81–98 (2011)
24. Shao, M., Yang, Y., Zhu, S., Cao, G.: Towards statistically strong source anonymity for sensor networks. In: Proc. IEEE INFOCOM (2008)
25. Lenstra, A.K., Verheul, E.R.: Selecting cryptographic key sizes. In: Imai, H., Zheng, Y. (eds.) PKC 2000. LNCS, vol. 1751, pp. 446–465. Springer, Heidelberg (2000)
26. Ghosh, A., Roughgarden, T., Sundararajan, M.: Universally utility-maximizing privacy mechanisms. In: ACM Symposium on Theory of Computing, STOC, pp. 351–360 (2009)
27. Li, Q., Cao, G.: Efficient privacy-preserving stream aggregation in mobile sensing with low aggregation error. Technical Report, The Pennsylvania State University (April 2013), http://www.cse.psu.edu/~qxl118/papers/li2013tr.pdf

Broadening the Scope
of Differential Privacy Using Metrics*

Konstantinos Chatzikokolakis[1,2], Miguel E. Andrés[2],
Nicolás Emilio Bordenabe[2,3], and Catuscia Palamidessi[2,3]

[1] CNRS
[2] LIX, Ecole Polytechnique
[3] INRIA

Abstract. Differential Privacy is one of the most prominent frameworks used to deal with disclosure prevention in statistical databases. It provides a formal privacy guarantee, ensuring that sensitive information relative to individuals cannot be easily inferred by disclosing answers to aggregate queries. If two databases are adjacent, i.e. differ only for an individual, then the query should not allow to tell them apart by more than a certain factor. This induces a bound also on the distinguishability of two generic databases, which is determined by their distance on the Hamming graph of the adjacency relation.

In this paper we explore the implications of differential privacy when the indistinguishability requirement depends on an arbitrary notion of distance. We show that we can naturally express, in this way, (protection against) privacy threats that cannot be represented with the standard notion, leading to new applications of the differential privacy framework. We give intuitive characterizations of these threats in terms of Bayesian adversaries, which generalize two interpretations of (standard) differential privacy from the literature. We revisit the well-known results stating that universally optimal mechanisms exist only for counting queries: We show that, in our extended setting, universally optimal mechanisms exist for other queries too, notably sum, average, and percentile queries. We explore various applications of the generalized definition, for statistical databases as well as for other areas, such that geolocation and smart metering.

1 Introduction

Differential privacy [1,2] is a formal definition of privacy which originated from the area of statistical databases, and it is now applied in many other domains, ranging from programming languages [3] to social networks [4] and geolocation [5].

Statistical databases are queried by analysts to obtain aggregate information about individuals. It is important to protect the privacy of the participants in the database, in the sense that it should not be possible to infer the value of an individual from the aggregate information. This can be achieved by adding random noise to the answer.

* This work is partially funded by the Inria large scale initiative CAPPRIS, the EU FP7 grant no. 295261 (MEALS), and the project ANR-12-IS02-001 PACE. Nicolás E. Bordenabe was partially funded by the French Defense procurement agency (DGA) with a PhD grant.

E. De Cristofaro and M. Wright (Eds.): PETS 2013, LNCS 7981, pp. 82–102, 2013.

Because of the focus on the single individual as the unit of protection, differential privacy relies in a crucial way on the notion of two databases being *adjacent*, i.e. differing only for an individual. A mechanism K is ϵ-differentially private if for any two adjacent databases x, x', and any property Z, the probability distributions $K(x)$, $K(x')$ differ on Z at most by e^ϵ, namely, $K(x)(Z) \leq e^\epsilon K(x')(Z)$. For two non-adjacent databases, there is no requirement other than the one induced by the transitive application of the property. Note that the set of all possible databases, together with the adjacency relation, forms a *Hamming graph*, and the graph distance $d_h(x, x')$ between x and x' is exactly the number of individuals in which x and x' differ. Then, for any databases x, x', it is easy to see (by transitivity on a path from x to x') that $K(x)(Z) \leq e^{\epsilon d_h(x,x')} K(x')(Z)$. We can view $\epsilon d_h(x, x')$ as the distinguishability level between two generic databases x, x': the smaller $\epsilon d_h(x, x')$ is, the more similar the probability distributions $K(x)$, $K(x')$ are required to be.

When the sensitive information to be protected is other than the value of a single individual, it is common to consider different notions of adjacency. For example, in cases of cohesive groups with highly correlated values, we could consider adjacent two databases differing in any number of individuals of the same group. Similarly, when dealing with friendship graphs in social networks, adjacency could be defined as differing in a single edge.

We argue that in some situations the distinguishability level between x and x' should depend not only on the number of different values between x and x', but also on the values themselves. We might require, for instance, databases in which the value of an individual is only slightly modified to be highly indistinguishable, thus protecting the *accuracy* by which an analyst can infer an individual's value.

More generally, we might want to apply differential privacy in scenarios when x, x' are not databases at all, but belong to an *arbitrary domain of secrets* $\mathcal{X}$. In such a scenario, there might be no natural notion of adjacency, but it is still reasonable to define a distinguishability level between secrets, and employ the same principle of differential privacy – i.e. the smaller the distinguishability level between x, x' is, the more similar the probability distributions $K(x)$, $K(x')$ are required to be – to obtain a meaningful notion of privacy. For instance, when dealing with geographic locations (aka, geolocation), it might be acceptable to disclose the fact that an individual is in Paris rather than in New York. However, disclosing the *precise* location of the individual within Paris is likely to be undesired (because, for instance, the individual is currently in Moulin Rouge rather than in his office in Place d'Italie). Thus it would be useful to have a distinguishability level that depends on the geographical distance.

In this paper we assume that we have a numeric function $\varepsilon(x, x')$, giving the distinguishability level between x, x', which depends on the application at hand and the privacy guarantees we wish to express. The corresponding notion of privacy is the requirement that for an arbitrary pair x, x' we have

$$K(x)(Z) \leq e^{\varepsilon(x,x')} K(x')(Z)$$

Note that standard ϵ-differential privacy is a particular case of this notion, that we obtain by setting $\varepsilon(x, x') = \epsilon d_h(x, x')$.

Since ε models distinguishability, there are some properties that it is expected to satisfy. First, it should be the case that any element is indistinguishable from itself, i.e.

$\varepsilon(x, x) = 0$. Second, the distinguishability level of x and x' should be the same as that of x' and x, i.e. $\varepsilon(x, x') = \varepsilon(x', x)$ (symmetry). Finally, if x_1 and x_2 are hardly distinguishable from x_3, then they should be also hardly distinguishable from each other. In other words, $\varepsilon(x_1, x_2)$ should be bounded by a function of $\varepsilon(x_1, x_3)$, $\varepsilon(x_2, x_3)$. In this paper we assume the triangle inequality, namely $\varepsilon(x_1, x_2) \leq \varepsilon(x_1, x_3) + \varepsilon(x_3, x_2)$, which means that ε is a metric. In the rest of this paper we use d (for "distance") instead of ε, and we call the corresponding privacy notion "d-privacy".

Similarly to the standard definition, d-privacy does not explicitly talk about the adversary's gain of knowledge. In order to better understand a privacy property, however, it is useful to provide interpretations that directly reason about the capabilities of the adversary. Two such interpretations exist for differential privacy: the first states that, regardless of side knowledge, the adversary's gain of knowledge by observing the reported answer is the same whether or not the individual's data were included in the database [1,6]. The second states that, an informed adversary who already knows all values except individual's i, gains no extra knowledge from the reported answer, regardless of side knowledge about i's value [2]. [1]

In the case of d-privacy, we provide two results that generalize the above interpretations, showing the privacy guarantees provided by a certain metric d. The first uses the concept of a *hiding* function $\phi : \mathcal{X} \rightarrow \mathcal{X}$. The idea is that ϕ can be applied to a secret x before the mechanism K, so that the latter has only access to a hidden version $\phi(x)$, instead of the real secret x. Then d-privacy implies that the adversary's conclusions (captured by his posterior distribution) are similar (up to a factor depending on ϕ) regardless of whether ϕ is applied to the secret or not. Moreover, we show that certain classes of hiding functions are "canonical", in the sense that if the property holds for those functions, it must hold in general.

The above characterization compares two posterior distributions and does not imply that the adversary learns no information, but that he learns the same regardless of whether the secret has been hidden or not. We then give a second characterization, comparing the adversary's conclusions (a posterior distribution) to his initial knowledge (a prior distribution). Since some information is allowed to be revealed, we cannot expect the two to be similar. Still, if we restrict to a neighborhood N of secrets that are close to each other, we can show that d-privacy implies that an informed adversary, knowing that the secret belongs to N, can gain little more information about the exact secret, regardless of his prior knowledge within N. Similarly to the previous characterization, we also show that certain classes of neighborhoods are canonical.

We give examples of privacy problems in various contexts, and show how to define appropriate metrics. In the context of statistical databases, we consider metrics that depend not only on the number of different values, but also on the values themselves. First, a stronger variant of differential privacy is given in which databases differing in a single individual are hardly distinguishable, but the distinguishability level becomes

---

[1] The knowledge increase of a non-informed adversary is not bounded by e^ε. Recalling the well-known example from [1], consider the side information that Terry Gross is two inches shorter than the average Lithuanian woman. Then obtaining the average height (even a noisy one) gives little additional information about Terry Gross to an informed adversary, but substantial information to a non-informed one.

even lower when the difference in the values is small. Moreover, this metric can be relaxed to obtain a privacy notion that focuses on protecting the accuracy of a value. This can be useful, for instance, in case an individual does not mind disclosing his age group, but wants to protect his exact birthday date (such precise information could in principle allow to identify the individual with little margin of error).

Departing from statistical databases, we consider smart meters, and the problem for privacy that can derive from accurate measurement of energy consumption at high frequency. Further, we consider the problem of hiding the exact position in location-based services. In all these examples, besides the proper metric notion, we construct also the canonical adversary which provides the operational interpretation.

Next, we turn our attention to the notion of utility, namely the accuracy of the reported answer, and in particular the Bayesian notion of utility [7,8], which takes into account the prior knowledge of the user. In general mechanisms may provide different degrees of utility for the same level of privacy, and obviously it is desirable to identify the optimal ones. Of particular interest are the *universally optimal* mechanisms, which provide optimal utility for all users (i.e., all priors). There are two well known results concerning universal optimality: the first [7] establishes that for counting queries the geometric and the truncated geometric mechanisms are universally optimal. The second [8] says that for any other kind of query no universally optimal mechanism exists.

We revisit these results in our framework and show that in contrast to the standard case, d-privacy allows to construct (for certain metrics) universally optimal mechanisms for many other kinds of queries. More precisely, we show that universally optimal mechanisms exist in the cases of (i) the sum, average and percentile queries for the Manhattan metric, and (ii) the average and percentile queries for the Maximum metric.

We also study the additional noise required to achieve privacy for databases queries, when we use a finer metric than the Hamming distance. Surprisingly, it turns out that in the case (i) above, the sensitivity of the queries remains the same as in the standard case. This means that, a standard ϵ-differentially private mechanism already incorporates "for free" the additional protection w.r.t. proximity of values.

Related Work. Several works in the differential privacy literature consider adjacency relations different than the standard one, effectively using a metric tailored to that application. Examples include group privacy [1] and edge privacy for graphs [9].

The generalization of differential privacy to arbitrary metrics was considered also in [10,3]. In those works, however, the purpose of extending the definition was to obtain compositional methods for proving differential privacy in programming languages, while in our work we focus on the implications of such extension for the theory of differential privacy. Namely, we aim at obtaining new meaningful definitions of privacy for various contexts through the use of different metrics (cf. the examples of the smart meters and of geolocation), and at investigating the existence of optimal mechanisms.

Another work closely related to ours is [11] in which an extended definition of differential privacy is used to capture the notion of fairness in classification. A metric d is used to model the fact that certain individuals are required to be classified similarly, and a mechanism satisfying d-privacy is considered fair, since it produces similar results for similar individuals. We view fairness as one of the many interesting notions that can be obtained through the use of metrics in various contexts, thus it encourages our goal of studying d-privacy. With respect to the actual metrics used in this paper, the difference is that we consider metrics that depend on the individuals' values, while [11] considers metrics between individuals.

Contribution. The main contributions of this paper are summarized below:

- We study d-privacy – an extension of differential privacy to arbitrary domains endowed with a metric d – in the general case, independently from any specific metric.
- We give two operational characterizations of d-privacy that directly constraint the capabilities of the adversary.
- We show examples of applications of d-privacy to privacy scenarios both in databases and in other contexts.
- We show that several queries (including the sum, average and percentile) admit universally optimal mechanisms for certain metrics. This contrasts sharply with standard differential privacy, where such mechanisms exist only for counting queries.

Plan of the Paper. In the next section we recall some preliminary notions about mechanisms, metrics, and differential privacy. Section 3 introduces the notion of d-privacy and presents two characterization results. In Section 4 we give a sufficient and necessary condition for the privacy of an oblivious mechanism, we discuss Laplace mechanisms, and we give sufficient conditions for a mechanism to be optimal. In Sections 5 and 6 we give several examples of applications of our notions, in statistical databases with an enriched notion of privacy, and in other domains, respectively. We also show how to construct universally optimal mechanisms for some of those examples in the cases of sum, average, and percentile queries. Section 7 concludes.

For space reasons we have omitted the proofs; they can be found in the report version of this paper [12].

2   Preliminaries

Mechanisms. Given two sets $\mathcal{X}$ and $\mathcal{Z}$, let $\mathcal{F}_{\mathcal{Z}}$ be a σ-algebra over $\mathcal{Z}$ and let $\mathcal{P}(\mathcal{Z})$ be the set of probability measures over $\mathcal{Z}$. A *mechanism* from $\mathcal{X}$ to $\mathcal{Z}$ is a (probabilistic) function $K : \mathcal{X} \to \mathcal{P}(\mathcal{Z})$. A mechanism K can be described in terms of probability density functions (pdf's), that is by a function $D : \mathcal{X} \to \mathcal{D}(\mathcal{Z})$ (where $\mathcal{D}(\mathcal{Z})$ denotes the space of the pdf's over $\mathcal{Z}$), such that $D(x)$ is the pdf of $K(x)$.

The composition $H \circ f$ of a deterministic function $f : \mathcal{X} \to \mathcal{Y}$ (called a *query*) and a mechanism $H : \mathcal{Y} \to \mathcal{P}(\mathcal{Z})$ is the mechanism $K : \mathcal{X} \to \mathcal{P}(\mathcal{Z})$ defined as $K(x) = (H \circ f)(x) = H(f(x))$. Mechanisms of this form are called *oblivious*.

Let π be a discrete probability measure on $\mathcal{X}$, called a *prior*.[2] Starting from π and using Bayes' rule, each observation $Z \in \mathcal{Z}$ of a mechanism $K : \mathcal{X} \to \mathcal{P}(\mathcal{Z})$ induces a *posterior* measure $\sigma = \mathbf{Bayes}(\pi, K, Z)$ on $\mathcal{X}$, defined as $\sigma(x) = \frac{K(x)(Z)\pi(x)}{\sum_{x' \in \mathcal{X}} K(x')(Z)\pi(x')}$.

---

[2] We restrict to discrete priors for simplicity; all results could be carried to the continuous case.

Metrics. A metric on a set $\mathcal{X}$ is a function $d_{\mathcal{X}} : \mathcal{X}^2 \to [0, \infty]$ such that $d_{\mathcal{X}}(x, y) = 0$ iff $x = y$, $d_{\mathcal{X}}(x, y) = d_{\mathcal{X}}(y, x)$, and $d_{\mathcal{X}}(x, z) \leq d_{\mathcal{X}}(x, y) + d_{\mathcal{X}}(y, x)$ for all $x, y, z \in \mathcal{X}$. The *diameter* of $A \subseteq \mathcal{X}$ is defined as $d_{\mathcal{X}}(A) = \sup_{x, x' \in A} d_{\mathcal{X}}(x, x')$.

A sequence $x_1, \ldots, x_n$ is called a *chain* from x_1 to x_n and denoted by $\tilde{x}$. The length $d_{\mathcal{X}}(\tilde{x})$ of a chain is defined as $d_{\mathcal{X}}(\tilde{x}) = \sum_{i=1}^{n-1} d_{\mathcal{X}}(x_i, x_{i+1})$. If $d_{\mathcal{X}}(\tilde{x}) = d_{\mathcal{X}}(x_1, x_n)$ then $\tilde{x}$ is called *tight*.

Of particular interest are metrics *induced by a graph* $(\mathcal{X}, \sim_{\mathcal{X}})$, where $\sim_{\mathcal{X}}$ is the graph's adjacency relation. In the induced metric, $d_{\mathcal{X}}(x, x')$ is the length of the shortest path from x to x' (or infinite if no path exists). Of great interest are also the Manhattan (or L_1), the Euclidean (or L_2) and the Maximum (or L_∞) metrics, denoted by d_1, d_2, d_∞ respectively. The numerical distance on the reals (which coincides with all d_1, d_2, d_∞) will be denoted by $d_{\mathbb{R}}$ for clarity. Finally, of great interest is the metric $d_{\mathcal{P}}$ on $\mathcal{P}(\mathcal{Z})$ defined as $d_{\mathcal{P}}(\mu_1, \mu_2) = \sup_{Z \in \mathcal{F}_{\mathcal{Z}}} \left| \ln \frac{\mu_1(Z)}{\mu_2(Z)} \right|$ with the convention that $\left| \ln \frac{\mu_1(Z)}{\mu_2(Z)} \right| = 0$ if both $\mu_1(Z), \mu_2(Z)$ are zero and ∞ if only one of them is zero.

Differential Privacy. We fix a finite domain of values $\mathcal{V}$, called the *universe*. A database $x \in \mathcal{V}^n$ consists of n records from $\mathcal{V}$ - each corresponding to an individual - that is x is a tuple $\langle x[1], \ldots, x[n] \rangle$, $x[i] \in \mathcal{V}$, where $x[i]$ is the value of the i-th individual in the database. We denote by $x[v/i]$ the database obtained from x by substituting the value v for individual i. The case when individuals are allowed to be absent from the database can be modeled by the universe $\mathcal{V}_\varnothing = \mathcal{V} \cup \{\varnothing\}$ where the null value $\varnothing$ denotes absence.

A crucial notion for differential privacy is that of *adjacency*: two databases x, x' are adjacent, written $x \sim_h x'$, if they differ in exactly one element. Let d_h be the distance induced by $\sim_h$ (i.e., $d_h(x, x')$ is the number of elements in which x, x' differ). The graph $(\mathcal{V}^n, \sim_h)$ is known as *Hamming graph*, and d_h as Hamming distance.

Let $\mathcal{Z}$ be a set of query outcomes; a mechanism $K : \mathcal{V}^n \to \mathcal{P}(\mathcal{Z})$ satisfies ϵ-differential privacy if adjacent databases produce answers with probabilities that differ at most by a factor e^ϵ:

$$K(x)(Z) \leq e^\epsilon \, K(x')(Z) \quad \forall x \sim_h x' \in \mathcal{V}^n, Z \in \mathcal{F}_{\mathcal{Z}} \tag{1}$$

Following [3], the definition can be expressed as $d_{\mathcal{P}}(K(x), K(x')) \leq \epsilon$ for all $x \sim_h x'$. Moreover, as explained in the introduction, we can rewrite it in terms of the Hamming distance: $d_{\mathcal{P}}(K(x), K(x')) \leq \epsilon d_h(x, x')$ for all $x, x' \in \mathcal{V}^n$.

A desirable feature of this definition is that it solely depends on the mechanism itself, without explicitly talking about the adversary's side knowledge, or the information that he learns from the reported answer. However, in order to get a better understanding of a privacy definition, it is useful to give an "operational" (or "semantic") interpretation that directly restricts the abilities of the adversary. To this end, we capture the adversary's side knowledge by a prior distribution π on $\mathcal{V}^n$, and his conclusions after observing Z by the posterior distribution $\sigma = \mathbf{Bayes}(\pi, K, Z)$.

There are two operational interpretations commonly given to differential privacy. The first can be informally stated as: "regardless of side knowledge, by observing the reported answer an adversary obtains the same information whether or not the individual's data were included in the database". This can be formalized as follows: consider a *hiding function* $\phi_{i,v} : \mathcal{V}^n \to \mathcal{V}^n$ replacing i's value by a fixed value v, i.e.

$\phi_{i,v}(x) = x[^v/_i]$, and let $\Phi_h = \{\phi_{i,v} \mid i \in 1..n, v \in \mathcal{V}\}$ be the set of all such functions. The mechanism $K \circ \phi_{i,v}$ behaves as K after removing i's value; hence we require the posterior distributions induced by $K, K \circ \phi_{i,v}$ to be similar. The resulting notion (called "semantic privacy" in [6])[3] can be shown to be implied by differential privacy.

Theorem 1 ([6]). *If a mechanism $K : \mathcal{V}^n \to \mathcal{P}(\mathcal{Z})$ satisfies ϵ-differential privacy then for all priors π on $\mathcal{V}^n$, all $\phi \in \Phi_h$, and all $Z \in \mathcal{F_Z}$:*

$$d_{\mathcal{P}}(\sigma_1, \sigma_2) \leq 2\epsilon \qquad \text{where } \sigma_1 = \mathbf{Bayes}(\pi, K, Z) \text{ and } \sigma_2 = \mathbf{Bayes}(\pi, K \circ \phi, Z)$$

Note that the above interpretation compares two *posterior* measures. This requirement does not imply that the adversary learns no information, but that he learns the same regardless of the presence of the individual's data. Both σ_1, σ_2 can be very different than the prior π, as the well-known example of Terry Gross [1] demonstrates.

A different interpretation can be obtained by comparing the posterior σ to the prior distribution π. Of course, we cannot expect those to be similar, since some information is allowed to be disclosed. Still, we can require the distributions to be similar when restricted to the value of a single individual, by assuming an informed adversary who knows all other values in the database. Let $N_i(x) = \{x[^v/_i] \mid v \in \mathcal{V}\}$ denote the set of databases obtained from x by modifying i's value, and let $\mathcal{N}_h = \{N_i(x) \mid x \in \mathcal{V}^n, i \in 1..n\}$. Knowing that the database belongs to a set $N \in \mathcal{N}_h$ means that we know all values except one. We denote by $\pi_{|N}$ the distribution obtained from π by restricting to N, i.e. $\pi_{|N}(x) = \pi(x|N)$. Requiring $\pi_{|N}, \sigma_{|N}$ to be similar brings us the definition of "semantic security" from [2], which is a full characterization of differential privacy.

Theorem 2 ([2]). *A mechanism $K : \mathcal{V}^n \to \mathcal{P}(\mathcal{Z})$ satisfies ϵ-differential privacy iff for all priors π on $\mathcal{V}^n$, all $N \in \mathcal{N}_h$, and all $Z \in \mathcal{F_Z}$:*

$$d_{\mathcal{P}}(\pi_{|N}, \sigma_{|N}) \leq \epsilon \qquad \text{where} \qquad \sigma = \mathbf{Bayes}(\pi, K, Z)$$

Note that if the adversary does not know $N \in \mathcal{N}_h$, then his knowledge can (and will in most cases) be increased. Note also that the above result does not imply that K allows the adversary to learn $N_i(x)$! In fact, this is clearly forbidden since it would violate the same condition for $N_j(x), j \neq i$, i.e. it would violate the other individuals' privacy.

3   Generalized Privacy

As discussed in the introduction, differential privacy can be generalized to the case of an arbitrary set of secrets $\mathcal{X}$, equipped with a metric $d_{\mathcal{X}}$.

Definition 1. *A mechanism $K : \mathcal{X} \to \mathcal{P}(\mathcal{Z})$ satisfies $d_{\mathcal{X}}$-privacy, iff $\forall x, x' \in \mathcal{X}$: $d_{\mathcal{P}}(K(x), K(x')) \leq d_{\mathcal{X}}(x, x')$, or equivalently:*

$$K(x)(Z) \leq e^{d_{\mathcal{X}}(x,x')} K(x')(Z) \quad \forall Z \in \mathcal{F_Z}$$

---

[3] The only difference between the semantic privacy of [6] and our formulation is that an "additive" metric between distributions is used instead of the "multiplicative" $d_{\mathcal{P}}$.

Intuitively, the definition requires that secrets close to each other wrt $d_\mathcal{X}$, meaning hardly distinguishable, should produce outcomes with similar probability. This is the same core idea as in differential privacy, which can be retrieved as $\mathcal{X} = \mathcal{V}^n, d_\mathcal{X} = \epsilon d_h$.

Note that Definition 1 contains no ϵ; the distinguishability level is directly given by the metric. In practice, the desired metric can be obtained from a standard one by scaling by a proper factor ϵ (recall that a scaled metric is also a metric). For instance, in the case of standard differential privacy, the Hamming distance between adjacent databases is 1, and we want their distinguishability level to be ϵ, hence we use the scaled version ϵd_h.

Note also that an *extended* metric (allowing $d_\mathcal{X}(x, x') = \infty$) can be useful in cases when we allow two secrets to be completely distinguished. The understanding of Definition 1 is that the requirement is always satisfied for those secrets. Similarly, *pseudo-metrics* (allowing $d_\mathcal{X}(x, x') = 0$ for $x \neq x'$) could be useful when we want some secrets to be completely indistinguishable (forcing $K(x)$ and $K(x')$ to be identical). To simplify the presentation, the results of this paper assume an extended metric (but not pseudo). An approximate version of $d_\mathcal{X}$-privacy can be defined, similarly to (α, δ) differential privacy [13]. We leave the study of such notion as future work.

Different metrics $d_\mathcal{X}, d_\mathcal{X}'$ on the same set $\mathcal{X}$ clearly give rise to different privacy notions. The "strength" of each notion depends on the distinguishability level assigned to each pair of secrets; $d_\mathcal{X}$-privacy and $d_\mathcal{X}'$-privacy are in general incomparable. However, lower distinguishability level implies stronger privacy.

Proposition 1. *If $d_\mathcal{X} \leq d_\mathcal{X}'$ (point-wise) then $d_\mathcal{X}$-privacy implies $d_\mathcal{X}'$-privacy.*

For example, some works consider an adjacency relation $\sim_r$ slightly different than $\sim_h$, defined as $x \sim_r x'$ iff $x' = x[\varnothing/i]$ (or vice versa), i.e. x' can be obtained from x by removing one individual. This relation gives rise to a metric d_r for which it holds that: $\frac{1}{2}d_r \leq d_h \leq d_r$. From Proposition 1, the two models are essentially equivalent; one can obtain ϵd_r-privacy from ϵd_h-privacy by doubling ϵ and vice versa.

Characterization 1. Similarly to standard differential privacy, $d_\mathcal{X}$-privacy does not explicitly talk about the adversary's gain of knowledge. To better understand the privacy guarantees provided by a certain metric $d_\mathcal{X}$, it is useful to directly reason about the capabilities of the adversary. Two such characterizations are given, generalizing the two interpretations of standard differential privacy (Theorems 1,2).

The first characterization uses the concept of a *hiding* function $\phi : \mathcal{X} \to \mathcal{X}$. The idea is that ϕ can be applied to x before the mechanism K, so that the latter has only access to a hidden version $\phi(x)$, instead of the real secret x. Let $d_\mathcal{X}(\phi) = \sup_{x \in \mathcal{X}} d_\mathcal{X}(x, \phi(x))$ be the maximum distance between a secret and its hidden version. We can show that $d_\mathcal{X}$-privacy implies that the adversary's conclusions (captured by his posterior measure) are the same (up to $2d_\mathcal{X}(\phi)$) regardless of whether ϕ is applied or not. Moreover, we show that certain classes of hiding functions are "canonical", in the sense that if the property holds for those, it must hold in general. We start be defining this class.

Definition 2. *Let Φ be a set of functions from $\mathcal{X}$ to $\mathcal{X}$, called* hiding functions. *A chain $\tilde{x}$ is called a* maximal Φ-chain *iff for every step i there exists $\phi \in \Phi$ s.t. $\phi(x_i) = x_{i+1}, \phi(x_{i+1}) = x_i$ and $d_\mathcal{X}(x_i, x_{i+1}) = d_\mathcal{X}(\phi)$. Then Φ is called* maximally tight *wrt $d_\mathcal{X}$ iff $\forall x, x' \in \mathcal{X}$ there exists a tight maximal Φ-chain from x to x'.*

Note that the above property requires hiding functions that *swap* the secrets x_i, x_{i+1}. This is not satisfied by the hiding functions $\phi_{i,v}$ introduced in the previous section, but will be satisfied by more general functions used later in the paper.

Theorem 3. *Let Φ be a set of hiding functions. If K satisfies $d_{\mathcal{X}}$-privacy then for all $\phi \in \Phi$, all priors π on $\mathcal{X}$, and all $Z \in \mathcal{F}_{\mathcal{Z}}$:*

$$d_{\mathcal{P}}(\sigma_1, \sigma_2) \leq 2\,d_{\mathcal{X}}(\phi) \quad \text{where} \quad \sigma_1 = \mathbf{Bayes}(\pi, K, Z) \text{ and } \sigma_2 = \mathbf{Bayes}(\pi, K \circ \phi, Z)$$

If Φ is maximally tight then the converse also holds.

The above characterization compares two posterior distributions; hence, it does not impose that the adversary gains no information, but that this information is the same regardless of whether ϕ has been applied to the secret or not.

Characterization 2. A different approach is to compare the adversary's prior and posterior distributions, measuring how much he learned about the secret. Since we allow some information to be revealed, we cannot expect these distributions to be similar. Still, if we restrict to a neighborhood N of secrets that are close to each other, we can show that $d_{\mathcal{X}}$-privacy implies that an informed adversary, knowing that the secret belongs to N, can gain little more information about the exact secret regardless of his side knowledge about N. Moreover, similarly to the previous characterization, we show that certain classes of neighborhoods are "canonical".

Definition 3. *Let $\mathcal{N} \subseteq 2^{\mathcal{X}}$. The elements of $\mathcal{N}$ are called* neighborhoods. *A chain $\tilde{x}$ is called a maximal $\mathcal{N}$-chain iff for every step i there exists $N \in \mathcal{N}$ such that $\{x_i, x_{i+1}\} \subseteq N$ and $d_{\mathcal{X}}(x_i, x_{i+1}) = d_{\mathcal{X}}(N)$. Then $\mathcal{N}$ is called* maximally tight *wrt $d_{\mathcal{X}}$ iff $\forall x, x' \in \mathcal{X}$ there exists a tight maximal $\mathcal{N}$-chain from x to x'.*

Theorem 4. *Let $\mathcal{N} \subseteq 2^{\mathcal{X}}$. If K satisfies $d_{\mathcal{X}}$-privacy then for all $N \in \mathcal{N}$, all priors π on $\mathcal{X}$, and all $Z \in \mathcal{F}_{\mathcal{Z}}$:*

$$d_{\mathcal{P}}(\pi_{|N}, \sigma_{|N}) \leq d_{\mathcal{X}}(N) \qquad \text{where} \qquad \sigma = \mathbf{Bayes}(\pi, K, Z)$$

If $\mathcal{N}$ is maximally tight then the converse also holds.

Using meaningful (and maximally tight) sets $\Phi, \mathcal{N}$, and applying the above characterizations, we can get an intuitive understanding of the privacy guarantees offered by $d_{\mathcal{X}}$-privacy. For example, in the case of databases, it can be shown that $\mathcal{N}_h$ is maximally tight wrt the d_h metric, hence the characterization of Theorem 2 can be obtained as a special case of Theorem 4. Theorem 1 can also be obtained from Theorem 3 (even though Φ_h is not maximally tight) since it only states an implication in one direction.

4   Answering Queries

To obtain the answer to a query $f : \mathcal{X} \rightarrow \mathcal{Y}$ in a private way, we can compose it with a mechanism $H : \mathcal{Y} \rightarrow \mathcal{P}(\mathcal{Z})$, thus obtaining an oblivious mechanism $H \circ f :$

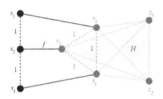

		z_1	z_2
y_1		$3/4$	$1/4$
y_2		$1/2$	$1/2$
y_3		$1/4$	$3/4$

Fig. 1. Counterexample to the converse of Fact 5. The table represents the distribution H. We note that $H \circ f$ satisfies $(\ln 2)$-privacy, and that f is 1-sensitive. However $H(y_1)(z_1) = 3/4 \nleq 2\,H(y_3)(z_1) = 2\,1/4$, hence H does not satisfy $(\ln 2)$-privacy.

$\mathcal{X} \to \mathcal{P}(\mathcal{Z})$. In this section, we first state the standard compositionality result about the privacy of $H \circ f$, relying on the notion of Δ-*sensitivity* (aka Lipschitz continuity), naturally extended to the case of d_x-privacy. Then, we introduce the concept of *uniform sensitivity*, and we use it to obtain the converse of the aforementioned compositionality result, which in turn allows to give optimality results later in the paper.

Definition 4. *f is Δ-sensitive wrt d_x, d_y iff $d_y(f(x), f(x')) \le \Delta d_x(x, x')$ for all $x, x' \in \mathcal{X}$. The smallest such Δ (if exists) is called the* sensitivity *of f wrt d_x, d_y.*

Fact 5. *Assume that f is Δ-sensitive wrt d_x, d_y and H satisfies d_y-privacy. Then $H \circ f$ satisfies Δd_x-privacy.*

Note that it is common to define a family of mechanisms $H_\epsilon, \epsilon > 0$, instead of a single one, where each H_ϵ satisfies privacy for a scaled version ϵd_y of a metric of interest d_y. Given such a family and a query f, we can define a family of oblivious mechanisms $K_\epsilon = H_{\epsilon/\Delta} \circ f, \epsilon > 0$, each satisfying ϵd_x-privacy (from Fact 5).

The converse of the above result does not hold in general, see Fig. 1 for a counterexample. However, it does hold if we replace the notion of sensitivity by the stronger notion of *uniform sensitivity*.

Definition 5. *Two elements $y, y' \in \mathcal{Y}$ are called Δ-expansive iff $d_y(y, y') = \Delta d_x(x, x')$ for some $x \in f^{-1}(y), x' \in f^{-1}(y')$. A chain $\tilde{y}$ is Δ-expansive iff all steps y_i, y_{i+1} are Δ-expansive. Finally, f is uniformly Δ-sensitive iff it is Δ-sensitive and for all $y, y' \in \mathcal{Y}$ there exists a tight and Δ-expansive chain from y to y'.*

Theorem 6. *Assume that f is uniformly Δ-sensitive wrt d_x, d_y. Then H satisfies d_y-privacy if and only if $H \circ f$ satisfies Δd_x-privacy.*

4.1 Laplace Mechanisms

Adding Laplace noise is the most widely used technique for achieving differentia privacy. The mechanism can be naturally adapted to any metric, using a variant of the exponential mechanism [14], by providing a properly constructed scaling function. Note that in the framework of d-privacy, we can express the privacy of the mechanism itself, on its own domain, without the need to consider a query or a notion of sensitivity.

(i) $\mathcal{Y} \subset \mathbb{R}, \quad \mathcal{Z} = \mathbb{R}$ $d_y = \epsilon d_{\mathbb{R}}$ $\lambda_\epsilon(z) = \dfrac{\epsilon}{2}$

(ii) $\mathcal{Y} \subset \mathbb{R}^2, \; \mathcal{Z} = \mathbb{R}^2$ $d_y = \epsilon d_2$ $\lambda_\epsilon(z) = \dfrac{\epsilon^2}{2\pi}$

(iii) $\mathcal{Y} \subset \mathbb{R}^2, \; \mathcal{Z} = \mathbb{R}^2$ $d_y = \epsilon d_1$ $\lambda_\epsilon(z) = \dfrac{\epsilon^2}{4}$

(iv) $\mathcal{Y} = \mathcal{Z} = q[0..k]$ $d_y = \epsilon d_{\mathbb{R}}$ $\lambda_\epsilon(z) = \begin{cases} \dfrac{e^{q\epsilon}}{e^{q\epsilon}+1} & z \in \{0, qk\} \\ \dfrac{e^{q\epsilon}-1}{e^{q\epsilon}+1} & 0 < z < qk \end{cases}$

Fig. 2. Instantiations of the Laplace mechanism

Definition 6. *Let $\mathcal{Y}, \mathcal{Z}$ be two sets, and let d_y be a metric on $\mathcal{Y} \cup \mathcal{Z}$. Let $\lambda : \mathcal{Z} \to [0, \infty)$ be a scaling function such that $D(y)(z) = \lambda(z) e^{-d_y(y,z)}$ is a pdf for all $y \in \mathcal{Y}$ (i.e. $\int_{\mathcal{Z}} D(y)(z) d\nu(z) = 1$). Then the mechanism $L : \mathcal{Y} \to \mathcal{P}(\mathcal{Z})$, described by the pdf D, is called a* Laplace mechanism *from $(\mathcal{Y}, d_y)$ to $\mathcal{Z}$.*

Fact 7 ([14]). *Any Laplace mechanism from $(\mathcal{Y}, d_y)$ to $\mathcal{Z}$ satisfies d_y-privacy.*

Figure 4.1 provides instantiations of the general definition for various choices of $\mathcal{Y}, \mathcal{Z}$ and d_y used in the paper, by properly adjusting $\lambda(z)$. The basic case (i) is that of the one-dimensional continuous Laplace mechanism. Similarly, we can define a two-dimensional continuous Laplace mechanism (used in Section 6.2), measuring the distance between points by either the Euclidean (ii) or the Manhattan (iii) metric. In the discrete setting, we obtain the Truncated Geometric mechanism TG_ϵ [7], given by (iv), using a quantized set of reals as input. We denote by $q[0..k]$ the set $\{qi \mid i \in 0..k\}$, i.e. the set of $k + 1$ quantized reals with step size $q > 0$.

4.2 Mechanisms of Optimal Utility

Answering a query privately is useless if the consumer gets no information about the real answer, thus it is crucial to analyze the mechanism's utility. We consider consumers applying Bayesian inference to map the mechanism's output to a guess that minimizes their expected loss. A consumer is characterized by a prior π on the set of secrets, and a loss function l (assumed to be monotone wrt a metric of reference, which is always $d_{\mathbb{R}}$ for the needs of this paper). The utility $\mathcal{U}(H, \pi, l)$ of a mechanism H for such a consumer is given by the expected loss (under an optimal remap strategy). This is the Bayesian notion of utility [7], but our results can be extended to risk-averse consumers.

A natural question to ask, then, is whether, for a *given query f*, there exists a mechanism that universally (i.e. for all priors and loss functions) provides optimal utility. Let $\mathcal{H}_f(d_x)$ be the set of all mechanisms $H : \mathcal{Y} \to \mathcal{Z}$ (for any $\mathcal{Z}$) such that $H \circ f$ satisfies d_x-privacy. All mechanisms in $\mathcal{H}_f(d_x)$ can be used to answer f privately, hence we are interested in the one that maximizes utility.

Definition 7. *A mechanism $H \in \mathcal{H}_f(d_x)$ is f-d_x-optimal iff $\mathcal{U}(H, \pi, l) \geq \mathcal{U}(H', \pi, l)$ for all $H' \in \mathcal{H}_f(d_x)$, all priors π and all loss functions l.*

The existence of (universally) optimal mechanisms is far from trivial. For standard differential privacy, a well-known result from [7] states that such a mechanism does exist for *counting* queries, i.e. those of the form "how many users satisfy property P".

Theorem 8 ([7]). *Let $\mathcal{Y} = [0..k]$ and let $f : \mathcal{V}^n \to \mathcal{Y}$ be a counting query. Then the TG_ϵ mechanism with input $\mathcal{Y}$ is $f\text{-}\epsilon d_h$-optimal for all $\epsilon > 0$.*

On the other hand, a well-known impossibility result [8] states that counting queries are essentially the only ones for which an optimal mechanism exists. This result is based on the concept of the *induced graph* $\sim_f$ of a query $f : \mathcal{V}^n \to \mathcal{Y}$, defined as: $y \sim_f y'$ iff $\exists x \sim_h x'$ s.t. $f(x) = y, f(x') = y'$.

Theorem 9 ([8]). *Let $f : \mathcal{V}^n \to \mathcal{Y}$ be a query such that $\sim_f$ is not a path graph. Then no $f\text{-}\epsilon d_h$-optimal mechanism exists for any $\epsilon < \ln 2$.*

Thus, most interesting queries, e.g. the sum and average, have no optimal mechanisms.

However, the above negative result and the concept of the induced graph are tied to the Hamming metric d_h. This raises the question of whether this special status of counting queries holds for any metric d_x. To answer this question, we give a sufficient condition for showing the optimality of TG_ϵ for an arbitrary query f and metric d_x, based on the concept of uniform sensitivity.

Theorem 10. *Let $\mathcal{Y} = q[0..k]$ and assume that $f : \mathcal{X} \to \mathcal{Y}$ is uniformly Δ-sensitive wrt $d_x, d_{\mathbb{R}}$. Then the TG_ϵ mechanism with input $\mathcal{Y}$ is $f\text{-}\Delta d_x$-optimal.*

In the following sections we show that this condition is indeed satisfied by several important queries, including the sum and average, for various metrics of interest.

5   Privacy in Statistical Databases

In this section, we investigate privacy notions in the context of statistical databases, other than the standard differential privacy. In contrast to the Hamming distance, which can be defined independently from the structure of the universe $\mathcal{V}$, we are interested in metrics that depend on the actual values and the distance between them. To this end, we assume that the universe is equipped with a metric d_v, measuring how far apart two values are. When the universe is numeric (i.e. $\mathcal{V} \subset \mathbb{R}$) then $d_v = d_{\mathbb{R}}$ is the natural choice. In the case of null values, we can extend a metric d_v from $\mathcal{V}$ to $\mathcal{V}_\varnothing$ by considering $\varnothing$ to be maximally distant from all other values, that is taking $d_v(\varnothing, v) = d_v(\mathcal{V}), v \in \mathcal{V}$. Note that this construction preserves the maximum distance between values, i.e. $d_v(\mathcal{V}_\varnothing) = d_v(\mathcal{V})$.

The first metric we consider, the normalized Manhattan metric, allows to strengthen differential privacy, obtaining a notion that not only protects the value of an individual, but also offers higher protection to small modifications of a value. Then we relax this metric, to obtain a weaker notion, that only protects the "accuracy" of an individual's value, but offers higher utility.

5.1   The Normalized Manhattan Metric

Differential privacy provides indistinguishability between databases differing in a single individual, but the level of distinguishability is independent from the actual value in those databases. Consider for example a database with salary information, and two adjacent databases $x \sim_i x'$ ($\sim_i$ denoting that they differ only in the value of the i-th individual) with $x[i] = v, x'[i] = v'$. A differentially private mechanism offers distinguishability level $\varepsilon(x, x') = \epsilon$, independently from v, v'. This means that when $v = 0, v' = 1M$, the indistinguishability level between x, x' will be the same as in the case $v = 20K$, $v' = 20.001K$.

One might expect, however, to have better protection in the second case, since the change in the individual's data is insignificant. Being insensitive to such small changes seems a reasonable privacy requirement since many queries (e.g. sum, average, etc) are themselves insensitive to small perturbations. The equal treatment of values is particularly problematic when we are obliged to use a "weak" ϵ, due to a high sensitivity. In this case, all values are only guaranteed to be weakly protected, while we could expect that at least close values would still enjoy high protection.

The normalized Manhattan metric $\tilde{d}_1$ expresses exactly this idea. Databases differing in a single value have distance at most 1, but the distance can be substantially smaller for small modifications of values, offering higher protection in those cases. The Manhattan metric d_1 on $\mathcal{V}^n$ and its normalized version $\tilde{d}_1$ are defined as:[4] $d_1(x, x') = \sum_{i=1}^{n} d_{\mathcal{V}}(x[i], x'[i])$ and $\tilde{d}_1(x, x') = \frac{d_1(x, x')}{d_{\mathcal{V}}(\mathcal{V})}$. Similarly to differential privacy, we use a scaled version $\epsilon \tilde{d}_1$ of the metric, to properly adjust the distinguishability level.

Concerning the operational characterizations of Section 3, the hiding functions and neighborhoods suitable for this metric are:

$$\phi_{i,w} = x[^{w(x[i])}/_i] \text{ for } w : \mathcal{V} \to \mathcal{V} \qquad N_{i,V}(x) = \{x[^v/_i] \mid v \in V\}$$
$$\Phi_1 = \{\phi_{i,w} \mid i \in 1..n, w : \mathcal{V} \to \mathcal{V}\} \qquad \mathcal{N}_1 = \{N_{i,V}(x) \mid x \in \mathcal{V}^n, i \in 1..n, V \subseteq \mathcal{V}\}$$

A hiding function $\phi_{i,w}$ replaces the value of individual i by applying an arbitrary substitution of values w (instead of replacing with a fixed value as $\phi_{i,v}$ does). Moreover, for the adversary, knowing $N_{i,V}(x)$ means that he knows the values of all individuals in the database but i, and moreover he knows that the value of i lies within V. Note that $\Phi_h \subset \Phi_1$ and $\mathcal{N}_h \subset \mathcal{N}_1$. We show that $\Phi_1, \mathcal{N}_1$ are "canonical".

Proposition 2. $\Phi_1, \mathcal{N}_1$ *are maximally tight wrt both* $d_1, \tilde{d}_1$.

From Theorem 3, we conclude that $\epsilon \tilde{d}_1$-privacy is equivalent to requiring that the adversary's posterior distributions with or without hiding i's value should be at most $2\epsilon \tilde{d}_1(\phi_{i,w})$ distant. Since $\tilde{d}_1(\phi_{i,w}) \leq 1$, hiding the individual's value in any way has small effect on the adversary's conclusions. But if i's value is replaced by one close to it, $\tilde{d}_1(\phi_{i,w})$ can be much lower than 1, meaning that the effect on the adversary's conclusions is even smaller.

---

[4] Note that in the differential privacy literature, the d_1 distance is often used on *histograms*. This metric is closely related to the standard d_h distance on $\mathcal{V}^n$ (it depends only on the record counts), and different than d_1 on $\mathcal{V}^n$ which depends on the actual values.

Then, from Theorem 4 we conclude that $\epsilon \tilde{d}_1$-privacy is equivalent to requiring that, for an informed adversary knowing the value of all individuals but i, and moreover knowing that i's value lies in V, his conclusions differ from his initial knowledge by at most $\epsilon \frac{d_V(V)}{d_V(\mathcal{V})}$. This difference is at most ϵ, but can be much smaller if values in V are close to each other, meaning that for an adversary who knows i's value with high accuracy, the gain is even smaller.

Intuitively, $\epsilon \tilde{d}_1$-privacy offers a stronger notion of privacy than ϵd_h-privacy:

Proposition 3. $\tilde{d}_1 \leq d_h$, thus $\epsilon \tilde{d}_1$-privacy implies ϵd_h-privacy.

Since distances in $\tilde{d}_1$ can be smaller than those in d_h, the sensitivity of a query wrt $\tilde{d}_1$ is in general greater than the sensitivity wrt d_h, which means that to achieve $\epsilon \tilde{d}_1$-privacy we need to apply more noise. However, for a general class of queries, it turns out that the two sensitivities coincide.

Definition 8. *A query f belongs to the family $\mathcal{C}$ iff $d_{\mathbb{R}}(f(x), f(x')) \leq d_V(x[i], x'[i])$ for all $i \in 1..n$ such that $x \sim_i x' \in \mathcal{V}^n$, and moreover $\exists x \sim_i x' \in \mathcal{V}^n$ such that $d_{\mathbb{R}}(f(x), f(x')) = d_V(\mathcal{V})$.*

Proposition 4. *Let $f \in \mathcal{C}$. The sensitivity of f wrt both $d_h, d_{\mathbb{R}}$ and $\tilde{d}_1, d_{\mathbb{R}}$ is $d_V(\mathcal{V})$.*

Intuitively, the class $\mathcal{C}$ contains queries for which the sensitivity is obtained for values that are maximally distant. For those queries, using the Truncated Geometric mechanism we can achieve a notion of privacy stronger than differential privacy *using the same amount of noise*!

Results About Some Common Queries. We now focus to some commonly used queries, namely the sum, average and p-percentile queries. Note that other commonly used queries such as the max, min and median queries are specific cases of the p-percentile query. In the following, we assume that the universe is $\mathcal{V} = q[0..k]_{\varnothing}$ with metric $d_{\mathbb{R}}$, and take $\mathcal{X} = \mathcal{V}^n \setminus \{\langle \varnothing, \ldots, \varnothing \rangle\}$, that is we exclude the empty database so that the queries can be always defined.

For these queries we obtain two results: first, we show that they belong to the $\mathcal{C}$ family, which means that we can achieve $\epsilon \tilde{d}_1$-privacy via the TG_ϵ mechanism, using the same amount of noise that we would need for standard differential privacy.

Proposition 5. *The* sum, avg, p-perc *queries belong to $\mathcal{C}$.*

More interestingly, we can show that the Truncated Geometric mechanism is in fact universally optimal wrt $\tilde{d}_1$ for such queries.

Theorem 11. *The* sum, avg *and* p-perc *queries are all uniformly qk-sensitive wrt $\tilde{d}_1, d_{\mathbb{R}}$.*

Corollary. $TG_{\epsilon/qk}$ *is* f-$\epsilon \tilde{d}_1$-*optimal for* $f \in \{$sum, avg, p-perc$\}$, $\epsilon > 0$.

5.2 The Manhattan Metric

In the previous section, we used the normalized Manhattan metric $\epsilon\widetilde{d}_1$, obtaining a strong privacy notion that protects an individual's value, while offering even stronger protection for small changes in an individual's value. This however, requires at least as much noise as standard differential privacy.

On the other hand, there are applications in which a complete protection of an individual's value is not required. This happens, for instance, in situations when the actual value is not sensitive, but knowing it with high accuracy might allow an adversary to identify the individual. Consider for example a database with the individuals' birthday, or the registration date and time to some social network. This information, by itself, might not be considered private, however knowing such information with minute-accuracy could easily allow to identify an individual. In such situations we might wish to protect only the accuracy of the value, thus achieving privacy with less noise and offering more accurate results.

This can be achieved by the Manhattan metric ϵd_1 (without normalization). This metric might assign a level of distinguishability higher than ϵ for adjacent databases, thus the privacy guarantees could be weaker than those of ϵ-differential privacy. However, adjacent databases with small changes in value will be highly protected, thus an adversary cannot infer an individual's value with accuracy.

Similarly to the previous section, we can obtain characterizations of ϵd_1-privacy using the same hiding functions Φ_1 and neighborhoods $\mathcal{N}_1$. The only difference is that $\epsilon d_1(\phi_{i,w})$ and $\epsilon d_1(N_{i,V})$ can be now higher than ϵ, offering weaker protection. However, when the adversary already knows i's value with high accuracy, meaning that values in V are close to each other, it is guaranteed that his knowledge will increase by a small factor (possibly even smaller than ϵ), ensuring that he cannot infer the value with even higher accuracy.

Note that the sensitivity of a query can be substantially lower wrt d_1 than wrt d_h. For example, the sum query is 1-sensitive wrt d_1 but qr-sensitive wrt d_h. This means that the noise we need to add could be substantially lower, offering better utility at the expense of lower privacy, but still sufficient for a given application.

Example 1. Consider a database containing the registration date on some social network, expressed as the number of days since Jan 1, 2000. We want to privately release the earliest registration date among individuals satisfying some criteria. A registration date itself is not considered sensitive, however from the result of the query it should be impossible to infer whether a particular individual belongs to that set. Since values can range between 0 and approximately 5.000, the sensitivity of the min query wrt d_h is 5.000, while wrt d_1 it is only 1.   By using ϵd_h we protect (up to the intended level ϵ) an individual's registration date within the whole range of values, while by using $\frac{\epsilon}{5}d_1$ we provide the intended protection only within a radius of 5 days. More precisely: in the first case two adjacent databases will always have distinguishability level ϵ, while in the second case such level of protection is guaranteed only if the individual's registration date differs by at most 5 days in the two databases (if they differ more the distinguishability level will increase proportionally). The second case, of course, offers less privacy, but, depending on the application, confusion within 5 days can be enough to prevent an individual from being identified. On the other hand, the trade-off with

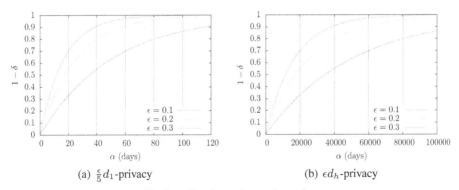

Fig. 3. Utility for various values of ϵ

utility can be much more favorable in the second case: In Figure 1 we show the utility of a Laplace mechanism for both metrics, in terms of (α, δ)-usefulness (meaning that the mechanism reports a result within distance α from the real value with probability at least $1 - \delta$).[5] Clearly, $\frac{\epsilon}{5}d_1$-privacy gives acceptable utility while ϵd_h-privacy renders the result almost useless.

Finally, the optimality result from the previous section also holds for d_1.

Theorem 12. *The* sum, avg *and* p-perc *queries are all uniformly* 1-*sensitive wrt* $d_1, d_{\mathbb{R}}$.

Corollary. TG_ϵ *is* f-ϵd_1-*optimal for* $f \in \{\mathrm{sum}, \mathrm{avg}, p\text{-perc}\}$, $\epsilon > 0$.

6   Privacy in Other Contexts

6.1   Smart Meters

A smart meter is a device that records the consumption of electrical energy at potentially very short time intervals, and transmits the information to the utility provider, thus offering him the capability to monitor consumption accurately and almost in real-time.

The problem. Although smart meters can help improving energy management, they create serious privacy threats: By analyzing accurate consumption data, thanks to appliance signature libraries it is possible to identify which electric devices are being used [15]. It has even been shown that, depending on the granularity of measurement and the resolution of data, it is possible to deduce what TV channels, and which movies are being watched [16].

Several papers addressed the privacy problems of smart metering in the recent past. The solution proposed in [17] is based on the use of techniques of (standard) differential privacy in order to send sanitized sums of the readings over some period of time (e.g. an hour, a day, a month) to the service provider. Since this solution is tailored to the use of smart metering for billing purposes, the noise added is assumed to be positive.

---

[5] Using Bayesian utility leads to similar results.

The Model. For the sake of generality, we assume here that the noise could be of any kind (not necessarily positive). We can regard the readings over the period $[1..n]$ as a tuple $x \in \mathcal{V}^n$, so that $x[i]$ represents the reading at the time i. Since [17] uses the standard differential privacy framework, the distinguishability metric on these tuples is assumed to be the Hamming distance, and therefore the privacy mechanism is tuned to protect the value of $x[i]$, regardless of whether the variation of this value is small or large. However, the solution proposed in [17] is general and can be adapted to a different distinguishability metric.

We argue that for the case of smart meters, the problem that derives from the extreme accuracy of the readings can be addressed with limited noise by adopting a metric that is sensitive also to the distance between values, and not only to the change of the value for a reading $x[i]$. The reason is the same as illustrated in previous section: if we want to protect small variations in the reading of $x[i]$, it is not a good idea to tune the sensitivity on the difference between the extremes values, because we would end up introducing a lot of noise. In fact, the experiments in [16] are performed on actual smart meters that are in the process of being deployed. These meters send readings to the service provider every 2 seconds. The solution proposed in [17] offers good privacy guarantees by completely protecting each measurement. However, such a definition is too strong if reporting values at short intervals is a requirement. With standard differential privacy, we cannot hope to fully protect each measurement without introducing too much noise. On the other hand, using a more relaxed metric, we can at least provide a meaningful privacy guarantee by protecting the accuracy of the values. Some privacy will still be lost, but the attacks described above where the individual's behaviour is completely disclosed, will be prevented.

The Manhattan distance d_1 on $\mathcal{V}^n$, however, is not suitable to model the privacy problem we have here: in fact d_1 is suitable to protect an individual $x[i]$ and its value, while here we want to protect *all the values at the same time*. This is because the adversary, i.e., the service provider, already knows *an approximation of all values*. Note the difference from the case of Section 5: there, the canonical adversary knows all exact values except $x[i]$, and for $x[i]$ he only knows an approximate value. (In the case of standard differential privacy, the canonical adversary knows all values except $x[i]$, and for $x[i]$ he does not even know an approximate value.)

The suitable distance, in this case, is the maximum distance between components, d_∞. In fact, we should consider x, x' "indistinguishable enough" (i.e. $d(x, x') \leq \delta$, for a certain δ) if and only if for each component i, $x[i], x'[i]$ are "indistinguishable enough" (i.e. $d(x[i], x'[i]) \leq \delta$, for the same δ). It is easy to see that the only distance that satisfies this property is $d(x, x') = d_\infty(x, x') = \max_i d_\mathcal{V}(x[i], x'[i])$.

Example 2. We illustrate the application our method to distort the digital signature of a tv program. The grey line in Fig. 4(a) represents the energy consumption of the first 5 minutes of Star Trek 11 [15]. The black line is (the approximation of) the signature produced by a smart meter that reports the true readings every 10 seconds (the samples are represented by the dots). The blue and the magenta dots in 4(b) are obtained by adding laplacian noise to the true readings, with ϵ values .1 and .5 respectively. As we can see, especially in the case of $\epsilon = .5$, the signature is not recognizable.

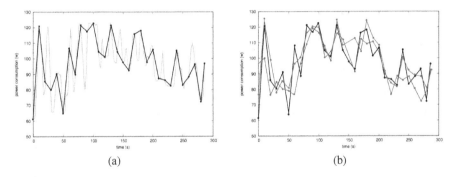

Fig. 4. Digital signature of a tv program (a) and its noisy reporting (b)

Concerning the characterization results, we use hiding functions substituting the value of all readings. Moreover, we use neighborhoods modelling an adversary that knows all readings with some accuracy, i.e. knows that each reading i lies within V_i.

$$\Phi_\infty = \{\phi_{1,w_1} \circ \ldots \circ \phi_{n,w_n} \mid w_i : \mathcal{V} \to \mathcal{V} \; \forall i \in 1..n\}$$
$$N_{\{V_i\}} = \{\langle v_1, \ldots, v_n \rangle \mid v_i \in V_i, i \in 1..n\}$$
$$\mathcal{N}_\infty = \{N_{\{V_i\}} \mid V_i \subseteq \mathcal{V}, i \in 1..n\}$$

We can show that $\Phi_\infty, \mathcal{N}_\infty$ are maximally tight.

Finally, we show that TG_ϵ is universally optimal for avg and p-perc.

Theorem 13. *The queries* avg *and* p-perc *are both uniformly* 1-*sensitive wrt* $d_\infty, d_\mathbb{R}$.

Corollary. TG_ϵ *is* f-ϵd_∞-*optimal for* $f \in \{\text{avg}, p\text{-perc}\}$, $\epsilon > 0$.

6.2 Geolocation

In this subsection we briefly describe an application of our framework to privacy-aware location-based systems. We refer to [18] for more details.

Privacy notions have been already studied in previous works. Some of these works [19,20,21] propose the use of the *expectation of distance error* of the attacker as the way to quantify the privacy offered by a mechanism. Others works [22,23,24] rely on the well-known concept of k-anonymity. The notion of *relevance* is also used to measure location privacy in [25]. A strong advantage of the use of d-privacy as privacy notion is that it abstracts from the side-knowledge of the attacker.

The Problem. In several situations it is desirable to know the location of an individual or a group of individuals in order to provide a service. For instance: In census-based statistics, to determine the population density in certain areas, in transportation industry, to estimate the average number of people who need to travel between two given stations, and in smartphone applications, to obtain points of interest nearby such as restaurants.

Due to privacy concerns, an individual may refuse to disclose his exact location to the service provider. Nevertheless, he may be willing to reveal approximate location information.It is worth noting that for several location-based systems it is usually enough to obtain an approximate location to be able to provide an accurate service. Note however, that in order to guarantee a non-negligible level of privacy, the random location cannot be generated naively. Therefore, if we want to develop a method to randomize location coordinates, we have to understand what kind of privacy the user expects to have, and how much information he is willing to reveal.

The Model. In this scenario, the privacy level depends on the accuracy with which an attacker can guess an individual's location from the reported one. We will therefore aim for a distance-dependent notion of privacy, requiring points that are close in distance to each other to be *indistinguishable* from the attacker's point of view. Our method will still allow the service provider to distinguish between points that are far from each other.

We consider the problem of geolocation on the Euclidean plane, which is a good approximation of the Earth surface when the area is not "too large". In this scenario, possible locations of an individual will be modeled with a set $\mathcal{X} \subseteq \mathbb{R}^2$, and possible reported values will be represented by a set $\mathcal{Z} \subseteq \mathbb{R}^2$. The metric $d_\mathcal{X}$ used in this context will be the Euclidean distance d_2.

Concerning the characterizations of Section 3, any function $\phi : \mathbb{R}^2 \to \mathbb{R}^2$ can be used as a hiding function. Moreover, a neighborhood can be any region $N \subseteq \mathbb{R}^2$, modelling an informed adversary who knows that the user is located within N. Hence we take $\Phi_2 = \mathbb{R}^2 \to \mathbb{R}^2$ and $\mathcal{N}_2 = 2^{\mathbb{R}^2}$, both of which are maximally tight wrt d_2.

In order to obtain a mechanism which satisfies ϵd_2-privacy, we can use the *Laplace* mechanism L_ϵ on $\mathbb{R}^2$ mentioned in Section 4.1, that is, the one described by the pdf $D_\epsilon(x)(z) = \frac{\epsilon^2}{2\pi} e^{-\epsilon d_2(x,z)}$ $x, z \in \mathbb{R}^2$. The results in Section 4.1 ensure that such mechanism satisfies ϵd_2-privacy.

7   Conclusion

Starting from the observation that differential privacy requires that the distinguishability of two databases depends on their Hamming distance, we have explored the consequences of extending this principle to arbitrary metrics. In this way we have obtained a rich framework suitable to model a large variety of privacy problems, and in domains other than statistical databases. Furthermore, even in statistical databases applications, whenever the privacy concern is related to disclosing small variations in the values of the individuals (rather than large ones), then our framework allows a more precise calibration of the noise necessary for achieving the intended level of privacy, and this results, in general, in a better utility than the one achievable under the constraint of standard differential privacy. We have investigated the trade-off between privacy and utility in this extended setting, and it turns out changing the metric has considerable implications on the existence of universally optimal mechanisms. In particular, for the Manhattan distance, the normalized Manhattan distance, and the max distance it is possible to define universally optimal mechanisms for several common queries like the sum, the average, and the percentile. This contrast sharply with the case of standard differential privacy, where universally optimal mechanisms exist only for counting queries. Finally, we have shown the applicability of our framework to various privacy problems in different domains, including smart meters and geolocation.

References

1. Dwork, C.: Differential privacy. In: Bugliesi, M., Preneel, B., Sassone, V., Wegener, I. (eds.) ICALP 2006. LNCS, vol. 4052, pp. 1–12. Springer, Heidelberg (2006)
2. Dwork, C., McSherry, F., Nissim, K., Smith, A.: Calibrating noise to sensitivity in private data analysis. In: Halevi, S., Rabin, T. (eds.) TCC 2006. LNCS, vol. 3876, pp. 265–284. Springer, Heidelberg (2006)
3. Reed, J., Pierce, B.C.: Distance makes the types grow stronger: a calculus for differential privacy. In: Proc. of ICFP, pp. 157–168. ACM (2010)
4. Narayanan, A., Shmatikov, V.: De-anonymizing social networks. In: Proc. of S&P, pp. 173–187. IEEE (2009)
5. Machanavajjhala, A., Kifer, D., Abowd, J.M., Gehrke, J., Vilhuber, L.: Privacy: Theory meets practice on the map. In: Proc. of ICDE, pp. 277–286. IEEE (2008)
6. Ganta, S.R., Kasiviswanathan, S.P., Smith, A.: Composition attacks and auxiliary information in data privacy. In: Proc. of KDD, pp. 265–273. ACM (2008)
7. Ghosh, A., Roughgarden, T., Sundararajan, M.: Universally utility-maximizing privacy mechanisms. In: Proc. of STOC, pp. 351–360. ACM (2009)
8. Brenner, H., Nissim, K.: Impossibility of differentially private universally optimal mechanisms. In: Proc. of FOCS, pp. 71–80. IEEE (2010)
9. Nissim, K., Raskhodnikova, S., Smith, A.: Smooth sensitivity and sampling in private data analysis. In: Proc. of STOC, pp. 75–84. ACM (2007)
10. Barthe, G., Köpf, B., Olmedo, F., Béguelin, S.Z.: Probabilistic relational reasoning for differential privacy. In: Proc. of POPL. ACM (2012)
11. Dwork, C., Hardt, M., Pitassi, T., Reingold, O., Zemel, R.S.: Fairness through awareness. In: Proc. of ITCS, pp. 214–226. ACM (2012)
12. Chatzikokolakis, K., Andrés, M.E., Bordenabe, N.E., Palamidessi, C.: Broadening the scope of Differential Privacy using metrics. Tech. rep., INRIA (2012), http://hal.inria.fr/hal-00767210
13. Dwork, C., Kenthapadi, K., McSherry, F., Mironov, I., Naor, M.: Our data, ourselves: Privacy via distributed noise generation. In: Vaudenay, S. (ed.) EUROCRYPT 2006. LNCS, vol. 4004, pp. 486–503. Springer, Heidelberg (2006)
14. McSherry, F., Talwar, K.: Mechanism design via differential privacy. In: Proc. of FOCS, pp. 94–103. IEEE (2007)
15. Lam, H., Fung, G., Lee, W.: A novel method to construct taxonomy electrical appliances based on load signatures. IEEE Trans. on Consumer Electronics 53(4), 653–660 (2007)
16. Greveler, U., Justus, B., Loehr, D.: Multimedia content identification through smart meter power use profiles. In: CPDP (2012)
17. Danezis, G., Kohlweiss, M., Rial, A.: Differentially private billing with rebates. IACR Cryptology ePrint Archive 2011, 134 (2011)
18. Andrés, M., Bordenabe, N., Chatzikokolakis, K., Palamidessi, C.: Geo-indistinguishability: Differential privacy for location-based systems. CoRR abs/1212.1984 (2012)
19. Shokri, R., Theodorakopoulos, G., Boudec, J.Y.L., Hubaux, J.P.: Quantifying location privacy. In: Proc. of S&P, pp. 247–262. IEEE (2011)

20. Shokri, R., Theodorakopoulos, G., Troncoso, C., Hubaux, J.P., Boudec, J.Y.L.: Protecting location privacy: optimal strategy against localization attacks. In: Proc. of CCS, pp. 617–627. ACM (2012)
21. Hoh, B., Gruteser, M.: Protecting location privacy through path confusion. In: SecureComm, pp. 194–205. IEEE (2005)
22. Kido, H., Yanagisawa, Y., Satoh, T.: Protection of location privacy using dummies for location-based services. In: Proc. of ICDE Workshops, p. 1248 (2005)
23. Shankar, P., Ganapathy, V., Iftode, L.: Privately querying location-based services with sybil-query. In: Proc. of UbiComp, pp. 31–40. ACM (2009)
24. Duckham, M., Kulik, L.: A formal model of obfuscation and negotiation for location privacy. In: Gellersen, H.-W., Want, R., Schmidt, A. (eds.) PERVASIVE 2005. LNCS, vol. 3468, pp. 152–170. Springer, Heidelberg (2005)
25. Ardagna, C.A., Cremonini, M., Damiani, E., De Capitani di Vimercati, S., Samarati, P.: Location privacy protection through obfuscation-based techniques. In: Barker, S., Ahn, G.-J. (eds.) Data and Applications Security 2007. LNCS, vol. 4602, pp. 47–60. Springer, Heidelberg (2007)

Turning Off GPS Is Not Enough: Cellular Location Leaks over the Internet

Hamed Soroush, Keen Sung,
Erik Learned-Miller, Brian Neil Levine, and Marc Liberatore

Dept. of Computer Science, University of Massachusetts, Amherst, USA
{soroush,ksung,elm,brian,liberato}@cs.umass.edu

Abstract. Many third parties desire to discover and disclose your location with the help of your cell phone. Using an embedded GPS, phone software will commonly reveal coordinates to carriers, advertisers, and applications. Can a remote party determine locational information absent explicit GPS information? For example, given a known starting or ending point, can a streaming music server distinguish the path you've taken through the physical world? We show that the path a cell phone and its owner take from or to a known location can be determined from remote observations of changes in TCP throughput. Empirically, our method can correctly determine with greater than 78% accuracy the path taken by phone from one of four paths, and with 63% accuracy the path taken from among eight paths.

1 Introduction

Information that is not part of the content of electronic communication, such as the location of the user, has almost no privacy protection in the U.S. Carriers inherently know to which towers mobile phones associate, and investigators can easily compel the release of such information. Mobile phones also expose location information to Internet services, apps [4], and advertising networks [9]. Location privacy in phones is limited to GPS access control per-app. In this paper, we demonstrate that mobile phones are subject to *Internet-based remote localization*. We show that the broad geographic path a cell phone and its owner take can be determined from remotely observed changes in TCP throughput. In short, we show that turning off GPS is not enough.

Many factors shape network traffic between a phone and a remote server. Some are ephemeral, including competing link- or TCP-layer flows. Others change only infrequently, such as the cellular infrastructure and the device's network stack. Signal strength is likely to have some geographical consistency, stemming from the location of radio towers, buildings, and the terrain; any user that lives on the edge of network coverage knows places where a call is likely to drop. A remote party communicating with a phone has a window into the complex interactions of these features. They can be used to reveal the phone's location, or at least significantly narrow the list of possible paths taken by a phone and its owner. This information is leaked regardless of application-level privacy settings.

E. De Cristofaro and M. Wright (Eds.): PETS 2013, LNCS 7981, pp. 103–122, 2013.

In this paper, we examine a restricted sub-problem of the general Internet-based remote localization problem. We approach the problem as an instance of the *time-sequence multi-class classification problem* [13], using network traffic traces as instances to be classified, and geographic paths as classes. We compare the accuracy of several classifiers that use only throughput measurements of music streamed to a mobile phone on a 3G/UMTS network. In our subproblem, we assume the attacker knows either the starting or ending location of the user's mobility, can isolate traffic belonging to the user, and can collect labeled training traces of phones traveling along a limited set of possible paths.

Consider a streaming audio service (like that provided by Spotify or Pandora) that wishes to localize users that have disabled GPS. For the service to discover an end point, it geolocates the user when they are connected to a broadband-supported Wi-Fi base station. Most mobile phones in the U.S. preferentially make these connections when they are available. To acquire training data, the service leverages their observations of users who do not disable GPS: travels within a cellular network provide training for throughput distributions over paths; connections from geographically static Wi-Fi provide the service with GPS coordinates of such access points.

Contributions. We collected hundreds of traces of music that we streamed to phones along four geographically separate routes in two directions each. We find that within small geographical areas, mean throughput is largely consistent and distinct. We examine the accuracy of three remote localization classifiers that leverage this consistency. Even a naive approach, trained on the mean throughput of each path, has some success. We trained an HMM classifier on the distribution of throughput values and achieved higher accuracy. Our best performing approach, a k-nearest neighbors (k-NN) classifier, trains on the ordered sequence of throughput values of each route. Empirically, the k-NN can correctly determine with greater than 78% accuracy the path taken by phone from one of four paths, and with 63% accuracy the path taken from among eight paths.

In sum, our main contributions are as follows.

- We define the Internet-based remote localization problem and demonstrate for the first time that cellular phones are subject to limited forms of it.
- We recorded 286 traces of music streamed over a 3G/UMTS cellular connection over one of four geographically distinct, bi-directional routes (8 paths total) over a one-month period. We also recorded 29 stationary traces.
- Our analysis shows statistically different throughput and signal strength means among small geographic areas (0.9 km^2 each). Phones that move between locations travel through consistent and distinct network conditions that are remotely observable.
- We examine the performance of the three classifiers listed above, demonstrating that both the k-NN and HMM approaches can distinguish between a small number of geographic routes taken by mobile users using only throughput measurements. The classifiers are also able to distinguish between mobile and stationary users. Only the k-NN is able to distinguish between two traces of the same route in opposite directions.

We explain classifiers performance by examining received signal strength at the target, its correlation with throughput, and the geographic consistency of both. We conjecture that the usual defenses against inference attacks, such as traffic padding and shaping, will help defend against this attack.

2   Problem Statement and Attacker Model

We are interested in a subset of the Internet-based remote localization problem: *Can an attacker, providing an Internet-based service to a mobile user that disabled GPS, infer the path taken by the mobile user, from among a limited set of paths, using only information visible at the server?* In later sections of this paper, we show that the answer is yes. Here, we elaborate on the problem, our assumptions, and our approach and its limitations.

Motivation. Solving this subproblem of the remote localization problem is an important step toward a solution to the more general problem. Aside from the research challenge, this problem is of interest to the general public. Particular users care about their own location being determined and shared without their consent. Further, society may judge phone-based location tracking of individuals as something to be regulated or otherwise controlled. For example, in a recent report [5], the U.S. Government Accountability Office notes that federal action could help protect consumer privacy; legislatively, the proposed Location Privacy Protection Act of 2012[1] and Mobile Device Privacy Act[2] both seek to protect this information in the U.S.

Assumptions. We assume the attacker is the remote end-point of the target's communication, as is the case for streaming services such as Spotify, Pandora, and many others; or has access (perhaps unauthorized) to network-level traces at this location. We assume that the carrier, who can localize the mobile node by examining the cell towers to which it has associated, is not assisting the attacker. We assume that the attacker does not have direct access to the internals of the cellular infrastructure or to the mobile device used by the target, and therefore will find it nearly impossible [1] to geolocate the user from its carrier-assigned IP address. (Carriers use a small pool of addresses that are re-used across the country from one minute to the next.) We assume the attacker does not have the ability to direct the mobile device to reveal its location overtly. The attacker only passively analyzes the communication between the mobile device and its server. Our attacker uses only throughput measurements of the target's data stream and not the content, which could be encrypted or otherwise unavailable – though we do assume the attacker could link flows if the remote end-point IP address changes. This assumption is reasonable given our attacker model. (We enumerate limitations of our evaluation in Section 5.)

Approach. Our approach builds models of the effects of mobility upon network traffic, and uses these models to determine the mobility of users. Specifically, the

---

[1] http://thomas.loc.gov/cgi-bin/query/z?c112:S.1223:

[2] http://markey.house.gov/document/2012/mobile-device-privacy-act-2012

attacker compares a trace of network traffic generated by a mobile user against a set of models representing specific paths through the world. The attacker creates these models by gathering information about TCP's performance on a set of possible routes that he assumes the target may take. The attacker may gather this information, which consists of traces of network traffic, during any period when the traffic observed would be similar — it need not be done strictly prior to the attack. This training information may be gathered from other users that have not disabled GPS. We conjecture that greater temporal locality will improve the attacker's performance, though we did not explicitly test this assumption.

Limitations. The traces we consider are on the order of tens of minutes long; we do not attempt to determine the shortest such trace that yields useful information. We do not attempt to solve short-duration instances of this problem, nor do we attempt to chain together small instances of the problem into a larger instance (i.e., from one instance of Wi-Fi access to a later one). We do not try to pinpoint the geographic location of the mobile, rather only the path taken from limited possibilities.

3   Data Collection and Exploratory Analysis

In this section, we describe our data and collection methodology, and we present an exploratory analysis of our data set. Our focus is on the geographic consistency of client-side signal strength and server-side throughput measurements. Our data set consists of 286 measurements of mobile phones traveling to and from a central location to four different locations, each about 25 minutes away (roughly a 360 km^2 area). We also collected 29 stationary traces, to serve as a simple baseline for our approach. In our analysis, we find that signal strength and throughput characteristics are tied to geography: in our data set, the mean throughput of 95% of 0.9 km^2 areas is statistically different from at least 90% of the other areas, and similar results hold for signal strength. The implication is that the route traveled by a mobile node is through a relatively unique sequence of mean throughputs that is classifiable.

3.1   Data Collection Methodology

Our measurements[3] are based on four Android cell phones instrumented to record traces of GPS location and signal strength. A server in our building streamed music continuously to the phones during measurement trials. We logged TCP traces at the server during trials. We later combined sets of corresponding phone and server traces, synchronizing by the timestamps within the traces. Note that it is impossible without carrier participation to take measurements at points inside the network along the path. Moreover, our goal was to take measurements that are available at the server without special access to cellular infrastructure, allowing for a weaker attacker. We took two sets of traces:

---

[3] Traces from our experiments are available for download from
http://traces.cs.umass.edu.

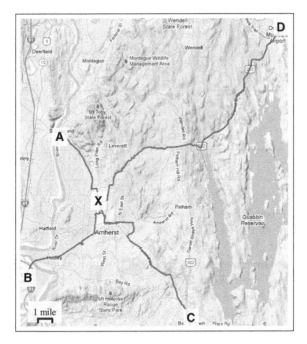

Fig. 1. We gathered data on four popular paths in our area, in two directions for each path. All paths intersect in Amherst, MA, labeled as "X".

- **Mobile 3G Measurement Set:** We used *Samsung Nexus S*, *Samsung Galaxy S*, *Motorola Atrix*, and *HTC Inspire* phones, all connected to the AT&T UMTS (3G) network, to record traces. The 802.11 radio on the phone remained powered off during the experiments. We collected data during a one-month period under varying traffic and weather conditions. Each measurement was taken as a phone traveled along one of four routes going either toward or away from our central location (point X in Figure 1). The individual paths are shown on a map in Figure 1 and summary statistics appear in Figure 2. In total, we recorded 286 traces in this set.
- **Stationary 3G Measurement Set:** We recorded 29 traces from stationary phones, connected to the UMTS (3G) network, located in different locations near our central location.

The phones collected traces of GPS location (with 10m accuracy) and signal strength[4]. Each element of the traces was sampled once per second. Traces of network activity on the server consist of standard `pcap` logs. We did not limit traces to periods of cellular connectivity, and some traces consisted of several TCP connections.

In the mobile sets, we hired several persons to collect data on these specific paths, and no person was assigned to a single path or phone. Our goal was to

---

[4] As reported by `android.telephony.SignalStrength.getGsmSignalStrength()`.

Route	Distance (mi)	Num. Traces Collected	Throughput (KB/s) mean ± s.d.	Duration (min) mean ± s.d.
X to A	8.7	68	143.1 ± 104.3	16.4 ± 4.3
A to X	8.7	63	167.2 ± 108.2	16.1 ± 4.2
X to B	9.2	28	49.8 ± 81.8	33.6 ± 9.0
B to X	9.2	24	67.0 ± 95.8	30.5 ± 4.8
X to C	12.7	31	127.3 ± 106.8	32.1 ± 7.9
C to X	12.7	29	123.4 ± 108.5	34.8 ± 7.4
X to D	22.2	24	47.6 ± 76.2	35.0 ± 10.3
D to X	22.2	19	36.5 ± 64.3	36.1 ± 5.1
Stationary	0	29	220.4 ± 120.3	20.4 ± 5.5

Fig. 2. Details of the traces in our Measurement Sets. Letters refer to landmarks labeled in Figure 1. In total, we recorded 286 mobile and 29 stationary traces.

avoid learning the phone model or user behind the movement. Each path differed in distance, and each took about 25 minutes on average to travel by car or bus. The travel time to location A was the shortest and D the longest. We discuss the implications of path duration on classifier bias in Section 5. Because we relied on a consumer phone platform, on some occasions the experiment failed because either the end time or start time were not recorded correctly, due to a GPS failure or write-to-flash failure. We did not attempt to even out the number of traces per path after our collection period completed. Though the number of traces per route and direction varies, we did not alter which traces to collect or which to use in the experiments for any reason (most importantly, to alter classification accuracy).

3.2   Geographic Analysis

We grouped all server-side throughput and client-side signal strength measurements into small geographic areas (much small than and having no correspondence to carrier cells) to determine if each area had consistent and differentiable mean throughput. The efficacy of any throughput-based remote localization scheme depends on such consistency. We found geographic consistency in both cases and a weak correlation between the two features.

Server-side throughput is influenced by the wireless link between the phone and cell tower [3], the network conditions and infrastructure [15] between the phone and server, the TCP algorithm [10], and other factors. Signal strength is just one factor that influences the wireless link but it is the factor with the strongest tie to geography. Received signal strength is influenced by many physical features, including occlusions between the radio and cell tower from tree foliage, the body of the person carrying the phone, buildings, and other structures.

The range of signal strength values are integers defined in GSM standard TS 27.007, with 0 referring to -113 dBm or less, 31 referring to -51 dBm or greater,

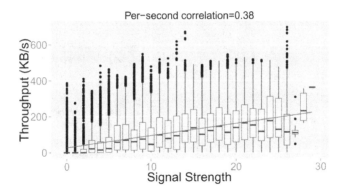

Fig. 3. On a per-second basis, the correlation between server-side throughput and client-side signal strength is 0.38. The plot shows a linear fit. Figures 13(left) and (right) show that this correlation increases to 0.58 and 0.89 on a per-trace and per-route basis, respectively.

and 99 referring to an undetectable signal. Each value between 1 and 30 is a linear increase from -111 to -53 dBm. We discarded values of 31, as the range it captures is too large for a meaningful regression. We treated values of 99 as 0.

We found a weak correlation between client-side signal strength and server-side throughput of 0.38 when considered as a per-second granularity. Figure 3 shows the distribution of throughput values per signal strength value as a boxplot. The figure also plots the least-squares linear fit of the two variables as a visual guide. In Section 5, we return to this correlation on a per-trace and per-route basis, showing the correlation increases to 0.58 and 0.89, respectively.

Figure 4 shows the mean throughput (left) and signal strength (right) of geographic areas in our measurements. The error bars of each mean indicate the 95% confidence interval of the mean. Each plot is sorted by an increasing mean value, and therefore the order of areas in the plots is not the same. Using a two-sided, 95% confidence interval t-test, we performed a pairwise comparison of the mean throughput of the areas. 95% of areas have means that are statistically different from at least 90% of other areas. The consistency of these values and the differences among areas suggests that latent information linking throughput and geography is available for training a classifier. Signal strength measurements have a similar consistency.

In Figure 5, we plot the mean throughput of each area on a geographical grid. Mobile nodes will travel through a sequence of areas that has a unique signature of mean throughputs. The task of classification is to match the observed throughput to a training set that captures these means. In the simplest approach, we can classify based on the mean throughput that a mobile device obtains from visiting a series of areas. In more advanced approaches, we can classify based on the ordered set of mean throughputs obtained, or the ordered set with timing information. We attempt all three approaches, detailed further in the next section.

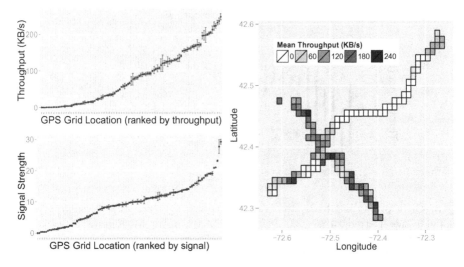

Fig. 4. The mean throughput (top) and signal strength (bottom) of geographical areas in our measurements. Each tic on the x-axis is a geographic area, and the order of areas is by increasing mean value; the order of areas in the plots is different. Error bars indicate the 95% c.i. of the mean. 95% of areas have throughput means that are statistically different from at least 90% of other areas (two-sided, 95% c.i. t-test). A similar result holds for signal strengths.

Fig. 5. The mean throughput of each area on a geographical grid. Mobile nodes will travel through a sequence of areas that has a unique signature of mean throughputs. The task of classification is to match the observed throughput to a training set that captures these means. Each area is approximately 0.9 km^2.

4   Classifiers for Mobile Throughput Traces

Given the attacker model and the data we've described in previous sections, it remains for us to detail how an attacker can use throughput traces to determine which path a mobile phone user takes. In this section, we describe several *classification* algorithms suited to this task.

Classifiers build models of labeled training instances of data, and use these models to decide to which class an unlabeled test instance belongs. The instances we considered were created from `pcap` files, and the specific data we were interested in was TCP throughput. We discretized this data into one-second intervals, and treated each instance as a sequence X of per-chunk median throughputs $(x_0, x_1, \ldots)$. With one second chunks, the index of each throughput value is the time since the start of the trace. The first algorithm, a straightforward k-nearest neighbor (k-NN) classifier, operates directly on these sequences. The second algorithm, based upon Hidden Markov Models (HMMs) requires some pre-processing of the sequences before operation, which we detail later.

4.1 Sequence-Based k-Nearest Neighbor Classifier

We build and use a k-NN classifier as follows. We train by simply storing training instances and their labels. To classify an unlabeled instance, we first compute the instance's *distance* from each labeled training instance. Given two instances X and Y, where $\text{len}(X) \leq \text{len}(Y)$, we define

$$\text{distance}(X, Y) = \sum_{i=0}^{\text{len}(X)-1} |x_i - y_i| + \sum_{i=\text{len}(X)}^{\text{len}(Y)-1} y_i \qquad (1)$$

The first summation is the per-chunk difference in throughput. The second summation is the remaining per-chunk throughputs; in effect, we are imputing zeros in the shorter trace.

We classify the instance as the label (i.e., the route) present in the largest fraction of the k-nearest neighbors. The choice of k tunes a smoothing effect in the data: A larger k reduces erroneous labeling due to matching against outliers, while too large of a k can result in simply choosing the most common training label. We used $k = 13$ for all experiments. All values between $k = 1 \dots 20$ performed roughly the same (59.4% to 67.1%, with a mean of 62.7%). For our data set, the choice of k is not critical. We don't expect the value is generalizable.

4.2 HMM-Based Classifiers

The data consists of frequent changes in throughput, and we construct an HMM classifier that models these changes. This classifier measures the consistency and volatility of the signal at certain levels along a path.

Overview. Figure 6 shows a simple HMM, with some details elided. This HMM represents one path through the world, and the corresponding changes in throughputs that are observed along that path. In this model, there are two states, corresponding to either a high or low throughput. In each state, the corresponding symbol is emitted with probability 0.95. There is an unspecified probability, $p_{\text{stay\_...}}$, that the HMM will stay in that state, or transition to the other state with probability $p_{\text{go\_...}}$. The exact probabilities can be set manually, or trained using measured data and the Baum-Welch algorithm. In this model, a more volatile signal may show higher transition probabilities than a more consistent signal, while a consistently high signal may result in a higher $p_{\text{stay\_high}}$ and a lower $p_{\text{stay\_low}}$.

Details. We build the HMM-based classifiers as follows. We start with the *sequences* of one-second chunks of throughput corresponding to the traces. The chunks are then symbolically labeled with one of n discrete symbols, where the cutoffs associated with each symbol are the equivalent quantiles. For example, $n = 2$ has a cutoff at the median and the symbols represent high and low throughputs, as illustrated in Figure 6(a). When $n = 4$, the cutoffs are at each quartile boundary, and so on. The sequence of symbols thus generated serves as input to our HMMs, as either labeled training data, or as unlabeled test data.

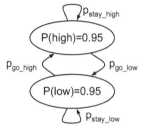

Route	p stay_low	P go_high	P go_low	P stay_high
A to X	0.91	0.09	0.08	0.92
X to A	0.88	0.12	0.06	0.94
B to X	0.96	0.04	0.10	0.90
X to B	0.95	0.05	0.05	0.95

(a) A simple HMM before training.

(b) HMM probabilities after training.

Fig. 6. A simple, untrained HMM as shown can be trained upon observed data. Trace data representing observed throughput is discretized into periods of high and low bandwidths, and the Baum-Welch algorithm is used to learn the most likely corresponding HMM. All emission probabilities converged to P(X)=1 from an initial setting of P(X)=0.95. For four such routes, four such two-state HMMs were learned using the Viterbi algorithm, with weights as shown in table (we used a 7-state HMM in our experiments).

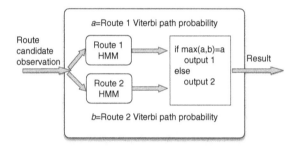

Fig. 7. The classification approach used for labeling traces corresponding to one of two candidate paths. Per-route HMMs are trained using the Baum-Welch algorithm on labeled traces. Classification of unlabeled traces is done by choosing the route corresponding to the HMM with the highest-probability Viterbi path.

The initial HMMs also have n states, where the state corresponding to each quantile has emission probability 0.95, and the other symbols are emitted with an equal division of the remaining 0.05 probability mass.

To train each HMM, we use the Baum-Welch algorithm, with an initial HMM as shown in Figure 6(a), where transition probabilities from each state are equiprobable. We apply Baum-Welch once for each labeled training sequence.

As an example, we show the resulting weights in Figure 6(b) for $n = 2$ to illustrate the differences between two such paths. Note that we show each direction separately, and that, as would be expected with an HMM in this scenario, the two machines for each path more closely resemble one another than those from the other path. In our traces, $n = 7$ produced best results; we tested values of n from 2 to 25. Values for n near 7 all performed nearly as well, and improvements past $n = 7$ were minimal and likely due to variance in the input data, given our relatively small data set. As with the choice of k for the k-NN classifier, our choice of n is tuned for our dataset and not generalizable.

The procedure for using our classifier is illustrated in Figure 7. We take an unlabeled sequence, and apply the Viterbi algorithm to it and each HMM, which produces an estimate of the probability that the HMM produced the observed sequence. We take the path corresponding to the most probable HMM as the prediction for that sequence.

5 Experimental Results

In this section, we report on our experiments. We begin with a brief overview of our approach and a list of our assumptions. We then describe the details of our experiments, and present and discuss our results.

5.1 Overview

Our experiments take the form of classification problems, where an attacker trains a classifier on training data, consisting of labeled sequences of throughput (training instances) as described in Section 4, and attempts to determine the class of an unlabeled instance (test instances). Varying the classifier and training and testing data allow us to determine how well the attacker can perform under different scenarios.

In all experiments, we use the standard definition of *accuracy* for a multi-class problem: the sum of correct classifications divided by the total number of classifications. Because each class is mutually exclusive as we have defined them (that is, the routes do not overlap and the classifier returns only a single result), accuracy is based on the sum of true positives for all classes and there are no true negatives possible. We trained and tested all classifiers in the same proportions on each data set, and we used leave-one-out cross-validation to measure accuracy.

Classifiers. We evaluate an attacker's accuracy using the k-nearest neighbor and throughput-based HMM classifiers described in Section 4. We also evaluate two naive approaches to classification. In the first naive approach, called *Throughput*, the classifier models each path as the mean of the mean of the throughputs associated with each path. This is among the simplest approaches to modeling a path that actually uses observed throughputs. In the other naive approach, called *Frequency*, the classifier simply chooses the class that was most common in the training data. Performing no better than Frequency, which uses no information from the data stream, implies a classifier models the situation poorly.

Summary of Experiments and Results. First, we show that an attacker can differentiate a mobile user from a stationary user, that is, make the binary choice of mobile or stationary. The attack succeeds with very high accuracy (77.4–91.2% for k-NN depending upon the exact scenario). Next, we show that given a user's starting or ending location and choice of four paths, an attacker can determine which path a user traveled, that is, choose correctly from among one of four options. This attack also succeeds with high accuracy (78.1–78.5% for k-NN depending on the scenario).

We then use our data to explore how well our method will scale to more choices. We show that given just the choice of four paths, an attacker can determine both the path and direction traveled (from among the eight possibilities) with good accuracy (63.3%). This problem parallels the problem of choosing from one of eight known paths given a starting or ending point, but is no easier: when forced to determine both path and direction, the attacker is choosing among paths where pairs are quite similar in some respects (since they are essentially mirror images of one another). We also show that in our data, the mirroring accounts for virtually none of the loss in accuracy for the k-NN classifier; for the other classifiers, the mirroring does cause a drop in accuracy.

Assumptions and Limitations. Our experiments are make many simplifying assumptions for this initial work. We assume the mobile target is always on one of n paths. We assume the attacker knows the starting location such that it can only be one of the starting points of the n paths. We assume the attacker has access to the streaming data as an end-point of the connection but cannot retrieve GPS information from the target's phone. In practice, to acquire training data, the attacker can leverage their observations of users who do not disable GPS; their travels within a cellular network and their connections to Wi-Fi provide the service with training data.

Our study is limited to one geographic location that is a small city with few tall buildings. Other small cities may be different, and cities replete with tall buildings may have very different characteristics. We don't consider situations where the user reverses direction or goes off-path. The speed of the mobile node was dictated by local traffic, but otherwise the driver went at speeds appropriate to each road. We have no data on walking or bicycling targets.

We used Subsonic[5] to stream a constant bitrate mp3 from our server to the phone, resetting the cache before each run. However, a real target might not stream data the entire length of the path (or at all), and hence we gave the attacker an advantage. Further, we did not model the complexities of commercial streaming services, which may not stream from a single location on the network. Finally, our measurements do not include any competing traffic flows to or from the phone during trace collection, which may complicate classification in practice.

5.2   Differentiating Stationary and Mobile Users

In our first experiment, we compare our instances of data from stationary phones against those from mobile phones. In this set of experiments, all stationary traces are one class, and mobile traces corresponding to each of the routes shown in Figure 1 are treated as the other class. The results are shown in Figure 8. In that figure, we see that the Throughput classifier performs about at parity with the more sophisticated techniques.

---

[5] http://www.subsonic.org

Path	Classes	k-NN	HMM	Thruput	Freq
X to A	2	**83.5%**	**87.6%**	72.2%	70.1%
A to X	2	80.4%	**88.0%**	65.2%	68.5%
X to B	2	**91.2%**	**89.5%**	**89.5%**	50.9%
B to X	2	77.4%	**90.6%**	**88.7%**	54.7%
X to C	2	**83.3%**	80.0%	78.3%	51.7%
C to X	2	**84.5%**	**86.2%**	**77.6%**	50.0%
X to D	2	81.1%	**84.9%**	**88.7%**	54.7%
D to X	2	87.5%	**93.8%**	**87.5%**	60.4%

Fig. 8. Classification accuracy for differentiating *stationary* vs. *mobile users*. Bolded entries have the highest accuracy; also bolded are entries that are not statistically different from the highest rate (one-sided, two-sample proportion test; 95% c.i.). In general, mean throughput is mostly sufficient to make this binary decision, but more sophisticated techniques do slightly better.

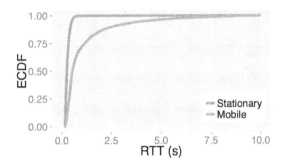

Fig. 9. The empirical CDF of server-side roundtrip time (RTT) estimates for long-running TCP connections when a mobile device is static or moving. The same device is used for both cases. The static scenario demonstrates a noticeably different distribution of estimated RTTs compared to the mobile scenario; RTT is a primary factor in TCP throughput [10].

Why does throughput-based classification work so well in this case? As we show in Figure 9, there are obvious differences in RTT estimates, and RTT is a prominent factor in TCP throughput [10]. Dramatic variations of the estimated RTT are likely the result of the increased number of local link-layer retransmissions, which seek to mitigate the impact of wireless losses on TCP [3]. These retransmissions are more common in our mobile scenarios.

5.3   Determining a User's Path

In our next set of experiments, we assume that user's starting or ending location is known, and that our goal is to determine which of four paths were taken by the mobile. Specifically, we train and test classifiers using only traces that are *Inward* to the central location ("...to X") described in Section 3; then we do so

Experiment	Classes	k-NN	HMM	Thruput	Frequency
4 paths × 1 direction (Inward)	4	**78.5%**	**75.6%**	67.4%	46.7%
4 paths × 1 direction (Outward)	4	**78.1%**	**70.9%**	48.3%	45.0%
4 paths × 2 directions	8	**63.3%**	39.5%	29.0%	23.8%
4 paths × either direction	4	**77.3%**	**72.7%**	57.3%	45.8%

Fig. 10. Classification accuracy for each classifier in different scenarios, discussed in Sections 5.3 and 5.4. Bold entries correspond to highest achieved values (following the same rule of significance from Figure 8).

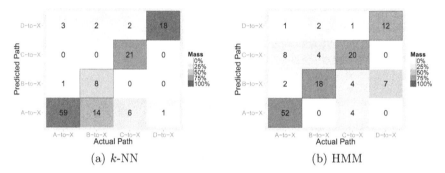

(a) k-NN   (b) HMM

Fig. 11. Confusion Matrices for the *Inwards* scenarios. The number in cell (x, y) shows the count of paths of type x that were classified as path y using our (a) k-NN and (b) HMM-based classifiers. Cells are shaded to show the mass of each distribution (by column); a perfect classifier would have non-zero entries on only the diagonal.

again, using only *Outward* ("X to ..."). Each set of experiments thus considers four classes. The results of these experiments are shown in Figure 10.

In these experiments, the k-NN and HMM-based classifiers significantly outperform the naive classifiers. In line with our intuition, we find that throughput alone does not adequately differentiate routes.

Figure 11 provides finer details on the k-NN and HMM classifier results for the *Inward* paths. While the classifiers do well in labeling most paths correctly, two particular types of error stand out. The k-NN classifier misclassifies many instances into the A-to-X class. This error is partly because throughput for a path may have an increased variance at times, particularly in areas of unstable signal. Since A-to-X is the most common class, it tends to win a majority in the voting if certain parts of a trace don't clearly match another class.

The HMM tends to conflate paths involving endpoints A and C, and paths involving B and D. Upon further analysis, we realized that these two paths contained instances that include long periods of high throughput (in the former case) or little to no throughput (in the latter) and thus there is more similarity between the HMMs trained for those classes. This effect can be seen in the distribution of throughputs for these routes in Figure 12. In general, paths that cover the same geographical area in different directions exhibit similar

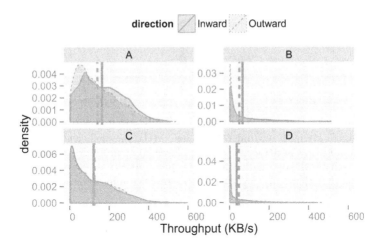

Fig. 12. Per-route distribution of throughput across all traces gathered on each path shown in Figure 1. Vertical lines denote the mean value for the corresponding distribution. Since per-route differences in throughput are the basis for classification, routes with similar distributions are more likely to be misclassified as one another, such as routes involving B and D in our experiments.

throughput distributions, resulting in a lowering of accuracy for classifiers that do not consider sequence information.

As we discussed in Section 3, the reason classification is possible is that throughput is geographically consistent in our dataset (See Figure 5). The experiments in this section demonstrate that path-level classification can make meaningful use of such consistency. Further, we see a correlation of signal strength and throughput at a path- and trace-level of granularity that is stronger than at the per-second granularity reported in Figure 3. The mean throughput observed at the server for each route has strong positive correlation of 0.89 with the median signal strength on that route. Figure 13(left) shows the linear fit for each of the eight paths in our mobile traces. The high correlation between per-route mean throughput and median signal strength suggests that route classification based on throughput means or distributions — as performed using the k-NN, HMM, or Closest Mean Throughput method — should capture some information about the location of the mobile phone.

We found a positive correlation of 0.58 at a per-trace level, shown in Figure 13(right). This drop in correlation — and the even smaller correlation of 0.38 at the per-second level — speaks to the challenge of this task: network performance is generally consistent for a path but it weakens significantly for shorter time scales. Additional features from the network traffic are likely needed to advance classification accuracy to work with finer time scales or geographies. In the next subsection, we investigate how these classifiers scale.

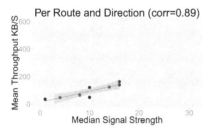
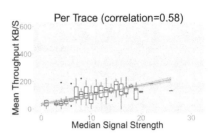

Fig. 13. The mean throughput for each route has strong positive correlation with the median signal strength on that route. The correlation coefficient is 0.89 per-route-and-direction, and 0.58 per-trace. (Note that it was 0.38 in Figure 3, which was a per-second granularity.) The correlation increases as granularity decreases, which supports our hypothesis that there are consistent effects of geography upon throughput.

Path	Classes	k-NN	HMM	Thruput	Frequency
A	2	**74.8%**	64.1%	60.3%	51.9%
B	2	**84.6%**	67.3%	57.7%	53.8%
C	2	**76.7%**	31.7%	46.7%	51.7%
D	2	**79.1%**	51.2%	**65.1%**	55.8%

Fig. 14. Classifier accuracy when determining direction of travel on a given path. Bold entries correspond to highest achieved categories (following the same rule of significance from Figure 8). Only the k-NN classifier includes sequence information in its model of paths, and it is consistently in the highest-achieving category.

5.4   Scaling and Direction-Insensitivity

Do our techniques scale beyond choosing one of four paths? While we cannot answer this question generally, we can artificially increase the number of choices the attacker has by considering each path in each direction as a separate class, giving us eight possible classes corresponding to the eight routes in Figure 2.

Our results are shown in the "2 directions" row of Figure 10. The accuracy of all methods except for the k-NN classifier collapses: it achieves a reasonable 63.3%, statistically significantly above the others. The HMM classifier at 39.5% scores statistically significantly above the Throughput and Frequency classifiers at 29.0% and 23.8%; the latter two are not significantly different from one another. Two questions arise: Why does performance decrease with more options? And why does the k-NN classifier do so much better than the others?

A key way that the k-NN classifier differs from the other three is that it considers the sequence information, whereas the other three discard or condense it. We conjecture that this additional information enables the k-NN classifier to perform well when some paths are essentially mirror images of one another, and we explore this conjecture with two more experiments.

First, we trained and tested the classifiers on each of the four paths in a direction-insensitive manner; that is, we gave paths from A to X and from X to A the same label (simply "A"), and so on. The results, in the row labeled "either direction" of Figure 10, show that the classifiers return to their previous level of accuracy in this scenario. Second, we trained and tested each classifier on four new scenarios. Each was a binary classification test where the classes were either paths from A to X or from X to A; then either from B to X or from X to B as a separate experiment; and so on. The results are shown in Figure 14; we see that the k-NN classifier consistently performs well, and the other classifiers are not able to distinguish the direction of a path.

Finally, a note on classifier bias. Because we could not control the duration of the paths, we verified that our sequence-based (k-NN) classifier did not perform well merely because paths were different lengths. We implemented a length-based classifier for this purpose (i.e., one that classified based on the duration of a trace). We found that while the length-based classifier performed better than frequency, the accuracy was driven by a different set of paths than the k-NN's correctly classified paths.

5.5   Approaches to Enhancing Privacy

We did not test any approaches for enhancing the privacy of users against this attack, but many existing techniques are likely to be effective. To prevent revealing their travel paths to nosy remote servers, phone users will need to traffic shape or otherwise perturb their data transmission, incurring a performance penalty.

For example, a trusted proxy located outside the cellular network can re-shape traffic before reaching the attacker. As noted in Section 2, we assume the carrier is not assisting the attacker. The proxy could be set up as a VPN, which we suggest not for the encryption but because it is a protocol widely supported by smart phones as a transparent method of redirecting traffic. It is feasible that the mobile device could reshape the traffic on its own. Most simply, it could limit throughput to a peak level that is reasonable across a wide area of the cell network. Or it could enforce regions of zero throughput. Of course, the challenge is to shape traffic in a way that does not overall reduce throughput or the interactivity needed by the application. This type of shaping may be easy for bulk file transfer (low interactivity required), moderately challenging for web browsing (where caching and pre-fetching may help mask throughput ceilings), and very challenging for interactive audio and video calls (where users are most sensitive to throughput limitations and network delay jitter).

6   Related Work

Mobile Phone Localization. Precisely localizing mobile phones or other similar devices on the basis of GSM and other location-explicit information is an active area of research, however, these works use information available only to the mobile user (such as which 802.11 base stations or cell towers are in range [6,11]) or their carrier (such as the pattern of handoffs [2] or other administrative details [14]). In our work, we focus on *remotely* localizing another party based only on a TCP traffic stream rather than local information.

Kune et al. [8] propose a technique to test if a user is present within a small area or absent from a large area by simply listening on the broadcast GSM channel. The focus of their work is on lower layers of GSM communication stack. We did not extend our study to analyze lower layers of 3G, because it is a legal violation in our jurisdiction. And again, our study is concerned with remote observation of network streams over cellular links, and largely treats the cellular infrastructure as a black box.

Xu et al. [14] present an approach for localizing performance measurements in 3G networks. They exploit the predictability of users' mobility pattern to develop a clustering algorithm for grouping related cell sectors and assigning IP performance measurements to fine-grained geographic regions. The proposed technique requires access to the cellular infrastructure. In contrast, our technique for network-based localization requires remote passive observation of the target, and data collection independent from the target and internals of the infrastructure.

Balakrishnan et al. [1] show that individual cell phones can expose different IP addresses to servers within time spans of a few minutes, and find that IP-based geo-localization is "impossible" in cellular networks. They show that application-level latencies can differ greatly among cities thousands of miles apart. Moreover, they show that the variation of latencies in short time spans is not high. Our work is complementary and extends similar notions further: we show the consistency of throughput at the finer granularity of square-kilometer regions, and we demonstrate successful classification experiments using such features.

Xu et al. [15] show that in contrast to wired Internet traffic, current cellular data traffic traverses through a limited number (4–6) of Gateway GPRS Support Node (GGSNs), which is the first IP hop of a data connection. The authors show that local DNS servers provide an appropriate approximation to estimate a user's network location (i.e., one of the 6 GGNs) for purposes of mobile content placement and server selection, due to the restricted routing in cellular networks. By assuming availability of partial information about the possible routes a user could be on, our approach aims at a much more granular localization than the DNS method proposed by Xu et al., which is limited to finding approximate network locations.

Other Remote Attacks. Kohno et al. [7] present a technique for fingerprinting a physical device remotely by exploiting clock skews. Their approach could be used to remotely identify the same device connected to the Internet at different times or using different IP addresses. Our approach, which is focused on detecting the routes taken by a mobile node, is orthogonal to this work and could benefit from it when locating the end-points of a target's travel path.

NAT and firewall policies of cellular carriers are explored in the work by Wang et al. [12]. They identify a set of such policies that directly impact performance, energy, and security of mobile devices. For instance, they show that NAT boxes and firewalls set timeouts for idle TCP connections, which sometimes lead to significant waste of energy on the mobile device. The authors show that in spite of deployment of firewalls, cellular networks are still vulnerable to denial of service and battery draining attacks. We explore another type of attack on the location privacy of mobile cellular users.

Case Law. Can the U.S. government, as a third party, obtain the throughput information needed for remote localization? Recently, in *U.S. v. Jones (No. 101259)*, the Supreme Court ruled that law enforcement need a warrant to remotely track a person's location through prolonged use of a GPS device. In that case, a GPS device was placed by the government on the target's car, which was considered a trespass by the majority opinion. In contrast, in our scenario the government would obtain only the size of packets received by a third party, assuming the government already knew through physical observation the starting or ending point of a target's journey. Acquisition of such signaling information does not usually require a warrant or wiretap because it is not content (see *Smith v. Maryland, 442 U.S. 735 (1979)*). Accordingly, recent cases involving acquisition of cell site information may be more relevant than *Jones*, but the issue is unsettled. For a summary of recent rulings on cell sites, see footnotes 8 and 9 in an opinion [6] from the *Jones* retrial.

7   Conclusion and Open Problems

We have demonstrated that the patterns of data transmission between a server on the Internet and a moving cell phone can reveal the geographic travel path of that phone. While the GPS and location-awareness features on phones explicitly share this information, phone users will likely be surprised to learn that disabling these features does not suffice to prevent a remote server from determining their general mobility. Our work shows that a simple k-nearest neighbor classifier can discover and exploit features of the geography surrounding possible travel paths to determine the path a phone took, using only data visible at the remote server on the Internet and training data collected independently.

It is an open and important problem to quantify the extent to which a user's location can be compromised in this fashion — with greater accuracy and among larger numbers of paths and different geographies — and to determine just how much information is needed to make these inferences. We conjecture that preprocessing of the data — smoothing or aligning the sequences — may more readily reveal patterns within a given path. Other algorithms may also improve the attacker's performance: for example, we have implemented a discrete left-right HMM, which models the sequence of changing throughput distributions along a path, with limited success. We anticipate that performance may improve with smoothed data or a more apt model, such as one with continuous observations. A model representing a user's position in 2-D space rather than along a specific path would allow an attacker to more easily identify user location in a real-world scenario. Finally, the ability to classify shorter traces would allow an attacker to deduce location with finer granularity.

---

[6] http://www.gpo.gov/fdsys/pkg/USCOURTS-dcd-1_05-cr-00386/pdf/
USCOURTS-dcd-1_05-cr-00386-9.pdf

Acknowledgements. This work was supported in part by NSF award CNS-0905349. We thank Mark Corner for early discussions of this work.

References

1. Balakrishnan, M., Mohomed, I., Ramasubramanian, V.: Where's that phone? Geolocating IP addresses on 3G networks. In: ACM IMC, pp. 294–300 (2009)
2. Becker, R.A., Caceres, R., Hanson, K., Loh, J.M., Urbanek, S., Varshavsky, A., Volinsky, C.: Route classification using cellular handoff patterns. In: ACM UbiComp, pp. 123–132 (2011)
3. Chan, M.C., Ramjee, R.: TCP/IP performance over 3G wireless links with rate and delay variation. In: ACM MobiCom, pp. 71–82 (2002)
4. Franken, A.: The Location Privacy Protection Act of 2011 (S. 1223) information sheet (2011), http://www.franken.senate.gov/files/documents/121011_LocationPrivacyProtection.pdf
5. Goldstein, M.L., et al.: Mobile Device Location Data (United States Government Accountability Office) (September 2012), http://www.gao.gov/assets/650/648044.pdf
6. Hightower, J., LaMarca, A., Smith, I.: Practical Lessons from Place Lab. IEEE Pervasive Computing 5(3), 32–39 (2006)
7. Kohno, T., Broido, A., Claffy, K.: Remote physical device fingerprinting. IEEE Trans. on Dependable and Secure Computing 2(2), 93–108 (2005)
8. Kune, D.F., Koelndorfer, J., Hopper, N., Kim, Y.: Location leaks on the GSM Air Interface. In: ISOC NDSS (February 2012)
9. Open Standards for Real-Time Bidding (RTB): OpenRTB Mobile RTB API v1.0 (February 2011), https://code.google.com/p/openrtb/downloads
10. Padhye, J., Firoiu, V., Towsley, D.F., Kurose, J.F.: Modeling TCP Reno Performance. IEEE/ACM Trans. Netw. 8(2), 133–145 (2000)
11. Thiagarajan, A., Ravindranath, L., Balakrishnan, H., Madden, S., Girod, L.: Accurate, Low-Energy Trajectory Mapping for Mobile Devices. In: USENIX NSDI (March 2011)
12. Wang, Z., Qian, Z., Xu, Q., Mao, Z., Zhang, M.: An untold story of middleboxes in cellular networks. In: ACM SIGCOMM, pp. 374–385 (August 2011)
13. Xing, Z., Pei, J., Keogh, E.: A brief survey on sequence classification. SIGKDD Explor. Newsl. 12(1), 40–48 (2010)
14. Xu, Q., Gerber, A., Mao, Z., Pang, J.: AccuLoc: practical localization of performance measurements in 3G networks. In: ACM MobiSys, pp. 183–196 (August 2011)
15. Xu, Q., Huang, J., Wang, Z., Qian, F., Gerber, A., Mao, Z.: Cellular data network infrastructure characterization and implication on mobile content placement. In: ACM SIGMETRICS, pp. 317–328 (2011)

How Others Compromise Your Location Privacy: The Case of Shared Public IPs at Hotspots

Nevena Vratonjic[1], Kévin Huguenin[1],
Vincent Bindschaedler[2,*], and Jean-Pierre Hubaux[1]

[1] School of Computer and Communication Sciences, EPFL, Switzerland
[2] Department of Computer Science, UIUC, USA

Abstract. Location privacy has been extensively studied over the last few years, especially in the context of location-based services where users purposely disclose their location to benefit from convenient context-aware services. To date, however, little attention has been devoted to the case of users' location being unintentionally compromised *by others*.

In this paper, we study a concrete and widespread example of such situations, specifically the location-privacy threat created by access points (e.g., public hotspots) using network address translation (NAT). Indeed, because users connected to the same hotspot share a unique public IP, a single user making a location-based request is enough to enable a service provider to map the IP of the hotspot to its geographic coordinates, thus compromising the location privacy of all the other connected users. When successful, the service provider can locate users within a few hundreds of meters, thus improving over existing IP-location databases. Even in the case where IPs change periodically (e.g., by using DHCP), the service provider is still able to update a previous (IP, Location) mapping by inferring IP changes from authenticated communications (e.g., cookies).

The contribution of this paper is three-fold: (i) We identify a novel threat to users' location privacy caused by the use of shared public IPs. (ii) We formalize and analyze theoretically the threat. The resulting framework can be applied to any access-point to quantify the privacy threat. (iii) We experimentally assess the state in practice by using real traces of users accessing Google services, collected from deployed hotspots. Also, we discuss how existing countermeasures can thwart the threat.

1 Introduction

With the ubiquity of mobile devices with advanced capabilities, it is becoming the norm for users to be constantly connected to the Internet; users can benefit from many online services while on-the-go. Among others, location-based services (LBSs) are increasingly gaining popularity. With an LBS, users share their location information with a service provider in return for context-aware services, such as finding nearby restaurants. Users also enjoy sharing location information with their friends on social networks (e.g., Facebook and Twitter) [26].

---

* Parts of this work were carried out while Vincent Bindschaedler was with EPFL.

E. De Cristofaro and M. Wright (Eds.): PETS 2013, LNCS 7981, pp. 123–142, 2013.

Although very convenient, the usage of LBSs raises serious privacy issues. Location privacy is a particularly acute problem as location information is valuable to many parties, because much of information can be inferred from users' locations (e.g., users' interests and activities). Location information is essential for many online service providers [13], especially for those whose business models revolve around personalized services. A prominent example is online advertising, an ever-increasing business with large revenues (e.g., $22.4 billion in the US in 2011 [28]), as so-called location-specific ads based on the location information are significantly more appealing to users [20].

Typically, users willingly disclose their location only to LBS providers. Yet, non-LBS providers can obtain users' locations through *IP-location*: determining the location of a device from its IP. Existing IP-location services rely either on (i) active techniques, typically based on network measurements [21], or (ii) passive techniques, consisting of databases with records of IP-location mappings [19, 24]. Active techniques provide more accurate results, however they incur high measurement overhead and a high response time (in the range of several seconds to several minutes) to localize a single IP. A passive approach is usually much faster and thus preferred by service operators. A number of IP-location databases are available, either free (e.g., HostIP [19]) or commercial (e.g., MaxMind [24]). Some databases contain records of landmark IPs for which the location can be inferred (e.g., institutions [37] or websites that post their location [17]) and other IPs are geolocated relatively to these landmarks. However, they provide at most a city-level accuracy and most of the entries refer only to a few countries [27]. For instance, MaxMind reports to correctly geo-locate, within a radius of 40 km, 81% of IP addresses in the US and 60%-80% in Europe. This level of accuracy is effective for regional advertising but is not sufficient for local businesses (e.g., bars) which require neighborhood or street-level accuracy [20]. Thus, major Web companies, including Google, are actively working on improving IP-location[1].

Service providers can also obtain a user's location via transitivity, relying on users to disclose their location and that of others in their vicinity: if a provider knows the location of user B and that user A is close to B, the provider knows roughly the location of A. Such situations arise when users report neighboring users (e.g., Bluetooth), or *check-in* on online social networks (OSNs) and tag friends they are with. In some cases, even if the proximity information is not directly revealed by users, a provider can still infer it, as we will show.

In this paper, we study a location-privacy threat users are exposed to on a daily basis. When a user connects to the Internet through the same access point (AP) as other users (e.g., a public hotspot, home router) who make LBS queries, the service provider learns the user's location. Indeed, because all of the devices connected to a public hotspot, implementing network address translation, share the AP's public IP, when users generate LBS queries, the service provider learns the location of the AP and maps it to the AP's public IP. IPs remain the same

---

[1] Google reports an accuracy of 95% at the region-level and 75% at the city-level, with high variance across countries, and seeks to improve it to the street-level [14].

for a certain amount of time, thus for any connection for which the source IP is the same as the AP's IP, the service provider can conclude that the device is located nearby the location of the AP. The accuracy of the estimated location depends on the range of the AP (typically under one hundred meters) and on the accuracy of the locations reported by users in LBS queries (typically under ten meters with GPS-geolocation). Thus, it is significantly more accurate than the existing IP-location databases. The fact that the threat is based on observing the user's IP, which might be inferred, e.g., by using a Java applet [25], even when the client tries to hide it, makes the threat even more difficult to evade.

The (IP, Location) mapping the adversary obtains for the AP stays valid until the IP changes. Dynamic IP addresses (provided that IPs are allocated to geo-diverse hosts), short DHCP leases, and systematic assignment of new IPs upon DHCP lease expiration therefore have a positive effect on location privacy. However, even when the IP is renewed and changes, service providers have means to learn about the IP change, for example, due to the widespread use of *authenticated* services (e.g., e-mails, OSNs). Consider a user connected to the AP who checks her e-mail shortly before and after an IP change. As a unique authentication cookie is appended to both requests, the service provider can conclude that the same user has connected with a new IP and can therefore update the (IP, Location) mapping with the new IP. In fact, it is sufficient that the service provider is able to link the requests to the same user, based on cookies, user agent strings, or any fingerprinting technique, e.g., [39].

The contribution of this paper is three-fold: (i) We identify the location-privacy threat that arises from the use of shared public IPs. Because the problem is inherent in the way networks (i.e., NAT) operate and its wide deployment, the potential impact of the threat is significant. The expected accuracy of locating affected users is about few hundreds of meters. (ii) We formalize and analyze the problem theoretically and we provide a framework to estimate the location-privacy threat, namely the probability of a user being localized by a service provider. The framework is easily applicable to any access point setting: it employs our closed-form solution and takes as input an AP's parameters (i.e., a few aggregated parameters, such as user connection and traffic rates, that can be extracted from logs) and it quantifies the potential threat. It is a light-weight alternative to extensive traffic analysis. The framework thus constitutes a valuable input to model sporadic location exposure. (iii) We evaluate experimentally the scale of the threat based on real traces of users accessing Google services, collected for a period of one month from deployed hotspots. Even at a moderately visited hotspot, we observe the large scale of the threat: the service provider, namely Google, learns the location of the AP only about an hour after users start connecting and within 24 hours he can locate up to 73% of the users. Finally, we discuss how existing countermeasures could thwart the threat. To the best of our knowledge, this is the first paper that addresses the problem of users' locations being exposed by others at NAT access points.

2 Background

In this section, we provide relevant background on the technical aspects under-lying the considered problem.

IPv4 (public) Address Allocation. To communicate on the Internet, hosts need public IP addresses. An IP can be either *static*, i.e., permanently fixed, or *dynamic*, i.e., periodically obtained from a pool of available addresses, typically through the Dynamic Host Configuration Protocol (DHCP). Dynamic IP is used for a limited amount of time specified by the *DHCP lease*. For convenience, upon DHCP lease expiration, hosts are often re-assigned the same IP. A large-scale study shows that over one month, less than 1% of the hosts used more than one IP and less than 0.07% used more than three IPs [4]. More than 62% of dynamic IPs on average remain the same over a period of at least 24 hours [38].

Network Address Translation (NAT). NAT hides an entire IP address space, usually consisting of private IPs, behind one or several public IPs. It is typically used in Local Area Networks (LANs), where each device has a private IP, including the gateway router that runs NAT. The router is connected to the Internet with a public IP assigned by an ISP. As traffic is routed from the LAN to the Internet, the private source IP in each packet is translated on-the-fly to the public IP of the router: traffic from all of the hosts in the LAN appears with the same public IP–the public IP of the NAT router. A study shows that about 60% of users are behind NATs [4].

Geolocation. Mobile devices determine their positions by using their embed-ded GPS or an online geolocation service. With a GPS, the computation takes place locally by using satellites' positions and a time reference. Commercial GPS provides highly accurate results (< 10 meters) [35], especially in "open sky" en-vironments. With online geolocation services (e.g., Skyhook) a device typically shares the list of nearby cell towers and Wi-Fi APs together with their signal strengths, based on which the server estimates the device's location by using a reference database. Such databases are built mostly by GPS-equipped mobile units that scan for cell towers and Wi-Fi APs and plot their precise geographic locations. Inputs of users with GPS-equipped devices, who provide both their positions and the surrounding stations, are also taken into account. Reported accuracy of such systems is about 10 meters [32].

3 System Model

In this section, we elaborate on the considered setting, notably NAT access points, the location-privacy threat, and the adversary.

3.1 Setting

We consider a *NAT Access Point* setting, a prevalent network configuration, where users connect to the Internet through an access point (AP), such as a public hotspot, a home (wireless) router or an open-community Wi-Fi AP (e.g., FON), as depicted in Fig. 1. An AP, located at (x_1, y_1), is connected to the Internet by a given ISP and provides connectivity to the authorized users. The AP has a single *dynamic public* IP that is allocated with DHCP by the ISP: The AP's public IP is selected from a DHCP pool of available IPs and is valid during the DHCP lease. When connecting to the AP, each device is allocated a *private* IP and the AP performs network address translation (NAT). Consequently, on the Internet, all connections originating from the devices connecting through the AP have the same source IP, which is the public IP of the AP.

While connected to the Internet through an AP, users make use of various online services including search engines, e-mail, social networks, location-based and online geolocation services. Services can be used either in an authenticated (e.g., e-mail) or unauthenticated way (e.g., search). We consider that the requests a server receives from the devices connected to the AP are of the following types:

1. Geolocation requests: `Geo-Req(MACs)`, where MACs refer to the MAC addresses of the APs and cell towers in the range of the device;
2. LBS requests: `LBS-Req((x_0, y_0))`, where (x_0, y_0) denotes the coordinates of the device[2] (assumed close to the AP's location (x_1, y_1)) shared by the user;
3. Authenticated standard (i.e., that are neither LBS nor Geolocation) requests: `Auth-Req(tok)`, where *tok* represents any information that allows for user authentication or linkability of user requests (e.g., a cookie or a username);
4. Unauthenticated standard requests: `Req()`.

With LBS requests, the service provider obtains the user's location under several forms and by different means. The user can specify her location in free-text (e.g., "bars close to Park and 57th, NYC") or by pin-pointing her location on a map. The location can also be determined by the user's device using one of the techniques described in Section 2 and communicated to the service provider by a mobile application or by her browser through the HTML 5 `getCurrentPosition` JavaScript function. Note that non-LBS applications and websites might access the user's location as well.

Both `Geo-Req` and `LBS-Req` contain an estimate of the AP's coordinates, thus they both enable the server to build the $(IP, (x_1, y_1))$ mapping. Consequently, there is no need to distinguish between these two types of requests, and we simply refer to both as LBS requests. For all types of request, the server knows the source IP, specifically the AP's public IP.

3.2 Adversary and Threat Models

We consider an adversary whose goal is to learn users' current locations, for instance, to make a profit by providing geo-targeted (mobile) ads and recommendations (e.g., a private company). The adversary has access to the information

---

[2] We assume that all LBS requests concern users' actual locations, or that the server has means to distinguish between such requests and other LBS requests. It is the case when the location is obtained directly (see Section 2), and sent to the server.

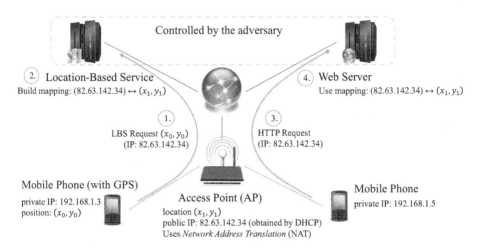

Fig. 1. System and threat model. Devices connect through a NAT access point and share a public IP. A user making an LBS request reveals her location (close to the AP) to the adversary (1) who then builds the (IP,Location) mapping (2). When another user connects to a different server controlled by the adversary (3), the adversary uses the (IP,Location) mapping to locate her as she connects with the same IP (4).

collected by a number of servers that provide online services described above. Companies, such as Google for instance, provide Web search (Google), e-mail (GMail), social networking (Google+), and geolocation and location-based services (Maps). As such, it receives requests of the four types and consolidates the information obtained [15]. The extent to which these services are used is exacerbated by their deep integration in the Android operating system. In addition, Google has an advertising network and thus has a strong incentive to obtain and monetize information about users' locations. As a matter of fact, Google is actively working on improving its IP-location based on users' traffic, in particular by mining queries associated with location (e.g., "best burgers NYC") [14].

Microsoft (with Bing, Hotmail, Bing Maps, and Windows Phones) and Apple (with iCloud and iPhone) are other relevant potential candidates for the considered adversary. Besides these major companies, an alliance of service providers can be envisioned to jointly build an IP-location database: each provider contributes IP-location records of its visitors with known locations and benefits from the database for the IPs of users connecting from unknown locations. This joint effort can be coordinated by an ad network that is common to the participating service providers. This approach extends the potential of the threat as it increases the set of potential adversaries: it alleviates the need for each service to receive all three types of requests and a significant fraction of user traffic.

In this paper, we focus on the case where the adversary has access to all four types of requests. The adversary is assumed to be *honest-but-curious*, meaning that he passively collects information but does not deviate from the specified protocol (e.g., implementing active techniques to retrieve users' locations).

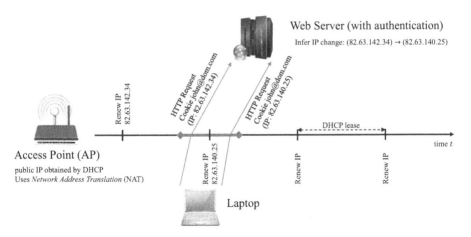

Fig. 2. AP's IP address renewal and updating of the (IP, Location) mapping. A user generates an authenticated request (with a unique cookie) during a DHCP lease interval in which the adversary has obtained the (IP, Location) mapping, shortly before the DHCP lease expires and the AP is assigned a new IP. Shortly after the IP change, the same user generates another authenticated request (with the same cookie) from the new IP. As both requests occurred in a short time interval, the adversary can infer that the AP's IP changed from 82.63.142.34 to 82.63.140.25 and update the mapping.

Given such an adversarial model, we consider the threat of the adversary who learns the location of a user without it being explicitly disclosed: The threat comes from the fact that the adversary can build mappings between an AP's IP and its geographic coordinates based on LBS requests he receives from other users connected to the AP. Because all requests (from devices connected through the AP) share the same public IP, the adversary can subsequently infer the location of the other users. More specifically, considering the example depicted in Fig. 1, when the LBS provider's server (controlled by the adversary) receives an LBS request for position (x_0, y_0), which is the actual position of the user (located close to the AP) determined by her GPS-equipped mobile phone, the server can map the AP's public IP (i.e., 82.63.142.34) to the approximated AP's location (i.e., $(x_1, y_1) \approx (x_0, y_0)$). Note that the accuracy of the AP's estimated location depends on the GPS accuracy of the user-reported location and the range of the AP. Later, when another user, connected through the AP, makes a request to a server (also controlled by the adversary), then the adversary exploits the obtained mapping and infers from the source IP that the second user is at the same location (i.e., (x_1, y_1)). The adversary can subsequently provide geo-targeted ads. If the adversary is interested in tracking users, he can locate any user who makes an authenticated request before the IP changes.

We assume that the IP addresses in the DHCP pool can be assigned to clients at very distant locations [10]. For instance, some nation-wide ISPs (e.g., SFR in France) assign IPs among the whole set of their clients scattered all over the country. Consequently, the fact that the AP's public IP is dynamic limits in time the extent of the threat: If the AP is assigned a new IP by the ISP, the mapping built by the adversary becomes invalid, unless he is able to infer the IP change. The inference can be based on authenticated requests as depicted in Fig. 2: A request, authenticated by cookie john@dom.com and originating from IP 82.63.142.34, is shortly followed by a request authenticated by the same cookie but originating from a different source IP (i.e., 82.63.140.25). There are two options: either the AP's IP has changed or the user has moved and is now connected from a different AP. If the inference time interval (delimited with diamonds in Fig. 2) around the IP renewal is short enough, then the adversary can infer, with high confidence, that the IP has changed and its new value.

In summary, the problem we study is as follows. Considering a single AP, time is divided into intervals corresponding to DHCP leases, during which the AP's public IP address remains the same. At a certain point in time, the adversary knows the location of the AP associated to the IP because (i) a user made an LBS request earlier in the time interval or (ii) the adversary knew the location corresponding to the public IP address from the previous interval **and** a user made an authenticated request shortly before and after the public IP address was renewed. The location-privacy threat is to be evaluated with respect to the number of users whose locations are known by the adversary. In the case of geo-targeted mobile ads, the adversary needs to know the location of the user *when* the user makes a requests: the victims are therefore the users who make a standard request *after* the adversary learns the (IP, Location) mapping (during the same DHCP lease). If the adversary is interested in tracking users, he can maintain a log of the users who connected during a DHCP lease and sent requests, and locate them *a posteriori* if he learns the (IP, Location) mapping at some point during the same DHCP lease: the victims are the users who make an authenticated request *during* a DHCP lease in which the adversary learns the (IP, Location) mapping. In this paper, we evaluate the threat with respect to an adversary who aims to exploit *current* location information through geo-targeted ads. However, it is possible to mount more powerful attacks on users' privacy (e.g., track users over time) based on the identified threat.

4   Formalization and Analysis

In this section, we model the aforementioned setting and we build a framework to quantify theoretically the location-privacy threat.

4.1   Model

We consider an access point AP, an honest-but-curious adversary $\mathcal{A}$, and a set of users who connect to AP and make requests to servers controlled by $\mathcal{A}$. We study the system over the continuous time interval $[0, +\infty)$. At each time instant t, AP has a single public IP. Every T time units, starting at time 0, the DHCP lease expires and AP is either re-assigned the same IP or allocated a new one. We model this by independent random variables drawn from a Bernoulli distribution:

with probability p_{New} AP is assigned a new IP, and with probability $1 - p_{\text{New}}$ it is re-assigned the same IP. We divide time into successive sub-intervals I_k, $k \geq 0$, of duration T, corresponding to the DHCP leases: $I_k = [kT, (k+1)T]$. Without loss of generality, we assume the duration of IP leases to be constant. Each sub-interval is aligned with a DHCP lease. Therefore, within each sub-interval AP's public IP remains unchanged. For any time instant t, we denote by $\bar{t}$, the relative time within the corresponding sub-interval, that is $\bar{t} = t \mod T$.

Users connect to AP, remain connected for a certain time and then disconnect. While connected, users make requests, each of which is of one of the following types: LBS, authenticated, or standard. All modeling choices in this section follow well-established conventions [30]–e.g., Poisson processes are known to fit well users arrival and access to services–and are backed up by several public Wi-Fi hotspot workload analysis (e.g., [11]). In addition, we assess the validity of these assumptions by using traffic traces, collected from a deployed network of access points, in [36]. We model users who arrive and connect to AP by a homogeneous Poisson process with intensity λ_{Arr}. We denote the time users stay connected to AP by T_{Dur}, which follows an exponential distribution with average $\frac{1}{\lambda_{\text{Dur}}}$. We assume the system to be stationary with respect to user connections and disconnections. Based on Little's law [30], the average number of connected users at any time instant t is constant and given by: $N_{\text{Con}} = \lambda_{\text{Arr}}/\lambda_{\text{Dur}}$.

Users generate requests independently of each other. For each user, the three types of requests she makes are also independent: Standard and authenticated requests are modeled by independent homogeneous[3] Poisson processes with intensity λ_{Std} and λ_{Auth}, respectively. We assume that each user makes a request when she connects to AP. For instance, e-mail or RSS clients automatically connect to a server when an Internet connection is available. We assume that only a proportion α_{LBS} of the users make LBS requests, and we model such requests by independent homogeneous Poisson processes with intensity λ_{LBS} for each user.

Fig. 3 depicts the user arrivals, departures, standard and LBS request processes and illustrates the key notations and concepts introduced in this section.

4.2   Threat

We first focus on a single sub-interval and quantify the location-privacy threat, with respect to the number of users whose locations are disclosed to the adversary because of others. Specifically, we call a *victim* a user who makes a standard request at a time at which the adversary knows the (IP, Location) mapping.

Quantifying the Threat in a Sub-interval. If at least one user connected to AP uses an LBS at some time instant (thus revealing her current location), $\mathcal{A}$ obtains the (IP, Location) mapping based on which it can locate other users.

We define the *compromise time* T_{Comp} as the first time within the sub-interval, when a user connected to AP uses an LBS. If such an event does not occur, the compromise time is equal to T. At any time, there are on average

---

[3] We use homogeneous Poisson processes for simplicity. A model using inhomogeneous processes with piece-wise constant intensity is available as a technical report [36].

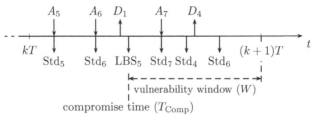

Fig. 3. Threat caused by a user making an LBS request. A_i and D_i represent User i's arrival and departure, respectively. Users 1 and 4 are already present at time kT. The time at which the first LBS request is made (LBS_5) is called the *compromise time* (T_{Comp}). From time T_{Comp} on, any user who makes a standard request is a victim. Users already connected at T_{Comp} are victims if they make a standard request after T_{Comp}, e.g., User 4. Users who connect after T_{Comp} are, *de facto*, victims as users make a standard request when they connect, e.g., User 7.

N_{Con} users connected to AP, out of which $\alpha_{\text{LBS}} N_{\text{Con}}$ potentially make LBS queries. The aggregated process of LBS requests is a Poisson process with intensity $\Lambda_{\text{LBS}} = \alpha_{\text{LBS}} N_{\text{Con}} \lambda_{\text{LBS}}$. Therefore, the expected compromise time is $\frac{1}{\Lambda_{\text{LBS}}}(1 - e^{-\Lambda_{\text{LBS}} T})$. We call $F_{\text{Comp}}(\bar{t})$ the probability that at least one LBS query (from the aggregated process) is made before time $\bar{t}$ in the sub-interval and f_{Comp} the corresponding probability density function. The time interval that spans from the compromise time to the end of the sub-interval is called the *vulnerability window* (see Fig. 3) and the expected value of its duration W is

$$\mathbf{E}\left[W\right] = T - \frac{1 - e^{-\Lambda_{\text{LBS}} T}}{\Lambda_{\text{LBS}}}. \tag{1}$$

Fig. 4 depicts the cumulative distribution function of the compromise time and its average value in an example setting. We observe that even with moderate AP popularity and LBS usage, the adversary obtains the mapping before the DHCP lease expires in 83% of the cases and he does so after 11 hours on average.

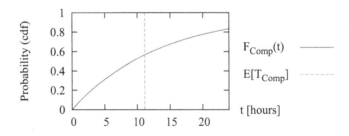

Fig. 4. Cumulative distribution function of the compromise time T_{Comp} (expressed in hours). The parameters were set to $T = 24$ h, $\lambda_{\text{Arr}} = 5$ users/h, $\lambda_{\text{Dur}} = 1/1.5$ (i.e., average connection time of one hour and a half), $\lambda_{\text{LBS}} = 0.05$ req./h, and $\alpha_{\text{LBS}} = 0.2$.

To compute the number of victims, we distinguish between two groups of users: those who were already connected when the first LBS request was made, e.g., User 6 in Fig. 3, and those who connected during the vulnerability window (and are, *de facto*, victims as they make a standard request when they connect), e.g., User 7. We call V the number of victims. It can be shown that (see [36]):

$$\mathbf{E}\left[V\right] = \frac{N_{\mathrm{Con}} \Lambda_{\mathrm{LBS}} \lambda_{\mathrm{Std}}}{(\lambda_{\mathrm{Std}} + \lambda_{\mathrm{Dur}}) - \Lambda_{\mathrm{LBS}}} \cdot \left[\frac{1 - e^{-\Lambda_{\mathrm{LBS}}T}}{\Lambda_{\mathrm{LBS}}} - \frac{1 - e^{-(\lambda_{\mathrm{Std}} + \lambda_{\mathrm{Dur}})T}}{(\lambda_{\mathrm{Std}} + \lambda_{\mathrm{Dur}})}\right] + \lambda_{\mathrm{Arr}}\left(T - \frac{1 - e^{-\Lambda_{\mathrm{LBS}}T}}{\Lambda_{\mathrm{LBS}}}\right). \quad (2)$$

This number has to be compared to the average number of users who have been connected at some point within the sub-interval: $V_{\mathrm{tot}} = N_{\mathrm{Con}} + \lambda_{\mathrm{Arr}}T$. It can be seen in Fig. 5 that the proportion of victims $\mathbf{E}\left[V\right]/V_{\mathrm{tot}}$ increases with T. This is because all users who connect after the compromise time are victims. When the DHCP lease expires, the location of more than half of the users is compromised.

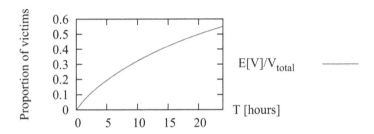

Fig. 5. Proportion of victims within a sub-interval of length T, corresponding to a DHCP lease. The parameters were set to: $\lambda_{\mathrm{Arr}} = 5$ users/h, $\lambda_{\mathrm{Dur}} = 1$ (i.e., average connection time of one hour), $\lambda_{\mathrm{Std}} = 10$ req./h, $\lambda_{\mathrm{LBS}} = 0.05$ req./h, and $\alpha_{\mathrm{LBS}} = 0.2$.

Inferring IP Change. We consider two successive sub-intervals, without loss of generality I_0 and I_1, and we look at the linking probability F_{Link} that the adversary infers the IP change from authenticated requests. This occurs if at least one user makes both an authenticated request at most ΔT time units ($\Delta T < T/2$) before, and another authenticated request at most ΔT time units after, the IP change. An expression of the probability F_{Link} of inferring the IP change can be derived by distinguishing between the users who were connected at time $T - \Delta T$ and those who connected within $[T - \Delta T, T]$ (see [36]).

The linking probability can be thought of as depending both on t and ΔT. Fig. 6a depicts the linking probability as a function of t. It remains constant for $t \geq T + \Delta T$ because only authenticated requests made in the time interval $[T - \Delta T, T + \Delta T]$ are taken into account to infer the IP change. Note that with a value of ΔT as small as 5 minutes, which provides high confidence, the adversary can still infer the IP change with a probability of 43%.

Fig. 6b depicts the linking probability at time $T + \Delta T$ as a function of ΔT. It can be observed that this probability rapidly converges to 1. Note that the fact that linking probability increases with ΔT is balanced by the decreased confidence of the adversary. This is because the probability that a user makes two authenticated requests from two distinct access points in the time interval $[T - \Delta T, T + \Delta T]$ (moving from one to the other) increases with ΔT.

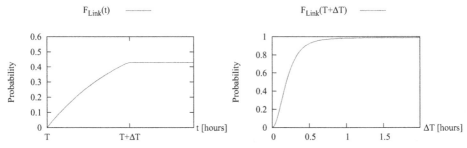

(a) Probability of inferring the IP change before time $t > T$ ($\Delta T = 5$ min)

(b) Linking probability at time $T + \Delta T$

Fig. 6. Linking probability. The parameters were set to $\lambda_{\text{Arr}} = 5$ users/h, $\lambda_{\text{Dur}} = 1/1.5$, $\lambda_{\text{Std}} = 10$ req./h, $\lambda_{\text{LBS}} = 0.05$ req./h, $\lambda_{\text{Auth}} = 2$ req./h, and $\alpha_{\text{LBS}} = 0.2$.

Quantifying the Threat over Multiple Sub-intervals. We now look at the probability (F_{Map}) of the adversary having the mapping, which is a combination of the probabilities that the compromise happens due to LBS usage (F_{Comp}) and the probability of having the mapping and inferring the IP change upon the lease expiration (F_{Link}), over successive sub-intervals. The probability $F_{\text{Map}}^{(k)}(t)$ that the adversary knows the mapping at time $t \in I_k$, $k \geq 1$ is

$$F_{\text{Map}}^{(k)}(\bar{t}) = F_{\text{Comp}}(\bar{t}) + (1 - F_{\text{Comp}}(\bar{t})) \cdot F_{\text{Map}}^{(k-1)}(T) \cdot ((1 - p_{\text{New}}) + p_{\text{New}} F_{\text{Link}}(\bar{t})) \quad (3)$$

with initial condition $F_{\text{Map}}^{(0)}(\bar{t}) = F_{\text{Comp}}(\bar{t})$. From Equation (3), it can be seen that $F_{\text{Map}}^{(k)}(T)$ obeys the following recursive equation:

$$F_{\text{Map}}^{(k)}(T) = a + b F_{\text{Map}}^{(k-1)}(T)$$

where $a = F_{\text{Comp}}(T)$ and $b = (1 - F_{\text{Comp}}(T)) \cdot ((1 - p_{\text{New}}) + p_{\text{New}} F_{\text{Link}}(T))$. This recursive equation has $a(1 - b^{k+1})/(1 - b)$ as a solution. As $b < 1$, $F_{\text{Map}}^{(k)}(T)$ converges to a finite value, i.e., $a/(1 - b)$.

The number of victims in the sub-interval I_k can be computed by replacing the density f_{Comp} with the density of $F_{\text{Map}}^{(k)}$ in the derivation of Equation (2) (see [36]). The probability that the adversary has the mapping (IP, Location) at time t in sub-interval I_k, i.e., $F_{\text{Map}}^{(k)}$ is illustrated in Fig. 7. It can be observed that the mapping probability increases over time and, after the convergence, the adversary successfully obtains the mapping before the DHCP lease expires in 79% of the cases and before the half-lease in 60% of the cases.

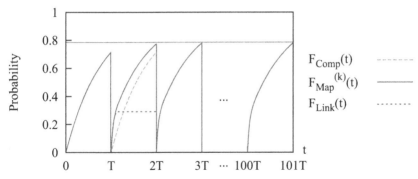

Fig. 7. Probability of knowing the (IP, Location) mapping at time t over several sub-intervals. The solid curve represents the probability of knowing the mapping at time t. The dashed curve represents the probability of obtaining the mapping from an LBS request. The dotted curve represents the probability of inferring the IP change. The parameters were set to $\lambda_{\text{Arr}} = 5$ users/h, $\lambda_{\text{Dur}} = 1/1.5$, $\lambda_{\text{Std}} = 10$ req./h, $\lambda_{\text{LBS}} = 0.035$ req./h, $\lambda_{\text{Auth}} = 0.2$ req./h, $T = 24$ h, $\Delta T = 2$ h, $\alpha_{\text{LBS}} = 0.1$, and $p_{\text{New}} = 1$. To highlight the respective contributions of the linking and compromise probabilities, some values differ from our previous setting (e.g., ΔT). In the first sub-interval, the linking probability is zero and the probability of having the mapping is the compromise probability. In subsequent sub-intervals, the probability $F_{\text{Map}}^{(k)}(t)$ increases due to the potential inference of IP changes: it becomes a combination of $F_{\text{Link}}(\bar{t})$ and $F_{\text{Comp}}(\bar{t})$ (and the probability of having the mapping by the end of the preceding sub-interval).

5   Experimental Results

In this section, we complement our theoretical analysis with experimental results based on traces from a network of Wi-Fi access points deployed at EPFL.

Dataset. Our dataset consists of daily user Wi-Fi *session traces, traffic traces* and *DNS traces* for a period of 23 days in June 2012. We aggregate the data of two APs (in a cafeteria and a library) located very close to each other ($\sim$15 meters), to emulate a single popular hotspot and to avoid side effects of micromobility, i.e., devices frequently changing the AP they are connected to.

Session traces contain information related to users connecting and disconnecting from the APs, obtained from the RADIUS logs. There are three types of RADIUS events: (i) `start` – upon successful authentication the device is assigned an IP denoting the beginning of a session; (ii) `update` – a periodic status message; and (iii) `stop` – a user disconnects denoting the end of the session. Each log entry contains a timestamp, the device's anonymized MAC address (i.e., encrypted with a key that is changed daily), the assigned IP, the ID of the AP the device is connected to, and an event type.

Traffic traces are obtained from the logs at a border router connecting the network to the Internet. Each log entry contains a timestamp, the source IP, and the destination (including the IP and port). The mapping between a user's assigned IP and her MAC address allows to correlate traffic with session traces.

DNS traces are obtained from the local DNS servers. Each log entry contains a timestamp, the source IP and the requested host name. Based on the source IPs, timestamps and requested resources, we correlate DNS with traffic traces.

In total, 4,302 users connected to the AP during 23 days. Users typically begin arriving around 7:AM. The average number of users connected to the AP over a day (averaged over 23 days) increases during the day and peaks around 6:PM (136 users on average). Very few users are connected after midnight.

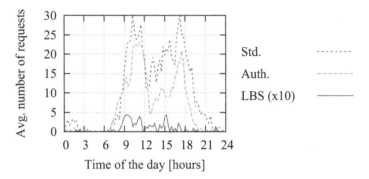

Fig. 8. Average number of std., auth. and LBS requests to the monitored services over a day (averaged over 23 days). For readability reasons, LBS traffic is multiplied by 10.

We filtered traffic to a number of Google services (including e-mail, search, LBS, analytics, advertising) and classified each request (i.e., standard, LBS, or authenticated) based on the destination IP, port and DNS requests. Details about the monitored services and the classification methodology can be found in citeRR. We sanitized the traffic data beforehand by appropriately grouping traffic traces into user-service sessions. To do so, we correlated traffic and DNS requests. This was possible because DNS replies for Google services are cached for a relatively short time (i.e., TTL of 300 seconds), and therefore a traffic request is very often preceded by a DNS request. Consequently, a request accounts for a user-service interaction, regardless of how much traffic the interaction generates.

Traffic to the monitored services (in terms of the number of user-service sessions) constitutes about 17% of the total traffic generated at the AP and 81.3% of users who connected have accessed at least one of the services. The average numbers of standard, authenticated and LBS requests (i.e., user-service interactions) during a day to the monitored services are depicted in Fig. 8. Standard requests are prevalent, followed by authenticated requests. The moderate usage of LBS can be explained with the location of the APs: most of the users visit this area almost on a daily-basis, therefore the need for location-based information is expected to be low. In our dataset, 9.5% of users generate LBS requests.

Results. First, we measure the compromise time and the proportion of victims based on the traces from our dataset. We compare the averaged experimental results with those from our theoretical analysis (Fig. 9). For the theoretical analysis, we use our framework with the parameters extracted from the real traces: $\lambda_{\mathrm{Arr}} = 14.54$ users/h and an average connection time of 2.17 hours ($\lambda_{\mathrm{Dur}} = 1/2.17$), obtained from the session traces; and traffic rates of $\lambda_{\mathrm{Std}} = 28.3$ req./h, $\lambda_{\mathrm{Auth}} = 14.6$ req./h and $\lambda_{\mathrm{LBS}} = 0.16$ req./h (with $\alpha_{\mathrm{LBS}} = 0.095$), obtained from the traffic traces. Because the theoretical model assumes a homogeneous user arrival rate, we compute the expected proportion of victims and compromise time as if the arrival process spanned from 7:30:AM–the time at which a significant number of users start connecting to the AP in our traces–to 7:PM. It can be observed that although the model does not capture the time-of-the-day effects of the user arrival and traffic processes, the theoretical and experimental expected proportions of victims match when considering the entire period of a day.

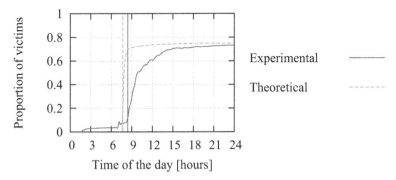

Fig. 9. Expected proportion of victims. Vertical lines represent average compromise times: theoretical $T_{\mathrm{Comp}} = 7$:42:AM and experimental $T_{\mathrm{Comp}} = 8$:25:AM.

We observe that around 8:AM (7:42AM estimated with our theoretical analysis and 8:25AM with our experimental results), only 1 hour after users typically start connecting to the AP, users' location privacy is compromised. By the end of the day, about 73% of the users who connected through the AP were compromised, out of which 90.5% did not make any LBS request ($\alpha_{\mathrm{LBS}} = 0.095$). With respect to the number of users who use Google services the proportion of victims actually corresponds to 90%. Thus, the result shows that Google is able to learn the location of 90% of its users who connect from the AP.

Once the adversary obtains the (IP, Location) mapping, it can maintain it over time by relying on authenticated requests to infer the IP changes upon DHCP lease expirations, as discussed in Section 4. Using traces from our dataset, we compute the probability of the adversary inferring the IP change for different renewal times during a day, considering the authenticated requests made at most ΔT minutes before and after the IP is changed. We consider three different values, $\Delta T = 1$, $\Delta T = 5$ and $\Delta T = 10$ minutes, and show the results in Fig. 10. Even with the smallest inference time window of 1 minute, the adversary can infer the IP change with the probability 1 between 2:PM and 5:PM. With higher values of ΔT the time during which the adversary can infer with probability 1 is even longer, i.e., from 11:AM to 7:PM with $\Delta T = 10$. However, the adversary's confidence decreases with larger ΔT. During the periods with less traffic (e.g., from 11:PM to 6:AM), the probability of the adversary inferring the mapping is

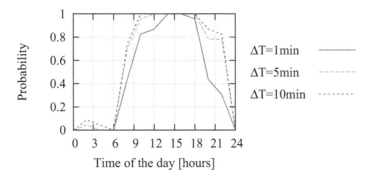

Fig. 10. Linking probability (i.e., probability of inferring the IP change) as a function of the renewal time, for different inference time window lengths (ΔT).

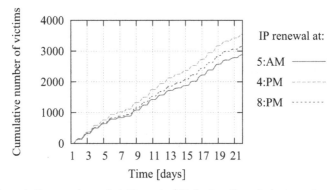

Fig. 11. Cumulative number of victims at AP during the whole experiment, for three different IP renewal times (the IP is changed every time the lease expires, $p_{New} = 1$).

smaller (less than 0.2) in all the cases. Between 5:AM and 6:AM, the adversary cannot infer the IP change, as there is no traffic during this time.

To further confirm the importance of the IP renewal time and its effect on the adversary's success, we plot the cumulative number of victims compromised at AP during three weeks, depending on the IP renewal time (Fig. 11). We set $\Delta T = 5$ minutes and we consider the renewal times at 5:AM, 4:PM and 8:PM, when the adversary is expected to be least successful, most successful and moderately successful, respectively. Indeed, from the results in Fig. 11, we confirm that the highest number of users (3,545 out of 4,302 users) is compromised when the IP renewal is at 4:PM, followed by 8:PM (3,149 victims). The adversary is least successful when the IP renewal is at 5:AM (compromising 2,879 users).

6   Countermeasures

Cryptographic primitives are efficient at protecting users' privacy, but because of the way networking protocols operate, they might not be sufficient, in particular, when the private information is the source IP address.

Hiding users' actual source IPs from the destination (i.e., the adversary) is a straightforward countermeasure against the considered threat and can be done in several ways. In relay-based anonymous communications, a user's traffic is forwarded from the source to the destination by several relay nodes, in a way that the destination cannot know the user's source IP. Examples of such networks include Tor [8], mix networks [5,7], or simple HTTP proxies. With Virtual Private Networks (VPNs), the user is assigned an IP that belongs to a remote network (e.g., a corporate network or commercial/public VPN). To the adversary, the user's requests appear to originate from within the remote network, whose location is different from that of the user. Unfortunately, such techniques are not widely adopted, especially in the case of mobile communications [34]. In addition, several techniques exist to identify the source IP of a client, even behind a NAT or a proxy, e.g., by using a Java applet [25].

Alternatively, these countermeasures can be implemented by ISPs, for instance, by deploying a country-wide NAT that aggregates traffic from all their subscribers at several gateways (e.g., Telefonica [33], Swisscom Hotspots) or by IP Mixing [29]. This also applies to operators of AP networks (e.g., Starbucks, AT&T Wi-Fi). However, they might lack incentives to implement such solutions.

Another approach to thwart the threat consists in degrading the knowledge of the adversary, by reducing the accuracy of the reported location and by increasing the uncertainty about the AP's location. Examples of location privacy enhancing technologies (PETs) reducing adversary's accuracy include spatial cloaking [2, 16] and adding noise to reported locations [1]. To increase adversary's uncertainty, [22] proposes to inject "dummy" requests, i.e., not related to users' locations. It is not easy for users to deploy these PETs, because some geolocation requests are implemented in operating systems, that can be controlled by the adversary (e.g., Google Android). Moreover, when these PETs are implemented in a non-coordinated fashion, the adversary might still be able to infer the actual location by filtering out requests that stand out from the bulk (increasing its certainty) and averaging the remaining requests (increasing its accuracy). Better results might be achieved if the AP operators implement the location-privacy preserving mechanisms, but they might lack incentives to do so.

Finally, as highlighted by our analysis, various other countermeasures can be implemented by the ISP or the AP's owner: reduce the DHCP lease, always allocate a new IP, trigger the IP change when the traffic is low (e.g., at 5:AM as suggested by our experimental results) or purposely impose silent periods around the renewal time (reducing the probability that the adversary infers the IP change from authenticated requests). Unfortunately, all these techniques have a negative effect on the quality of service and impose a significant overhead in network management. Thus, they are unlikely to be deployed in practice. Besides technical countermeasures, we envision a "Do-not-geolocalize" initiative, similar to "Do-not-track" [9], letting users to opt-out of being localized.

7   Discussion

Scale and Implications of the Threat. The threat enables an adversary to build an IP-location system, to obtain (at least) sporadic user locations and to profit from delivering location-targeted information when users access the services. However, we can also envision a different type of adversary, whose goal is to mount more powerful attacks on user privacy. In fact, once the adversary has access to sporadic user location, he is able to reconstruct entire trajectories, produce patterns of user-movement habits, or infer other information about the user, e.g., users' real identities, interests and activities. For example, in [31] it is shown how an adversary that observes each user's sporadic locations (that could be noisy and anonymized) can de-anonymize the users, compute the probability that a given user is at a given location at a given time, and construct users' full trajectories. By using various techniques, it has been shown that users can be identified by inferring where they spend most of their time (notably their home and workplace) [3,12,18,23]. In these cases, the identified location-privacy threat can serve as a building block that enables other, more powerful attacks.

In this paper, we focus on how an adversary can obtain the sporadic user-location information that is needed for commercial needs of service providers. Other attacks that are enabled by this location-privacy threat are beyond the scope of this paper and are largely addressed by the research community, as previously discussed. However, our work provides a framework that can be used to quantify sporadic location exposure upon which the community can build.

Business Opportunities. The presented (IP, Location) mapping technique can be used as a novel IP-location solution potentially improving on existing solutions [27,37]. Service providers, such as Google, can build and monetize this service by simply utilizing user traffic they receive. Additional advantages of this approach are that it does not require a dedicated infrastructure or network measurements. Such a system can be used on its own, or as a complementary to the existing ones. Because ISPs control the IP allocation and can prevent service providers from building the mapping (using the aforementioned countermeasure) they can make a profit by selling IP locations to service providers (e.g., Verizon in the US [6]) – some ISPs sell geographic information on the topology of their networks [25] – or by selling privacy-protection services to users.

8   Conclusion

In this paper we have presented a practical threat, demonstrating that the location privacy of users connecting to access points can be compromised by others. The scale of the threat is significant because it leverages on the way most networks are designed (i.e., NAT). When successful, the service provider can locate users within a few hundreds of meters, i.e., more accurately than existing IP-location databases. Our theoretical analysis provides a framework that enables us to quantify the threat for any access-point setting and to identify the key parameters and their impact on the adversary's success. The framework serves as a light-weight alternative to an extensive traffic analysis to estimate the threat. We experimentally investigate the state in practice, by analyzing real traces of users accessing Google services, collected from deployed Wi-Fi access points. We observe the large scale of the threat even with a modest use of LBS services. We survey possible countermeasures and we find that adequate ones can be used to protect individual users' location privacy, but they need to be widely deployed.

We intend to further study this threat by focusing on the following aspects: (i) the accuracy of a IP-location service, based on (IP, Location) mappings; (ii) the refinement of the model by modeling users' arrivals by an inhomogeneous Poisson process to capture time-of-the-day effects; (iii) the adversary's inference of IP changes, studying the trade-off between the probability of inferring the IP change and the adversary's confidence; and (iv) the adversary's ability to track users as they move and connect to different APs over time.

References

1. Agrawal, R., Srikant, R.: Privacy-Preserving Data Mining. In: SIGMOD (2000)
2. Ardagna, C.A., Cremonini, M., De Capitani di Vimercati, S., Samarati, P.: An Obfuscation-Based Approach for Protecting Location Privacy. IEEE Transactions on Dependable Secure Computing 8(1), 13–27 (2011)
3. Beresford, A., Stajano, F.: Location Privacy in Pervasive Computing. IEEE Perv. Comp. 2, 46–55 (2003)
4. Casado, M., Freedman, M.J.: Peering Through the Shroud: The Effect of Edge Opacity on IP-Based Client Identification. In: NSDI (2007)
5. Chaum, D.L.: Untraceable Electronic Mail, Return Addresses, and Digital Pseudonyms. Communications of the ACM 24(2), 84–90 (1981)
6. CNN: Your Phone Company is Selling Your Personal Data (2011), http://money.cnn.com/2011/11/01/technology/verizon_att_sprint_tmobile_privacy
7. Danezis, G., Dingledine, R., Hopwood, D., Mathewson, N.: Mixminion: Design of a Type III Anonymous Remailer Protocol. In: S&P, pp. 2–15 (2003)
8. Dingledine, R., Mathewson, N., Syverson, P.: Tor: The Second-generation Onion Router. In: USENIX Security (2004)
9. Federal Trade Commission: Protecting Consumer Privacy in an Era of Rapid Change: A Proposed Framework for Businesses and Policymakers. Report (2010)
10. Freedman, M.J., Vutukuru, M., Feamster, N., Balakrishnan, H.: Geographic Locality of IP Prefixes. In: IMC (2005)
11. Ghosh, A., Jana, R., Ramaswami, V., Rowland, J., Shankaranarayanan, N.: Modeling and Characterization of Large-Scale Wi-Fi Traffic in Public Hot-Spots. In: INFOCOM (2011)
12. Golle, P., Partridge, K.: On the Anonymity of Home/Work Location Pairs. In: Tokuda, H., Beigl, M., Friday, A., Brush, A.J.B., Tobe, Y. (eds.) Pervasive 2009. LNCS, vol. 5538, pp. 390–397. Springer, Heidelberg (2009)
13. Goodell, G., Syverson, P.: The right place at the right time. Communications of the ACM 50(5), 113–117 (2007)
14. Google Engineering Center Zurich: Technology and Innovation for Web Search. Private communication (October 2012)
15. Google Privacy Policy (2012), http://www.google.com/intl/en/policies/privacy/

16. Gruteser, M., Grunwald, D.: Anonymous Usage of Location-Based Services Through Spatial and Temporal Cloaking. In: MobiSys (2003)
17. Guo, C., Liu, Y., Shen, W., Wang, H., Yu, Q., Zhang, Y.: Mining the Web and the Internet for Accurate IP Address Geolocations. In: INFOCOM (2009)
18. Hoh, B., Gruteser, M., Xiong, H., Alrabady, A.: Enhancing Security and Privacy in Traffic-Monitoring Systems. IEEE Perv. Comp. 5, 38–46 (2006)
19. HostIP: My IP Address Lookup and Geotargeting Community Geotarget IP Project, http://www.hostip.info/
20. Targeting Local Markets: An IAB Interactive Advertising Guide. Interactive Advertising Bureau (2010)
21. Katz-Bassett, E., John, J.P., Krishnamurthy, A., Wetherall, D., Anderson, T., Chawathe, Y.: Towards IP Geolocation Using Delay and Topology Measurements. In: IMC (2006)
22. Kido, H., Yanagisawa, Y., Satoh, T.: An Anonymous Communication Technique using Dummies for Location-Based Services. In: ICPS, pp. 88–97 (2005)
23. Krumm, J.: Inference Attacks on Location Tracks. In: LaMarca, A., Langheinrich, M., Truong, K.N. (eds.) Pervasive 2007. LNCS, vol. 4480, pp. 127–143. Springer, Heidelberg (2007)
24. Geolocation and online fraud prevention by MaxMind, http://www.maxmind.com/
25. Muir, J.A., Oorschot, P.C.V.: Internet Geolocation: Evasion and Counterevasion. ACM Computing Survey 42, 4:1–4:23 (2009)
26. Patil, S., Norcie, G., Kapadia, A., Lee, A.: "Check Out Where I Am!": Location-Sharing Motivations, Preferences, and Practices. In: CHI (2012)
27. Poese, I., Uhlig, S., Kaafar, M.A., Donnet, B., Gueye, B.: IP Geolocation Databases: Unreliable? ACM SIGCOMM CCR 41, 53–56 (2011)
28. PricewaterhouseCoopers: Internet Advertising Revenue Report (2011)
29. Raghavan, B., Kohno, T., Snoeren, A.C., Wetherall, D.: Enlisting ISPs to Improve Online Privacy: IP Address Mixing by Default. In: Goldberg, I., Atallah, M.J. (eds.) PETS 2009. LNCS, vol. 5672, pp. 143–163. Springer, Heidelberg (2009)
30. Ross, S.M.: Stochastic Processes. Wiley (1995)
31. Shokri, R., Theodorakopoulos, G., Le Boudec, J.Y., Hubaux, J.P.: Quantifying Location Privacy. In: S&P (2011)
32. Skyhook Location Perf, http://www.skyhookwireless.com/location-technology
33. Telefonica implement NAT for DSL users (2012), http://bandaancha.eu/articulo/7844/usuarios-adsl-movistar/compartiran-misma-ip-mediante-nat-escasear-ipv4
34. Tor Metrics Portal, https://metrics.torproject.org
35. USA Department of Defenses: Global Positioning System: Standard Positioning Service Performance Standard (2008)
36. Vratonjic, N., Huguenin, K., Bindschaedler, V., Dubovitskaya, A., Hubaux, J.P.: Location Privacy Threats at Public Hotspots. Tech. rep., EPFL (2013)
37. Wang, Y., Burgener, D., Flores, M., Kuzmanovic, A., Huang, C.: Towards Street-Level Client-Independent IP Geolocation. In: NSDI (2011)
38. Xie, Y., Yu, F., Achan, K., Gillum, E., Goldszmidt, M., Wobber, T.: How Dynamic are IP Addresses? In: SIGCOMM (2007)
39. Yen, T.F., Xie, Y., Yu, F., Yu, R.P., Abadi, M.: Host Fingerprinting and Tracking on the Web: Privacy and Security Implications. In: NDSS (2012)

The Path Less Travelled: Overcoming Tor's Bottlenecks with Traffic Splitting*

Mashael AlSabah, Kevin Bauer, Tariq Elahi, and Ian Goldberg

Cheriton School of Computer Science
University of Waterloo
{malsabah,k4bauer,mtelahi,iang}@cs.uwaterloo.ca

Abstract. Tor is the most popular low-latency anonymity network for enhancing ordinary users' online privacy and resisting censorship. While it has grown in popularity, Tor has a variety of performance problems that result in poor quality of service, a strong disincentive to use the system, and weaker anonymity properties for all users. We observe that one reason why Tor is slow is due to low-bandwidth volunteer-operated routers. When clients use a low-bandwidth router, their throughput is limited by the capacity of the slowest node.

With the introduction of *bridges*—unadvertised Tor routers that provide Tor access to users within censored regimes like China—low-bandwidth Tor routers are becoming more common and essential to Tor's ability to resist censorship. In this paper, we present Conflux, a dynamic traffic-splitting approach that assigns traffic to an overlay path based on its measured latency. Because it enhances the load-balancing properties of the network, Conflux considerably increases performance for clients using low-bandwidth bridges. Moreover, Conflux significantly improves the experience of users who watch streaming videos online.

Through live measurements and a whole-network evaluation conducted on a scalable network emulator, we show that our approach offers an improvement of approximately 30% in expected download time for web browsers who use Tor bridges and for streaming application users. We also show that Conflux introduces only slight tradeoffs between users' anonymity and performance.

1 Introduction

Tor [10] is a widely used low-latency anonymity network, which offers strong privacy guarantees by tunnelling a user's Internet traffic through virtual circuits consisting of multiple intermediate overlay routers using a layered encryption scheme based on onion routing [40]. Beyond enabling anonymous communications online, Tor has become an essential tool in the fight against Internet censorship. Today, regimes around the world continue to aggressively filter [61], monitor [36], or explicitly block access [34] to certain types of online content. While Tor serves an estimated 400,000 users on a daily basis [54], its public infrastructure of over 3000 public relays can be easily blocked. In response, Tor uses special unlisted relays called *bridges* to aid users residing within regimes, such as China, that explicitly block the Tor network. Unfortunately, bridges generally provide a lower quality of service than Tor's public infrastructure.

---

* An extended version of this paper is available [1].

E. De Cristofaro and M. Wright (Eds.): PETS 2013, LNCS 7981, pp. 143–163, 2013.

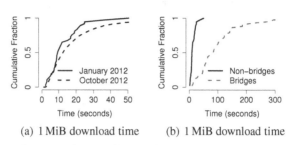

(a) 1 MiB download time   (b) 1 MiB download time

Fig. 1. Figure 1(a) shows the time required to download 1 MiB files over Tor in Jan. and Oct. 2012. Observe the long tail of the download time distribution. Figure 1(b) shows a download time comparison between Tor users who use public entry guards and those who use bridges.

Although Tor's primary goal is to support *real-time interactive* applications such as web browsing, the network suffers from a variety of performance problems [11] that are manifested as high and variable delays which result in a poor user experience. This poor experience discourages Tor's adoption and ultimately results in a smaller user base and weaker anonymity for all users [9].

Dynamic Traffic Splitting for Tor. In this work, we recognize that the diversity of bandwidth provided by Tor's volunteer-operated routers, and in particular the low-bandwidth bridges, degrades performance. We also recognize the significance of improving the performance of some high-throughput applications, such as streaming web videos, for Tor users. We propose an unconventional approach to improving performance when using low-bandwidth routers and bridges: *Tor users should split their traffic across multiple semi-disjoint circuits.*

In the context of Tor, traffic splitting can improve load balancing. When routers become over-utilized and experience congestion, splitting traffic across semi-disjoint paths can ease the burden on the congested circuit; under our scheme, circuits need only share a common exit router. Second, by splitting data over multiple circuits, the user's throughput can achieve up to the aggregate throughput of all circuits rather than a single one. This is particularly useful when a circuit uses a low-bandwidth router. Tor's router selection algorithm favors routers that have higher bandwidths to ensure sufficient throughput to transport users' traffic and to balance the traffic load across Tor's routers. However, individual Tor routers can have vastly different bandwidth capacities, ranging from 20 KiB/s to over 20 MiB/s. Figure 1(a) shows a long-tailed distribution of download times for 1 MiB files over the course of two different months: January and October 2012.[1] These slower downloads often correspond to circuits that used at least one low-bandwidth router. By combining multiple circuits with low-bandwidth nodes, the attainable throughput is no longer bound by the bottleneck node, but is instead the aggregate of each individual circuit's throughput.

Our Approach. We design, implement, and evaluate *Conflux*,[2] a novel congestion-aware traffic splitting and load balancing algorithm for anonymous communication

---

[1] This data was obtained from The Tor Metrics Portal [52].
[2] Conflux: a flowing together of rivers or streams.

networks. Conflux forwards a client's individual cells down multiple circuits that share a common exit router. Our algorithm dynamically measures the throughput of each constituent circuit and assigns traffic to each in proportion to its observed throughput. Our approach performs sub-stream traffic splitting, which provides a fine granularity of load balancing, as splitting can be performed at the individual cell level. This allows the traffic that is sent on a circuit to correspond to its desired load. The circuit's endpoints (the client and the exit router) are responsible for splitting the traffic at one endpoint and buffering, re-ordering, and delivering in-order cells to the application at the other end of the circuit. This approach can be deployed incrementally, as only clients and exit routers need to upgrade to support it.

To quantify the performance benefits of our proposed design, we perform a variety of live and whole-network experiments on an emulation-based Tor network testbed [4]. Our evaluation indicates that our approach can result in decreased queueing delays and increased throughput for users, particularly those who rely on low-bandwidth bridges to access the Tor network. We also find that, under light traffic loads, Conflux improves performance for clients who use Tor to access streaming videos (such as blocked YouTube videos[3]). Improving performance for such users is important, as streaming video websites are becoming a dominant source of Internet traffic [27,41].

We also critically evaluate the security implications of utilizing additional circuits in light of the end-to-end traffic confirmation attack [43, 45]. Our analyses indicate that our scheme only slightly increases users' vulnerability to this attack. Anonymity is also slightly decreased when the adversary uses powerful selective denial of service tactics [3,6,7,56] to maximize the number of circuits that can be compromised.

Contributions. This paper offers these contributions.

1. To improve performance for bridge and streaming application users, we design, implement, and evaluate a dynamic traffic splitting scheme that distributes the traffic load across circuits according to each circuit's bandwidth capacity.

2. Our live performance analysis indicates that Conflux results in an expected improvement of 30% in a typical Tor client's queueing delay and up to 75% in total download time. Whole-network experiments show that noticeable improvements are possible even when most or all clients adopt Conflux.

3. We analyze the security of Conflux and provide quantitative results showing that there is a small tradeoff between users' anonymity and performance gains.

Outline. The remainder of this paper is organized as follows: Section 2 describes Tor's design at a high level and Section 3 presents the Conflux design and an algorithm for splitting traffic in a manner that balances the traffic load over each circuit. We evaluate our proposal in Section 4 and offer a security analysis in Section 5. We discuss a variety of open issues and enumerate avenues of future work with our design in Section 6, contrast our contributions with related work in Section 7, and conclude in Section 8.

---

[3] Note that while Tor's browser bundle disables Flash by default, it is now possible to stream videos over Tor using HTML5. We expect this use case of streaming video over Tor to increase in popularity in the near term.

2   Background

How Tor Works. The Tor overlay network involves three kinds of nodes: Onion Proxies (OP), Onion Routers (OR), and directory authorities. OPs run on end-users' machines (clients). OPs start their operation by contacting the directory authorities to download the *network consensus*, which contains information about all ORs in the Tor network. ORs are volunteer-run relays (or *nodes*) that are responsible for relaying users' traffic to other nodes or to destinations outside of Tor, such as web servers.

The OP constructs a number of *circuits*—Tor-network paths through which the client's traffic is relayed in fixed-sized (512-byte) units called *cells*. To construct a circuit, the OP chooses three relays, each in a manner that weights a relay's selection in proportion to its bandwidth capacity. With Tor's decentralized architecture, only the exit node can observe the user's traffic and only the *entry guard* knows the identity of the user. Clients use the same set of three entry guards for a long period of time (currently 30–60 days), to mitigate the threat of the predecessor attack [60] and other attacks that seek to correlate entry and exit traffic to link senders with their respective receivers [35]. If both the entry guard and exit node cooperate, they can use traffic analysis to link the initiator to her destination [24, 45].

Circuits and Streams. A single TCP connection is used between any two ORs in the network. However, this single TCP connection is used to multiplex several circuits that may or may not belong to the same user. To identify different circuits, each OR assigns different circuit IDs to circuits. In addition to circuit multiplexing, the OP can multiplex several TCP *streams* over one circuit, which generally has a lifetime of ten minutes. To ensure flow control of data in flight, Tor employs an end-to-end window-based flow control mechanism in which every time the OP (or exit OR) receives 100 cells, it acknowledges windows of data cells using SENDME (or acknowledgement) cells.[4] We leverage these end-to-end control cells as a means to infer a circuit's bandwidth capacity, as we describe in Section 3.

Evading Censorship with Bridges. In addition to anonymous communications, Tor is an important tool in the fight against censorship. Tor helps users around the world visit blocked websites. In some cases, Tor's infrastructure of directory authorities and routers has been blocked, for example by the so-called "Great Firewall of China" [25]. To facilitate entry to the Tor network despite such blocking, Tor has introduced *bridges*, which are unlisted Tor routers that are distributed to censored users via out-of-band mechanisms such as HTTPS queries to bridges.torproject.org. To ensure that a censor cannot collect all bridges and simply block them, Tor currently limits the number of bridges that are distributed to each /24 IP address block [55]. Currently, clients use bridges in lieu of an entry guard, to keep the total circuit length at three routers.

While bridges provide an essential service to an estimated 30,000 censored users as of November 2012 [54], they are believed to be operated by Tor clients who often reside on low-bandwidth broadband networks. To confirm this hypothesis, we obtained 221, of approximately 700 [53], bridges in January 2012 using Tor's standard HTTPS

---

[4] For more details about Tor's flow control mechanisms, see AlSabah *et al.* [2].

request service from PlanetLab hosts on 55 different /24 IP networks.[5] Figure 1(b) compares the performance of a live Tor client that downloads 1 MiB files using entry guards versus bridges. Clearly, the low-bandwidth bridges are a significant source of poor performance. Furthermore, Tor bridges are becoming integrated into ubiquitous devices such as wireless access points to simplify the process of configuring and running a bridge on a broadband Internet link at home [50]. Thus, because low-bandwidth bridges will likely become even more common in the near future, in this work we seek to improve performance for bandwidth-limited bridge clients.

Adapting Tor to the Changing Web. Unlike previous efforts which seek to enhance the experience of web browsers in Tor by throttling bulk downloads (specifically file-sharing applications) [19,31], we recognize that some emerging classes of bulk transfers should actually be improved rather than throttled. In fact, recent Internet traffic studies have revealed that file sharing applications are consuming less bandwidth,[6] while streaming video applications are starting to account for an increasingly large fraction of Internet traffic by volume [27,41]. Therefore, in order to survive and continue to attract new users, it is crucial for Tor to meet the demands of its users and the changing web by improving the experience for streaming users. Although The Tor Project mainly welcomes web browsing, it is hard these days to separate streaming from web browsing. If a user visits a blocked news website via Tor, the user may also want to view videos associated with the stories accessed.

While streaming websites (such as Youtube and Netflix) sometimes use strategies that consist of buffering data followed by transmitting ON-OFF bursts to users, it has also been shown that one streaming strategy can be considered as simple file downloads [38]. We adopt the strategy of the simple file downloads to model streaming videos in our experiments in Section 4

3   Conflux's Design

We next shift attention to the design of our system. An OP that uses Conflux builds a number of circuits (two or more) that intersect at a common exit OR. We refer to the OP and common exit OR as the *end points* of a multipath. The OP receives and sends data to the client's application (such as a web browser), while the exit OR sends and receives data from an external server (such as a web server). Each end point receives data and splits it into cells, adding sequence numbers to the cell headers. Next, the end point divides the cells across the circuits of the multipath according to a traffic splitting scheme. When the other end point receives the cells, it collects and reorders them according to their sequence numbers before delivering their contents to their destinations. We note that this approach does not replace Tor's bandwidth-weighted router selection algorithm, but complements it.

---

[5] This procedure for enumerating bridges is described in more detail by Ling *et al.* [26]. Automatically enumerating Tor bridges is more difficult at present because clients have to solve CAPTCHAs. For our experimental evaluation in Section 4.2, we use a smaller, more recent list of bridges.

[6] Note that P2P traffic on Tor is also likely to drop with the rise of UDP-based P2P applications [5].

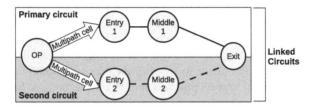

Fig. 2. Multipath construction and stream linking

Our approach to cell-level traffic splitting consists of three parts: 1) multipath construction, 2) throughput-informed sub-stream traffic splitting, and 3) sequencing, buffering, and reordering. We next describe each part in turn.

Constructing the Multipath. As shown in Figure 2, the client constructs the first circuit, called the *primary circuit*, according to Tor's bandwidth-weighted router selection. Then, if the client wishes to use Conflux, the client forms another circuit that uses different entry and middle ORs, which are also selected according to the bandwidth-weighted algorithm. The only constraint our system requires on the second circuit is that its exit OR has to be the same as the primary circuit's exit OR. Next, the OP sends a new type of command cell, which we call the "multipath" cell, through both circuits to the common exit OR. The multipath cell contains a 32-byte random nonce that is common to each of the OP's linked circuits. This nonce enables the exit router to associate the OP's TCP streams with its linked circuits.[7] The OP uses the primary circuit to command the exit OR to establish the TCP connections to Internet destinations. Closing a multipath is no different from closing circuits in Tor. If a circuit in a multipath exceeds its lifetime (ten minutes by default), and if it is idle, the circuit is torn down. Closing one circuit does not affect the operation of other circuits. Since a Tor client already builds many spare circuits by default, we do not expect any additional load being introduced by Conflux.

Dynamic Sub-stream Traffic Splitting. To improve load balancing, we designed and implemented a dynamic load balancing algorithm where the splitting end point assigns different amounts of traffic to each circuit depending on its observed throughput relative to the other linked circuits. The advantage of this approach is that it is reactive to network dynamics, such as the congestion state of a circuit and its available capacity relative to the other circuits.

This scheme works as follows. First, the splitting end point (the OP for client-to-server traffic, or the exit OR for server-to-client traffic) measures the latency of each of the linked circuits. This can be done by storing the time every 100th cell is sent down a particular circuit, and noting the time that the corresponding circuit-level SENDME arrives. This allows the splitting end point to compute the current round-trip-time (RTT) of cells on the circuit; this will be inversely proportional to the circuit throughput, as cells are of fixed size.

---

[7] As usual, a malicious exit router can trivially observe all circuits it handles, including linked ones.

CircID	Relay Cmd	Data Cmd	Recognized?	StreamID	Digest	Length	**Seq No**	**Data**
2	1	1	2	2	4	2	4	494

Fig. 3. The 512-byte data cell format with each field's length (in bytes) for Conflux

The splitting end point periodically updates the throughput measurements assigned to each linked circuit. Next, every time a data cell is ready to be transmitted on a multipath, the particular circuit used to send the cell is selected with a probability proportional to its throughput.

Sequencing, Buffering, and Reordering. Before any splitting can be performed on TCP streams across different circuits, we have to ensure that the receiver will be able to reorder cells before delivering them to their destination (client program or exit TCP connection). Therefore, we implement sequencing of data cells before sending them down our multipaths. Tor's standard data cell consists of a circuit identifier, a "relay" command type, a "data" sub-type, a "recognized" field to identify whether the cell is to be delivered locally, a stream identifier, a message digest to ensure integrity, a data length, and the data. We modify the cell format slightly, to reserve the first four bytes of the payload for the sequence numbers, as shown in Figure 3. This reduces the amount of data that can fit into each cell's payload by less than 1%.

Because we divide a single TCP stream across circuits, we expect that cells may arrive out of order. Therefore, the two end points of a multipath, the OP and exit OR, are responsible for buffering and reordering cells that arrive out of order. First, as long as the cells arrive in order, they are immediately delivered to the client application (or the TCP exit connection) when the receiver is the OP (or the exit OR). Also, we keep track of the sequence number of the last delivered cell. If a cell arrives out of order, it is stored in a sorted list of cells. When the next expected cell arrives, it is delivered to the OP (or TCP exit connection) along with any buffered cells with subsequent sequence numbers that have already arrived.

Implementation Details. We implemented the multipath construction and cell sequencing, buffering, and reordering in the Tor source code (version 0.2.3.0-alpha-dev). We also implemented the weighted traffic splitting algorithm as described above. Conflux can be turned on or off as a configuration option. Note that only the circuit's end points (e.g., the client and the exit router) are required to upgrade to run Conflux. Thus, Conflux can be incrementally deployed as individual exit routers and clients upgrade. Our full implementation consists of roughly 2,000 lines of code.

4 Performance Evaluation

In order to empirically demonstrate the potential performance benefits of the proposed scheme, we present a series of live and large-scale experiments.

Table 1. Network model for whole-network experiments

Attribute	Data Source
Pairwise link latency	King dataset [15]
Tor router bandwidth	Tor consensus (Nov. 2011)
Tor client bandwidth	Ookla Net Index dataset [33]
Traffic characteristics	Tor traffic study [28]

4.1 Experimental Setup

Live Experiments. First, we seek to measure the potential benefits of deploying a modified Tor router on the currently deployed Tor network. Since only the Tor exit router needs to be modified in order to use Conflux, we deploy a single exit router and conduct a series of performance measurements using a Tor client that we control.

Each measurement is collected as follows: First, a Conflux multipath circuit is built using two entry routers $entry_1$ and $entry_2$, two middle routers $middle_1$ and $middle_2$, and our modified exit router *exit*. In order not to expose other clients' traffic, we set the exit policy of *exit* so that it can only connect to a specific web server. This means that *exit* will act as an exit router only for our traffic, but it can be a middle or an entry node for other clients' encrypted traffic. Using Conflux, our client fetches 320 KiB, 1 MiB and 5 MiB files. These file sizes were chosen to approximate web pages and larger files [37]. For comparison, the stock Tor client downloads the files over different circuits it builds using Tor's default bandwidth-weighted router selection algorithm.[8] Measurements were collected from December 2012–January 2013, during which time our exit router was configured with a bandwidth rate of 200 KB/s.

To evaluate the performance benefits for people using low-bandwidth Tor bridges, we also collect measurements where our client uses Tor bridges as its entry nodes. We collected 36 bridges by using Tor's standard HTTPS request service and we manually solved CAPTCHAs. The bridge clients work as follows. Every thirty minutes, our stock Tor and Conflux clients choose six bridges randomly from the list of 36 bridges we obtained, and use them as the first hop on each circuit they construct.

Whole-Network Experiments. One of the limitations of a live performance evaluation is that it is generally not possible to understand how performance might change when all participants of the network adopt the new design. To help understand these *whole-network effects*, we also perform experiments using the ExperimenTor testbed [4]. ExperimenTor is a Tor network testbed and toolkit that enables whole-network Tor experiments on a network topology with realistic delay, bandwidth, and other characteristics using the Modelnet [57] network emulation platform.

One challenge in conducting such an evaluation is that one must faithfully model the dynamics of the live network such as network latency, bandwidth, and traffic characteristics and replicate them in isolation. To enhance the realism of our experiments, we use a variety of empirical data sources, summarized in Table 1, to construct a network topology based on realistic link latencies, Tor router bandwidths sampled uniformly

---

[8] To reduce any bias in the performance results due to the selection of particularly fast or slow entry guards, we disable the use of entry guards for this experiment.

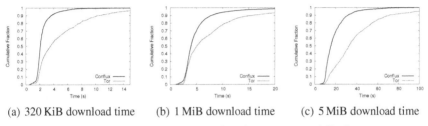

(a) 320 KiB download time   (b) 1 MiB download time   (c) 5 MiB download time

Fig. 4. Live performance comparison between Tor and Conflux

from a Tor consensus document from November 1, 2011, and asymmetric Tor client bandwidths assigned by sampling from the Ookla Net Index broadband data set [33] (the interquartile ranges are 4–13 Mbit/s downstream, 0.5–1.9 Mbit/s upstream).

Client Traffic Models. In addition to building a realistic network topology, it is important to replicate the dynamics of the network's traffic. Since Tor's users are anonymous, it is inherently difficult to characterize real Tor traffic. One such study [28] exists, which reported that over 92% of TCP connections leaving a Tor exit router result from web browsing and make up nearly 60% of the network's aggregate traffic volume. However, BitTorrent accounts for only about 3% of connections, but comprises over 40% of the aggregate traffic volume. We employ these empirical observations in developing realistic traffic models for our whole-network experiments. Beyond modeling the dynamics of the past and present Tor network, we also consider emerging trends in Internet traffic. We model two types of clients in our experiments: First, web browsing clients are modelled as fetching 320 KiB files (the median web page size on the Internet [37]) with random think time pauses between 1–30 seconds (chosen uniformly at random). A similar distribution of "think times" between web requests was measured by Hernández-Campos *et al.* [18]. Second, bulk clients (e.g., streaming video) download 5 MiB files with uniformly random delays of 1–5 minutes between fetches. This download size and delay distribution approximates observations of YouTube video sizes and viewing durations [22]. As mentioned in Section 2, we model streaming clients by large file downloads [38].

To highlight the performance benefits for bandwidth-deprived bridge clients, we also conduct whole-network experiments in which clients use a bridge in lieu of an entry guard. Since bridges are typically run by Tor clients themselves, we configure five bridges to run on asymmetric broadband-like Internet connections chosen from the Ookla Net Index data set.

4.2   Results

Performance Metrics. To evaluate the performance of our technique, we measure *time-to-first-byte* and *download time*. The time-to-first-byte is the time it takes the client to receive the first cell of data after it issued a request; it is a good measure of both the responsiveness of the network and its congestion state. The other metric we consider is download time, which is simply the time it takes for the client to receive the last byte of data after issuing a request (download time includes the time-to-first-byte).

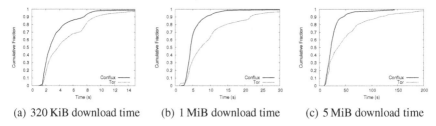

(a) 320 KiB download time   (b) 1 MiB download time   (c) 5 MiB download time

Fig. 5. Download time performance comparison between Tor and Conflux using live Tor network bridges

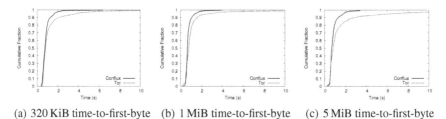

(a) 320 KiB time-to-first-byte (b) 1 MiB time-to-first-byte (c) 5 MiB time-to-first-byte

Fig. 6. Time-to-first-byte performance comparison between Tor and Conflux using live Tor network bridges

Live Performance. Figure 4 compares the time for a client to download 320 KiB, 1 MiB, and 5 MiB files using Tor and Conflux. We observe a noticeable improvement in download times for all file sizes. However, improvements are more visible with larger file sizes. For example, the median improvement in download time for the 320 KiB and 1 MiB files is 42% and 25%, respectively. For the 5 MiB files, the improvement is around 54%. The reason why improvements are more visible for larger file sizes is the mechanics of TCP congestion control (see the extended version of this work [1, Appendix A] for details).

Live Performance for Bridge Users. When we apply Conflux with clients who use low-bandwidth bridges as their entry nodes, we also observe significant improvement in performance, regardless of the download size. Figures 5(a), 5(b) and 5(c) show that the download times for 320 KiB, 1 MiB, and 5 MiB files are significantly improved; the performance improvement is most significant for the 5 MiB download, which experiences an improvement of over 50% relative to Tor.

Furthermore, Figures 6(a), 6(b) and 6(c) compare the times-to-first-byte for clients who use bridges to download 320 KiB, 1 MiB, and 5 MiB files using Tor and Conflux. Regardless of the download size, the Conflux clients experience faster response times compared to Tor. By using multiple circuits, if one circuit is congested, Conflux is able to send cells down a second, possibly uncongested circuit.

Whole-Network Deployment. We next seek to evaluate the performance of our technique if all our browsing bridge users and bulk clients in the network upgraded. In our large-scale experiments, we deploy a 20-router Tor network on our ExperimenTor testbed. Next, we fix the number of the total Tor clients to 400. Of the 400 clients, 30

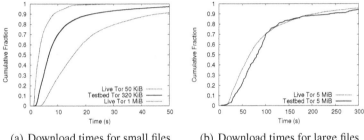

(a) Download times for small files   (b) Download times for large files

Fig. 7. Performance comparison between ExperimenTor (testbed), when 370 web browsers and 30 bulk clients are used, and the live Tor network using torperf. These graphs show that our testbed setup realistically reproduces the performance of the live Tor network.

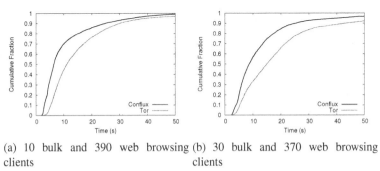

(a) 10 bulk and 390 web browsing (b) 30 bulk and 370 web browsing
clients   clients

Fig. 8. Download time comparison between Tor and Conflux for web clients that download 320 KiB using bridges in whole-network deployment experiments

clients act as bulk downloaders and 370 clients act as the interactive web browsers. Our initial experiments revealed that if all web clients who use entry guards use Conflux, those clients observe no performance benefits because the exit routers would be slower than the entry guards and would become the bottlenecks in circuits constructed by Conflux. Therefore, for our whole-network deployment experiments, we focus on browsing *bridge users*, since they have more performance incentives to use Conflux.

Before we present our whole-network deployment results, we first compare the stock Tor download time measurements obtained from our testbed, when 370 web and 30 bulk clients are used, with the live Tor network measurements maintained by the Tor metrics portal [52]. Figure 7(a) shows that the stock Tor download time distribution, of 320 KiB files obtained using ExperimenTor, fits between the download time distributions of the 50 KiB and 1 MiB files obtained from the live Tor network. Note that the Tor project only maintains the download times of 50 KiB, 1 MiB and 5 MiB file sizes over the live Tor network.

Second, Figure 7(b) demonstrates that our testbed's download time distribution of 5 MiB files closely approximates the respective distribution obtained from the live Tor network. In fact, the results look accurate for the fourth quartile of the download times, and for the first three quartiles, the testbed performance is only 15% slower than the live Tor network.

Although we believe that using 370 web and 30 bulk clients produces an accurate approximation, we also experiment with a lighter load of 390 web and 10 bulk clients, as there are continual efforts to reduce the load in the network by throttling the bulk downloaders [19, 31]. Furthermore, in each experiment, among the 390 or 370 web clients, we fix the number of bridge users to 50. We also run an additional five low-bandwidth routers that act as bridges.[9] Those bridges are neglected by non-bridge users.

Next, we present the results for the web browsing bridge users (for bulk clients' results, see the extended version of this paper [1, Appendix B]). Figure 8 shows the significant performance gains in download times experienced by bridge users using Conflux when the network is lightly loaded with 10 bulk clients and 390 web browsers. At the median, it takes a Tor client 11 seconds to finish downloading the 320 KiB file, whereas with Conflux, it takes only 6 seconds, which is approximately a 45% improvement. When we increase the load to 30 bulk clients to match the performance of the current Tor network, we still observe significant download time improvements. For Tor clients, the download times are degraded by 4 seconds, as the download time reaches 15 seconds at the median, whereas with Conflux, the degradation is only 2 seconds, as downloads complete in 8 seconds. Therefore, even with congestion, Conflux maintains the performance advantage of roughly 46%.

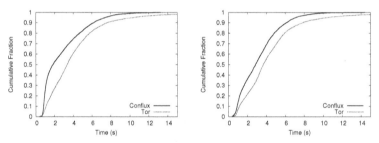

(a) 10 bulk and 390 web browsing clients (b) 30 bulk and 370 web browsing clients

Fig. 9. Time-to-first-byte comparison between Tor and Conflux for web clients that download 320 KiB using bridges in whole-network deployment experiments

Figure 9 tells us a similar story for the time-to-first-byte results. Under a light load of 10 bulk clients, Conflux needs only 1.8 seconds before the browser starts changing for the bridge user at the median. The respective waiting time for the Tor client is 3.3 seconds, which is a 45% improvement in time-to-first-byte using Conflux. When

Table 2. Relative download time comparison at the 80th percentile for Conflux and Tor under increasing traffic loads

User type	Light load	Regular load
Web browsing bridge users	Improved by 32%	Improved by 34%
Streaming (bulk) users	Improved by 17%	Improved by 3%
Other clients	Not affected	Not affected

---

[9] Since little is known about the total number and behavior of bridge users, we make reasonable assumptions in designing these experiments.

we increase the load to 30 bulk clients, the median time-to-first-byte is still improved by roughly 23% when Conflux is used. Therefore, our large-scale experiments confirm our live experiments, in which we observed large performance benefits when Conflux is used for bridge users. Table 2 summarizes our whole-network experimental results.

5   Security Analysis

We next investigate how the multipath routing scheme in Conflux affects the probability of the adversary linking together a circuit's source and destination. This linking, or *circuit compromise*, occurs when the adversary controls both endpoints of a given circuit [48] and applies timing analysis [24, 45] to reveal the communication patterns between the client and its corresponding destination. We first analyze the potential for path compromise due to passive attacks. Active attacks are considered in Section 5.3.

5.1   Identifying Bridge Users

Exit ORs can easily recognize which clients are using Conflux. Therefore, to prevent exit ORs from identifying bridge users, both bridge users and non-bridge users are encouraged to use Conflux. In fact, non-bridge browsing users can benefit from Conflux because browsing activity often involves streaming or downloading large files or images. In such situations, non-bridge users can observe between 3% to 17% performance improvements as we have seen in the results of our whole-network deployment experiments summarized in Table 2. This substantial improvement provides them with strong incentives to use Conflux and thereby aid in increasing the anonymity set of bridge users who adopt Conflux.

5.2   Path Compromise

We next examine the effect Conflux has on client exposure and compare it to Tor. We look at both client compromise rates as well as individual circuit compromise rates to provide a more thorough discussion of the security implications of Conflux.

For client compromise, we adopt the model used by Elahi *et al.* [13], which provides a realistic and empirical approach to determining client exposure due to real-world network phenomena such as guard churn. In their model, clients are considered compromised whenever there is a malicious relay in their guard set. Note that if a client has a guard set containing malicious guards, then the number of circuits created before choosing a malicious guard would be sightly smaller for Conflux as compared to Tor. However, such a client would be deanonymized with either Tor or Conflux, and so from a *client compromise* point of view, we consider either situation to be equally bad. (We will consider *circuit compromise*, in which one cares about how *often* a client's circuits are compromised, below.) This captures the upper bound on the absolute compromise levels of the client population. The reason why only clients with all guards honest are assured safety is that if even one of the guards is malicious then the client will eventually pick a malicious guard at the same time as picking a malicious exit, and will be exposed.

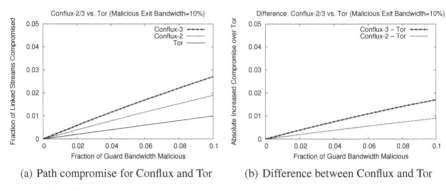

(a) Path compromise for Conflux and Tor   (b) Difference between Conflux and Tor

Fig. 10. Security of Conflux with two and three circuits compared to stock Tor

This model depends only on the distribution of the guards amongst the clients' guard sets and is not affected by the multipath scheme Conflux utilizes. Conflux does not alter how guards are selected by clients into their guard sets nor how guards are selected for circuits. This makes the guards clients pick with Conflux identical to those picked with Tor, and hence both systems have identical exposure rates.

Under certain circumstances, individual circuit compromise rates can be just as important as client compromise rates. The following formula captures the probability of a compromised multipath in Conflux.

$$P(\text{Compromised}) \triangleq f_{xbw} \cdot (1 - (1 - f_{gbw})^k) \tag{1}$$

Here, k is the number of guard nodes[10] used in the multipath, while the adversary controls a proportion f_{xbw} of the network's exit bandwidth and a proportion f_{gbw} of the network's guard bandwidth. The equivalent value for Tor is $f_{xbw} \cdot f_{gbw}$, the probability of selecting both a malicious exit and guard. Note that, as expected, this is the same as the expression for Conflux when $k = 1$.

In order to understand the implications of this formula, we compare Conflux — denoted Conflux-2 where two guards are used on a multipath and Conflux-3 where three guards are used — with Tor and plot the results in Figure 10(a). It is clear that while Conflux-2/3 increases the chance of a compromised circuit, it is very slight in absolute terms; at 10% compromised exit bandwidth it is 0.9% in Conflux-2 and 1.72% in Conflux-3, as shown in Figure 10(b). The tradeoff between this slight increase and that of increased performance can be evaluated depending on the needs of the client.

We further analyze the probability distribution (B_m) of a client having m malicious guards in its guard set as well as the probability (P_m) of constructing compromised circuits given m compromised guards. Assuming 10% malicious exit bandwidth, Table 3 provides the probabilities of picking 0 or more malicious guard relays as well as the probabilities of constructing malicious circuits under those conditions. *Note that*

---

[10] This analysis is also applicable to bridge relays since Conflux utilizes them in the same manner as guard relays.

Table 3. Compromised circuit rates at different values of k (the number of entry guards used for a (multi)path) given m malicious relays in the user's guard set at 10% malicious guard bandwidth (for the computation of B_m) and 10% malicious exit bandwidth (for the computation of P_m)

Malicious Relays in Guard Set (m)	Probability of m (B_m)	P_m(Compromised)		
		$k = 1$ (Tor)	$k = 2$ (Conflux-2)	$k = 3$ (Conflux-3)
0	72.9%	0%	0%	0%
1	24.3%	3.33%	6.67%	10%
2	2.7%	6.67%	10%	10%
3	0.1%	10%	10%	10%

because malicious guards are chosen infrequently, Conflux often adds no additional vulnerability to path compromise over and above Tor.[11]

The same analysis follows for AS-level adversaries that can observe the connections between clients and their guards/bridges, and between exit relays and the destinations. Substituting the fraction of circuits observed by the adversary between the two end points, i.e. $f_{client-guard}$ and $f_{exit-destination}$, for f_{gbw} and f_{xbw} respectively in Equation 1, we can calculate compromise rates in similar fashion to those in Table 3. While it is difficult to estimate realistic adversarial AS coverage, Edman and Syverson [12] and Wacek *et al.* [58] provide values of between 18–25% for the parameters above.

5.3 Selective Denial of Service

We now consider active attacks, in the form of selective denial of service (SDoS) [3,6,7, 56]. Under this attack the adversary actively breaks circuits he is part of if he finds that either end point is not controlled by him. This causes the client to create compromised circuits at a higher rate. The adversary can choose to either SDoS circuits immediately or be strategically patient.

Recall that Conflux establishes *primary circuits* first, to which further (secondary) circuits are linked to form multipaths. Hence, this mechanism provides two avenues for the SDoS attack: first at the primary circuit building stage and second at the circuit linking stage. We analyze each in turn.

We model the likelihood of primary circuit compromise with SDoS by inputing Formula 1 from Section 5.2 in the following formula, proposed by Das and Borisov [7], where f is the fraction of malicious relay bandwidth:

$$P(SDoS) \doteq \frac{P(\text{Compromised})}{P(\text{Compromised}) + (1 - f)^3} \tag{2}$$

With SDoS, the only primary circuits that are possible will either be compromised ($P(\text{Compromised})$) or entirely honest ($(1 - f)^3$). At 10% malicious bandwidth this

---

[11] As of July 2012, the Tor network had roughly 1,200 MiB/s aggregate guard bandwidth and roughly 600 MiB/s aggregate exit bandwidth [51]. We believe that an adversary in possession of 10% of each of these bandwidths is a powerful, high-resource attacker. Thus, this should be considered a worst-case security analysis.

attack increases the likelihood to 2.54% from 1.9% for Conflux-2 and to 3.57% from 2.7% for Conflux-3. Compare this to Tor where the same attack increases the likelihood to 1.35% from 1%. The increases here are due to the primary circuit creation phase and not due to Conflux's multipath linking scheme.

The strategic adversary servicing a primary circuit with a compromised exit relay may gain an added advantage by performing SDoS exclusively on the secondary circuits being linked to the primary. At 10% malicious bandwidth the probability of this scenario is 9%. Under Conflux-2, employing SDoS on such secondary circuits exclusively gains the adversary 0.23% whereas Conflux-3 gains the adversary 0.41%. The adversary needs to balance the cost of this strategy in terms of bandwidth used to service the uncompromised primary and the added advantage it provides.

A possible countermeasure is to ensure that the OP will retry the linked circuit using the same guard and will not switch to another (potentially malicious) guard. After a few retries, if it is unable to build a *secondary circuit* for the linked stream, the OP will give up but without impacting the client whose traffic still flows over the uncompromised primary circuit.

6   Discussion

Congestion. Conflux does not introduce any additional traffic to the network as our multipaths are bounded by the window of the primary circuit and by the bandwidth of the exit routers. Indeed, in our large-scale experiments, we found that the windows are not exhausted when Conflux is used. As indicated by our results, congestion is reduced because Conflux dynamically senses latency on each circuit as a congestion indicator, which allows our traffic splitting approach to perform smart load balancing so that congestion can be avoided. Moreover, Conflux is complementary to incentive schemes that seek to increase the number of exit routers and bridges.

Computational Cost. One might wonder if Conflux adds more complexity to the operation of routers since it requires building more circuits resulting in more public key (PK) operations. Since Tor clients build spare idle circuits by default, Conflux can use those circuits as secondary circuits in order not to add more PK operations in building multipaths. For circuits that must be built on demand, Conflux doubles the cost of building circuits (assuming only two paths are used). However, those costs can be significantly reduced if Conflux uses Tor 0.2.4's ntor handshake [8], which eliminates PK decryptions at routers during circuit construction.

Experimental Limitations. The results we obtained show an improvement in a testbed environment. In our experiments, we emulate the network behaviour and traffic load using ExperimenTor, since it allows us to set up different network topologies with different bandwidth and link settings. For practical purposes, we scaled the network down to 20 routers, which is not reflective of the real Tor network. However, we strived in our experiments to perform and obtain realistic performance measurements under different traffic loads. Performing large-scale experiments using different network models such as the ones recently proposed by Jansen *et al.* [20] and Wacek *et al.* [58] and performing a large-scale performance evaluation on the live Tor network are areas for future work.

Future Work. Recall that our dynamic traffic splitting technique is based only on two circuits. One area we want to explore is using Conflux with more than two circuits. Since we found the performance improvements to be significant with two circuits, we suspect that we may find even more performance benefits with more than two circuits. We leave exploring the performance benefits of splitting traffic over more than two circuits for future investigation.

Another avenue for future work is to evaluate alternative methods for measuring circuit latency. Recall that we opportunistically measure the latency of a circuit in order to access its performance using Tor's existing circuit-level SENDME cells that a client sends to the exit router after receipt of every 100th data cell. This allows us to measure circuit latency/congestion for free (e.g., with no additional overhead to the network). An alternative technique is to introduce a new cell type that clients send to exits and perform more frequent measurements. A potential advantage of this approach is that it might detect sudden changes in latency and thereby react to congestion faster. However, a downside is that this approach is more hostile to the network, because it places more probe traffic onto the network.

7   Related Work

Multipath TCP (MPTCP). MPTCP [17] is a transport layer protocol that allows applications to send data over several interfaces/addresses, whereas Conflux is implemented at the overlay layer. Because data is source-routed in Tor, we can choose our multipaths and ensure they are only joined at the exit routers. In MPTCP, routing decisions are done by IP routers, and a TCP source cannot choose the Internet path. MPTCP is more useful if divergent paths are available (multi-homing).

Multipath to Improve Anonymity. In the context of high-latency Chaumian mix networks, Serjantov and Murdoch [42] show that sending packets over multiple disjoint routes through the mix network may increase anonymity against a partial passive adversary. Also, Feigenbaum et al. [14] proposed multipath routing to mitigate timing attacks [43,45] in low-latency anonymity networks, using a layered mesh topology.

Multipath to Improve Performance. In the context of low-latency onion routing networks, MORE [23] routes every packet through a different path of onion routers, half of which are chosen by the sender and half chosen by the receiver. While this approach offers the ability to create highly dynamic paths—which can have desirable performance, load balancing, and anonymity properties—the requirement that communicating parties participate in the anonymity network may reduce MORE's practicality.

To increase throughput in Tor, Snader [46] presents preliminary experiments in which clients receive n different streams over n disjoint circuits. In particular, multiple circuits are shown to reduce the time to download 1 MB files. However, it is unclear whether performance is improved for smaller web-like streams; furthermore, since this scheme uses more entry and exit points into the Tor network, it may increase the threat of end-to-end traffic confirmation attacks (as in Bauer et al. [3]).

Combination with Other Tor Performance Work. There are several proposals that aim to improve the performance of Tor in different ways such as congestion control and avoidance [2, 16, 39, 49, 59], improved router selection [44, 47], scalability [29, 30], and applying incentive schemes to increase the number and bandwidth of Tor relays [21, 31, 32]. Conflux is complementary to these previous approaches and we expect that even greater performance benefits are possible by combining these proposals together. We leave this for future investigation.

8   Conclusion

Motivated by the need to improve the performance of Tor, we presented the design, implementation, and analysis of Conflux, a dynamic congestion-aware traffic splitting scheme that is designed to improve the load balancing of the network which is particularly useful for clients using low-bandwidth routers such as bridges. We evaluated Conflux using a series of small-scale experiments on the live network, and using large-scale experiments on an isolated testbed. Our results indicate that significant performance benefits can be obtained at the expense of a slight decrease in anonymity.

Acknowledgements. We would like to thank Eugene Vasserman and the anonymous reviewers for their helpful input in improving the quality of this work. We also thank our sponsors: NSERC, ORF, The Tor Project Inc., and Qatar University.

References

1. AlSabah, M., Bauer, K., Elahi, T., Goldberg, I.: The Path Less Travelled: Overcoming Tor's Bottlenecks with Traffic Splitting. Tech. Rep. CACR 2013-16 (2013), http://www.cacr.math.uwaterloo.ca/techreports/2013/cacr2013-16.pdf
2. AlSabah, M., Bauer, K., Goldberg, I., Grunwald, D., McCoy, D., Savage, S., Voelker, G.M.: DefenestraTor: Throwing out Windows in Tor. In: Fischer-Hübner, S., Hopper, N. (eds.) PETS 2011. LNCS, vol. 6794, pp. 134–154. Springer, Heidelberg (2011)
3. Bauer, K., McCoy, D., Grunwald, D., Kohno, T., Sicker, D.: Low-Resource Routing Attacks against Tor. In: Proceedings of the Workshop on Privacy in the Electronic Society (WPES 2007), pp. 11–20 (October 2007)
4. Bauer, K., Sherr, M., McCoy, D., Grunwald, D.: ExperimenTor: A Testbed for Safe and Realistic Tor Experimentation. In: Proceedings of the USENIX Workshop on Cyber Security Experimentation and Test (CSET), pp. 51–59 (August 2011)
5. Blond, S.L., Manils, P., Chaabane, A., Kaafar, M.A., Castelluccia, C., Legout, A., Dabbous, W.: One Bad Apple Spoils the Bunch: Exploiting P2P Applications to Trace and Profile Tor Users. In: Proceedings of the 4th USENIX Conference on Large-scale Exploits and Emergent Threats, LEET 2011. USENIX Association (2011)
6. Borisov, N., Danezis, G., Mittal, P., Tabriz, P.: Denial of Service or Denial of Security? How Attacks on Reliability can Compromise Anonymity. In: Proceedings of CCS 2007, pp. 92–102 (October 2007)
7. Das, A., Borisov, N.: Securing Tor Tunnels under the Selective-DoS Attack. In: Proceedings of Financial Cryptography and Data Security (February 2013)
8. Dingledine, R., Mathewson, N.: Tor protocol specification, https://gitweb.torproject.org/torspec.git/blob/HEAD:/tor-spec.txt
9. Dingledine, R., Mathewson, N.: Anonymity Loves Company: Usability and the Network Effect. In: Workshop on the Economics of Information Security, pp. 547–559 (June 2006)

10. Dingledine, R., Mathewson, N., Syverson, P.: Tor: The Second-Generation Onion Router. In: Proceedings of the 13th USENIX Security Symposium, pp. 303–320 (2004)

11. Dingledine, R., Murdoch, S.: Performance Improvements on Tor or, Why Tor is Slow and What We're Going to Do about It (March 2009), http://www.torproject.org/press/presskit/2009-03-11-performance.pdf

12. Edman, M., Syverson, P.F.: AS-awareness in Tor path selection. In: Proceedings of the 2009 ACM Conference on Computer and Communications Security (CCS), pp. 380–389 (2009)

13. Elahi, T., Bauer, K., AlSabah, M., Dingledine, R., Goldberg, I.: Changing of the Guards: A Framework for Understanding and Improving Entry Guard Selection in Tor. In: Proceedings of the Workshop on Privacy in the Electronic Society (WPES 2012). ACM (October 2012)

14. Feigenbaum, J., Johnson, A., Syverson, P.: Preventing Active Timing Attacks in Low-Latency Anonymous Communication. In: Atallah, M.J., Hopper, N.J. (eds.) PETS 2010. LNCS, vol. 6205, pp. 166–183. Springer, Heidelberg (2010), http://portal.acm.org/citation.cfm?id=1881151.1881161

15. Gil, T.M., Kaashoek, F., Li, J., Morris, R., Stribling, J.: King Data Set, http://pdos.csail.mit.edu/p2psim/kingdata (accessed August 2011)

16. Gopal, D., Heninger, N.: Torchestra: Reducing Interactive Traffic Delays over Tor. In: Proceedings of the 2012 ACM Workshop on Privacy in the Electronic Society, WPES 2012, pp. 31–42. ACM, New York (2012)

17. Han, H., Shakkottai, S., Hollot, C.V., Srikant, R., Towsley, D.: Multi-path TCP: A Joint Congestion Control and Routing Scheme to Exploit Path Diversity in the Internet. IEEE/ACM Trans. Netw. 14(6), 1260–1271 (2006)

18. Hernández-Campos, F., Jeffay, K., Smith, F.D.: Tracking the Evolution of Web Traffic: 1995-2003. In: Proceedings of the 11th IEEE/ACM International Symposium on Modeling, Analysis and Simulation of Computer Telecommunication Systems (MASCOTS), pp. 16–25 (2003)

19. Jansen, R., Syverson, P., Hopper, N.: Throttling Tor Bandwidth Parasites. In: Proceedings of the 21st USENIX Security Symposium (August 2012)

20. Jansen, R., Bauer, K., Hopper, N., Dingledine, R.: Methodically Modeling the Tor Network. In: USENIX Workshop on Cyber Security Experimentation and Test (CSET) (August 2012)

21. Jansen, R., Hopper, N., Kim, Y.: Recruiting New Tor Relays with BRAIDS. In: Proceedings of ACM CCS, pp. 319–328 (October 2010)

22. King, A.: Average Web Page Size Septuples Since 2003. Website Optimization, LLC, http://www.websiteoptimization.com/speed/tweak/average-web-page (accessed February 14, 2012)

23. Landsiedel, O., Pimenidis, A., Wehrle, K., Niedermayer, H., Carle, G.: Dynamic Multipath Onion Routing in Anonymous Peer-to-Peer Overlay Networks. In: IEEE Global Telecommunications Conference, pp. 64–69 (November 2007)

24. Levine, B.N., Reiter, M.K., Wang, C., Wright, M.: Timing Attacks in Low-Latency Mix-Based Systems. In: Juels, A. (ed.) FC 2004. LNCS, vol. 3110, pp. 251–265. Springer, Heidelberg (2004)

25. Lewman, A.: China Blocking Tor: Round Two (March 2010), https://blog.torproject.org/blog/china-blocking-tor-round-two (accessed August 2011)

26. Ling, Z., Luo, J., Yu, W., Yang, M., Fu, X.: Extensive Analysis and Large-Scale Empirical Evaluation of Tor Bridge Discovery. In: Proceedings of the 31st IEEE International Conference on Computer Communications (INFOCOM) (March 2012)

27. Maier, G., Feldmann, A., Paxson, V., Allman, M.: On Dominant Characteristics of Residential Broadband Internet Traffic. In: Proceedings of the 9th ACM SIGCOMM Conference on Internet Measurement Conference, pp. 90–102 (November 2009)

28. McCoy, D., Bauer, K., Grunwald, D., Kohno, T., Sicker, D.: Shining Light in Dark Places: Understanding the Tor Network. In: Borisov, N., Goldberg, I. (eds.) PETS 2008. LNCS, vol. 5134, pp. 63–76. Springer, Heidelberg (2008)
29. McLachlan, J., Tran, A., Hopper, N., Kim, Y.: Scalable Onion Routing with Torsk. In: Proceedings of the 16th ACM Conference on Computer and Communications Security, CCS 2009, pp. 590–599. ACM, New York (2009)
30. Mittal, P., Olumofin, F., Troncoso, C., Borisov, N., Goldberg, I.: PIR-Tor: Scalable Anonymous Communication Using Private Information Retrieval. In: Proceedings of the 20th USENIX Security Symposium (August 2011)
31. Moore, W.B., Wacek, C., Sherr, M.: Exploring the Potential Benefits of Expanded Rate Limiting in Tor: Slow and Steady Wins the Race with Tortoise. In: Proceedings of the 27th Annual Computer Security Applications Conference, ACSAC 2011, pp. 207–216 (2011)
32. "Johnny" Ngan, T.-W., Dingledine, R., Wallach, D.S.: Building Incentives into Tor. In: Sion, R. (ed.) FC 2010. LNCS, vol. 6052, pp. 238–256. Springer, Heidelberg (2010)
33. Ookla: Net Index by Ookla — Source Data, http://www.netindex.com/source-data (accessed on January 27, 2012)
34. The OpenNet Initiative: YouTube Censored: A Recent History, http://opennet.net/youtube-censored-a-recent-history (accessed February 6, 2012)
35. Øverlier, L., Syverson, P.: Locating hidden servers. In: Proceedings of the 2006 IEEE Symposium on Security and Privacy, pp. 100–114 (May 2006)
36. Piatek, M., Kohno, T., Krishnamurthy, A.: Challenges and Directions for Monitoring P2P File Sharing Networks-or: Why My Printer Received a DMCA Takedown Notice. In: Proceedings of the 3rd Conference on Hot Topics in Security, pp. 12:1–12:7 (July 2008)
37. Ramachandran, S.: Web Metrics: Size and Number of Resources, https://code.google.com/speed/articles/web-metrics.html (accessed August 2011)
38. Rao, A., Legout, A., Lim, Y.S., Towsley, D., Barakat, C., Dabbous, W.: Network Characteristics of Video Streaming Traffic. In: Proceedings of the Seventh Conference on Emerging Networking EXperiments and Technologies, CoNEXT 2011, pp. 25:1–25:12. ACM, New York (2011)
39. Reardon, J., Goldberg, I.: Improving Tor Using a TCP-over-DTLS Tunnel. In: Proceedings of the 18th USENIX Security Symposium (August 2009)
40. Reed, M.G., Syverson, P.F., Goldschlag, D.M.: Anonymous Connections and Onion Routing. IEEE Journal on Selected Areas in Communication 16(4), 482–494 (1998)
41. Sandvine: Sandvine Global Internet Phenomena Report — Fall 2011 (October 2011), http://www.sandvine.com/downloads/documents/10-26-2011_phenomena/Sandvine%20Global%20Internet%20Phenomena%20Report%20-%20Fall%202011.pdf
42. Serjantov, A., Murdoch, S.J.: Message Splitting Against the Partial Adversary. In: Danezis, G., Martin, D. (eds.) PET 2005. LNCS, vol. 3856, pp. 26–39. Springer, Heidelberg (2006)
43. Serjantov, A., Sewell, P.: Passive Attack Analysis for Connection-Based Anonymity Systems. In: Snekkenes, E., Gollmann, D. (eds.) ESORICS 2003. LNCS, vol. 2808, pp. 116–131. Springer, Heidelberg (2003)
44. Sherr, M., Blaze, M., Loo, B.T.: Scalable Link-Based Relay Selection for Anonymous Routing. In: Goldberg, I., Atallah, M.J. (eds.) PETS 2009. LNCS, vol. 5672, pp. 73–93. Springer, Heidelberg (2009)
45. Shmatikov, V., Wang, M.H.: Timing Analysis in Low-Latency Mix Networks: Attacks and Defenses. In: Gollmann, D., Meier, J., Sabelfeld, A. (eds.) ESORICS 2006. LNCS, vol. 4189, pp. 18–33. Springer, Heidelberg (2006)
46. Snader, R.: Path Selection for Performance- and Security-Improved Onion Routing. Ph.D. thesis, University of Illinois at Urbana-Champaign (2010)

47. Snader, R., Borisov, N.: A Tune-up for Tor: Improving Security and Performance in the Tor Network. In: Proceedings of the Network and Distributed Security Symposium (NDSS) (February 2008)

48. Syverson, P., Tsudik, G., Reed, M., Landwehr, C.: Towards an Analysis of Onion Routing Security. In: Federrath, H. (ed.) Anonymity 2000. LNCS, vol. 2009, pp. 96–114. Springer, Heidelberg (2001)

49. Tang, C., Goldberg, I.: An Improved Algorithm for Tor Circuit Scheduling. In: Proceedings of the 17th ACM Conference on Computer and Communications Security, pp. 329–339. ACM, New York (2010)

50. The Tor Project: Codename: Torouter, `https://trac.torproject.org/projects/tor/wiki/doc/TorouterAssignedTicketstothisproject` (accessed August 2011)

51. The Tor Project: Tor Metrics Portal: Bandwidth History by Relay Flags, `https://metrics.torproject.org/network.html?graph=bwhist-flags&start=2012-07-01&end=2012-07-02&dpi=72#bwhist-flags` (accessed July 2012)

52. The Tor Project: Tor Metrics Portal: Data, `https://metrics.torproject.org/data.html#performance` (accessed November 2012)

53. The Tor Project: Tor Metrics Portal: Network, `http://metrics.torproject.org/network.html?graph=networksize&start=2012-01-01&end=2012-01-31&dpi=72#networksize` (accessed November 2012)

54. The Tor Project: Tor Metrics Portal: Users, `http://metrics.torproject.org/users.html` (accessed November 2012)

55. The Tor Project: Tor Bridges Specification (May 2009), `https://gitweb.torproject.org/torspec.git/blob_plain/HEAD:/bridges-spec.txt` (accessed August 2011)

56. Tran, A., Hopper, N., Kim, Y.: Hashing It out in Public: Common Failure Modes of DHT-based Anonymity Schemes. In: ACM Workshop on Privacy in the Electronic Society, pp. 71–80 (November 2009)

57. Vahdat, A., Yocum, K., Walsh, K., Mahadevan, P., Kostić, D., Chase, J., Becker, D.: Scalability and Accuracy in a Large-Scale Network Emulator. SIGOPS Oper. Syst. Rev. 36, 271–284 (2002)

58. Wacek, C., Tan, H., Bauer, K., Sherr, M.: An Empirical Evaluation of Relay Selection in Tor. In: Proceedings of the Network and Distributed Security Symposium (NDSS) (February 2013)

59. Wang, T., Bauer, K., Forero, C., Goldberg, I.: Congestion-aware Path Selection for Tor. In: Keromytis, A.D. (ed.) FC 2012. LNCS, vol. 7397, pp. 98–113. Springer, Heidelberg (2012)

60. Wright, M.K., Adler, M., Levine, B.N., Shields, C.: The Predecessor Attack: An Analysis of a Threat to Anonymous Communications Systems. ACM Trans. Inf. Syst. Secur. 7(4), 489–522 (2004)

61. Xu, X., Mao, Z.M., Halderman, J.A.: Internet Censorship in China: Where Does the Filtering Occur? In: Spring, N., Riley, G.F. (eds.) PAM 2011. LNCS, vol. 6579, pp. 133–142. Springer, Heidelberg (2011)

How Low Can You Go: Balancing Performance with Anonymity in Tor

John Geddes[1], Rob Jansen[2], and Nicholas Hopper[1]

[1] University of Minnesota, Minneapolis, MN
[2] U.S. Naval Research Laboratory, Washington, DC

Abstract. Tor is one of the most popular anonymity systems in use today, in part because of its design goal of providing high performance. This has motivated research into performance enhancing modifications to Tor's circuit scheduling, congestion control, and bandwidth allocation mechanisms. This paper investigates the effects of these proposed modifications on attacks that rely on network measurements as a side channel. We introduce a new class of *induced throttling* attacks in this space that exploit performance enhancing mechanisms to artificially throttle a circuit. We show that these attacks can drastically reduce the set of probable entry guards on a circuit, in many cases uniquely identifying the entry guard. Comparing to existing attacks, we find that although most of the performance enhancing modifications improve the accuracy of network measurements, the effectiveness of the attacks is reduced in some cases by making the Tor network more homogeneous. We conclude with an analysis of the total reduction in anonymity that clients face due to each proposed mechanism.

1 Introduction

The Tor [10] network is a widely-used anonymity and censorship-circumvention tool that provides anonymous Internet access to millions of users every day. This anonymity is provided by routing user traffic through a *circuit* of three relays, using layered encryption to prevent any single relay from seeing more than the next and previous links in the circuit, so that a relay may know the origin or destination of a connection, but not both. The Tor network allows users to participate as clients without contributing as relays, to build a greater variety of plausible uses of the network and provide a larger anonymity set.

One of the key design choices of the Tor system is the goal of building a large anonymity set by providing high performance to as many users as possible, while sacrificing some level of protection from large-scale (global) adversaries. For example, Tor does not attempt to protect against an end-to-end correlation attack that certain mix systems try to prevent [7, 14, 25], as they introduce large costs in increased latency making such systems difficult to use. This performance focus has led researchers to investigate a variety of methods to improve performance, such as using different circuit scheduling algorithms [30], better congestion control [2], and throttling high bandwidth clients [13, 22, 26]. Several

E. De Cristofaro and M. Wright (Eds.): PETS 2013, LNCS 7981, pp. 164–184, 2013.

of these mechanisms have been or will be incorporated into the Tor software as a result of this research.

One overlooked side effect of these improvements, however, is that in some cases improving the performance of users can also improve the performance of attacks against the Tor network. For example, several attacks have been proposed [12, 17, 24, 27] that rely on measuring the latency or throughput of a Tor circuit to draw inferences about its source and destination. If an algorithm improves the throughput or responsiveness of Tor circuits this can improve the accuracy of the measurements used by these attacks either directly or by averaging a larger sample. Thus it is important to analyze how these modifications to Tor interact with attacks based on network measurements.

In this paper we investigate this interaction. We start by introducing a new class of attacks based on network measurement, which we call *induced throttling* attacks. In these attacks, an adversarial exit node exploits congestion or traffic admission control algorithms to artificially throttle and unthrottle a chosen circuit without directly sending data through the circuit or relay. This leads to a recognizable pattern in other circuits sharing resources with the target circuit, leaking information about the connection between the client and entry guard. We show that there are highly effective induced throttling attacks against most of the proposed scheduling, flow control, and admission control modifications to Tor, allowing an adversary to uniquely identify entry guards in many cases.

We also examine the effect these algorithms have on previous attacks [17, 24] to see if the improvement in performance, and therefore in network measurements, leads to more successful attacks. Through large-scale simulation, we find that for throughput attacks, the improved network measurements are essentially "cancelled out" by the reduced variance in performance provided by these improvements. We also find that nearly all of the proposed improvements increase the effectiveness of latency-based attacks, in many cases leading to a 10% or higher loss in "degree of anonymity."

Finally, we perform a comprehensive analysis of the combined effects of throughput, induced throttling and latency-measurement attacks. We show that using induced throttling, the combined attacks can in many cases uniquely identify the source of a circuit by a likelihood ratio test. These results indicate that flow and admission control algorithms can have considerable impact on the security as well as performance of the Tor network, and new proposals must be evaluated for resistance to induced throttling.

2 Background and Related Work

This section discusses the proposed performance-enhancing algorithms for and attacks against Tor to facilitate an understanding of our work.

2.1 Tor

As previously mentioned, Tor is the most popular anonymity and censorship-circumvention system, currently consisting of roughly 3000 relays and millions of daily users. During the circuit building process, each client chooses the entry relay into the Tor network from a small set of relays (currently three). Every circuit built by the client will begin with one of these *guard relays* in order to prevent passive logging attacks [28, 32]. It is generally considered feasible for an adversary to eventually de-anonymize a client by combining knowledge of a client's guard nodes with other attacks [4, 17].

2.2   Circuit Scheduling

Tor traditionally used a round robin [15] fair queuing algorithm to determine which among the active circuits on an onion-routing connection to send from next. Although the round robin algorithm is still the software default, the network directory authorities are currently distributing configuration options that enable an EWMA-based algorithm. The EWMA algorithm selects the circuit with the lowest exponentially weighted moving average throughput, and was suggested by Tang and Goldberg [30] in order to reduce latency and prioritize performance for low throughput circuits.

2.3   Congestion Control

The high client-to-relay ratio in Tor causes performance problems that have been the focus of a considerable amount of previous research. The main congestion control mechanism used by Tor is an end-to-end window based system, where the exit relay and client use SENDME control cells to infer network level congestion. Tor separates data flowing inbound from data flowing outbound,[1] and congestion control mechanisms operate independently on each flow. Each circuit starts with an initial 1000 cell window which is decremented by the source edge node for every cell sent. When the window reaches 0, the source edge stops sending. Upon receiving 100 cells, the receiver edge node returns a SENDME cell to the source edge, allowing the source edge to increment its circuit window by 100 and continue sending more cells.

Tor's *end-to-end* congestion control is slow to react to congestion that occurs in the middle of circuits. Therefore, AlSabah *et al.* introduced N23 [2], a link based algorithm that can instead detect and react to congestion on every *link* in the circuit. Similar to the native congestion control mechanism in Tor, each relay in an N23-controlled circuit initializes its credit balance to $N2 + N3$ and decrements it by one for every cell it forwards. After a node has forwarded $N2$ cells, it returns back a flow control cell containing the number of forwarded cells to the backward relay. Upon receiving a flow control cell from the forward relay, the backward relay updates its credit balance to be $N2+N3$ minus the difference in cells it has forwarded and cells the forward relay has forwarded.

---

[1] Throughout this paper, we use *inbound* to indicate the direction toward the client edge of a circuit, and *outbound* to indicate the direction toward the exit relay edge of a circuit. Relatedly, we use *forward* to indicate the direction of the destination of a data flow, and *backward* to indicate the direction of the source of a data flow.

2.4   Traffic Admission Control

Guard nodes in Tor have the ability[2] to throttle clients using a basic rate limiter [9]. The algorithm uses a token bucket whose size and refill rate are configurable to enforce a long-term average throughput while allowing short-term data bursts. The intuition behind the algorithm is that a throttling guard node will limit the client's rate of requests for new data, which will lower the outstanding amount of data that exists inside the network at any given time and generally reduce congestion and improve performance.

There have been many proposed uses of and alterations to the approach outlined above, some of which vary the connections that are throttled [1, 22, 26] and others that vary the throttle rate [13, 22, 26]. Of particular interest are algorithms that dynamically utilize the number of client-to-guard (C-G) connections to adjust throttling rates [22]: the *bitsplit* algorithm divides its configured BandwidthRate evenly among C-G connections; the *flag* algorithm uses the number of C-G connections to determine the rate over which a client will get flagged as "high throughput" and throttled; and the *threshold* algorithm throttles the loudest fraction of C-G connections.

2.5   Known Attacks

Murdoch and Danezis previously proposed a Tor circuit clogging attack [27] in which the adversary sends data through a circuit in order to cause congestion and change its latency characteristics. The adversary correlates the latency variations of this circuit with those of circuits through other relays in order to identify the likely relays of a target circuit. The attack requires significant bandwidth in order to produce a signal strong enough for correlation, and it has been shown to be no longer effective [12]. There have been numerous variations on this attack, some of which have simple defenses [12, 18] and others that have low success rates [4]. This work does not consider these "general" congestion attacks where the main focus is keeping bandwidth usage small enough to remain practical. Instead, we focus on the feasibility and anonymity effects of new induced throttling attacks introduced by recent performance enhancing algorithm proposals.

Mittal *et al.* recently proposed "stealthy" throughput attacks [24] where an adversary that controls an exit node of a circuit attempts to find its guard relay by using "probe" clients that measure the attainable throughput through each relay.[3] The adversary may then correlate the circuit throughput measured at the exit node with the throughput of each of its probes to find the guard node with high probability. Some of our attacks also utilize probe clients in order to recognize the signal produced once throttling has been induced on a circuit. Hopper *et al.* [17] propose an attack where an adversary injects malicious javascript into a webpage in order to measure the round trip time of a circuit. The adversary may use these measurements to narrow the possible path the

---

[2] Tor does not currently enable throttling by default.

[3] The attack is active in that an adversary launches it by sending data to relays, but stealthy in that its data streams are indistinguishable from normal client streams.

target circuit is taking through the network and approximate the geographical location of the client. As our techniques are similar to both of these attacks, we include them in our evaluation in Section 4 and analysis in Section 7.

3 Methodology

The remainder of this paper will focus on the proposed changes to Tor's internal algorithms that aim to reduce congestion or throttle circuits as discussed in Section 2. In particular, we consider three classes of algorithms that have been recently proposed: EWMA circuit scheduling [30]; N23 congestion control [2]; and bitsplit, flag, and threshold throttling [22]. We will also consider an *ideal* throttling algorithm that has perfect knowledge of the traffic type of every stream.[4]

3.1 Metrics

We will explore new algorithm-specific attacks we have developed, as well as previously published generic attacks [17, 24], and quantify the extent to which the attacks affect anonymity. In analyzing the algorithms, we can expect them to have one of two effects: the algorithms may improve the effectiveness of statistical attacks by making side channel *throughput* and *latency* measurements more accurate, improving the adversary's ability to de-anonymize the client; or the algorithms may reduce the noise that an adversary uses to eliminate entry guards and clients from the potential candidate set, frustrating the attacks and improving client anonymity. We will use the following metrics to determine the extent to which our attacks affect anonymity:

Percentile. The *percentile* for a candidate target T of an attack is defined as the percent of other candidate targets (i.e., members of the anonymity set) with a lower score than T, based on statistical information the attacker uses to score each candidate as the true target. A higher *percentile* for T means there is a greater likelihood that T is the true target. Percentiles allow an attacker to reduce uncertainty by increasing confidence about the true target, or increasing confidence in rejecting candidates unlikely to be the true target.

Degrees of Anonymity. In order to measure the actual level of anonymity lost in the attacks for each algorithm, we first analyze reduction in terms of *entropy* [8, 29] and then compute the *degree of anonymity* [8]. Entropy quantifies uncertainty an adversary has about a target, while the degree of anonymity loss provides us with how much total information a system is leaking. We create a reduced anonymity set based on a threshold value determining what entities to include or discard, then for each possible threshold value we calculate the degree of anonymity *loss*. While this may not show the direct implications of anonymity

---

[4] The algorithm throttles high throughput nodes at a rate of 50 KiB/s and approximates the difftor approach of AlSabah *et al.* [1].

loss on each client, we can determine the best case scenario for a potential adversary by examining the maximum amount of information leakage possible. Perhaps more importantly, it allows us to do cross experimental comparisons to determine the effect that different algorithms have under different attack scenarios.

Client Probability. In order to determine the total reduction in anonymity, we consider the probability distribution that clients have before and after an attack. Given a set of relays R, the *a priori* probability that a relay R_i is the guard node G is $P[G = R_i] = \frac{1}{|R|}$. In addition, for each relay R_i and a set of clients C, the *a priori* probability that a client C_i is the victim V is $P[V = C_i|R_j] = \frac{1}{|C|}$. Therefore, we define the probability that any client C_i is the victim as: $P[V = C_i] = \sum_j P[V = C_i|R_j]P[G = R_j]$. For our purposes, an attack can affect this metric in one of two ways: it either will attempt to identify possible entry guards, thus changing the probability distribution $P[G = R_i]$; or it tries to reduce the set of possible clients given that it knows a potential entry guard, in which case the distribution $P[V = C_i|R_j]$ is updated for each relay R_j.

3.2 Experimental Setup and Model

Our experiments will utilize the Shadow simulator [19, 21], an accurate discrete event simulator that runs the real Tor code over a simulated network. Shadow allows us to configure large scale experiments running on network sizes not feasible using traditional distributed network testbeds [5] while offering precise control over network topology, latency, and bandwidth characteristics. Shadow also allows us to: control Tor's circuit creation process; experiment with our attacks in a safe environment; and run repeatable experiments while only modifying the algorithm or attack scenario of interest, resulting in more controlled and accurate evaluations and comparisons.

We developed a model of the Tor network based on work by Jansen *et al.* [20], and use it as the base of each large scale experiment in the following sections. We will discuss necessary changes to the following base configuration as we explore each specific attack scenario: 160 exit relays, 240 nonexit relays, 2375 web clients, 125 bulk clients, 75 small TorPerf clients, 75 medium TorPerf clients, 75 large TorPerf clients, and 400 HTTP servers. The web client downloads a 320 KiB file from one of the randomly selected servers, after which it sleeps for a time between 1 and 60 seconds drawn uniformly at random before starting the next download. The bulk clients repeatedly download a 5 MiB file with no wait time between downloads. Finally, the TorPerf clients only perform one download every 10 minutes, where the small, medium and large clients download 50 KiB, 1 MiB and 5MiB files respectively. This distribution of clients is used to approximate the findings of McCoy *et al.* [23], Chaabane *et al.* [3] and data from Tor [31].

4   Algorithmic Effects on Known Attacks

This section evaluates how recently proposed performance enhancing algorithms affect previously known guard and client identification attacks against Tor.

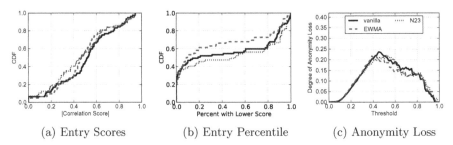

(a) Entry Scores   (b) Entry Percentile   (c) Anonymity Loss

Fig. 1. Results for throughput attack with vanilla Tor compared to EWMA and N23 scheduling and congestion control algorithms

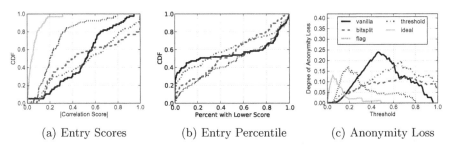

(a) Entry Scores   (b) Entry Percentile   (c) Anonymity Loss

Fig. 2. Results for throughput attack with vanilla Tor compared to different throttling algorithms

4.1   Throughput as a Signal

We first explore the scenario of Mittal *et al.* [24], where an attacker is able to identify the guard relay of a circuit with high probability by correlating throughput measured at an adversarial exit node to probe measurements made through a set of entry guards.

We first ran our base experiment from Section 3.2 to discover the circuits that each bulk client created. Then, for every entry G that was not a middle or exit relay for any bulk client, we instantiated a probe client that created a one-hop circuit through G in order to measure its throughput. This was done to minimize the interference of other probes on bulk circuits, where they only potentially affect the circuit they are measuring and no other. We compared vanilla Tor with 6 different algorithms: EWMA circuit scheduling [30], N23 congestion control [2], bitsplit, flag, and threshold throttling [22], and ideal throttling.

The results for the EWMA and N23 algorithms can be seen in Figure 1. Figure 1a shows the correlation of each entry's throughput to that measured by its assigned probe client as a cumulative distribution function (CDF). High correlation scores mean changes in the true entry's throughput strongly corresponds with changes in the probe's throughput. Figure 1b shows, for each candidate entry, the percent of other candidates with a lower score (see Section 3.1). Correlation scores and percentiles can help the attacker reduce uncertainty about the entry node of the target circuit. Figure 1c shows the degree of anonymity loss while varying the threshold value, that is, the minimum correlation score an entry guard must have to be included in set of possible guards. Our results indicate that there are more candidates that match well with the true entry with EWMA (i.e., more uncertainty about the true entry). However, both EWMA and N23 result in insignificant anonymity loss compared to vanilla Tor.

Results for the throttling algorithms are shown in Figure 2. We found incredibly low entry guard correlation scores for the ideal and flag algorithms in Figure 2a, and Figure 2b shows that 48% of entry guards are in the top quintile of the list based on correlation score in vanilla Tor, while only 22-41% of the guards in the throttling algorithm experiments made it in the top quintile. Figure 2c shows a much larger peak in anonymity loss for vanilla Tor compared to all other algorithms, indicating that an adversary would expect more information leakage when choosing the threshold correctly. This implies that the throttling algorithms would actually result in a *larger* anonymity set for the adversary, making the attack less accurate. Intuitively, the throughput of throttled circuits tend to be more similar than the throughput of unthrottled circuits, increasing the uncertainty during the attack. The throttling algorithms effectively smooth out circuit throughput to the configured long-term throttle rate, making it more difficult to distinguish the actual entry guard from the set of potential guards.

4.2   Latency as a Signal

We now explore the latency attack of Hopper *et al.* [17]. They show how an adversarial exit relay, having learned the identity of the entry guard in the circuit, is able to estimate the latency between the client and guard. This is accomplished by creating two ping streams through the circuit, one originating from the client and one from the attacker. The ping stream from the attacker is used to estimate the latency between the entry guard and the exit relay which, when subtracted from the ping times between the client and exit relay produces an estimate of latency·between the client and guard. Using network coordinates to compile the set of "actual" latencies between potential clients and guards, the adversary is then able to reduce the anonymity set of clients based on the estimated latency. Since this attack relies on the accuracy of the estimated latency measurements, the majority of the algorithms have the potential to *decrease* the anonymity of the clients by allowing an adversary to discard more potential clients.

For our experiments, we use the same base configuration with 400 relays and 2500 clients, with an additional 250 victim clients setup to send pings through the Tor circuit every 5 seconds. Then, for each victim client a corresponding attacker client is added, which creates an identical circuit to the one used by the victim, and then sends a ping over this circuit every 5 seconds. These corresponding ping clients are used to calculate the estimated latency between the victim and entry guard as discussed above. In order to determine the actual latencies between the clients and guard node, we utilize the fact that Shadow determines the latency distribution that is sampled from between each node that communicates in the experiment, so we merely assign the median latency of these distributions

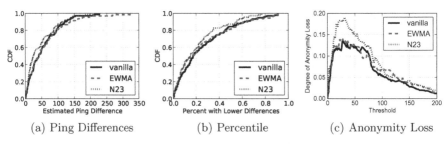

(a) Ping Differences   (b) Percentile   (c) Anonymity Loss

Fig. 3. Results of latency attack on EWMA and N23 algorithms

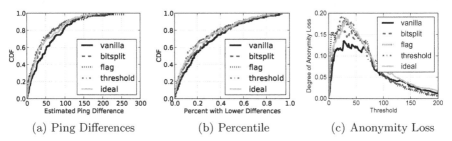

(a) Ping Differences   (b) Percentile   (c) Anonymity Loss

Fig. 4. Results of latency attack on the various throttling algorithms

as the actual latencies between nodes. This would correspond to the analysis done in [17] where it is assumed that these quantities were known *a priori*, so we believe using this "insider information" doesn't contradict any assumptions made in the initial paper outlining the attack. Furthermore, since we're ultimately concerned with how the attacks differ using various algorithms, the analysis should hold.

Similar to the original attack, we take the minimum of all observed ping times seen over both the victim and attacker circuit, denoted T_{VX} and T_{AX} respectively. Then, an estimate of the latency between the victim and entry guard, T_{VE}, is calculated as $\hat{T}_{AE} = T_{VX} - T_{AX} + T_{AE}$, where T_{AE} is the latency between the attacker and entry guard as calculated above. Figures 3a and 4a show the difference in estimated latency computed by an adversary and the actual latency between the client and guard, while Figures 3b and 4b show how these compare with the differences between the estimate and other possible clients. While these graphs only show a slight improvement for every algorithm except EWMA, the degree of anonymity loss in Figures 3c and 4c shows a noticeable increase in the maximum possible information gain an adversary can achieve. Even though there is only a slight improvement in the accuracy of the latency estimation, this allows an adversary to consider a smaller window around the estimation to filter out potential clients while still retaining similar accuracy rates. This results in a smaller set of potential clients to consider, and thus a higher reduction in anonymity of the victim client.

5   Induced Throttling via Congestion Control

We now look at how an attacker is able to use specific mechanisms in the congestion control algorithms to induce throttling on a target circuit.

5.1   Artificial Congestion

Recall from Section 2.3, the congestion control algorithms send control cells backward to notify edge nodes to send more data. If there is congestion and the nodes go long enough without receiving these cells, they stop sending data until the next control cell is received. Using these mechanisms, an adversarial exit node can implicitly control when a client can and cannot send data forward, thereby inducing artificial congestion.

To demonstrate the effectiveness of such techniques, we introduce a more detailed "torrent" client that models the BitTorrent protocol and mimics a "tit-for-tat" scheme [6]. Instead of downloading a file from a server as is done by the existing web and bulk clients, the torrent client swaps 16 KiB blocks of data with a peer. This swapping causes large amounts of data to both be uploaded and downloaded and allows us to demonstrate attacks that induce artificial congestion. In our experiment, a bulk and torrent client create connections over the same circuit, where each relay was configured with 128 KiB/s bandwidth. The exit relay would then periodically hold all torrent client control cells in an attempt to throttle the connection. Figure 5 shows the observed throughput of both clients, where the shaded regions indicate periods when the exit relay was holding control cells bound for the torrent client. We can see that approximately 30 seconds into these periods, the torrent client runs out of available cells to send and goes into an idle state, leaving more resources to the bulk client resulting in a rise in the observed throughput.

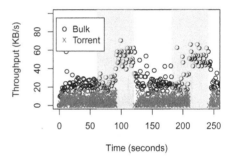

Fig. 5. The effects of using artificial congestion to induce throttling

Next we want to identify how a potential adversary could utilize this in an attempt to identify entry guards used in a circuit. We can see the intuition behind the attack in Figure 5: when throttling of a circuit is repeatedly toggled, the throughput of all other circuits going through those nodes will increase and then decrease, producing a noticeable pattern which an adversary may be able to detect. We assume a scenario similar to previous attacks [12,24,27], where an adversary controls an exit node and wants to identify the entry guard of a circuit going through them. The adversary creates one-hop probe circuits through possible entry guards by extending circuits through middle relays that the adversary controls, and measures the throughput and congestion on each circuit at a constant interval. The adversary then periodically throttles the circuit by holding control cells and tests for an increase in throughput for the duration of the attack. By repeatedly performing this action an attacker should be able to reduce the possible set of entry guards that the circuit might be using.

5.2 Small Scale Experiment

To test the feasibility of such an attack, we designed a small scale experiment with 20 relays, 190 web clients and 10 bulk clients. One of the exit relays was designated as the adversary and one of the bulk clients was designated as the victim. The victim bulk client was then configured to use the torrent client while creating circuits using the adversary as their exit relay. Then, for each of the 19 remaining non-adversarial relays, a probe client was added and configured to create one-hop circuits through the relay, measuring observed throughput in 100 ms intervals. The adversarial exit relay would then wait until the victim client created the connection, then every 60 seconds would toggle between normal mode in which all control cells are sent as appropriate, and throttle mode where all control cells are held.

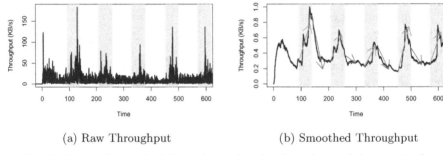

(a) Raw Throughput   (b) Smoothed Throughput

Fig. 6. Raw and smoothed throughput of probe through guard during attack

Figure 6a shows the observed throughput at the probe client connected to the entry guard that the victim client was using, where the shaded regions correspond to the periods where the victim client runs out of available cells to send and is throttled. During these periods the probe client sees a large spike in observed throughput as more resources become available at the guard relay. While these changes are visually identifiable, we need a quantitative test that can deal with noise and variability in order to analyze a large number of probe clients and reduce the set of possible guards.

5.3 Smoothing Throughput

The first step is to smooth out the throughput measurements for each probe client in order to filter out any noise. Given throughput measurements (t_i, b_i), we first compute the exponentially weighted moving average (EWMA), using $\alpha = 0.01$. We then take the output from EWMA and pass it through a cubic spline smoothing algorithm [16] with smoothing parameter $\lambda = 0.5$. The result of this process can be seen in Figure 6b with the normalized smoothed throughput plotted over the shaded attack windows.

5.4   Scoring Algorithm

The intuition behind the scoring algorithm can be seen in Figure 6b. Over each attack window marked by the shaded regions, the guard probe client should see large increases and decreases in throughput at the beginning and end of the window. Here we want the scoring algorithm to place heavy weight on consistent large increases and decreases that align with all the windows, while at the same time minimizing false positives from potentially assigning too much weight to large spikes that randomly happen to align with the attack window.

The first step of the scoring algorithm is to calculate a linear regression on the smoothed throughput over the first δ seconds[5] at the start and end of each attack window and collect the slope values s_i and e_i for the start and end regression. Then for each window i, first sort all probe clients based on their s_i slope value from highest to lowest, and for each probe client record their relative rank r_{s_i}. Repeat this for the slope value e_i, only instead sort the clients from lowest to highest, again recording their relative rank r_{e_i}. Rankings are used instead of the raw slope value in order to prevent the false positives from large spikes mentioned previously. Now that each probe client has a set of ranks $\{r_{s_1}, r_{e_1}, \ldots, r_{s_n}, r_{e_n}\}$ over n attack windows, the final score assigned to each client is simply the mean of all the ranks, where the lower the score the higher chance the probe client connected through the entry guard.

5.5   Large Scale Experiments

In order to test the accuracy of this attack on a large scale, we used the base experiment setup discussed in Section 3.2, with the addition of one-hop probe clients to connect through each relay. For each run, a random circuit used by a bulk node was chosen to be the attack circuit and the exit node used in the circuit was made an attacker node. The bulk node was then updated to run a torrent client, and the probe clients that were initially set up to probe the middle and exit relays were removed. For each algorithm, we performed 40 runs with the different attack circuits chosen for each run. We configure the experiments with the vanilla Tor algorithm which uses SENDME cells for congestion control, and the N23 congestion control algorithm with $N3 = 500$ and $N3 = 100$. We experimented with having the torrent client send 1, 2, 5, and 10 streams over the circuit. The single stream results are shown in Figure 7 and the multiple stream results in Figure 8.

Figure 7a shows the CDF of the average score computed by the ranking algorithm for the entry guards' probe client, while Figure 7b shows the CDF of the percent of probe clients with a higher rank (i.e. worse score) than the true guard's probe client. Interestingly, even though in vanilla Tor not a single entry

---

[5] Through empirical evaluation we found $\delta = 30$ seconds to be ideal.

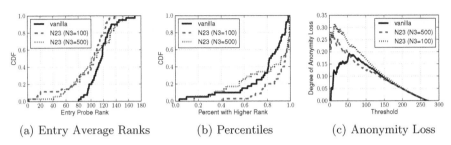

(a) Entry Average Ranks   (b) Percentiles   (c) Anonymity Loss

Fig. 7. Large-scale induced throttling via congestion control. The torrent client sends a single stream over the circuit.

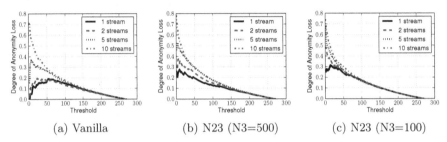

(a) Vanilla   (b) N23 (N3=500)   (c) N23 (N3=100)

Fig. 8. Large-scale induced throttling via congestion control. The torrent client sends multiple streams over the circuit. The anonymity loss is higher when the torrent client utilizes more streams.

guard probe had a score better than 150 out of 400, we still see about 80% of the entry guard probe clients were in the 25th percentile amongst all probe clients. Furthermore, we see that the attack is much more successful with the N23 algorithm, especially with $N3 = 100$, with peaks in degree of anonymity loss at 31%, compared to 27% with $N3 = 500$ and 19% in vanilla Tor. This is due to the fact that it is easier to induce throttling with N23, especially when the $N3$ value is low. In vanilla Tor, the initial window is set at 1000 cells, while for the N23 algorithm this would be $N2 + N3$, which works out to 510 and 110 cells for $N3 = 500$ and $N2 = 100$ respectively (default value for $N2$ is 10). The outcome is that for N23 with $N3 = 100$, we were able to throttle the attack circuit around 12 times, resulting in 24 comparison points over all attack windows, while both with $N3 = 500$ and vanilla Tor we see around 7 attack windows, resulting in 14 comparison points. The reason that we see slightly better entry probe rankings with $N3 = 500$ than vanilla Tor is because with N23, each node buffers cells when it runs out of credit, while vanilla Tor buffers cells at the client. This means when the congestion control cell is finally sent by the attacker, it would cause the entry guard to flush the circuits buffer and cause an immediately noticeable change in throughput and thus a higher rank score for the entry guard.

While using one circuit for one stream is the ideal greedy strategy for a BitTorrent client using Tor, it may not always be feasible to accomplish this. To explore what effects sending multiple streams over a circuit has on the attacks, for each algorithm we experimented having our torrent client send 2, 5, and 10 streams over the circuit that the attacker throttles. The results are shown in Figure 8. For each algorithm, we can see how the degree of anonymity loss changes as more streams are multiplexed over a single Tor circuit. Not surprisingly, all three algorithms have a high degree of anonymity loss when sending 10 streams over the circuit, as this dramatically increases the amount of data being sent over the circuit. Thus, when the artificial throttling is induced, there will be larger variations and changes in observed throughput at the entry guard's probe client. Even adding a single extra stream to the circuit can in some cases cause a noticeable reduction in the degree of anonymity, as particularly exemplified by the N23 algorithm with $N3 = 100$ (Figure 8c).

6   Induced Throttling via Traffic Admission Control

We now explore how an attacker is able to use specific mechanisms in proposed traffic admission control algorithms to induce throttling on a target circuit, creating a throughput signal at much lower cost than the techniques required in [24].

6.1   Connection Sybils

Recall that each of the algorithms proposed in [22] relies on the number of client-to-guard connections to adaptively adjust the throttle rate (see Section 2). Unfortunately, this feature may be controlled by the adversary during an active sybil attack [11]: an adversary may either modify a Tor client to create multiple connections to a target guard relay instead of just one, or boot multiple Tor clients that are each instructed to connect to the same target.[6] As a result, the number of connections C at the target will increase to $C = C_n + C_s$, where C_n is the number of normal connections and C_s is the number of sybil connections. The throttling algorithms will be affected as follows: the *bitsplit* algorithm will lower the throttle rate to $\frac{\texttt{BandwidthRate}}{C_n + C_s}$; the *flag* algorithm will throttle any connection whose average throughput has ever exceeded $\frac{\texttt{BandwidthRate}}{C_n + C_s}$ to the configured flag rate; and the *threshold* algorithm will throttle the loudest fraction f of connections to the throughput of the quietest of that throttled set (but no less than a floor of 50 KiB/s).[7] Therefore, the attacker may cause the throttle rate at any guard relay to reduce dramatically in all of the algorithms by using enough sybils. In this way, an adversary controlling an exit node can determine the guard node belonging to a target circuit with high probability. Note that the attacker need not use any bandwidth or computational resources beyond that which is required to establish the connections from its client(s) to the target guard relay.

We test the feasibility of this attack in Shadow. We configure a network with 5 relays, a file server, and a single victim client that downloads a large file from the server through Tor for 300 seconds. The adversary controls the exit relay on

---

[6] A similar attack was previously described in [22], Section 5.2, Attack 4.

[7] We use a flag rate of 5 KiB/s and a threshold of $f = 0.10$ as advised in [22]

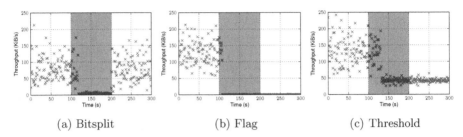

(a) Bitsplit   (b) Flag   (c) Threshold

Fig. 9. Small scale sybil attack on the bandwidth throttling algorithms from [22]. The shaded area represents the period during which the attack is active. The sybils cause an easily recognizable drop in throughput on the target circuit.

the client's circuit and therefore is able to compute the client's throughput. The attacker starts multiple sybil nodes at time $t = 100$ seconds that each connect to the same entry relay used by the victim. The sybil nodes are shut down at $t = 200$, after being active for 100 seconds.

The results of this attack on each algorithm are shown in Figure 9, where the shaded area represents the time during which the attack was active. Figure 9a shows that the *bitsplit* algorithm is only affected while the attack is active, after which the client throughput returns to normal. However, the client throughput remains degraded in both Figures 9b and 9c—the *flag* algorithm flagged the client as a high throughput node and did not unflag it while the *threshold* algorithm continued to throttle at the 50 KiB/s floor. Further, notice that the throttling does not occur until roughly 10 to 20 seconds after the attack has begun. This is due to the size of the token bucket, i.e., the `BandwidthBurst` configuration: the attack causes the refill rate to drop dramatically, but it takes time for the client to use up the existing tokens in the bucket. In addition to the delay associated with the token bucket size, Figure 9c shows added delay in the *threshold* algorithm because it only updates throttle rates once per minute.

6.2   Large Scale Experiments

We further explore the sybil attack on a large scale in Shadow. In addition to the base experiment setup discussed in Section 3.2, we add a victim client who downloads a large file through a circuit with an adversarial exit and a known target guard. The adversary starts sybil nodes and instructs them to connect to the known target guard at time $t = 100$. The sybil nodes cycle through 60 second active and inactive phases, and the adversary measures the throughput of the circuit.

The results of this attack on each algorithm are shown in Figure 10, where the shaded area again represents the time during which the attack was active. In the large scale experiment, only the *bitsplit* algorithm (Figure 10a) produced a repeatable signal while the throttle rate remained constant after the first phase for both *flag* (Figure 10b) and *threshold* (Figure 10c). Also, these results show the importance of correctly computing the attack duration: the signal was missed

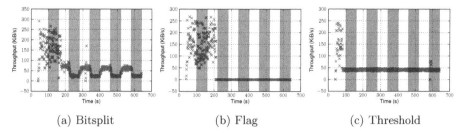

(a) Bitsplit   (b) Flag   (c) Threshold

Fig. 10. Large scale sybil attack on the bandwidth throttling algorithms from [22]. The shaded area represents the period during which the attack is active. Due to token bucket sizes, the throughput signal may be missed if the attack phases are too short.

during the first phase for both *bitsplit* and *flag* because the token bucket had not yet fully drained.

6.3 Search Extensions

Because the drop in throughput during the attack is easily recognizable, it is much easier to carry out than those discussed in Section 5. Therefore, in addition to statistical correlations that eliminate potential guards from a candidate set for a given circuit, a *search strategy* over the potential guard set will also be useful. In a linear search, the adversary would attack each candidate guard one by one until the throughput signal on the target circuit is recognized. This strategy is simple, but it may take a long time to test every candidate. A binary search, where the attacker tests half of the candidates in each phase of the search, would significantly reduce the search time. Note that a binary search may be ineffective on certain configurations of the *flag* and *threshold* algorithms because of the lack of a repeatable signal (see Figures 9 and 10).

Regardless of the search strategy, a successful attack will contain enough sybils to allow the adversary to recognize the throughput signal, but otherwise be as fast as possible. Given our results above, the attack should consider the token bucket size and refill rate of each candidate guard to aid in determining the number of sybils to launch and the length of time each sybil should remain active. An adversary who controls the circuit exit may compute the average circuit throughput and estimate the amount of time it would take for the circuit to deplete the remaining tokens in a target guard's bucket during an attack. Each sybil should then remain active for at least that amount of time. Figure 10 shows that the throughput signal may be missed without these considerations.

7 Analysis

Having seen how the algorithms perform independently in different attack scenarios, we now want to examine the overall effects on anonymity that each algorithm has. For our analysis, we use client probability distributions as discussed in Section 3.1 to measure how much information is gained by an adversary. Recall that we have the probability that a client is the victim being

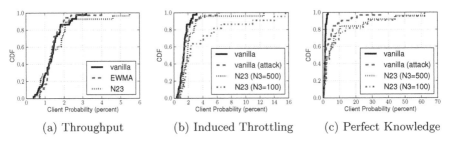

(a) Throughput   (b) Induced Throttling   (c) Perfect Knowledge

Fig. 11. Victim client probabilities, various congestion control attack scenarios

$P[V = C_i] = \sum_j P[V = C_i|R_j]P[G = R_j]$ for a set of relays R and clients C. Now we need to determine how to update the probability distributions for $P[G = R_j]$ and $P[V = C_i|R_j]$ based on the attacks we've covered.

There are three attacks discussed that are used to learn information about the guard node used in a circuit, determining $P[G = R_j]$. The throughput attack and artificial throttling attack both attempt to reduce the set of possible entry guards by assigning a score to each guard and using a threshold value to determine the reduced set. For each attack, we compile the set of scores assigned to the *actual* guard nodes, and use this set as input to a kernel density estimator in order to generate an estimate of the probability density function, $\hat{P}$. Then, given a relay R_j with a score $score(R_j)$ we can compute $P[G = R_j] = \hat{P}[X = score(R_j)]$. For the sybil attacks on the throttling algorithms we were able to uniquely identify the entry guard, so we have $P[G = R_j] = 1$ if R_j is the guard, otherwise it's 0. Therefore, denoting R_G as the guard relay, we have $P[V = C_i] = P[V = C_i|R_G]$.

For determining the probability distribution for $P[V = C_i|R_j]$, recall that the latency attack computes the difference between the estimated latency $\hat{T}_{VE}$ and the actual latency T_{VE} as the score, and ranks potential clients that way. Using the absolute value of the difference as the score, we compute the probability density function $\hat{P}$ in the same way as we did for $P[G = R_j]$. Therefore, to compute $P[V = C_i|R_j]$, we let $lat_{C_iR_j}$ be the actual latency between client C_i and relay R_j, and $\hat{T}_{VE}$ be the estimate latency between the client and entry guard. Then, with $diff = |lat_{C_iR_j} - \hat{T}_{VE}|$ we have $P[V = C_i|R_j] = \hat{P}[X = diff]$ from the computed probability density function.

Our analysis first concentrates on how the algorithms perform with the throughput and latency attack compared to vanilla Tor. We then focus on the new induced throttling attacks shown in Section 5 and 6 to see if there are improvements over either vanilla Tor or the throughput attack with the algorithms. For each attack we use a set of potential victims $\{V_i\}$ and their entry guards G_i and compute the probabilities $P[V = V_i]$ as shown above.

The results for the algorithms EWMA, N23, and the induced throttling attacks described in Section 5 are shown in Figure 11. We can see in Figure 11a that with just the throughput and latency attack, vanilla Tor leaks about the same amount of anonymity of a client as EWMA and N23. The exception to this is that a tiny proportion of clients have probabilities ranging from 4-6% which

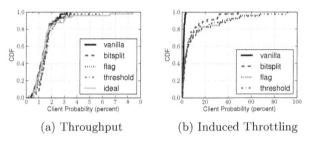

(a) Throughput   (b) Induced Throttling

Fig. 12. Victim client probabilities, various traffic admission control attack scenarios

is outside the range in vanilla Tor. Referring back to Figure 3 we see that these algorithms, N23 in particular, leak slightly more information than vanilla Tor based on latency estimation. While sometimes this information gain might be counteracted by the amount of possible entry guards that need to be considered, there are a small amount of cases where the guard set is reduced enough that the extra information from the latency attack translates into a higher probability for the client.

When replacing the throughput attack with the induced throttling attack we start to see a larger divergence in client probabilities, as shown in Figure 11b. While the induced throttling attack with vanilla Tor leaks slightly more information than vanilla Tor with the throughput attack, N23 with $N3 = 500$ has higher client probabilities than both attacks on vanilla Tor and higher than N23 with just the throughput attack. Furthermore, N23 with $N3 = 100$ does significantly better than all previous algorithms, leaking more information than vanilla Tor for almost half the clients, reaching probabilities as high as 15%.

The results in Figure 11b assume that the client only sends one stream over the circuit, the worst case scenario for an adversary. As shown in Figure 8, as the number streams multiplexed over the circuit increases, the degree of anonymity loss sharply approaches 100% implying that an adversary would be able to uniquely identify the entry guard. An analysis with this assumption of "perfect knowledge" can be seen in Figure 11c, where $P[G = R_j] = 1$ when R_j is the entry guard. Here we see a dramatic improvement from when a client only sends a single stream over the circuit, with some clients having probabilities as high as 60%, compared to a peak of 15% with a single stream.

Using the throughput attack with the traffic admission control algorithms produces similar results as N23 and EWMA, as shown in Figure 12a. There is a slightly higher upper bound in the client probability caused by the threshold and ideal throttling algorithms, but for the most part these results line up fairly closely to what was previously seen. Given that the throttling algorithms all had similar peaks to N23 with respect to the loss of anonymity in the latency attacks, these results aren't too surprising. Even with the improved performance of the latency attack, these gains are wiped out by the fact that the throughput attack results in too many guards that need to be considered in relation to the clients. However, when using the sybil attack to induce throttling under the assumption that the adversary is able to uniquely identify the entry guard in use, we see dramatically higher client probabilities. Figure 12b shows the result of this analysis, where at the extreme end we see clients with probabilities as high as 90%. This is due to the fact that with the sybil attack we are able to identify the exact entry guard used by each victim, thus reducing the noise from having to consider the latency of clients based on other possible relays. This very effectively demonstrates the level of anonymity lost when an adversary is able to significantly reduce the set of candidate entry guards.

8   Conclusion

While high performance is vital to the Tor system, algorithms which seek to improve allocation of network resources via more advanced congestion control or traffic admission algorithms need to take into account the implications on anonymity, both with respect to existing attacks and the potential for new ones. To this effect, we introduce a new class of *induced throttling* attacks and demonstrate the effectiveness across a wide variety of performance enhancing algorithms, resulting in dramatic information leakage on victim clients. Using the new class of attacks, we perform a comprehensive analysis on the implications on anonymity, showing both the effects the algorithms have on existing attacks, as well as showing the increase in information gain from the new attacks.

Preventing these new attacks isn't straightforward, as in many cases the adversary is merely exploiting the underlying mechanisms in the algorithms. With the *induced throttling* attacks on vanilla and N23 congestion control, an adversary acts exactly as they should under heavy congestion, so prevention or detection becomes difficult without completely changing the algorithm. In these cases it comes down to the performance/anonymity trade-off. However, in the throttling algorithms the adversary is taking advantage of the fact that only the raw number of open connections are considered when calculating the throttling rate, allowing Sybil connections to be created using negligible resources. A throttling algorithm might prevent this by considering only *active* connections which have seen a minimum amount of bandwidth over a certain time period, forcing the attacker to spend a non-trivial amount of resources to significantly affect the throttle rate. The throttling rate could also be weighted by each connection's average bandwidth, creating a direct correlation between the bandwidth an adversary must provide and its influence on the throttling rate. Alternatively, throttling algorithms that do not directly consider the number of connections would not be vulnerable to the attacks in this paper.

Acknowledgments. We would like to thank our shepherds Roger Dingledine and Damon McCoy and the anonymous reviewers for their comments that helped improve this paper. This work was supported by NSF grant 0915145.

References

1. AlSabah, M., Bauer, K., Goldberg, I.: Enhancing Tor's performance using real-time traffic classification. In: Proceedings of the 2012 ACM Conference on Computer and Communications Security. ACM (2012)
2. AlSabah, M., Bauer, K., Goldberg, I., Grunwald, D., McCoy, D., Savage, S., Voelker, G.M.: DefenestraTor: Throwing out windows in Tor. In: Fischer-Hübner, S., Hopper, N. (eds.) PETS 2011. LNCS, vol. 6794, pp. 134–154. Springer, Heidelberg (2011)
3. Chaabane, A., Manils, P., Kaafar, M.A.: Digging into anonymous traffic: A deep analysis of the tor anonymizing network. In: 2010 4th International Conference on Network and System Security (NSS) (2010)
4. Chakravarty, S., Stavrou, A., Keromytis, A.D.: Traffic Analysis Against Low-Latency Anonymity Networks Using Available Bandwidth Estimation. In: Gritzalis, D., Preneel, B., Theoharidou, M. (eds.) ESORICS 2010. LNCS, vol. 6345, pp. 249–267. Springer, Heidelberg (2010)
5. Chun, B., Culler, D., Roscoe, T., Bavier, A., Peterson, L., Wawrzoniak, M., Bowman, M.: PlanetLab: an overlay testbed for broad-coverage services. SIGCOMM Computer Communication Review 33 (2003)
6. Cohen, B.: Incentives build robustness in BitTorrent. In: Workshop on Economics of Peer-to-Peer Systems, vol. 6 (2003)
7. Danezis, G., Dingledine, R., Mathewson, N.: Mixminion: Design of a type III anonymous remailer protocol. In: Proc. of IEEE Security and Privacy (2003)
8. Díaz, C., Seys, S., Claessens, J., Preneel, B.: Towards measuring anonymity. In: Dingledine, R., Syverson, P.F. (eds.) PET 2002. LNCS, vol. 2482, pp. 54–68. Springer, Heidelberg (2003)
9. Dingledine, R.: Adaptive throttling of Tor clients by entry guards. Technical Report 2010-09-001, The Tor Project (September 2010)
10. Dingledine, R., Mathewson, N., Syverson, P.: Tor: The Second-Generation Onion Router. In: Proceedings of the 13th Usenix Security Symposium (2004)
11. Douceur, J.R.: The Sybil Attack. In: Druschel, P., Kaashoek, M.F., Rowstron, A. (eds.) IPTPS 2002. LNCS, vol. 2429, pp. 251–260. Springer, Heidelberg (2002)
12. Evans, N.S., Dingledine, R., Grothoff, C.: A practical congestion attack on Tor using long paths. In: Proceedings of the 18th USENIX Security Symposium (2009)
13. Gopal, D., Heninger, N.: Torchestra: Reducing interactive traffic delays over Tor. In: Proc. of the Workshop on Privacy in the Electronic Society (2012)
14. Gulcu, C., Tsudik, G.: Mixing E-mail with Babel. In: Proceedings of the Symposium on Network and Distributed System Security (1996)
15. Hahne, E.: Round-robin scheduling for max-min fairness in data networks. IEEE Journal on Selected Areas in Communications 9(7) (1991)
16. Hastie, T.J., Tibshirani, R.J.: Generalized additive models, vol. 43 (1990)
17. Hopper, N., Vasserman, E.Y., Chan-Tin, E.: How much anonymity does network latency leak? In: Proceedings of the 14th ACM Conference on Computer and Communications Security. ACM (2007)
18. Houmansadr, A., Borisov, N.: SWIRL: A Scalable Watermark to Detect Correlated Network Flows. In: Proc. of the Network and Distributed Security Symp. (2011)
19. Jansen, R.: The Shadow Simulator, http://shadow.cs.umn.edu/
20. Jansen, R., Bauer, K., Hopper, N., Dingledine, R.: Methodically Modeling the Tor Network. In: Proceedings of the 5th Workshop on Cyber Security Experimentation and Test (August 2012)

21. Jansen, R., Hopper, N.: Shadow: Running Tor in a Box for Accurate and Efficient Experimentation. In: Proceedings of the 19th Network and Distributed System Security Symposium (2012)
22. Jansen, R., Syverson, P., Hopper, N.: Throttling Tor Bandwidth Parasites. In: Proceedings of the 21st USENIX Security Symposium (2012)
23. McCoy, D., Bauer, K., Grunwald, D., Kohno, T., Sicker, D.: Shining light in dark places: Understanding the Tor network. In: Borisov, N., Goldberg, I. (eds.) PETS 2008. LNCS, vol. 5134, pp. 63–76. Springer, Heidelberg (2008)
24. Mittal, P., Khurshid, A., Juen, J., Caesar, M., Borisov, N.: Stealthy traffic analysis of low-latency anonymous communication using throughput fingerprinting. In: Proceedings of the 18th ACM Conference on Computer and Communications Security. ACM (2011)
25. Möller, U., Cottrell, L., Palfrader, P., Sassaman, L.: Mixmaster protocol version 2. Draft (July 2003)
26. Moore, W.B., Wacek, C., Sherr, M.: Exploring the Potential Benefits of Expanded Rate Limiting in Tor: Slow and Steady Wins the Race With Tortoise. In: Proceedings of 2011 Annual Computer Security Applications Conference (2011)
27. Murdoch, S.J., Danezis, G.: Low-cost traffic analysis of Tor. In: 2005 IEEE Symposium on Security and Privacy. IEEE (2005)
28. Øverlier, L., Syverson, P.: Locating Hidden Servers. In: Proceedings of the 2006 IEEE Symposium on Security and Privacy (2006)
29. Serjantov, A., Danezis, G.: Towards an information theoretic metric for anonymity. In: Dingledine, R., Syverson, P.F. (eds.) PET 2002. LNCS, vol. 2482, pp. 41–53. Springer, Heidelberg (2003)
30. Tang, C., Goldberg, I.: An improved algorithm for Tor circuit scheduling. In: Proceedings of the 17th ACM Conference on Computer and Communications Security. ACM (2010)
31. The Tor Project: The Tor Metrics Portal, https://metrics.torproject.org/
32. Wright, M., Adler, M., Levine, B.N., Shields, C.: Defending Anonymous Communication Against Passive Logging Attacks. In: Proceedings of the 2003 IEEE Symposium on Security and Privacy (May 2003)

OSS: Using Online Scanning Services
for Censorship Circumvention

David Fifield[1], Gabi Nakibly[2], and Dan Boneh[1]

[1] Computer Science Department, Stanford University
[2] National EW Research & Simulation Center,
Rafael – Advanced Defense Systems Ltd.

Abstract. We introduce the concept of a web-based online scanning service, or OSS for short, and show that these OSSes can be covertly used as proxies in a censorship circumvention system. Such proxies are suitable both for short one-time rendezvous messages and bulk bidirectional data transport. We show that OSSes are widely available on the Internet and blocking all of them can be difficult and harmful. We measure the number of round trips and the amount of data that can be pushed through various OSSes and show that we can achieve throughputs of about 100 KB/sec. To demonstrate the effectiveness of our approach we built a system for censored users to communicate with blocked Tor relays using available OSS providers. We report on its design and performance.

1 Introduction

Nowadays many nations regularly filter Internet traffic by blocking news sites, social networking sites, search sites, and even public mail sites like Gmail. The OpenNet Initiative, which tracks public reports of Internet filtering, lists a large number of countries that filter Internet traffic. Over half of the 74 countries tested in 2011 imposed some degree of filtering on the Internet [1].

In response, several proxy systems have emerged to help censored users freely browse the Internet. Most notable among these is Tor [2], which, while originally designed to provide anonymity, has also seen wide use in circumvention. Other proposals include Telex [3], Infranet [4] and Ultrasurf [5] as well as several enhancements to Tor [6–8]. The existence of circumvention systems makes the censor's job harder: The censor must block all circumvention tools in order to remain effective.

Network censorship techniques fall into two broad classes: blocking by address and blocking by content. This work is mainly about the former: We seek to enable a censored user to communicate with a network host even when a censor blocks all traffic to and from that host's IP address. Flash proxy [6] is an example of a system resistant to address blocking; it creates a large number of short-lived proxies. Blocking by content, that is, the inspection of packet contents and other traffic characteristics such as timing, requires different circumvention techniques, for example mimicking other common protocols, as StegoTorus [7] does, or making the traffic look like no protocol in particular, as obfsproxy [8]

E. De Cristofaro and M. Wright (Eds.): PETS 2013, LNCS 7981, pp. 185–204, 2013.

does. Combining resistance to both kinds of censorship is a subject of active development. Even though we are primarily concerned with blocking by address, Sect. 7 considers mitigations for content blocking in the system of this paper.

The system proposed in this paper is especially well suited to be used as a *rendezvous* protocol. A rendezvous protocol is an important component of a proxy-based circumvention system that allows a censored user to send a small amount of information (a few bytes) outside the censored region for the purpose of introducing the user to a proxy. Rendezvous protocols are low-bandwidth and designed to be difficult to block.

A complete circumvention system must also address secure client software distribution, an install system, and secure integration with a web browser. We have implemented our system as a Tor pluggable transport [9] so that it can use the Tor Project's existing infrastructure that addresses these concerns.

Our Contributions. In this paper we propose a new approach to building proxies. In particular, we identify a large set of widely available web services that can be covertly made into proxies.

Our starting point is the observation that many web services take a URL as user input and then scan the web page behind that URL. We give many examples in Sect. 3, but for concreteness consider PDFmyURL, a service that does exactly what its name suggests: Given a URL it returns a PDF of the target page. With a URL as input, software on the server uses WebKit to fetch the page, render it, and convert it to PDF. The page is fetched immediately after the user clicks the submit button. We emphasize that pdfmyurl.com is just an example – there are *many* available services, including malware analysis sites and many others, that take a URL as input and then retrieve the page that the URL points to.

Now, suppose that the URL provided as input to pdfmyurl.com points to a site A.com that when accessed over HTTP returns a 302 redirect response to another site B.com. The server at pdfmyurl.com will dutifully follow the redirect and issue another HTTP request to the new target site B.com. Suppose now that B.com also returns a 302 redirect response back to A.com, but with a slightly modified path. pdfmyurl.com will follow the redirect back to A.com. Then A.com issues another redirect back to B.com and so on. This redirect ping-pong can go on for a while and the pdfmyurl.com server will obediently bounce back and forth between the two sites A.com and B.com. By embedding data in the URLs provided in each redirect, the two sites A.com and B.com can communicate using pdfmyurl.com as a proxy. Figure 1 illustrates this.

We refer to a service like PDFmyURL as an *Online Scanning Service* or OSS for short. For our purposes, an OSS must satisfy the following requirements:

1. It is not blocked by the censor.
2. It makes the initial HTTP scanning request in real time (within a few seconds of being asked).
3. It follows at least one redirect, where a "redirect" is any of a number of methods described in Sect. 4 (for example, we can use frames, refresh headers, or JavaScript to cause the redirects).

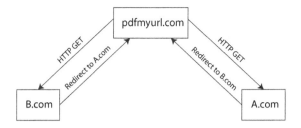

Fig. 1. Illustration of the redirection process

Requirement 3 means that there is a way to respond to an OSS's HTTP request that causes the OSS to make another request to a URL of our choice. We use the OSS as a proxy by embedding data in these requests and redirecting it between two hosts. When used for rendezvous rather than bidirectional data transfer, Requirement 2 is relaxed (in some cases it is acceptable if rendezvous takes a few minutes) and Requirement 3 is unnecessary (rendezvous messages fit in a single request and do not require a reply).

There are many OSS-like services on the web. It is an advantage of this circumvention technique that there is no canonical list of "supported OSSes" that must be known in advance. One host may use any convenient OSS to communicate with the other, as long as it satisfies the three requirements above, without prior arrangement with the other host. What the OSS may do behind the scenes is not important for the purpose of data transfer; we use only its ability to make requests and follow redirects.

A comparison with the flash proxy system [6] is instructive. Where the flash proxy system uses the abundant resource of web browser IP addresses, our system uses online scanning services, which are less numerous but potentially more costly to block as they may host important services.

In principle, censors can counter this circumvention system by blocking all OSS providers. However, as we show in Sect. 3, OSSes are so prevalent that it would be difficult to discover all of them. Furthermore, blocking all OSSes on the Internet would cause economic hardship and block legitimate popular services that have nothing to do with censorship circumvention.

In Sect. 2 we detail the threat model we address in this paper. In Sect. 3 we survey many existing OSS services and survey which are suitable for circumvention and which have undesirable side effects. Section 4 describes a number of redirect methods and measure their performance with each OSS. Section 5 has measurements of the performance characteristics of several OSSes, with experimental results for overall throughput. In Sect. 6 we describe the system we built that allows censored users to communicate with blocked sites through arbitrary OSS providers. A security analysis of the system follows in Sect. 7. Ethical considerations of using OSSes in this way are the subject of Sect. 8. Section 9 concludes.

2   Threat Model

Our work deals with five entities, whose relationship is summarized in Fig. 2.

1. Censored user – a user within the filtered region who tries to access a target web site outside the filtered region.
2. Censor – an authority that monitors and blocks traffic between the censored user and the outside world. An example of a censor is a national government, censoring at the borders of a country. The censor is the adversary we try to circumvent.
3. OSS – an online web service used as an intermediary in communication. It is located outside the filtered region. It is assumed that the censor does not block traffic between the censored user and the OSS. The OSS may be oblivious to the circumvention effort: It does not generally actively assist circumvention, but neither does it work with the censor to frustrate circumvention.
4. Cooperating proxy – a server located outside the censored region that relays traffic to and from the target web site. An example of such a proxy is a Tor bridge. The censor blocks traffic between the censored user and the cooperating proxy; otherwise, the user would contact it directly.
5. Target web site – a web site located outside the filtered region. The censor blocks traffic between the censored user and the target web site.

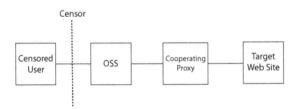

Fig. 2. Illustration of the relationship between the principal entities. Our system enables indirect communication between the censored user and the cooperating proxy, otherwise prohibited by the censor.

The censor may inspect all traffic passing through it and may block any packet it wishes. However, it does not do stateful tracking, namely keeping state on every monitored data session or IP endpoint. We assume the censor does not control the user's computer (through a backdoor or similar) and that the user is able to get and install circumvention software. The censor is motivated to minimize "collateral damage" caused by its blocking: Access to innocuous or economically important targets is allowed while a relatively small subset of traffic is blocked. In other words, the censor will not block web services that can be used as OSSes unless they are associated with circumvention – and even then, only if the cost of blocking them is not too high.

The OSS is independent of the censor and does not collude with the censor to prevent circumvention. The OSS is untrusted and may read or modify traffic passing through it.

Our security goals are to communicate with a blocked endpoint without exchanging traffic directly with it; to be expensive for the censor to block (in economic and social terms); and to be covert in the sense that it should not be possible to pinpoint a user without specifically focusing on that user's traffic.

3 Online Scanning Services

To demonstrate the feasibility of our circumvention method, we investigated a number of existing OSS providers listed below. We divide them into the categories of security, advertising, web diagnostics, processed retrieval, and link shorteners. In this section we list example OSSes in each category, and in the next we analyze their characteristics as applied to circumvention.

3.1 Security Scanners

This category consists of services that scan a web page for malicious content. The scans are initiated by submitting a URL in a web form.

Dr.Web `http://vms.drweb.com/online/`
An online scanner using the Dr.Web antivirus engine.

NoVirusThanks `http://vscan.novirusthanks.org/`
NoVirusThanks is a security company with a free multi-engine antivirus scan.

VirusTotal `https://www.virustotal.com/#url`
VirusTotal scans uploaded files and URLs with a variety of antivirus engines.

3.2 Contextual Advertising

Contextual advertising attempts to match advertisements to the web pages on which they appear. The ad network scans web pages containing advertisements to find keywords or other context.

Google AdSense `https://www.google.com/adsense/`
An AdSense advertisement is a piece of JavaScript code. It sends the URL of the page it is on to the AdSense servers in order to find out what to display. If the URL is not in the servers' cache, the servers begin an immediate scan. (The structure of our URLs ensures that they will not be found in cache.) Our experiments show that the AdSense crawler will crawl arbitrary URLs, not only those on a domain belonging to an AdSense customer.

3.3 Web Diagnostics

This category includes services that analyze the contents of a web page.

vURL Online `http://vurldissect.co.uk/`
Dissects web markup and extracts some information for analysis. The information includes such things as image and link references.

W3C Markup Validation `http://validator.w3.org/`
Checks the markup of web documents in formats like HTML and XHTML.

3.4 Processed Retrieval Services

Services that return a web document after filtering it in some way.

GoMo `http://www.howtogomo.com/`
Renders a web site as it appears on a smartphone.

IE NetRenderer `http://netrenderer.com/`
Renders a web site as it appears in various versions of Internet Explorer.

PDFmyURL `http://pdfmyurl.com/`
Converts a web page into PDF.

3.5 Link Shorteners

Link shorteners turn a URL and into another, usually shorter, URL that redirects
to the original.

Google URL Shortener `https://goo.gl/`
The goo.gl shortener makes an HTTP request to the target page in order to
show a thumbnail preview. We were not able to drive this OSS programmatically, as shortening a link and retrieving the preview is a complicated process
involving a Google Account and JavaScript code. For this reason, and because initiating a scan has the side effect of creating a permanent short link,
goo.gl is not a high-quality OSS for our purposes.

Twitter Link Shortener `https://t.co/`
Links posted on Twitter are shortened by the mandatory URL shortening
service t.co [10]. As a side effect of creating a short link, a number of scanners retrieve the URL. To initiate a scan, we programmatically post a tweet
containing the URL to be scanned. Like goo.gl, Twitter leaves a record of
each scan request in the form of a short link and a tweet.

3.6 Discussion

The throughput of an OSS depends on the specific redirect method used, but
overall some are faster than others. In addition, some OSSes are not suitable
for circumvention: Twitter and goo.gl create a record of each communication in
the form of a short URL, and require using an account that ties circumvention
to a long-term (potentially pseudonymous) identity. We make this division of
tested OSSes into those that are fast, those that are slow, and those that have
deficiencies that make them unsuitable for circumvention:

High-rate: Dr.Web, GoMo, NoVirusThanks, PDFmyURL.
Low-rate: AdSense, NetRenderer, VirusTotal, vURL, W3C.
Unsuitable: goo.gl, Twitter.

The fast OSSes can be used for bulk data transfer while slow ones are best
suited for rendezvous. Section 5 tests a selection of the best OSSes and redirect
methods.

The number of OSSes we study in this paper was limited only by our resources. Other potential OSSes are translation services, photo printing services, file hosts, RSS aggregators, and image sharing sites. We tested common web browsers as if they were OSSes, and found that browsers are capable of acting as circumvention proxies. However, proxying over redirects in browsers offers no real advantages over using custom code as in the flash proxy system [6], so we omit the results of browser testing.

4   Using an OSS for Communication

In this section we show how to use an OSS as a traffic relays. We then measure the performance characteristics of each of the OSSes from Sect. 3. In what follows we refer to the censored user as the *client*, and the remote cooperating proxy as the *server*.

Initiating Communication. Each OSS is started differently. To name two examples, the W3C markup validator requires only a single GET request containing the URL to be scanned as a query parameter; VirusTotal requires first retrieving the home page to get a cross-site request forgery (CSRF) token, then including the token in a POST request along with the URL to be scanned. Once initiated, however, the client and server may communicate without knowing the details of the underlying OSS.

We describe a variety of techniques for causing an OSS to request a URL: HTTP redirects, refresh, frames, and JavaScript. We group all of these techniques under the general term "redirect methods." What they have in common is that they allow an HTTP response to control some aspect of a subsequent request. The easiest part of a request to control is the URL. Some redirect methods, such as the JavaScript-based ones, also allow control over the request body, which we take advantage of in order to send more data per round trip.

Relaying Traffic. The URL is our primary vehicle for communication. Our URLs follow this format:

$$\text{http://}host\text{:}port/random/id/seq/ack?query$$

random is a random string, changing with every request, whose purpose is to inhibit caching by the OSS. *id* identifies the URL as being part of a particular data stream or session; it allows a server to handle multiple simultaneous clients. *seq* and *ack* carry information about what what bytes each endpoint has received. (OSSes do not in general follow an unlimited number of redirects; they effectively drop the last communication in a redirect chain. The client and server retransmit unacknowledged bytes until they are received.) *query* contains a `data` parameter encoding the payload (except for the redirect methods that carry data in the request body instead). `data` is base64-encoded using the URL-safe alphabet [11]. *query* additionally contains metadata like the client's "return address" (the URL to which the server's redirects will be directed), the name of the redirect method to use, and a `fin` marker for end-of-stream. A typical URL is

http://*host*:*port*/4a931e1d/e16813d8/0/0?data=SGVsbG8g...

Measurements. What follows in the rest of this section are descriptions of each redirect method, and the results of testing each redirect method against each OSS. In the performance tables, a redirect method/OSS combination is summarized by a triple of numbers. An example summary is

redirects	capacity	delay
10	2047	0.5

The three numbers in order are

- Maximum number of redirects followed. We cut off testing above 250 requests; services that did not stop before this limit are reported as ∞. The number of redirects matters because the client must kick off a new redirect chain once a previous chain is exhausted.
- Maximum data capacity per redirect, in bytes. For redirect methods that embed data in URLs, this is the maximum URL length allowed. The amount of useful payload data can be derived from the URL length by subtracting a constant to account for non-data parts of the URL, then multiplying by 3/4 to account for base64 encoding. For redirect methods that send data in request bodies, the number is the maximum body size allowed. We cut off testing above 512 KB; services that did not stop before this limit are reported as ∞.
- Delay, in seconds, between initiating a scan and when the OSS's first request is received. For some services the delay is variable, so we report an approximate average. For goo.gl, which was tested by manually copying URLs, the delay column is empty.

We tested the limits on number of redirects using a program that redirected to itself and kept a count of requests until a timeout. To measure payload limits, we did a binary search over URL and request body lengths.

Unusual results in the tables are called out with footnotes. We speculate that some services have limits in place other than those we measured, for example a limit on clock time. An unanticipated finding was that some services have multiple backend scanners with different characteristics. For this reason, some table entries contain more than one number, separated by slashes. In the code samples that follow, `http://example.com/` takes the place of a data-carrying transport URL.

4.1   HTTP Redirects

The specification of HTTP 1.1 [12, Sect. 10] defines a number of status codes that effect redirects: 300 Multiple Choices, 301 Moved Permanently, 302 Found, 303 See Other, and 307 Temporary Redirect.

Table 1. Performance characteristics of HTTP redirects

| | 300 | | | 301/302/303/307 | | |
OSS	redirects	capacity	delay	redirects	capacity	delay
AdSense	0	0	0.3	5	2047	1.1
Dr.Web	∞	8181	0.5	∞	8181	0.5
GoMo	15	∞	3.5	15	∞	3.9
goo.gl	15	2047	–	15	2047	–
NetRenderer	10	2083	1.2	10	2083	1.2
NoVirusThanks[1]	10	≈128000	1.3	10	≈128000	1.4
PDFmyURL	0	0	0.9	∞	∞	1.1
Twitter[2]	0	0	2.5	4/25	>2047	2.3
VirusTotal[3]	5/20	2047	5.9	5/20	2047	4.2
vURL[4]	20	≈128000	22.6	20	≈128000	22.5
W3C	0	0	0.8	7	8181	0.7

[1] NoVirusThanks appears to be time-limited. We were able to send about 128000 bytes per redirect but the exact number fluctuated around this value.
[2] Posting on Twitter was observed to cause up to three requests from different /24 IP address ranges, each with its own characteristics. At least one of the scanners supports payloads of at least 2048 bytes.
[3] The behavior of VirusTotal was variable, probably because of different backend scanners. Sometimes 5 and sometimes 20 redirects were allowed. Sometimes the payload was limited to 2047 and sometimes apparently unlimited.
[4] vURL, like NoVirusThanks, appears to be time-limited.

All these status codes have in common the Location header, whose value is the URL to redirect to. They have some differences, both in specification and in implementation. For example, 303 requires that the redirect be followed using the GET method, while 307 repeats the method used in the original request.

Table 1 shows the performance of each OSS using 300-series redirects. We tested each of the five redirect codes separately. 301, 302, 303, and 307 had the same performance and level of support in our tests, so they are shown in a single table column. 300 was somewhat less widely supported. Support for HTTP redirects other than 300 is universal. HTTP redirects are the only working method for NoVirusThanks, Twitter, vURL, and W3C.

We generally embed data in URL parameters over GET requests. It is tempting to try to use 307 with a POST request in order to carry data in request bodies, but unfortunately this does not work. After receiving a 307 redirect, the OSS makes a request to the new location using its original request body, not the body returned along with the 307. Changes to request bodies do not survive the "ping-pong" the way that changes to URLs do. In order to make use of POST and request bodies we turned to JavaScript-based redirects, described later.

4.2   Refresh

Another method of redirecting an HTTP request is the "meta-refresh" technique and the related Refresh header, which are widely supported despite being

Table 2. Performance characteristics of HTTP refresh

OSS	meta-refresh			Refresh header		
	redirects	capacity	delay	redirects	capacity	delay
AdSense	5	2047	1.3	5	2047	1.2
Dr.Web	0	0	0.6	0	0	0.4
GoMo	∞	∞	5.0	∞	∞	4.0
goo.gl	30	2047	–	30	2047	–
NetRenderer	1	2083	1.0	1	2083	1.0
NoVirusThanks	0	0	0.5	0	0	0.5
PDFmyURL	∞	∞	1.8	∞	∞	2.9
Twitter	0	0	1.0	0	0	2.6
VirusTotal[1]	0/≈150	0/∞	6.0	0/≈150	0/∞	4.5
vURL	0	0	22.3	0	0	22.9
W3C	0	0	0.8	0	0	0.8

[1] One of VirusTotal's scanners is apparently time-based; we were able to make about 150 refreshes in 60 seconds. Another scanner allowed no refreshes.

deprecated and non-standard [13]. A meta-refresh is a piece of HTML that instructs the user agent to go to another URL after a delay of 0 seconds:

```
<meta http-equiv="refresh" content="0; url='http://example.com/'">
```

The same effect can be accomplished with a Refresh HTTP header.

```
Refresh: 0; url='http://example.com/'
```

Meta-refresh and the Refresh header have identical performance characteristics within every OSS. Table 2 shows the performance of refresh-based redirects.

4.3 Frames

Recursively loaded resources can serve the same purpose as redirects. An HTML document may contain a frameset or iframe; those may in turn contain frames, and so on, up to an implementation-defined limit on nesting. Using the frameset method, each response contains HTML like this example:

```
<frameset><frame src="http://example.com/"></frame></frameset>
```

Using iframe, responses look like this:

```
<iframe src="http://example.com/"></iframe>
```

Table 3 shows how frames are treated by each OSS. Limits on frame nesting vary. PDFmyURL, which does not limit other redirect methods, limits frame nesting to 201 levels.

Table 3. Performance characteristics of HTML frames

OSS	frameset			iframe		
	redirects	capacity	delay	redirects	capacity	delay
AdSense	0	0	0.6	0	0	0.7
Dr.Web	1	≈450000	0.6	1	≈450000	0.5
GoMo	201	∞	3.8	201	∞	4.3
goo.gl	9	2047	–	9	2047	–
NetRenderer[1]	≈80	2083	1.6	≈80	2083	1.2
NoVirusThanks	0	0	0.6	0	0	0.5
PDFmyURL	201	∞	1.8	201	∞	1.7
Twitter	0	0	2.0	0	0	2.2
VirusTotal[2]	0/9	0/∞	5.0	0/9	0/∞	9.3
vURL	0	0	22.4	0	0	22.3
W3C	0	0	0.6	0	0	0.7

[1] NetRenderer's limit appears to be time-based. We were able to make about 80 redirects in 30 seconds.

4.4 JavaScript

JavaScript provides another way for one web resource to load another. JavaScript has the ability to control request bodies via the POST method – an advantage because services typically allow more data in request bodies than in URLs.

JavaScript-based redirects' higher bandwidth is offset by less widespread support. Only goo.gl, GoMo, NetRenderer, and PDFmyURL usefully followed JavaScript-based redirects.

We tried two different ways of loading a URL in JavaScript. The first builds an HTML form containing the payload and submits it in the document's `onload` handler:

```
<body onload="document.f.submit();">
  <form name="f" method="post" action="http://example.com/">
    <input name="data" value="SGVsbG8g..."/>
  </form>
</body>
```

The second uses XMLHttpRequest to load a new HTML page (which contains its own XMLHttpRequest), and replaces the current page with the loaded page.

```
<script type="text/javascript">
  xhr = new XMLHttpRequest();
  xhr.open("POST", "http://example.com/");
  xhr.setRequestHeader("Content-type", "application/x-www-form-urlencoded");
  xhr.onreadystatechange = function() {
    if (xhr.readyState == xhr.DONE && xhr.status == 200) {
      document.open();
      document.write(xhr.responseText);
      document.close();
    }
  };
  xhr.send("data=SGVsbG8g...");
</script>
```

Table 4. Performance characteristics of JavaScript redirects

OSS	onload			XMLHttpRequest		
	redirects	capacity	delay	redirects	capacity	delay
AdSense	0	0	0.5	0	0	0.7
Dr.Web	0	0	0.6	0	0	0.5
GoMo	∞	∞	7.1	∞	∞	3.2
goo.gl	30	∞	–	15	∞	–
NetRenderer	0	0	1.0	0	0	1.0
NoVirusThanks	0	0	0.5	0	0	0.7
PDFmyURL	∞	∞	2.5	∞	∞	1.4
Twitter	0	0	2.6	0	0	2.9
VirusTotal	0	0	4.4	0	0	4.0
vURL	0	0	22.3	0	0	22.5
W3C	0	0	0.7	0	0	0.7

Table 4 is a summary of JavaScript-based redirects. goo.gl, which tightly limits the lengths of URLs to 2047 bytes, has no equivalent restriction on the length of request bodies.

5   Experiments

5.1   Implementation

To evaluate the performance of the circumvention scheme we implemented client and server programs. Both programs have similar capabilities: Each listens for HTTP requests, identifies the stream to which an incoming request belongs, extracts the payload, and redirects the request back to the peer with a portion of buffered payload data. The client program presents a SOCKS [14] interface to the local host. The programs can be used with or without Tor, and we tested both configurations.

The main difference between the programs is that only the client initiates scan requests to OSSes, while the server remains passive and must wait for an HTTP requests from an OSS before sending data back to the client. This design choice requires the client to refresh redirect chains when they reach their limits, and to poll the server for data periodically, even if the client has nothing to send. This model has advantages but is not the only possibility; see Sect. 6 for further discussion.

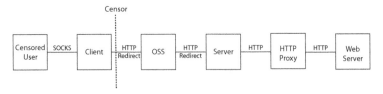

Fig. 3. End-to-end data flow between a censored user and an HTTP proxy

Figure 3 shows an end-to-end flow for communicating with an HTTP proxy. The censored user connects to the client with SOCKS and requests a connection to the server. The client program chooses an OSS and initiates a request for it to scan the server. The scan request contains a random stream ID, a return address on which the client is listening, and a redirect method. The redirect method is needed because the server may not know what redirect methods the OSS supports. The server receives the scan request, extracting the stream ID and data payload. The server immediately redirects the OSS back to the client's return address. The server is configured to feed its concatenated payloads to the HTTP proxy. When the HTTP proxy returns data to the server, the server buffers it until it receives another request from the client with the same stream ID to which it can respond with a payload.

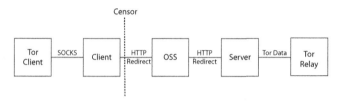

Fig. 4. End-to-end data flow between a censored user and a Tor relay

Figure 4 shows the end-to-end flow when configured to use Tor. The use of a SOCKS interface means that both client and server work as Tor pluggable transports [9]. In this configuration, the Tor relay serves as a general-purpose proxy. Not shown are the additional hops that packets would take through the Tor network before reaching the target web server.

5.2   Throughput Measurements

We now present the results for the throughput measurements for different OSS and redirection method combinations. For these measurements we used only a single redirect chain at a time. After a chain is exhausted as a result of reaching the redirection limit, a new scan request is initiated. In these tests, both client and server programs were on the same host, that is, traffic went out over the Internet and then returned to the same place. We timed the download of a 1 MB file. The available bandwidth between our test machine and the location of the remote file is high enough that the time taken to download mostly reflects OSS overhead. Table 5 lists the measured throughput for each OSS and redirect combination. In general, two different redirection methods in the same category yield roughly similar results given the same OSS. If there is a difference we show the higher throughput.

Though Sect. 3 has examples of OSSes allowing half a megabyte or more of payload, larger payload sizes bring diminishing improvements in asymptotic bandwidth, while increasing latency. In our transport programs, we limited payloads to 32 KB.

Table 5. Throughput measurement results (bytes per second)

method / OSS	HTTP redirects	refresh	frames	JavaScript
AdSense	500	500	–	–
Dr.Web	20K	–	–	–
GoMo	22K	28.2K	28.2K	175K
goo.gl	350	400	410	110K
NetRenderer	850	–	1.3K	–
NoVirusThanks	21K	–	–	–
PDFmyURL	220K	160K	180K	265K
Twitter	2.4K	–	–	–
VirusTotal	1K	–	–	–
vURL	250	–	–	–
W3C	4.6K	–	–	–

It is evident from Table 5 that the throughputs of different OSS/redirect combinations vary widely. The lowest throughput we measured, 250 B/s, was with vURL/302 and the highest, 265 KB/s, came from PDFmyURL/onload.

The user may increase available throughput by simultaneously initiating multiple scan requests, to the same OSS or to different OSSes. We tested this technique for every OSS and redirection method by creating two concurrent streams, and observed their aggregate throughput to be twice that of a single stream, with the exception of AdSense. AdSense seems to impose a limit on the resources allocated at any given time to handle scan requests received from the same IP address. Two simultaneous scan requests caused the time for the OSS to act upon a received redirect to double. The other OSS that is operated by Google, goo.gl, does not impose such limits.

We repeated the tests using with the programs configured to use Tor. We tested several OSS and redirection method combinations and found that they generally produce about the same throughput as with a bare HTTP proxy.

6   The Overall System

Redirect techniques in OSSes can be used to carry data – in some configurations with high enough bandwidth and low enough latency to support comfortable web browsing. In this section we describe how to use this facility as part of a larger circumvention system in two scenarios: as a rendezvous method and as a bulk bidirectional data transport.

Anonymity is important for circumvention. For this reason, we use Tor as the target of OSS proxies, even though the idea of using HTTP requests for communication is not tied to Tor. Traffic passed over Tor is encrypted, so it is unreadable by the censor and, importantly, by the OSS. Tor traffic is additionally authenticated, so that a malicious OSS cannot cause communication to be redirected to something other than a Tor relay without the client noticing. Tor by itself is widely used for circumvention, but in places where Tor is blocked, it should not be necessary to give up on Tor's protections while using an OSS.

In the discussion so far, redirects have been used as a means of decreasing delay, with only the client making HTTP requests and initiating new redirect chains. Before continuing, we note an alternative design that has both client and server mutually initiating single scans of each other. This alternative has the advantage of not requiring the OSS to support redirects, relying only on its ability to make single requests. Disadvantages are higher overhead and delay – both client and server now receive the HTTP response to their every scan request, in addition to the HTTP requests made by the OSS – as well as increased server-side complexity. Another disadvantage is that the circumvention server has to support all of the potential OSSes, and know how to initiate a request with each of them. This eliminates the client's ability to choose its own unblocked OSS independently of the circumvention server.

An important property of the system is that every user has the freedom to choose which OSSes will be used without coordination with the cooperating proxy, the OSS, or other users. Even without such coordination, finding OSSes in the first place requires some expertise of the user. We leave unspecified how a user might find OSSes on an ongoing basis.

Both censored client and cooperating proxy act as HTTP servers that must be able to receive requests from the OSS, which acts as an HTTP client. This unfortunately requires that both client and server be able to receive TCP connections, which in particular means that neither may be behind network address translation (NAT). The cooperating proxy is a server on the Internet that can be assumed to be able to receive connections, but many censored users in the real world are behind NAT. For those users, using an OSS for communication will require the technical ability to do port forwarding, when port forwarding is even possible. NAT does not pose a problem for rendezvous, which only requires sending in one direction.

6.1   OSS as Rendezvous

Recall that a rendezvous protocol allows a censored client to send a small amount of information out through the censor in a way that is very hard to block. The usual goal is to bootstrap a higher-bandwidth transfer mechanism. Rendezvous over OSS is simple and doesn't even involve redirects. The client just encodes the data it wants to send in a URL pointing to the server it wants to send the data to. Rendezvous messages are short, so one request is enough, and the client doesn't have to receive a reply. If the OSS uses encryption, it is not possible for the censor to selectively block rendezvous messages by looking for distinctive URLs. It may be expensive to block all traffic to an OSS, if the OSS is commonly used for purposes other than circumvention.

Rendezvous is by nature low-bandwidth and infrequent. Ideally, just one short message is sent at the beginning of a session lasting hours. There is a lower risk of OSS administrator annoyance and blocking when the system is used in this way, compared to high-bandwidth uses.

There exists the danger of an eavesdropping OSS; the OSS should be regarded as an untrusted network router capable of seeing the traffic that passes through it. Our implementation of OSS-based rendezvous for the flash proxy system additionally encrypts messages before encoding them into URLs, as a measure of protection against OSSes that log the requests they are asked to make.

6.2   OSS as Bidirectional Data Channel

It certainly works to use a public OSS connected to a Tor relay as a general-purpose proxy. With heavy use, though, there is a chance of detection and blocking, not by the censor but by the OSS itself. (During our tests, we were blocked by PDFmyURL and Twitter.) The operators of an OSS cannot be assumed to care about the cause of circumvention, and a large number of unusual requests and redirects are likely to be unwanted if noticed. As an example, PDFmyURL's page on overusage [15] explicitly lists the conditions that may result in blocking:

> *Your IP or domain can be excluded if you overuse the service. You'll get a blocked message if you make a combination of:*
> 1. *more than 100 PDFs in two hours with a single IP, and*
> 2. *all these 100+ PDFs take more than 1000 seconds to process on our servers, and*
> 3. *use more than 10% of CPU resources.*

We suspect that what led to our blocking was heavy bandwidth tests, which transferred several megabytes using URLs as long as 32 kilobytes. Shorter and less bandwidth-intensive applications are less likely to be problematic. While using an OSS as a data channel may be useful in some special circumstances, we think that use as a rendezvous is more universally applicable.

7   Security Analysis

In this section we evaluate the system for unique traffic characteristics. We analyze each characteristic relative to the threat model outlined in Sect. 2 and discuss whether it can be used by the censor to flag traffic produced by our mechanism. In addition, we consider some possible extensions to the system that increase its resistance to content blocking.

Cooperating Proxy Address. Both the initial scanning requests as well as the redirection responses coming from the censored user contain a URL, the IP address or domain name of which belongs to the cooperating proxy. The censor can block flows that contain the address or domain name of a blocked host.

It may seem that HTTPS encryption is the easy solution to this problem, but the censored client can't be assumed to have a certificate that will be considered valid by the OSS. Requests to the client, and the client's redirection responses, must be in plain HTTP. Using the alternative design mentioned in Sect. 6 that does not use redirects, HTTPS works to hide the cooperating proxy's address; as there are no redirects, there is no need to send the location to redirect to.

A mitigation of the problem is to obfuscate the proxy's name in the traffic that goes between the censored user and the OSS. There are several ways to do this obfuscation. With the JavaScript redirection methods, the censored user can use code to generate the proxy address in URLs, rather than embedding the address directly. Blocking becomes more costly as the censor must run JavaScript code to find the other endpoint of a communication.

Domain names are a cheap and abundant resource. Multiple domain names that resolve to the same IP address serve as aliases that increase the cost of blocking. Using a rendezvous protocol, every censored user may learn a single domain name alias for their chosen OSS.

Instead of using many domain names for the proxy one can use many shortened URLs that all point to the same proxy name. To do this one must use a URL shortening service that allows to attach to the shortened URL custom parameters. An example shortener that allows parameters is `http://para.ms/`. It copies parameters attached to the shortened URL to the original long URL. This way the censored user may request that the OSS scan the shortened URL with custom parameters and the OSS will be redirected to the proxy using the same parameters.

Incoming Connections. A censored user receives incoming connections from the OSS. By disallowing incoming connections to residential users a censor would be able to block our mechanism. Although it is much more common for a residential user to initiate connections rather than receive them, it is our assumption that incoming connections are common enough that the censor will be reluctant to block them wholesale.

An alternative blocking strategy is be to block only incoming requests coming from known OSSes. This strategy will have less collateral damage. However, as we have shown potential OSSes are abundant and it is hard for the censor to discover and block them. Furthermore, blocking incoming connections from known OSSes may incur economic damage. For example, disallowing Google from initiating connections to the filtered region would inhibit web sites inside the filtered region from appearing on Google's search results or from using AdSense.

URL Pattern. The system uses distinctive URLs containing hexadecimal strings and well-known query string parameters. An alternative URL design may encode all the information in a single query string parameter with a predefined obfuscated structure. The parameter name may be arbitrary. It may be necessary to avoid using very long URLs (the censor may filter on length), potentially reducing bandwidth.

Number of Redirects. A censored user responds to HTTP requests with some form of redirection. It may be suspicious if a large fraction of HTTP responses are redirects. However, only HTTP redirects and refresh redirects are straightforward to detect. In addition, a censor limited as described in our threat model (Sect. 2) is not able to do stateful monitoring on the entire volume of monitored traffic. Therefore, it is impossible for the censor to gather the number of redirects for every endpoint in the filtered region. The censor might be able to do stateful monitoring only of connections to known OSSes. However, as we have stated above it is hard for the censor to discover all potential OSSes.

Number of Outgoing Connections. A censored user may initiate many outgoing connections to the same OSS. An large number of outgoing connections may be suspicious. Again, due to the stateless monitoring constraint the censor is not be able to measure the number of outgoing connections for every endpoint in the filtered region. Statefully monitoring only those endpoints that communicate with known OSSes may be feasible, but it is hard for a censor to discover all potential OSSes.

Eavesdropping by the OSS. Our threat model assumes that the OSS is not colluding with the censor; however it is not necessarily a trusted entity. An OSS can intercept all communications between the user and the cooperating proxy. In this sense the OSS resembles an ISP, Tor entry relay, or other network router that lies on the path between the user and the cooperating proxy. Traffic should be encrypted and authenticated, as the Tor protocol is, to prevent eavesdropping and tampering by the OSS.

8   Ethical Considerations

Our proposal uses web services for a purpose they were not designed for. Fortunately, there are measures that will allow an OSS to curb or eliminate its use as a circumvention relay.

One such measure is for the cooperating proxy (i.e. the Tor bridge) to send with every redirect message a signal that will indicate that this redirect is part of a censorship circumvention data flow. If an OSS does not wish to take part in the data flow, it may refuse to follow that redirect. The signal between the cooperating proxy and the OSS can take many forms as long as it is known to all proxies and OSSes. An example of such a signal is a distinguished HTTP header included in the HTTP response to the OSS. Note that this signal does not compromise the security of the circumvention method because the traffic between the proxy and the OSS is not monitored by the censor.

9   Conclusions

We have shown that general-purpose web services that scan a given URL can be covertly used to relay information between a user in a censored region and a blocked web site. Blocking *all* these general-purpose services is practically impossible to do and would severely cripple the web in the censored region, disabling security scanners, URL shortening services, advertisers, and many others.

After identifying a large class of online scanning services (OSSes), we analyzed their performance as proxies. We showed that many common services can handle many round trips and provide decent throughput. Some OSSes can be used to proxy live session data while others provide limited bandwidth and would mostly be used only for rendezvous. We experimented with a system that can relay information between a browser and server using these OSSes as a relay. The system is available as an experimental rendezvous for the flash proxy system [6] and is part of Tor's pluggable-transports web browser bundles starting with the 2.4.11-alpha-1 release [16]. Source code and experimental results are available from `https://gitweb.torproject.org/user/dcf/oss.git`.

Acknowledgments. The work is supported by DARPA and Space and Naval Warfare Systems Center Pacific under Contract No. N66001-11-C-4022. Opinions, findings and conclusions or recommendations expressed in this material are those of the author(s) and do not necessarily reflect the views of the Defense Advanced Research Project Agency and Space and Naval Warfare Systems Center Pacific. Distrib. Statement "A:" Approved for Public Release, Distribution Unlimited.

References

1. The OpenNet Initiative: OpenNet Initiative Internet censorship data (November 2011), `http://opennet.net/research/data`
2. Dingledine, R., Mathewson, N., Syverson, P.: Tor: The second-generation onion router. In: Proceedings of the 13th USENIX Security Symposium (August 2004)
3. Wustrow, E., Wolchok, S., Goldberg, I., Halderman, J.A.: Telex: Anticensorship in the network infrastructure. In: Proc. 20th USENIX Security Symposium (2011)
4. Feamster, N., Balazinska, M., Harfst, G., Balakrishnan, H., Karger, D.: Infranet: Circumventing web censorship and surveillance. In: Proceedings of the 11th USENIX Security Symposium (2002)
5. Ultrareach Internet Corp.: Ultrasurf proxy, `http://www.ultrasurf.us/`
6. Fifield, D., Hardison, N., Ellithorpe, J., Stark, E., Boneh, D., Dingledine, R., Porras, P.: Evading censorship with browser-based proxies. In: Fischer-Hübner, S., Wright, M. (eds.) PETS 2012. LNCS, vol. 7384, pp. 239–258. Springer, Heidelberg (2012)
7. Weinberg, Z., Wang, J., Yegneswaran, V., Briesemeister, L., Cheung, S., Wang, F., Boneh, D.: StegoTorus: a camouflage proxy for the Tor anonymity system. In: ACM Conference on Computer and Communications Security, pp. 109–120 (2012)
8. Kadianakis, G., Mathewson, N.: Obfsproxy architecture (December 2011), `https://www.torproject.org/projects/obfsproxy`
9. Appelbaum, J., Mathewson, N.: Pluggable transports for circumvention (October 2010), `https://gitweb.torproject.org/torspec.git/blob/HEAD:/proposals/180-pluggable-transport.txt`
10. Twitter: FAQs about Twitter's link service, `https://support.twitter.com/entries/109623`
11. Josefsson, S.: The base16, base32, and base64 data encodings. RFC 4648 (Proposed Standard) (October 2006)
12. Fielding, R., Gettys, J., Mogul, J., Frystyk, H., Masinter, L., Leach, P., Berners-Lee, T.: Hypertext transfer protocol – HTTP/1.1 (1999)

13. Jacobs, I., Chisholm, W., Vanderheiden, G.: HTML techniques for web content accessibility guidelines 1.0. Technical report, W3C (December 2000), http://www.w3.org/TR/2000/NOTE-WCAG10-HTML-TECHS-20001106, latest version available at http://www.w3.org/TR/WCAG10-HTML-TECHS/
14. Leech, M., et al.: SOCKS protocol version 5 (1996)
15. PDFmyURL: Over usage (limited use) (October 2011), http://support.pdfmyurl.com/topic/getting-help-overusage
16. Fifield, D., Allaire, A.: Ticket #7559: Registration via indirect URL request (March 2013), https://trac.torproject.org/projects/tor/ticket/7559

The Need for Flow Fingerprints
to Link Correlated Network Flows

Amir Houmansadr[1] and Nikita Borisov[2]

[1] The University of Texas at Austin
amir@cs.utexas.edu
[2] University of Illinois at Urbana-Champaign
nikita@illinois.edu

Abstract. Linking network flows is an important problem in the detection of stepping stone attacks as well as in compromising anonymity systems. Traffic analysis is an effective tool for linking flows, which works by correlating their communication patterns, e.g., their packet timings. To improve scalability and performance of this process, recent proposals suggest to perform traffic analysis in an *active* manner by injecting invisible *tag*s into the traffic patterns of network flows; this approach is commonly known as *flow watermarking*. In this paper, we study an *under-explored* type of active traffic analysis that we call it *flow fingerprinting*. Information theoretically, flow watermarking aims at conveying a *single bit* of information whereas flow fingerprinting tries to reliably send *multiple bits* of information, hence it is a more challenging problem. Such additional bits help a fingerprinter deliver extra information in addition to the existence of the tag, such as the network origin of the flow and the identity of the fingerprinting entity. In this paper, we introduce and formulate the flow fingerprinting problem and contrast its application scenarios from that of the well-studied flow watermarking. We suggest the use of coding theory to build fingerprinting schemes based on the existing watermarks. In particular, we design a non-blind fingerprint, Fancy, and evaluate its performance. We show that Fancy can reliably fingerprint millions of network flows by tagging only as few as tens of packets from each flow.

Keywords: Flow fingerprinting, traffic analysis, linear codes, network security.

1 Introduction

Linking network flows is an important problem in different applications, including stepping stones detection [13,28] and compromising anonymity [22,23]. For instance, it is widely known that attackers can de-anonymize a low-latency anonymity system by linking its egress and ingress flows. Since network flows are commonly encrypted in such applications, linking flows is feasible only through correlation of communication patterns such as packet timings, packet counts, and packet sizes [13,22,23]; this is known as *traffic analysis*.

E. De Cristofaro and M. Wright (Eds.): PETS 2013, LNCS 7981, pp. 205–224, 2013.

Traditional traffic analysis links network flows *passively*, i.e., through observing and correlating patterns inherent in network flows such as packet timings [3,28]. Unfortunately, this suffers from high rates of false positive errors due to the intrinsic correlation that exists among network flows, even if they are not related [13]. For instance, HTTP connections to the same webpage exhibit highly correlated packet timings [14], even if they are initiated independently by individuals residing in different network locations. In response to this, researchers have suggested an *active* approach for traffic analysis. In this approach, communication patterns of network flows are slightly perturbed, e.g., by delaying packets, such that this perturbation is detectable from the flows even after passing through a noisy network like the Internet. The existing designs for active traffic analysis are referred to as *flow watermarks*. A flow watermarking system is composed of *watermarkers*, who tag network flows by perturbing their patterns, and *detectors*, who analyze intercepted flows to identify those carrying the watermark perturbation.

In this paper, we study *flow fingerprinting*, an under-explored[1] variant of active traffic analysis. Flow fingerprinting is similar to flow watermarking in that it *tags* network flows by slightly perturbing their communication patterns—we call these tags *flow fingerprints*. Flow fingerprinting, however, differs from flow watermarking in the amount and the kind of information that it embeds: *A watermark tag contains a "single bit", which solely states that the carrying flow has been tagged by "some" tagger (watermarker); on the other hand, a fingerprint tag contains "multiple bits" of information, which convey additional information about the flows being tagged.* In simpler words, for each observed flow a watermark detector only seeks the answer to the following question: *"Has this flow been tagged by any of our watermarking agents?"* A fingerprint extractor, however, looks for additional information about the intercepted flow, such as the network origin of that flow, its relation to other observed flows, the identity of its tagger, and so on. Example questions asked by a fingerprint extractor are: *"Which specific fingerprinter (out of all fingerprinters) tagged this flow?"* *"Which specific flow is related to the observed flow?"* *"In which region of the network has this flow been tagged?"* etc.

The Need for Flow Fingerprints. While flow watermarking and fingerprinting look very similar in how they operate, they have different capabilities and limitations. To illustrate this better, consider the following application scenario. Previous research [22, 23] have designed flow watermarking systems in order to attack anonymity systems by linking their egress and ingress flows. Such watermarks, however, can only conduct a *targeted* attack in this scenario, i.e., they can identify the egress flows corresponding to a "single" target, ingress flow. On the other hand, one might need to perform a *non-targeted* attack in this case, i.e., to simultaneously identify the egress flows corresponding to "many" ingress flows observed; this can not be accomplished through flow watermarking [10,13,19,23,27]

---

[1] By fingerprinting we mean fingerprinting of traffic patterns, not packet contents. The latter is orthogonal to the problem studied in this paper, and is widely studied.

as they do not have efficient mechanisms to confidently distinguish among various watermark tags. Performing such a non-targeted attack requires a flow fingerprinting scheme that embeds various tags on different ingress flows, and that is reliably able to extract them from the egress flows. In Section 2 we elaborate more on the differences between flow watermarking and fingerprinting.

A Gap in the Literature. The literature on active traffic analysis has mainly studied the flow watermarking problem [10,13,19,23,27] while **entirely ignoring flow fingerprinting**. This comes as a surprise given that, in several important applications of traffic analysis, flow fingerprinting *is* indeed the solution to the problem, not watermarking (see Section 2). As fingerprinting aims at the reliable extraction of multiple information bits its design is *more challenging* than flow watermarking, which only conveys a single bit of information. One might design a **naive fingerprinting scheme by having a flow watermarker insert different tags into different flows**. The problem, however, is that the watermark detectors will not able to distinguish among a *large number* of distinct watermarks as they are not designed to do so (they might be able to distinguish within a small set of watermarks though). Note that in several flow watermarking systems [10, 13, 17, 19] a watermark signal is composed of a sequence of numbers, often referred to by the *misleading* term of watermark "bit"s. These watermark bits, however, do not correspond to different "information bits," but they all help to the reliable transmission of a single information bit. To make this more clear, consider the cell-counter attack of [17]. This attack uses a Tor-specific [7] flow watermark that embeds a secret sequence of watermark bits on each Tor flow by modifying its cell counters [6]. In this setting, a single Tor cell delivers a 0 watermark bit and a triplet Tor cells sent together denotes a 1 watermark bit. As network congestion and network delay can separate and merge cells in a circuit, the authors in [17] design a *recovery* mechanism to detect the distorted watermark sequences. While this mechanism is able to *detect* the presence of the watermark sequence on a distorted flow, it is not able to reliably *extract* the watermark bits. For instance, suppose that each watermarker inserts only one of these two watermarks: "010" and "00000". Once a detector receives a flow with a "010" cell pattern, it will return positive correlations against *both* "010" and "00000" watermark sequences due to its recovery mechanism (for "0000" the detector assumes that the triplet cells carrying the 1 bit are split by the Tor routers). In simpler words, the detector can tell, with high assurance, that a flow contains *a* watermark, but it can not tell which one.

As another example, consider RAINBOW [13], which is the basis of our Fancy fingerprint. For a specific set of RAINBOW parameters, i.e., a watermark amplitude of $10ms$ and a watermark length of 500, RAINBOW achieves a false negative rate of around 10^{-6} (Figure 4 of [13]), i.e., it misses only one out of a million watermark tags. For the same parameters, the average correlation between the embedded watermark and the extracted one is about 0.55 (Figure 6 of [13]), meaning that it roughly misses one third of the watermark bits with unknown positions, despite its very high watermark detection ratio. Similarly, *all* of the proposed flow watermarks [10, 13, 17, 19] are only able to detect the presence of the watermark, but cannot extract the watermark bits reliably.

Our Contributions. In this paper, we introduce and formulate the flow fingerprinting problem and contrast its application scenarios from that of the well-studied flow watermarking. We also design a class of flow fingerprints, called Fancy, that uses a non-blind architecture similar to the RAINBOW [13] watermark. Fancy utilizes communication codes for the reliable extraction of fingerprint bits. We investigate the use of three classes of coding schemes in the design of Fancy, namely block codes, convolutional codes, and turbo codes [21]. We simulate Fancy using real-world network traces and evaluate its fingerprinting performance for different coding algorithms and under different conditions. The simulation results show that it is possible to reliably send dozens of fingerprint bits over very short lengths of network flows. Our methodology in using coding theory can motivate the design of other fingerprints based on existing watermarking systems. In summary, in this paper we make the following main contributions:

- We introduce and formulate the problem of flow fingerprinting, and discuss its necessity in several applications;
- We design the very first flow fingerprinting scheme, called Fancy;
- Through massive simulations on real-world network traces we show the promising reliability of Fancy in fingerprinting network flows and discuss different performance trade-offs.

In this paper, we **do not** study tag invisibility, robustness to active attacks, and similar issues common to flow watermarks. While these issues are important, they have been extensively studied in the watermarking literature. In particular, the invisibility and robustness evaluations of [13, 16] apply to the Fancy fingerprint designed in this paper.

Paper's Organization. The rest of this paper is organized as follows: in Section 2, we introduce flow fingerprinting and elaborate on its differences with flow watermarking by mentioning their application scenarios. In Section 3 we describe the design of our proposed flow fingerprinting scheme, Fancy. We design efficient codes for Fancy and evaluate their performance in Section 4. We discuss the related work in Section 5 and the paper is concluded in Section 6.

2   Network Flow Fingerprinting

As described above, active traffic analysis has mainly been studied in the concept of flow watermarking, leaving flow fingerprinting unexplored. In this section, we define the flow fingerprinting problem by describing its components and goals. Then, we discriminate flow fingerprinting from its dual, flow watermarking, by explaining their application scenarios.

2.1   Problem Statement

A fingerprinting system is composed of two main components: *fingerprinters* and *fingerprint extractors*. A typical implementation of a fingerprinting system may consist of several fingerprinters and extractors mounted at different network locations. A fingerprinter slightly modifies communication patterns of an observed network flow, e.g., its packet timings, so that it modulates an ℓ-bits *fingerprint tag* into that flow. This ℓ-bits fingerprint conveys some information about the carrying flow, e.g., its network origin, hence it might have different values across different flows. A fingerprinted flow passes through a noisy network, e.g., the Internet, before it is intercepted by a fingerprint extractor who, then, tries to extract its ℓ-bits fingerprint tag. A fingerprint tag should be *robust* to the network noise, i.e., an extractor should be able to extract *all* ℓ bits correctly. Also, as with flow watermarks, a fingerprint should be *invisible*, i.e., an entity not part of the fingerprinting system should not be able to distinguish between a fingerprinted flow and a regular flow.

2.2   Application Scenarios

Active traffic analysis is traditionally suggested for two applications: detection of stepping stone attacks [10,13,19], and compromising anonymity systems [17,22]. In the following, we introduce these two applications and discriminate fingerprinting and watermarking in each of these cases.

Compromising Anonymity Systems. An anonymity system like Tor [7] maps a number of input flows to a number of output flows while hiding the exact relationships between them. The goal of an attacker, then, is to link an incoming flow to its outgoing flow (or vice versa). Previous research [22,23] has suggested the use of flow watermarks for performing this attack. To do so, an attacker tags the flows entering the anonymity network and watches output flows for the inserted watermark. Such an attack can be performed in two manners, *targeted* and *non-targeted*. As we discuss in the following, flow watermarking is only able to conduct the targeted form of this attack, whereas conducting the non-targeted attack requires flow fingerprinting.

1) Targeted attack. Consider a malicious website who intends to identify users who visit that website through an anonymity system (see Figure 1a). To do so, the malicious website inserts a tag on all flows between itself and the anonymizing system. An accomplice who can eavesdrop on a link to the anonymity system (e.g., a malicious Tor entry node, or an ISP) can identify the users browsing the malicious website by looking for the inserted tag. Note that, in this case, the malicious website suffices to insert *the same tag* on any flow that it tags, i.e., it inserts a watermark. This is because the accomplice only needs to check for the existence of the tag, but not its value.

2) Non-targeted attack. Now consider a different scenario in which two (or more) compromised/malicious Tor [7] nodes intend to de-anonymize Tor's connections (see Figure 1b). We argue that this application requires flow fingerprinting as a solution. Suppose that the malicious nodes A and B intercept traffic from n and m number of distinct users, respectively. If flow watermarking was used by the attackers, the node A would insert the same tag (i.e., a watermark) on the traffic of all of its n users, and the node B would look for that single watermark on the traffic of all of its m users. In this case, if B detects the watermark on the traffic of one of its m users, namely $U_{B,k}$, the attackers can only infer that $U_{B,k}$ is communicating with *one of* the n users observed by A, but they can not tell with which of them. Alternatively, suppose that flow fingerprinting is used by the attackers. In this case, A inserts a different, customized tag (i.e., a fingerprint) on the traffic of each of its n users, e.g., it inserts the fingerprint f_i on the traffic of user $U_{A,i}$. Now, if B observes that the traffic to one of its users, $U_{B,k}$, contains the fingerprint f_i the attackers can infer that users $U_{A,i}$ and $U_{B,k}$ are communicating through the anonymity system.

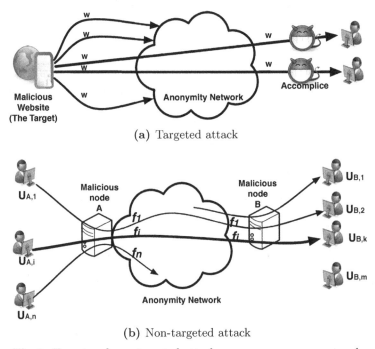

(a) Targeted attack

(b) Non-targeted attack

Fig. 1. Target and non-targeted attacks on an anonymous network

Stepping Stone Detection. A stepping stone is a host that is used to relay an attacking traffic to its victim destination, in order to hide the true origin of the attack. To defend, an enterprise network should be able to identify the ingress flows that are linked (correlated) with some egress flow. The situation is therefore very similar to an anonymous communication system, with n flows entering the enterprise and m flows leaving. There are two objectives for active traffic analysis in this case, as described in the following; the first one is achievable using flow watermarking while the second one requires flow fingerprinting.

1) Detecting relayed flows. As previous research [13, 19] suggests, flow watermarks can be used to detect relayed network flows in this scenario. Suppose that the enterprise network consists of two border routers A and B. To do so, the border router A inserts a watermark tag w on all flows that enter the enterprise network. On the other side, the border router B inspects all egress network flows, looking for the watermark w. Suppose that A intercepts n flows and B intercepts m network flows at a given time. If B detects that a network flow $F_{B,k}$ is carrying the watermark tag w, the security officer of the enterprise network infers that $F_{B,k}$ is a traffic relayed through the enterprise. However, the security officer can not tell which of the n flows observed by A is the source of $F_{B,k}$, since A inserts the same watermark tag on all intercepted flows.

2) Detecting relayed flows and their origins. Flow fingerprinting can be used to not only detect the relayed flows, but also identify their sources. Consider the case in which the border router A inserts different tags (i.e., fingerprints) on each of the n intercepted flows (that is, the fingerprint f_i is inserted into the i-th flow, $F_{A,i}$). Now, suppose that B detects the fingerprint f_i on the network flow $F_{B,k}$. In this case, the security officer infers two facts: first, $F_{B,k}$ is a relayed traffic and, second, the source of this relay traffic is the network flow $F_{A,i}$. A watermark, however, is not able to identify the source of the relayed traffic.

3   Fancy Fingerprinting Scheme

In this section, we describe the design of our flow fingerprinting system, Fancy. Fancy consists of two main elements: a *fingerprinter* that embeds fingerprint messages inside intercepted flows by slightly modifying their timing patterns, and a *fingerprint extractor* (extractor in short) that analyzes the timing patterns of the intercepted flows, trying to extract the fingerprint messages. Fancy uses a *non-blind* architecture similar to the RAINBOW watermark [13]: the fingerprinter communicates with fingerprint extractors some information about the flows being fingerprinted, which is required for efficient fingerprint extraction. To perform this communication, Fancy uses a third element in its design, *IPDs registrar*, which is accessible by fingerprinters and fingerprint extractors. A Fancy fingerprinter stores some information about the intercepted flows on the IPDs registrar, which is periodically accessed by Fancy extractors. Figure 2 shows the high-level block diagram of Fancy.

3.1   Embedding Fingerprints

Figure 3 illustrates a Fancy fingerprinter. Suppose that a network flow, n, with packet timings of $t = \{t_i | i = 1, ...\}$ enters the fingerprinter (e.g., a router) where it is to be fingerprinted. The fingerprinter generates an ℓ-bits fingerprint message, $f = \{f_i | f_i = \pm 1, i = 1, .., \ell\}$, that especially corresponds to the intercepted flow n. That is, a different fingerprint sequence is generated for each intercepted flow, however a fingerprint sequence can be re-used for another flow once the first flow has terminated. This fingerprinter records n's fingerprint message, f, along with

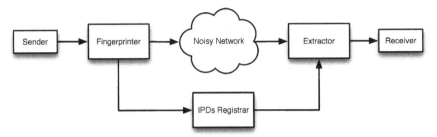

Fig. 2. The main model of Fancy fingerprinting system

the last ℓ^c inter-packet delays (IPDs) of n, i.e., $\boldsymbol{\tau} = \{t_i|\tau_i = t_{i+1} - t_i, i = 1, .., \ell^c\}$, in the IPDs registrar (ℓ^c is the length of the fingerprinted flows, as described later). In addition to recording the flow's fingerprint in the IPDs registrar, the fingerprinter embeds $\boldsymbol{f}$ on the intercepted flow n, as described in the following (in Section 3.3, we discuss the reason for both embedding the fingerprint into the flow and recording it in the IPDs registrar).

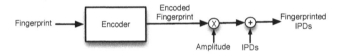

Fig. 3. Fingerprinting scheme of Fancy

The fingerprinter embeds the fingerprint $\boldsymbol{f}$ into the intercepted flow n by delaying its packets by an amount such that the IPD of the i-th fingerprinted packet is

$$\tau_i^c = \tau_i + a \cdot f_i^c \tag{1}$$

The constant a is the *fingerprint amplitude* and $\boldsymbol{f}^c = \{f_i^c|f_i^c = \pm 1, i = 1, ..., \ell^c\}$ is the *encoded fingerprint* sequence, which is generated from $\boldsymbol{f}$ as described in the following. The value a is chosen to be small enough so that the artificial jitter caused by fingerprinting is invisible to non-fingerprinting parties and to the users.

Fingerprint Generation: Suppose that Fancy intends to insert an ℓ-bits fingerprint $\boldsymbol{f} = \{f_i|i = 1, ..., \ell\}$ on a candidate flow. Since each fingerprint bit takes one of the +1 and -1 values, the number of all distinct fingerprint sequences is 2^ℓ. A fingerprinter encodes an ℓ-bits fingerprint sequence, $\boldsymbol{f}$, into an ℓ^c-bits encoded fingerprint $\boldsymbol{f}^c$ by passing $\boldsymbol{f}$ through the encoder block of Fancy fingerprinter. For a given encoding algorithm, we define the *redundancy* of our fingerprinting system, r, to be the redundancy of the utilized encoder, i.e.,

$$r = \ell^c/\ell. \tag{2}$$

3.2   Extracting Fingerprints

Suppose that a Fancy extractor receives the fingerprinted flow n after passing the noisy network, e.g., the Internet. Let us consider that $\boldsymbol{\tau}^{c,r} = \{\tau_i^{c,r} | i = 1, .., \ell^c\}$ are the IPDs of n as observed by the extractor (the superscript c denotes being encoded/fingerprinted and the superscript r denotes being received after passing the noisy network). As described above, the Fancy fingerprinter has recoded n's IPDs before getting fingerprinted, i.e., $\boldsymbol{\tau}$, in the IPDs registrar, along with the embedded fingerprint message $\boldsymbol{f}$. The extractor uses this recorded information to perform fingerprint extraction by accessing the IPDs registrar.

The IPDs registrar contains *flow records*, which are generated by fingerprinters. Each flow record is a pair $R_k = (\boldsymbol{\tau}^k, \boldsymbol{f}^k)$, where k is the index of the record in the IPDs registrar, $\boldsymbol{\tau}^k$ is the original IPDs sequence of a fingerprinted flow, and $\boldsymbol{f}^k$ is the fingerprint embedded into that flow. For each received flow, the extractor loops through the IPDs registrar to find the right flow record corresponding to it (if any).

For any flow record in the IPDs registrar, e.g., $(\boldsymbol{\tau}^k, \boldsymbol{f}^k)$, the extractor performs the following steps:

1. The extractor derives the following sequence:

$$f_i^{r,k} = (\tau_i^{c,r} - \tau_i^k)/a \qquad i = 1, .., \ell^c \tag{3}$$

   where $\tau_i^{c,r}$ is the i-th IPD of the received flow.

2. Then, the extractor passes the ℓ^c-bits $\boldsymbol{f}^{r,k} = \{f_i^{r,k} | i = 1, .., \ell^c\}$ through a *decoder* block that outputs an ℓ-bits sequence $\boldsymbol{f}^{d,k} = \{f_i^{d,k} | f_i^{d,k} = \pm 1, i = 1, .., \ell\}$. This decoder is the corresponding decoder for the encoder block used by Fancy fingerprinter.

3. The extractor declares that the received flow contains the fingerprint sequence $\boldsymbol{f}^k$ if it is the same as the decoder's output, i.e., if we have that:

$$f_i^{d,k} = f_i^k, \qquad \forall i \in \{1, .., \ell\} \tag{4}$$

4. If (4) does not hold the extractor uses the next flow record from the IPDs registrar and repeats the steps above until the end of the database.

We claim that the described algorithm results in reliable extraction of Fancy fingerprints. Let us consider the following two cases:

Case 1 (True match): Suppose that the extractor has picked the flow record that corresponds to the received flow, i.e., $\boldsymbol{\tau}^k = \boldsymbol{\tau}$ and $\boldsymbol{f}^k = \boldsymbol{f}$. We have that

$$\tau_i^{c,r} = \tau_i^c + \delta_i \tag{5}$$

where δ_i is the network jitter applied to the i-th IPD and τ_i^c is the fingerprinted IPD. In this case, using (1), (5), and (3) we get that:

$$f_i^{r,k} = (\tau_i^{c,r} - \tau_i^k)/a \tag{6}$$
$$= (\tau_i + \delta_i + a f_i^c - \tau_i)/a \tag{7}$$
$$= f_i^c + \delta_i/a \tag{8}$$

In other words, using the right flow record from the registrar the step 1 of our extraction process will generate a perturbed version of the coded fingerprint. As a result, passing this perturbed coded fingerprint through the decoder (step 2) is likely to return the embedded fingerprint, depending on the noise conditions and the decoder performance (in Section 4 we design decoders that perform very well in our application). Since this decoded fingerprint is the same as the one contained in the flow record, step 3 of the algorithm will result in a correct fingerprint extraction.

Case 2 (False match): Now, let us consider a case where the extractor is using a non-relevant flow record from the registrar. In this case, the second step of the above algorithm will result in an arbitrary fingerprint sequence. The odds that this arbitrary fingerprint is the same as the one contained in the flow record is $2^{-\ell}$. For the values of ℓ used in our design (e.g., 25) this results in a tiny false extraction rate, so we neglect this case in our performance evaluation. Note that the overall probability for a received flow getting false matched with some flow record is $2^{-\ell} \times Y$, where Y is the number of flow records matched against from the IPDs registrar; the following filtering process minimizes Y.

Filtering Flow Records: In order to speed up the extraction process, also to decrease the possibilities of false matches, for a received flow the extractor leaves out a large number of flow records in the registrar by using simple filters. One very simple, yet efficient, filter is the packet count of the registered flows: the extractor does not consider flow records whose corresponding flows have packet counts much larger or much smaller than the packet count of the received flow. A second filter that we use is the *IPDs-distance* metric, which leaves out the records with non-similar IPDs. We define the IPDs-distance metric between a received flow with IPDs $\boldsymbol{\tau}^r$ and a flow record $R_k = (\boldsymbol{\tau}^k, \boldsymbol{f}^k)$ to be:

$$d(\boldsymbol{\tau}^r, \boldsymbol{\tau}^k) = \frac{1}{\ell^c} \sum_{i=1}^{\ell^c} (\tau_i^r - \tau_i^k - f_i^c) \tag{9}$$

If R_k is the right record corresponding to the received flow this distance metric will return the average network jitter on the path, which is a small number. The extractor considers only those records from the registrar whose distance from the received flow are smaller than a threshold, η. By putting η equal to four times the standard deviation of the network jitter the odds that the right record is left out is approximately 10^{-4} (we model the network jitter as Laplace distribution [13]).

3.3 Alternative Designs

As described above, to fingerprint a flow n with the fingerprint message $\boldsymbol{f}$, the fingerprinter performs two tasks: a) it records the fingerprint $\boldsymbol{f}$ in the IPDs registrar, along with the IPD values of the flow, and, b) it embeds $\boldsymbol{f}$ into the network flow n. Alternatively, one could suggest to only record the fingerprint in the registrar, or to only embed it into the flow. In the following, we back our design decision by discussing the performance degradation of the two alternatives.

Passive Fingerprinting. An alternative approach to Fancy is to only record fingerprint sequences in the IPDs registrar along with their corresponding IPDs sequences, *without* embedding the fingerprints into the flows. In fact, this approach is passive traffic analysis, which has extensively been studied in the literature [3, 9, 25]. Unfortunately, this approach may result in high rates of false detection, especially when the evaluated flows are cross-correlated. The common examples for correlated network flows are web traffic (to the same destination), and file transfers. To validate this, we simulate an optimum passive traffic analysis scheme [14] on real web traffic that are generated by different users to the same websites. Our results (Table 1) show that even this optimum passive traffic analysis scheme produces very large false positive errors in linking the correlated web traffic.

Table 1. False positive error rates of the optimum passive traffic analysis [14] in linking web traffic that are generated by different users to the same websites (N is the flow length).

Website	$N=25$	$N=50$	$N=100$
baidu.com	0.29	0.07	0.08
blogger.com	0.97	0.63	1
facebook.com	0.91	0.97	0.96
live.com	1	1	0.38
wikipedia.org	0.94	0.44	0.46
yahoo.co.jp	0.66	0.33	0.05
yahoo.com	1	1	0.23
yandex.com	0.89	0.08	0.02

Only Embedded into Flows. As another alternative, one could only embed fingerprints in network flows *without* recording them in the IPDs registrar. This, also, results in high rates of false extraction errors. For a received flow at the extractor, the use of a non-corresponding flow record from the registrar will most likely lead the extractor to retrieve some *valid* fingerprint sequence that is different from the embedded fingerprint. By recording the fingerprints in the registrar as well the extractor can detect this by simply comparing the extracted fingerprint with the one recorded in the IPDs registrar.

4   Code Design and Simulations

We investigate the use of different coding algorithms as the encoder/decoder block of Fancy. In particular, we investigate the use of several linear block codes [21] considering our communication channel. Based on our measurements over

Planetlab [1] the standard deviation of network jitter (δ) between randomly selected nodes varies between $6ms$ and $12ms$. For a fingerprinting amplitude of $a = 10ms$, the SNR [2], given by $SNR = 20log(a/\delta)$, varies between -1.5836 and 4.4370 (i.e., an average of 1.4267). Also, we aim at having a flow length of around $n \approx 100$ for fingerprinting, since larger lengths would take longer to extract. For these parameters, we look for appropriate coding algorithms to be used by Fancy's encoder. Dolinar et al. [8] compare the performance of several block codes for different lengths of information bits, along with the theoretical capacity limits. In particular, they illustrate the appropriate block size values for different coding algorithms, i.e., the range of block sizes that a coding algorithm performs close enough to the channel capacity. Based on such evaluations (Figure 12 in [8]) we identify several codes that are expected to work well for our system parameters. In particular, we investigate the use of three types of linear codes in our simulations, which are Reed-Solomon (RS) Codes, convolutional codes, and turbo codes. The simulations are done in Matlab using network traces gathered over Planetlab [1], and by using Matlab's built-in coding functions and the CML coding library [4].

Evaluation metrics – We define the following metrics to evaluate the extraction performance of Fancy.

- **Extraction Rate (P_E):** This metric is the ratio of the number of fingerprinted flows successfully extracted by a Fancy extractor to the number of all fingerprinted flows.
- **Miss Rate (P_M):** This is the ratio of the number of fingerprinted flows declared as non-fingerprinted by a Fancy extractor to the number of all fingerprinted flows. We have that $P_M = 1 - P_E$.

The goal of a Fancy extractor is to maximize the extraction rate (i.e., minimize the miss rate).

4.1   Reed-Solomon (RS) Codes

Reed-Solomon (RS) codes [21] are a class of linear block codes that are maximum distance separable (MDS), i.e., they meet the equality criteria of the *singleton bound* [21]. In fact, the RS codes are the only known instances of the MDS codes. The encoding structure of the RS codes makes them suitable for M-ary communication schemes where the noise is applied in bursts over a message bit stream (e.g., satellite communications). This makes them a good candidate for applications where bursty noise may happen to inter-packet delays, e.g., due to network congestion. We use the notation (n, k)-RS for an RS code that encodes each k message symbols into n encoded symbols, where each symbol is m bits and $m = \log_2(n + 1)$ (e.g., an n-bit RS coded message consists of $m \times n$ binary bits).

We design a Fancy fingerprint, called Fancy-RS, that utilizes RS encoders as part of its encoding algorithm. More specifically, Fancy-RS generates an ℓ^c-bits coded fingerprint $\boldsymbol{f}^c$ from an ℓ-bits fingerprint sequence $\boldsymbol{f}$ by passing $\boldsymbol{f}$ through an (n,k)-RS encoder. We have that $\ell^c = n/k\ell$.

We simulated Fancy-RS in Matlab. We use traces of network jitter gathered over Planetlab [1] to simulate the effect of the noisy network over the finger-printing performance. Note that we do not include the original IPDs in our simulations, since as discussed in Section 3.2 the extractor is able to reliably pick the original IPD sequence from the IPDs registrar and subtract it from the received flow before performing the extraction. In the first experiment, we measure and compare the performance of our fingerprint extractor for different parameters of the (n,k)-RS encoder. We set $a = 10ms$ and $p = 2$. We also set $\ell = mk$ (generally, ℓ should be an integer multiplication of mk) and vary the m and k parameters of our RS encoder (each experiment is run for 1000 times with different randomly generated fingerprints and different network jitter). Figure 4 shows the extraction rate (P_E) for different values of m and k (the bars show the 95% confidence intervals). As can be seen, for a given m, decreasing k improves the extraction performance since it increases the redundancy of our RS encoder, i.e., $(2^m - 1)/k$. Figure 5 shows the coding redundancy of Fancy-RS for different parameters of the RS code.

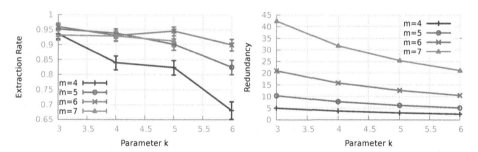

Fig. 4. Extraction rate of Fancy-RS for different RS encoders. ($a = 10ms$, and $\ell = mk$)

Fig. 5. Coding redundancy of Fancy-RS for different RS encoders. ($a = 10ms$, $p = 2$, and $\ell = mk$)

Finally, the number of distinct fingerprints, N, that can be embedded and extracted reliably by Fancy-RS is given by

$$N = 2^{mk} \tag{10}$$

For instance, for $k = 5$, and $m = 5$ (i.e., $\ell = 25$) we have that $N \approx 10^7$.

In order to evaluate the effect of the fingerprint amplitude (a), we measure the extraction rate for different values of a. This is illustrated in Figure 6, where $m = 5$, and $k = 5$. As intuitively expected, increasing a rapidly improves the true detection and miss rate such that for $a = 20ms$ we have that $P_T = 1$ and $P_M = 0$. Note that increasing the fingerprint amplitude a makes the fingerprint less invisible, as discussed in [13].

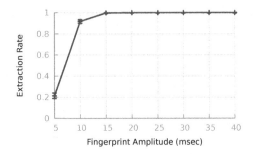

Fig. 6. Extraction rate of Fancy-RS for different fingerprint amplitudes. ($m = 5$, $k = 5$, i.e., the redundancy is 6.2)

4.2 Convolutional Codes

Convolutional codes are another class of linear error-correcting codes that have use in several different applications [21]. An (n, k) convolutional code, (n, k)-Conv, is a function with k inputs and n outputs. The input stream, i.e., $\boldsymbol{f} = \{f_i | f_i \in \{0, 1\}, i = 1, 2, ...\}$, is split into k streams entering the inputs of the encoder. Each of the n output streams of this encoder is evaluated by convolving some of the input streams with a generator function $\boldsymbol{G}$. The length of the generator function is called the *constraint length* v, and $u = v - 1$ is the memory of the encoder. An easy-to-implement decoder for convolutional codes is an ML decoder based on the Viterbi algorithm [21].

We design a variant of Fancy fingerprint, called Fancy-Conv, that uses convolutional coding for its encoding process. More specifically, an ℓ-bits fingerprint sequence $\boldsymbol{f}$ passes through the (n, k)-Conv encoder of Fancy-Conv, which generates the final encoded fingerprint $\boldsymbol{f}^c$ consisting of ℓ^c bits.

We implemented Fancy-Conv in Matlab using the CML [4] coding libraries. We use a constraint length of $v = 9$, and a randomly created generator function G. We run several experiments to measure the performance of Fancy-Conv for different parameters, where each experiment is run for 1000 randomly generated fingerprints. In the first experiment, we measure the effect of our encoder's redundancy on the fingerprinting performance, where $a = 10ms$, and $\ell = 24$. Figure 7 shows the extraction rate (with bars showing the 95% confidence intervals) for different redundancies of (n, k)-Conv. As can be seen, increasing the redundancy, r, improves the extraction rate; this, however, increases the flow length required to embed the fingerprint, which is linear with redundancy, i.e., $\ell^c = r\ell$.

We also measure the effect of the fingerprint amplitude on the detection performance. As can be seen from Figure 8, increasing the fingerprint amplitude improves the extraction rate ($\ell = 18$, and the convolutional code's redundancy is 8). This comes at the price of less fingerprint invisibility. A fingerprint amplitude of $a = 20ms$ results in a very good extraction rate, while at the same time provides a promising invisibility.

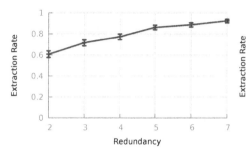 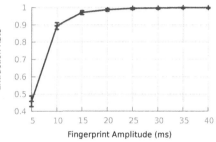

Fig. 7. Extraction rate of Fancy-Conv for different encoder redundancies. ($a = 10ms$)

Fig. 8. Extraction performance of Fancy-Conv for different fingerprint amplitudes. ($\ell = 18$, and the convolutional code's redundancy is 8)

Finally, the number of distinct fingerprints, N, that can be embedded and extracted reliably by Fancy-Conv is given by $N = 2^\ell$. For instance, for $\ell = 24$, we have that $N \approx 10^7$.

4.3 Turbo Codes

Turbo codes are a class of high-performance error correction codes and are the first practical capacity-approaching codes [18]. A turbo code is generated by concatenating two or more *constituent* codes, where each constituent code can be a convolutional or a block code. Usually some *interleaver* reorders the data at the input of the inner encoders. Turbo codes are decoded through iterative schemes. There are two types of Turbo codes: *Block Turbo Codes* (BTC), and *Convolutional Turbo codes* (CTC).

In this paper, we consider the use of BTC codes in the design of Fancy fingerprints. A BTC code works by encoding a $k_x \times k_y$ matrix of data, D, into a $n_x \times n_y$ matrix C as follows: a (n_x, k_x) systematic code encodes each row of D, a block interleaver reorders the rows of the resulted matrix, and finally, a (n_y, k_y) systematic code encodes the columns of the resulted matrix to generate the final $n_x \times n_y$ dimensional matrix C. The systematic codes used for BTC codes are the cyclic codes, e.g., Hamming, Single Parity Check, and Extended Hamming [18]. The constituent block codes can be generated using polynomials.

We design Fancy-BTC, a fingerprint that uses BTC codes as its encoding block. Our BTC code uses two convolutional codes as its horizontal and vertical constituent codes. We use the CML [4] coding library to simulate Fancy-BTC in Matlab. We randomly create the generator functions of the convolutional codes that constitute our BTC encoder (with constraint lengths of v_x and v_y for the horizontal and vertical codes, respectively). To encode a fingerprint f with length ℓ our encoder reorders f into a $k_x \times k_y$ matrix D, where $k_x = k_y = round(\sqrt{\ell})$ and $round(\cdot)$ rounds to the nearest larger number. The encoder also fills the first $B = k_x \times k_y - \ell$ bits of this matrix with zeros. We use an iterative detector that stops only if either a maximum number of iterations has reached, or the additional iterations do not change the decoded fingerprint.

In our first experiment, we measure the effect of the number of iterations on the extraction performance (each experiment is run for 1000 randomly generated fingerprints). We use a fingerprint amplitude of $a = 10ms$, a fingerprint length of $\ell = 25$, and our code is designed such that $v_x = v_y = 6$, $k_x = k_y = 5$, $B = 0$ and the code redundancy is 5.95. Figure 9 shows the extraction rate for different values of the maximum decoder iteration, along with the 95% confidence intervals. As can be seen, even though the detection performance improves rapidly for small numbers of iterations it does not change significantly after several iterations. Considering the added processing overhead for more iterations, we choose 8 as the maximum number of iterations performed by our detector, being used in all of our consecutive simulations.

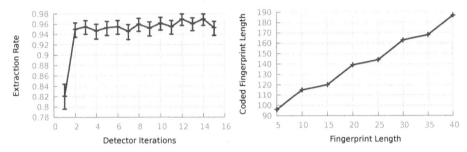

Fig. 9. Extraction rate of Fancy-BTC for different values of maximum decoder iteration. ($a = 10ms$, $\ell = 25$, and $r = 5.95$)

Fig. 10. The length of the coded fingerprint for different fingerprint lengths for Fancy-BTC

In the second experiment, we keep $v_x = v_y = 6$ and $a = 10ms$, but vary the fingerprint length ℓ. Figure 10 shows the length of the coded fingerprint for different values of the fingerprint length. As before, the number of distinct fingerprints, N, is exponential with ℓ. As can be seen from the figure, increasing ℓ only linearly increases the length of the encoded fingerprint, while it exponentially increases N. Note that in the figure the code redundancy is around 6, but varies a bit with ℓ since our BTC encoder can not produce all redundancy values for any given ℓ.

In the third experiment, we evaluate the performance of Fancy-BTC using BTC codes with different redundancies. More specifically, we set $a = 10ms$, $\ell = 25$, and $k_x = k_y = 5$ and try BTC codes with different constraint lengths (v_x and v_y), resulting in various redundancies. Figure 11 shows the extraction rate for codes with different redundancies. As can be seen, Fancy-BTC does not perform well for small values of code redundancies, however increasing the code redundancy rapidly improves its performance. In fact, such an improved performance comes at the price of longer fingerprinted flows.

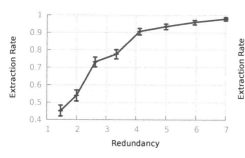

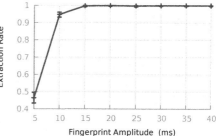

Fig. 11. Extraction rate of Fancy-BTC for different redundancies of the BTC code. ($a = 10ms$, $\ell = 25$)

Fig. 12. Extraction rate of Fancy-BTC for different values of fingerprint amplitude. ($\ell = 25$, and $r = 4$)

Finally, we illustrate the effect of the fingerprint amplitude on the extraction performance. As can be seen from Figure 12, increasing a rapidly improves the extraction, such that $a = 20ms$ results in an extraction rate of in 1000 runs of the experiment.

4.4 Comparison

We also compare the performance of the three versions of Fancy, i.e., Fancy-RS, Fancy-Conv, and Fancy-BTC. Figure 13 shows the extraction rate of the three schemes for different values of encoder redundancy (for all three schemes we have that $\ell = 25$, and $a = 10ms$). As can be seen, for very small redundancies the Fancy-RS outperforms the other two, even though all of the schemes perform poorly for such small values of redundancy. As the redundancy increases, all schemes improve their performance and, in particular, the Fancy-BTC outperforms the other two schemes for high redundancies.

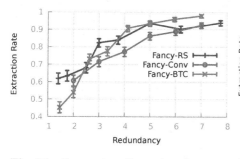

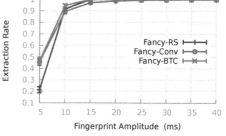

Fig. 13. Comparing the extraction performance of Fancy-RS, Fancy-Conv, and Fancy-BTC for different code redundancies

Fig. 14. Comparing the extraction performance of Fancy-RS, Fancy-Conv, and Fancy-BTC for different fingerprint amplitudes (with a similar redundancy of around 6)

We also compare the three schemes for different fingerprint amplitudes. Figure 14 shows the extraction performance of Fancy-RS, Fancy-Conv, and Fancy-BTC for different values of a, with $\ell = 25$. Also, the redundancies of Fancy-RS, Fancy-Conv, and Fancy-BTC are 6.2 , 6, and 5.96, respectively (note that it is not possible to produce an exact value of r for any given ℓ). As intuitively expected, increasing the fingerprint amplitude significantly improves the extraction performance at the cost of larger perturbations applied to the fingerprinted flows.

5   Related Work

Traffic analysis has long been studied for linking network flows. Early traffic analysis schemes [5, 9, 20, 24, 26, 28] work in a passive manner, i.e., they record the communication characteristics of incoming flows and correlate them with that of the observed outgoing flows. The right place to do this is often at the border router of an enterprise, so the overhead of this technique is the space used to store the stream characteristics long enough to check against correlated relayed streams, and the CPU time needed to perform the correlations. In a complex application with many interconnected networks, a relayed connection, e.g., through a stepping stone, may enter and leave the monitored network through different points; in such cases, there is also an additional communications overhead for transmitting traffic statistics between the border routers.

To address some of the efficiency concerns of passive traffic analysis, researchers have suggested to perform traffic analysis in an active manner. Active traffic analysis improves upon passive traffic analysis in two ways. First, by inserting a pattern that is uncorrelated with any other flows, they can improve the detection efficiency, requiring smaller numbers of packets to be observed (hundreds instead of thousands) and providing lower false-positive rates (10^{-4} or lower, as compared to 10^{-2} with passive watermarks) [14]. Second, they can operate in a *blind* fashion [25]: after an incoming flow is watermarked, there is no need to record or communicate the flow characteristics, since the presence of the watermark can be detected independently. The detection is also potentially faster as there is no need to compare each outgoing flow to all the incoming flows within the same time frame.

Wang et al. borrowed the QIM watermarking idea from the multimedia literature to perform active traffic analysis [25]. This approach, however, is fragile to packet-level modifications, e.g., a single dropped packet would completely destroy the watermark pattern. To provide robustness to such packet-level perturbations several proposals apply the watermark modifications on the timing "intervals" of network flows [19,23,27]. Kiyavash et al. [12,15] demonstrated that applying the interval-based watermarks identically on different flows can give away the embedded watermark to an attacker who observes several watermarked flows. This affected the design of the successor watermarking schemes [10,13], which apply the watermark patterns to network flows depending on the features of the candidate flow. Note that such schemes do not insert different watermark tags on different flows, but they apply the same watermark tag differently on different flows. Houmansadr et al. [11] use repeat-accumulate codes to improve the detection performance of watermarks.

While most of the proposals for flow watermarking use timing patterns for their modifications, other traffic patterns are also used for watermark insertion. For instance, Yu et al. [27] design a watermarking system that tags flows by modifying their packet rates in different time intervals. As another example, Ling et al. [17] propose a watermarking attack on Tor [7] that works by modifying packet sizes. The attack works by modifying the counts of Tor cells [6] carried by network packets.

6 Conclusions

In this paper, we shed light on an unexplored, yet important, variant of active traffic analysis, flow fingerprinting. We designed the first flow fingerprinting scheme, Fancy, and demonstrated its reliability in tagging large numbers of distinct flows. We explored the use of different linear codes in the design of Fancy and compared their performance. In particular, we showed that Fancy can reliably tag millions of distinct network flows using flows as short as tens of packets.

Acknowledgements. The authors would like to thank Roger Dingledine and anonymous reviewers for their insightful comments. This work was supported in part by the National Science Foundation grant CNS 0831488 and the Boeing Trusted Software Center at the Information Trust Institute at the University of Illinois.

References

1. Bavier, A., Bowman, M., Chun, B., Culler, D., Karlin, S., Muir, S., Peterson, L., Roscoe, T., Spalink, T., Wawrzoniak, M.: Operating Systems Support for Planetary-Scale Network Services. In: NSDI (2004)
2. Benedetto, S., Biglieri, E.: Principles of Digital Transmission: With Wireless Applications. Information Technology: Transmission, Processing, and Storage. Kluwer Academic/Plenum Press (1999)
3. Blum, A., Song, D., Venkataraman, S.: Detection of Interactive Stepping Stones: Algorithms and Confidence Bounds. In: Jonsson, E., Valdes, A., Almgren, M. (eds.) RAID 2004. LNCS, vol. 3224, pp. 258–277. Springer, Heidelberg (2004)
4. The coded modulation library (cml), http://www.iterativesolutions.com/Matlab.html
5. Danezis, G.: The Traffic Analysis of Continuous-Time Mixes. In: PETS (2004)
6. Dingledine, R., Mathewson, N.: Tor Protocol Specification, https://gitweb.torproject.org/torspec.git?a=blob_plain;hb=HEAD;f=tor-spec.txt
7. Dingledine, R., Mathewson, N., Syverson, P.: Tor: The Second-Generation Onion Router. In: USENIX Security Symposium (2004)
8. Dolinar, S., Divsalar, D., Pollara, F.: Code Performance as a Function of Block Size. Technical report, TMO Progress (1998)

9. Donoho, D.L., Flesia, A.G., Shankar, U., Paxson, V., Coit, J., Staniford, S.: Multiscale Stepping-stone Detection: Detecting Pairs of Jittered Interactive Streams by Exploiting Maximum Tolerable Delay. In: Wespi, A., Vigna, G., Deri, L. (eds.) RAID 2002. LNCS, vol. 2516, pp. 17–35. Springer, Heidelberg (2002)

10. Houmansadr, A., Borisov, N.: SWIRL: A Scalable Watermark to Detect Correlated Network Flows. In: NDSS (2011)

11. Houmansadr, A., Borisov, N.: Towards Improving Network Flow Watermarks using the Repeat-accumulate Codes. In: ICASSP (2011)

12. Houmansadr, A., Kiyavash, N., Borisov, N.: Multi-Flow Attack Resistant Watermarks for Network Flows. In: ICASSP (2009)

13. Houmansadr, A., Kiyavash, N., Borisov, N.: RAINBOW: A Robust And Invisible Non-Blind Watermark for Network Flows. In: NDSS (2009)

14. Houmansadr, A., Kiyavash, N., Borisov, N.: Non-blind Watermarking of Network Flows. CRR, arXiv:1203.2273v1 (2012)

15. Kiyavash, N., Houmansadr, A., Borisov, N.: Multi-Flow Attacks Against Network Flow Watermarking Schemes. In: USENIX Security Symposium (2008)

16. Lin, Z., Hopper, N.: New Attacks on Timing-based Network Flow Watermarks. In: USENIX Security (2012)

17. Ling, Z., Luo, J., Yu, W., Fu, X., Xuan, D., Jia, W.: A New Cell Counter Based Attack Against Tor. In: CCS, New York, USA (2009)

18. Mackay, D.J.C.: Information Theory, Inference and Learning Algorithms, 1st edn. Cambridge University Press (June 2003)

19. Pyun, Y., Park, Y., Wang, X., Reeves, D.S., Ning, P.: Tracing Traffic through Intermediate Hosts that Repacketize Flows. In: INFOCOM (2007)

20. Staniford-Chen, S., Heberlein, L.T.: Holding Intruders Accountable on the Internet. In: IEEE S&P (1995)

21. van Lint, J.H.: Introduction to Coding Theory, 3rd edn. Springer, Berlin (1998)

22. Wang, X., Chen, S., Jajodia, S.: Tracking Anonymous Peer-to-peer VoIP Calls on the Internet. In: CCS (2005)

23. Wang, X., Chen, S., Jajodia, S.: Network Flow Watermarking Attack on Low-Latency Anonymous Communication Systems. In: IEEE S&P (2007)

24. Wang, X., Reeves, D.S., Wu, S.F.: Inter-Packet Delay Based Correlation for Tracing Encrypted Connections Through Stepping Stones. In: Gollmann, D., Karjoth, G., Waidner, M. (eds.) ESORICS 2002. LNCS, vol. 2502, pp. 244–263. Springer, Heidelberg (2002)

25. Wang, X., Reeves, D.S.: Robust Correlation of Encrypted Attack Traffic Through Stepping Stones by Manipulation of Interpacket Delays. In: CCS (2003)

26. Yoda, K., Etoh, H.: Finding a Connection Chain for Tracing Intruders. In: Cuppens, F., Deswarte, Y., Gollmann, D., Waidner, M. (eds.) ESORICS 2000. LNCS, vol. 1895, pp. 191–205. Springer, Heidelberg (2000)

27. Yu, W., Fu, X., Graham, S., Xuan, D., Zhao, W.: DSSS-Based Flow Marking Technique for Invisible Traceback. In: IEEE S&P (2007)

28. Zhang, Y., Paxson, V.: Detecting Stepping Stones. In: USENIX Security Symposium (2000)

How Much Is Too Much?
Leveraging Ads Audience Estimation
to Evaluate Public Profile Uniqueness

Terence Chen[1,2], Abdelberi Chaabane[3], Pierre Ugo Tournoux[4],
Mohamed-Ali Kaafar[1,3], and Roksana Boreli[1,2]

[1] National ICT Australia
firstname.lastname@nicta.com.au
[2] School of Electrical Engineering & Telecommunications, UNSW, Australia
[3] INRIA, Grenoble, France
firstname.lastname@inria.fr
[4] IREMIA, LIM, Université de la Réunion, France
tournoux@gmail.com

Abstract. This paper addresses the important goal of quantifying the threat of linking external records to public Online Social Networks (OSN) user profiles, by providing a method to estimate the uniqueness of such profiles and by studying the amount of information carried by public profile attributes. Our first contribution is to leverage the Ads audience estimation platform of a major OSN to compute the information surprisal (IS) based uniqueness of public profiles, independently from the used profiles dataset. Then, we measure the quantity of information carried by the revealed attributes and evaluate the impact of the public release of selected combinations of these attributes on the potential to identify user profiles. Our measurement results, based on an unbiased sample of more than 400 thousand Facebook public profiles, show that, when disclosed in such profiles, *current city* has the highest individual attribute potential for unique identification and the combination of *gender*, *current city* and *age* can identify close to 55% of users to within a group of 20 and uniquely identify around 18% of users. We envisage the use of our methodology to assist both OSNs in designing better anonymization strategies when releasing user records and users to evaluate the potential for external parties to uniquely identify their public profiles and hence make it easier to link them with other data sources.

1 Introduction

The potential to uniquely identify individuals by linking records from publicly available databases has been demonstrated in a number of research works, e.g. [11, 19, 23]. In [23] Sweeney reported on the uniqueness of US demographic data based on the 1990 census and showed that, 87% of the US population can be uniquely identified by *gender*, *ZIP code* and *date of birth*. The resulting loss of privacy, i.e. the potential for re-identification of a person's private data which

E. De Cristofaro and M. Wright (Eds.): PETS 2013, LNCS 7981, pp. 225–244, 2013.

may exist in any other publicly released dataset, was also demonstrated by the author. A more recent study [11] also produced similar conclusions. Therefore, anonymization of databases (*e.g.* medical records or voting registers) with the aim of protecting the privacy of individual's records when such are publicly released, in reality cannot be successful if the released database contains potentially unique combinations of attributes relating to specific individuals.

Today, with the proliferation of public online data, Online Social Networks (OSNs) are a rich source of information about individuals. For either social or professional purposes, users upload various, in most cases highly personal and up to date information, to their OSN accounts. User's personal data exposure is managed by public profiles, which contain a selected (in some case mandatory) subset of the total information available in their private OSN profiles. In fact, public profiles represent an easily accessible public dataset containing user's personal details which, depending on the OSN, can include their age, gender, contact details [1] for home and workplace, interests, etc (for a full list, see [15]).

The existence of public profiles creates a valuable new source of information that has to be considered when releasing anonymized personal records. Also, the anonymized OSN private (profile) data is being released by OSN's to profiling and advertising companies, including in some cases additional information (e.g. political orientation such as in [1]), thus increasing the number of already available anonymized datasets used e.g. for medical or other research. These can be henceforth linked to public profiles, allowing the re-identification (and the de-anonymization) of the personal records i.e. the exposure of individual's identities[2] Previous research has addressed the release of online data in public OSN profiles [14,15] and re-identification mechanisms aimed at e.g. anonymized OSN graphs [20].

In this paper, we aim to revisit the study of the uniqueness of demographics, however we consider *online public data* available for individuals. As a first step towards such analysis, we consider the evaluation of the uniqueness of public OSN profiles, consisting of the publicly available attributes e.g. *gender, age, location*, etc. associated with individual OSN accounts. We use information surprisal and entropy, established information theory metrics for measuring the level of information contained in random variables, to quantify the level of uniqueness. Having a higher information surprisal of the attribute values released in the public OSN profile can be directly related to being more unique in a set of OSN users, and therefore more easily re-identifiable when combining with other publicly available datasets containing the same attribute values. Then, this work also answers the question of the appropriate selection of attributes to be included when releasing anonymized personal records.

We note that quantifying the user's revealed information is a challenging task, as data that needs to be acquired in order to obtain a reliable estimation of profile uniqueness, is either only partially accessible (private attributes are

---

[1] Recently released Graph Search (`https://www.facebook.com/about/graphsearch`) service from Facebook illustrates well the ease of access to individual profiles.

[2] The policy of major OSNs is to use real names (`http://goo.gl/2DkG6`).

by definition hidden), protected by OSNs providers, or of too large volume for the data collection to be practical. Our study provides a novel probabilistic framework that leverages the global private attribute statistics retrieved from a major OSN ad platform (Facebook), to obtain an *unbiased* quantification of uniqueness. We present an approach that takes user specific privacy policy into account and allows us to calculate the uniqueness of public profiles, computed over the entire Facebook dataset.

The first contribution of our paper is our proposed **methodology for computing the uniqueness of public OSN profiles**, independently from the dataset on which the analysis is performed. This methodology can, more generally, be applied to any set of attributes that comprise a user's profile. To calculate the probability of publicly revealing a combination of attributes and evaluate the measure of uniqueness, we combine statistics derived from the captured dataset of publicly revealed attributes and the ads audience estimation platform. We consider both independence and dependence of the probabilities to reveal different attributes.

Our second contribution is that we **evaluate the quantity of information** carried in individual attributes and attribute combinations present in user's profiles of a major OSN (Facebook). We show that there is a wide range of values for the amount of identifying information carried by different attributes, with *gender* being the lowest with $1.3bits$ of entropy and *current city* the highest with the entropy of $13.6bits$.

In our third contribution, we **identify the key attribute combinations that contribute to profile uniqueness in Facebook**. Consistent with reported results for linking anonymous US datasets [11, 23] but also applicable globally, we show that the combination of *gender*, *place of residence* and *age* (directly related to date of birth used in [11,23]) has the highest impact on the potential for re-identification of user's anonymized data. The higher information granularity available in [11,23] and the difference in the type of community studied (online and global versus US population) results in a lower, although still significant, potential for identification. We show that 55% of Facebook users that reveal this attribute combination can be identified as a group of 20 and around 18% of such users can be considered unique with an information surprisal of $29bits$.

Finally, we **show the impact of user's privacy policy on the amount of information carried in Facebook public profiles** and highlight how policy uniqueness contributes to potential re-identification of users in anonymized datasets. We show that some attributes may allow users to hide in the crowd if revealed, as opposed to hiding them from public access.

The remainder of this paper is organized as follows. In Section 2 we provide a summary of the datasets used for this study. In Section 3 we describe the methodology for computing the uniqueness of public profiles. We present results and identify the key attributes that contribute to uniqueness in Section 4, followed by the discussion in Section 5. Related work is presented in Section 6 and we conclude in Section 7.

2   Our Data Source

For the purpose of our study, we have collected two datasets from Facebook: a set of public user profiles and a set of statistics collected from the **F**acebook **A**ds audience estimation **P**latform (hereafter referred to as FAP). In the following, we start by providing a brief description of user's profile as implemented by Facebook, then we describe the methodology used to collect the data in use in this paper. Finally, we describe the characteristics of our datasets.

2.1   Facebook Profiles

Facebook, similarly to a number of other OSNs, utilizes user profiles that are a collection of attributes which describe the user's personal data. An attribute may take one of a pre-determined set of values, e.g. *gender* can be male or female, while *current country* may take any of the global country names. Also, some attributes may be in free form text and may also have a number of values, e.g. *interests* may include books, movies, shopping, etc. The availability of these attributes conforms to a set of privacy rules (i.e., ACL) defined by Facebook and selected (with the exception of a small number of mandatory attributes) by the user. According to the privacy settings, an attribute can be visible to anyone, shared with (a set of) user's social links (e.g., friends) or only visible to the owner of this profile. Hereafter, we consider an attribute (resp. a set of attributes, i.e. profile) to be *public* if it is visible to anyone and *private* otherwise.

2.2   Public Facebook Profiles Dataset

Collecting data from a large OSN is a challenging task, as the huge volume of data necessitates use of a sampling approach, which should produce a uniform representation of the overall dataset. In this study we use the dataset of Facebook public profiles from [5]. This dataset was obtained by first scraping all unique user names in the latin character part of the the Facebook public directory[3], resulting in 100 Million user identifiers (IDs). Then, we sampled, randomly, a subset of 494,392 IDs for which we retrieved the corresponding public profiles (i.e. attributes). We finally processed the collected data to unify the values of country of origin and current country using the Geocoding API[4]. This resulted in a set of 445,024 profiles[5] used for this study, that we refer to as PubCrawl.

It is worthwhile noting that, as per [10], an unbiased sample of a population can be obtained by True Uniform sampling of the total population, i.e. for Facebook, by sampling the 32-bit space of user IDs. However, in practice only 25% of

---

[3] http://www.facebook.com/directory/

[4] https://www.developers.google.com/maps/documentation/geocoding/

[5] The size's mismatch is due to profiles where the geolocation was unsuccessful or simply could not be used (e.g. some of the 49 K profiles that have been removed correspond to locations in China for which at the time of the data collection the Ads platform did not provide demographic information. Note that currently the FB ads platform provides no information for Iran, while China has been enabled).

this space is currently allocated to existing users. A close approximation of True Uniform sampling for Facebook IDs can be achieved by randomly sampling the Facebook public directory which lists all IDs of searchable profiles. We have verified the number of searchable profiles in Facebook public directory, as of April 2013, was 1.14 Billion. This is very close to the reported number of Facebook monthly users for December 2012, 1.06 Billion[6] (whether the corresponding profiles are searchable or not[7]). We believe then that our dataset extracted from the Facebook public directory is a good representative of the Facebook population of public profiles.

2.3 Facebook Ads Platform Dataset

Facebook offers a platform to estimate the audience of targeted ad campaigns[8]. Advertisers can select different criteria such as user's *locations* (country or city), *gender*, *age* (or range of ages), etc.[9] These criteria can also be combined in a conjunctive manner. According to the selected combination, FAP outputs the *audience* which represents the number of Facebook users that match the criteria.

Although there is no full report on how Facebook generates the audience values, Facebook document [10] states that it uses *all* provided information to calculate the audience size for targeted ads which implies that both public and private attributes are utilized. The only exception is the use of IP address to determine the current location of users (i.e. *current city* and *current country*)[11] To build the FAP dataset we proceed as follows. We use a subset of six attributes: *gender, age, relationship status, Interested in, current city* and *current country*. First, for every Facebook profile in PubCrawl, we extract the set of revealed attribute's values (e.g., male, New York). Then, for each extracted attribute set, we retrieve the corresponding audience size from FAP. In addition, we collect statistics for each attribute and for all possible attribute values (e.g., all possible locations).

To collect the statistics from FAP, we have developed a customized automated browser based on the Selenium WebDriver[12] which sends requests to FAP with an acceptable rate. We share our collected dataset on: `http://planete.inrialpes.fr/projects/Adsstatistics`. Finally, it is interesting to note that Facebook deliberately reduces the granularity of estimated audience size by

---

[6] `http://goo.gl/GEJyH`

[7] Note that with the current privacy settings in Facebook, users can no longer opt-out of the Facebook public directory (`http://goo.gl/AufHN`).

[8] `http://www.facebook.com/advertising/`

[9] The advertiser can also target user's interests (e.g., beer and wine), interested-in (men or/and women), relationship, language, education and workplace.

[10] `http://goo.gl/wxcgX`

[11] We acknowledge that users connecting to the OSN service through e.g. proxies may introduce errors into the location distributions extracted from Facebook statistics compared to actual values.

[12] `http://seleniumhq.org/`

only returning "fewer than 20" for audience numbers lower than 20 users. In our methodology presented in the following section, we conservatively consider "fewer than 20" as being exactly 20 users.

3 Methodology for Computation of Public Profile Uniqueness

This section presents our proposed method to leverage the ad platform audience estimation provided by OSNs operators (focusing on Facebook) to estimate the uniqueness of users profiles. The uniqueness of a random variable is related to the amount of information that it carries and is commonly measured by Information Surprisal (IS) and entropy. These are probability based metrics, therefore to compute the IS or entropy associated with a user's profile, we need a way to estimate the probability to observe the set of attribute values comprising the profile, independently from the population of profiles we consider.

We first introduce the required theoretical background and notations used in this paper, followed by the description of our mechanism to estimate the profile uniqueness.

Table 1. Notations used in this paper

$\mathcal{A}$	A set of attributes $(a_1, a_2, ...)$.
$V(a_i)$	The values of attribute a_i.
$u^{\mathcal{A}}$	A profile defined over the attributes in $\mathcal{A}$.
pub, priv	Denote the public and private OSN profiles.
$\varnothing^{a_i}$	The set of profiles in which an attribute a_i is not available.
$P^{\varnothing}(a_i)$	Probability that the attribute a_i is not present in a profile.
$P^{rev}(\mathcal{A})$	Probability to publicly reveal every attribute in $\mathcal{A}$ knowing that they are present in the private profile.

3.1 IS and Entropy Computation for OSN Profiles

Table 1 introduces the notations used in this paper. We denote Tot as the set of *all* user profiles of a given OSN. Every user profile $u^{\mathcal{A}}$ in Tot comprises a set of k attributes $\mathcal{A} = (a_1, .., a_i, .., a_k)$. The profile $u^{\mathcal{A}}$ and all the associated variables may refer to a private, priv or a public, pub profile. An attribute a_i can be seen as a random variable, X^{a_i}, with values in $V(a_i) = \{x_1^{a_i}, x_2^{a_i}, .., x_n^{a_i}\}$ which follow a discrete probability function $P(a_i = x_j^{a_i})$. Similarly, a user's profile $u^{\mathcal{A}}$ defined on a set of k attributes $\mathcal{A}$ can be seen as the outcome of the k-dimensional random vector $(X^{a_1}, X^{a_2}, .., X^{a_k})$.

Information Surprisal and Entropy. IS or self-information measures the amount of information contained in a specific outcome of a random variable. IS of a user profile u which includes a set of attributes $\mathcal{A}$ is given by: $IS(u^{\mathcal{A}}) = -log_2(P(u^{\mathcal{A}}))$, with $P(u^{\mathcal{A}}) = \frac{|u^{\mathcal{A}}|}{|Tot|}$ *i.e.* the proportion of users having the values of $u^{\mathcal{A}}$ for the set of attributes $\mathcal{A}$. IS is measured in bits and every bit of surprisal adds one bit of identifying information to a user's profile and thus halves the size of the population to which $u^{\mathcal{A}}$ may belong.

Entropy, denoted $H(\mathcal{A})$, on the other hand, quantifies the amount of information contained in a random variable (here a multi-dimensional random vector). Entropy and IS are closely related, as entropy is the expected value of the information surprisal, i.e. $H(\mathcal{A}) = E(IS(u^{\mathcal{A}}))$. The entropy of a set of attributes $\mathcal{A}$ is given by: $H(\mathcal{A}) = -\sum_{u^{\mathcal{A}} \in V(\mathcal{A})} P(u^{\mathcal{A}})IS(u^{\mathcal{A}})$, and can be seen as the amount of information carried by the attributes in $\mathcal{A}$. E.g. a user in our public dataset of $4.45 \cdot 10^5$ profiles is unique if IS reaches $19bits$. For the Facebook population estimate, we use the value provided by FAP of 722 Million users, therefore a user profile is unique with an IS of $29bits$.

In the following, we focus on the use of the IS and entropy as a convenient way to measure the uniqueness of $u^{\mathcal{A}}$ amongst the OSN user profiles, which can be further utilised to derive the related level of anonymity of user profiles e.g. by using k-anonymity [24].

The freq Method – Is PubCrawl Enough. A naive approach to compute the uniqueness of profiles is to rely on an unbiased sample of the entire OSN's profiles, such as PubCrawl, and adopt a frequency-based approach (denoted freq) to provide a rough approximation of the probability $P(u^{\mathcal{A}})$, used to compute IS and entropy. Assuming we have a dataset of $|Tot|_{crawl}$ profiles, we can then estimate the probability of each profile simply as $\frac{|u^{\mathcal{A}}|}{|Tot|_{crawl}}$ if u^{A} belongs to PubCrawl, and 0 otherwise, where $|u^{\mathcal{A}}|$ represents the number of occurrences of $u^{\mathcal{A}}$ in PubCrawl. In the remainder of the paper, we will refer to the frequency-based computation of IS as IS_{freq}, computed by:

$$IS_{\text{freq}} = -log_2\left(\frac{|u^{\mathcal{A}}|}{|Tot|_{crawl}}\right) \tag{1}$$

This approach has at least two drawbacks. Unless all possible combinations of attribute values (as observed in the entire set of profiles Tot) are collected in the PubCrawl dataset, the frequency-based approach would provide a very coarse estimation and the IS value is lower bounded by the sample size of the dataset. Therefore if freq method is used, a maximum value of $19bits$ can be reached, as opposed to the maximum IS value of $29bits$, based on a full dataset. For the same reason, we would not be able to estimate the uniqueness of profiles corresponding to a set of attribute values that are not in PubCrawl. Whereas collecting such a large dataset is technically challenging, we propose a new methodology based on the audience estimation provided by the advertising systems of OSNs, which, as per Section 2, have access to the full set of private user's profiles.

3.2   Computing Profile Uniqueness from Advertising Audience Estimation

Ideally, to compute IS and entropy of a set of attributes $\mathcal{A}$ that are free from sampling bias and granularity constraints, we need to know the frequency of each profile, i.e. $|u^{\mathcal{A}}|$, in the full dataset Tot. Leveraging the audience size estimation from the OSN ad platform, we are now able to obtain such statistics that are based on the entire set of profiles. As discussed in Section 2.3, the audience size is estimated from both public and private profiles, resulting in overestimation of frequency for public profiles. This is because user's privacy policy limits the amount of information released on public profiles, which is often significantly lower than that available in private profiles and as such $|\varnothing^{\mathcal{A}}|_{pub} \gg |\varnothing^{\mathcal{A}}|_{priv}$.

However, the bias induced by users' privacy policy can be corrected by noting that: $|u^{\mathcal{A}}|_{pub} = |u^{\mathcal{A}}|_{priv} \cdot P^{rev}(\mathcal{A})$, where $P^{rev}(\mathcal{A})$ is the probability to publicly reveal attributes in $\mathcal{A}$ knowing that they are disclosed in the private profile.

In the following, we propose two methods to compute P^{rev}, trading off accuracy of the IS estimation and measurement costs (reflected by the number of requests to the ad platform) as discussed in Section 3.2. These methods are respectively denoted indep and dep, as they differ in the assumption regarding the mutual independence of the probabilities to reveal specific attributes.

The indep Method – Assuming Independence between the Likelihood of Revealing Specific Attributes. Here, we assume the probabilies to reveal selected attributes in user's public profile are mutually independent. The probability to reveal an attribute a_i, $P^{rev}(a_i)$, can then be obtained as follows.

First, we highlight the fact that the total number of public and private profiles is equal, $|Tot|_{pub} = |Tot|_{priv}$, i.e. there will always exist a corresponding public and private user's profile. We also observe that the number of public profiles in which an attribute is not present, i.e. $|\varnothing^{a_i}|_{pub}$, strictly depends on the probability that this attribute isn't publicly present, i.e. $P^{\varnothing}_{pub}(a_i)$, and as such: $|\varnothing^{a_i}|_{pub} = P^{\varnothing}_{pub}(a_i) \cdot |Tot|_{pub}$. Similarly, we can calculate the probability that an attribute is not disclosed in private profiles as: $|\varnothing^{a_i}|_{priv} = P^{\varnothing}_{priv}(a_i) \cdot |Tot|_{priv}$.

The number of profiles which define a_i as a private attribute but in turn hide this attribute from public access can then be obtained from equation (2):

$$|\varnothing^{a_i}|_{pub} - |\varnothing^{a_i}|_{priv} = P^{\varnothing}_{pub}(a_i) \cdot |Tot|_{pub} - P^{\varnothing}_{priv}(a_i) \cdot |Tot|_{priv} \tag{2}$$

On the other hand, we note that $(|Tot|_{priv} - |\varnothing^{a_i}|_{priv})$ accounts for the number of private profiles where a_i is revealed, and that $P^{rev}(a_i) \cdot (|Tot|_{priv} - |\varnothing^{a_i}|_{priv})$ is the total number of public profiles where a_i is revealed. Hence, the difference $(|Tot|_{priv} - |\varnothing^{a_i}|_{priv}) - P^{rev}(a_i) \cdot (|Tot|_{priv} - |\varnothing^{a_i}|_{priv})$ accounts for the number of users who have profiles where a_i is revealed on private but not on public profiles. We can then compute:

$$|\varnothing^{a_i}|_{pub} - |\varnothing^{a_i}|_{priv} = (1 - P^{rev}(a_i)) \cdot (|Tot|_{priv} - |\varnothing^{a_i}|_{priv}) \tag{3}$$

Hence from equations (2) and (3) we have:

$$P^{\varnothing}_{pub}(a_i) \cdot |Tot|_{pub} - P^{\varnothing}_{priv}(a_i) \cdot |Tot|_{priv} = (1 - P^{rev}(a_i)) \cdot (|Tot|_{priv} - |\varnothing^{a_i}|_{priv})$$

i.e.

$$P_{pub}^{\varnothing}(a_i) - P_{priv}^{\varnothing}(a_i) = (1 - P^{rev}(a_i)) \cdot (1 - P_{priv}^{\varnothing}(a_i))$$

$$P^{rev}(a_i) = 1 - \frac{P_{pub}^{\varnothing}(a_i) - P_{priv}^{\varnothing}(a_i)}{1 - P_{priv}^{\varnothing}(a_i)} \tag{4}$$

with $P_{pub}^{\varnothing}(a_i)$ is the probability that attribute a_i is not available in public profiles.

Note that $P_{pub}^{\varnothing}(a_i)$ is computed from PubCrawl: $P_{pub}^{\varnothing}(a_i) = \frac{|\varnothing^{a_i}|_{pub}}{|Tot|_{crawl}}$. On the other hand, $P_{priv}^{\varnothing}(a_i)$, the probability that attribute a_i is not available in private profiles, is computed from FAP dataset: $P_{priv}^{\varnothing}(a_i) = \frac{|\varnothing^{a_i}|_{priv}}{|Tot|_{priv}}$, where $|\varnothing^{a_i}|$ is not directly available but can be computed by using the aggregate number of profiles queried from the ad platform for all possible values of the attribute a_i:

$$|\varnothing^{a_i}|_{priv} = |Tot|_{priv} - \sum_{u^{a_i} \in V(a_i)} |u^{a_i}|_{priv}$$

For example, for the attribute *age*, the number of private profiles in which this attribute is not included can be obtained by: $|\varnothing^{age}|_{priv} = |Tot|_{priv} - \sum_{j=13}^{j=65^+} |u^{age=j}|_{priv}$ (*age* can be queried from FAP for a range of values between $13 - 65^+$, where 65^+ refers to the "Nomax" *age* attribute in FAP).

According to the assumed independence between attributes a_i, the probability to reveal every attribute in $\mathcal{A}$ is obtained by: $P_{indep}^{rev}(\mathcal{A}) = \prod_{a_i \in \mathcal{A}} P^{rev}(a_i)$

Finally, the IS estimation of public profile $u^{\mathcal{A}}$ using indepmethod can be computed as:

$$IS_{indep} = -log_2(\frac{|u^{\mathcal{A}}|_{priv} \cdot P_{indep}^{rev}(\mathcal{A})}{|Tot|_{priv}}) \tag{5}$$

The dep Method – Considering Dependence between the Likelihood of Revealing Specific Attributes. Although the indep method offers a simple way to compute $P^{rev}(\mathcal{A})$, the estimation of probabilities can be inaccurate if the independence assumption does not hold. To verify this, we evaluate the dependence between the likelihood of revealing specific attributes, based on our PubCrawl dataset. Table 2 shows the calculated probabilities to reveal each of the six example attributes: *gender, interested in, relationship, age, current city,* and *country* along the rows knowing that another attribute along the columns has been already revealed. Table 2 also includes the overall probability to reveal specific attributes $(1 - P_{pub}^{\varnothing}(a_i))$.

We can observe that there is indeed a correlation between probabilities to reveal specific attributes on public profiles. To properly assess the correlation between two attributes, the probability $P(a_i = revealed|a_j = revealed)$ must be considered jointly with $1 - P_{pub}^{\varnothing}(a_i)$, the overall probability to publicly reveal a_i. The highest dependance can be observed for users' interest (*Interested In*),

Table 2. Probabilities to reveal attribute a_1 (rows) knowing that attribute a_2 is shown on public profile, e.g. $P(gender = revealed|age = revealed) = 0.86$

$1 - P^{\varnothing}_{pub}(a_i)$	0.76	0.15	0.22	0.024	0.21	0.23
	Gend.	Int. In	Rel.	Age	City	Country
Gender	1.00	0.88	0.86	0.86	0.8	0.8
Interested In	0.17	1.00	0.46	0.35	0.24	0.24
Relationship	0.25	0.68	1.00	0.48	0.33	0.33
Age	0.01	0.04	0.03	1.00	0.03	0.03
City	0.23	0.34	0.32	0.41	1.00	0.97
Country	0.23	0.35	0.33	0.43	0.99	1.00

where users who reveal this attribute have a much higher probability to reveal any other attributes, *e.g.* the probability to reveal the *relationship status* when *Interested In* is revealed is over three times higher than the overall probability to reveal the *relationship status*.

We note that the values of the probabilities from Table 2 may be driven either by information sensitivity and user's privacy awareness, or simply by natural dependency between attributes from a semantic perspective, however the dependency analysis is out of the scope of this paper.

In the following, we present a methodology to compute $P^{rev}(\mathcal{A})$ taking into account the dependency between probabilities to reveal attributes. Addressing the dependency between $P^{rev}(a_i)$ with $a_i \in \mathcal{A}$, requires us to compute the frequency of a disclosed combination of these attributes.

$P^{rev}_{dep}(\mathcal{A})$ can be computed similarly to equation (4), as:

$$P^{rev}_{dep}(\mathcal{A}) = 1 - \frac{P^{\varnothing}_{pub}(\mathcal{A}) - P^{\varnothing}_{priv}(\mathcal{A})}{1 - P^{\varnothing}_{priv}(\mathcal{A})} \tag{6}$$

with $P^{\varnothing}_{pub}(\mathcal{A})$ and $P^{\varnothing}_{priv}(\mathcal{A})$, the probability that a set of attributes $\mathcal{A}$ is not available in a public (resp. private) profile being defined as : $P^{\varnothing}_{pub}(\mathcal{A}) = P(\bigvee_{a_i \in \mathcal{A}} a_i = \varnothing)$ and

$$P^{\varnothing}_{priv}(\mathcal{A}) = \frac{|Tot|_{priv} - \sum_{u^{\mathcal{A}} \in V(\mathcal{A})} |u^{\mathcal{A}}|_{priv}}{|Tot|_{priv}} \tag{7}$$

We note that the computation of $P^{\varnothing}_{priv}(\mathcal{A})$, and $P^{rev}_{dep}(\mathcal{A})$, requires the audience estimation of every value $u^{\mathcal{A}}$ in $V(\mathcal{A})$. This is implemented by requesting every possible set of attributes from the ad platform. For example, to obtain $P^{\varnothing}_{priv}(\mathcal{A})$ where $\mathcal{A} = \{Interested\ In, gender\}$, we query the ad platform for the number of profiles corresponding to all combinations of $gender = \{man, woman\}$ and $Interested\ In = \{man, woman, both\}$.

This represents an overhead in terms of measurement costs for the dep method, as compared to the indep method which requires a fewer number of queries. However, we note that this overhead may not be prohibitive, as the audience size estimation requests are sent to the ad platform only once for any set of attribute values.

The IS of the public profile $u^{\mathcal{A}}$, assuming the dependency of publicly revealing attributes, denoted by IS_{dep}, can be estimated as:

$$IS_{\text{dep}} = -log_2(\frac{|u^{\mathcal{A}}|_{priv} \cdot P_{\text{dep}}^{rev}(\mathcal{A})}{|Tot|_{priv}}) \tag{8}$$

4   Findings on Public Profile Attributes

In this section we study the uniqueness of users within the PubCrawl dataset, using the methodology presented in Section 3. We stress that our main focus is on the uniqueness resulting from the presence of specific attributes and attribute combinations in user's public profile, in line with our goal to have a generic mechanism for evaluating uniqueness. The impact of specific values is only presented for selected examples and used for illustration purposes and a comprehensive analysis based on attribute values is subject for further study.

4.1   Information Surprisal for a Single Attribute

We first consider the IS and entropy (average IS) for individual attributes, calculated using the freq and indep/dep methods and based on the PubCrawl and FAP datasets. Note that in this section, as we are calculating IS (and entropy) for a single attribute, the IS_{dep} and IS_{indep} (and corresponding entropy) values are identical, and denoted as $IS_{\text{dep/indep}}$.

Figure 1 (a)–(l) shows the PDF and CDF of the calculated IS values (y-axis, left and right hand side, respectively). For the sake of clarity, entropy H is included as a numerical value on top of each sub-figure (a)–(l). In addition, an absence of an attribute value may also be related to the profile uniqueness. To illustrate this, suppose that all users but one show their gender, as such the user who is hiding this information is *uniquely* identifiable since he has a unique "disclosing" pattern. Hence, the entropy is not only derived from the attribute value, but also from its presence (or absence). Therefore, we also show above each of sub-figures 1 (a)–(l) the number of users who hide a specific attribute and the associated IS as numerical values.

Overall, we can observe that there is a considerable difference in the range of IS and entropy values for selected attributes, with *gender* shown in Figure 1 (c)–(d) having the lowest and *current city* shown in Figure 1 (k)–(l) the highest entropy (and IS) values, respectively 1.3*bits* and 13.6*bits*. This follows the definitions of IS and entropy, which are related to the number of values an attribute may take and the number of users with specific attribute values, so higher information granularity and lower number of users for a specific value both result in a higher uniqueness.

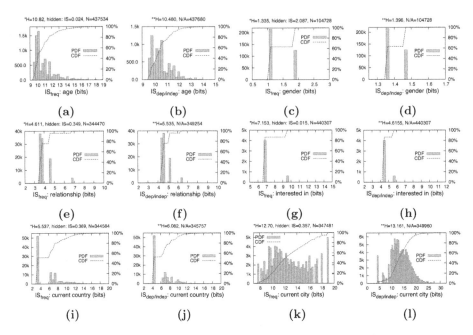

Fig. 1. PDF (left) and CDF (right) of *IS* values and Entropy *H* (shown on top of the sub-figures) for single attribute computed by IS_{freq} and $IS_{dep/indep}$ methods (note $IS_{dep} = IS_{indep}$ for single attribute). Values are shown for: *age, gender, relationship, interested in, current city* and *country*. * hidden IS=information surprisal for users hiding this attribute; N: number of users who hide this attribute; ** N/A: Total of N and the number of users for whom the disclosed attribute value is not available on FAP, e.g. age > 65

Age: Considering the $IS_{dep/indep}$ values in Figure 1 (b), we can observe that over 70% ($\sim$ 5.5k) of users have an IS value higher than $10.5bits$, corresponding to an identifying user group size of about 500k users. This supports the conclusion that *age* is an identifying attribute which users should be careful about disclosing. In line with this, the users who hide this attribute (representing 98.4% of the total population) are highly anonymous with an IS value of $0.024bits$. We remind the reader that each bit of information increase in IS halves population size to which the user represented by their public profile with corresponding IS may belong.

Gender: We can observe that Facebook users who reveal the *gender* attribute disclose less information (with average $IS_{freq} = 1.34bits$ shown in Figure 1 (c) and average $IS_{dep/indep} = 1.4bits$) shown in Figure 1 (d) than the users who consider this information private (with IS of $2.08bits$). In Section 4.4 we will show the impact of hiding a common combination of attributes, including *gender*. Note that this is a highly popular attribute, with around 75% of Facebook users disclosing it in their profiles. Consequently, the population that hides it displays a high IS value for this attribute.

Relationship Status: The calculated IS_{freq} shows, in Figure 1 (e)–(f), that for more than 60% of the users, the *relationship status* reveals a low value of IS, with $IS_{freq} = 4bits$ and $IS_{dep/indep} = 4.4bits$. Hiding this information has a very low associated IS of $0.35bits$. We note that only a subset of IS results are presented here, due to the supported values in FAP [13].

Interested In: We observe in Figure 1 (g)-(h) that the vast majority of profiles in our dataset do not disclose this attribute, resulting in a low IS value for such users ($0.24bits$). The average IS_{freq} values for users who display this attribute are moderate ($7.53bits$). Similarly, the $IS_{dep/indep}$ values also do not indicate high user uniqueness, with users being identifiable to within a group of 3.9 Million, only by revealing this single attribute.

Current Country: There is a wide range of IS values for users who have disclosed this attribute, as can be seen in Figure 1 (i)–(j). The average IS values are moderately high, with $IS_{freq} = 5.54bits$ and $IS_{dep/indep} = 6.08bits$, while hiding this information reveals very little ($0.4bits$). We note that 210 different countries appear as values for this attribute in our PubCrawl dataset. By examining the data values, we have observed that close to half of the total population (of those who have revealed their *current country*) have US as this attribute value. Therefore, the corresponding IS, for both IS_{freq} and $IS_{dep/indep}$ methods, is low with a value of around $4bits$. For all other users with the *current country* attribute set, the calculated IS values for both methods range between a moderate value of $7bits$ to $15bits$, a significant amount of information which increases the uniqueness of the user resulting in an identifiable group of around 22k users.

   When comparing the IS_{freq} and $IS_{dep/indep}$ values, we can observe a lower IS_{freq} for the US, indicating that the IS_{freq} method overestimates the representation of US in the IS calculation.

Current City: The large range of potential values for this attribute and correspondingly high potential to distinguish users intuitively flags it as sensitive personal information. We can observe from Figure 1 (k)–(l) that the average IS values are quite high, with $IS_{freq} = 12.7bits$ and $IS_{dep/indep} = 13.16bits$, while hiding this information reveals very little ($0.4bits$). Also, more than 75% of the users who display this attribute value lose more than $11bits$ (based on both IS_{freq} and $IS_{dep/indep}$ values). Note than more than 20% of the users in PubCrawl reveal this information, which makes it a valuable attribute for unique identification.

4.2 Expected Information Surprisal as a Function of the Number of Attributes

We now consider multiple attributes in IS calculations. Figure 2 shows the expected IS and the average entropy values calculated for a varying number of

---

[13] The Facebook Ads Platform (FAP) allows display of *relationship* statistic based only on a subset of values supported in Facebook profiles: single, married, engaged and in a relationship; queries based on divorced and widowed status are not supported.

attributes. We show the minimum, 25th percentile, median, 75th percentile and maximum of the IS values for all users. Both IS and entropy are averaged over all combinations of the selected number of attributes. As can be expected, increasing the number of disclosed attributes results in higher IS and entropy values and the corresponding amount of revealed information about the users. In Section 4.3, we will explore the specific attribute combinations which will result in higher IS values and therefore present a higher privacy risk for users.

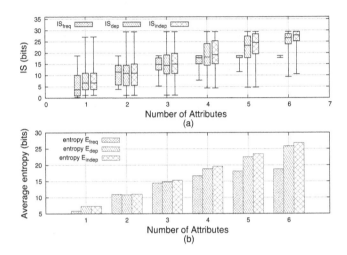

Fig. 2. (a) Information surprisal and;(b) Expected entropy for a varying number of attributes

Comparing the results obtained using the three calculation methods, in Figure 2 we can observe that the values of IS_{freq} are consistently lowest for all attribute combinations, followed by IS_{dep} and IS_{indep}. As previously discussed, IS_{freq} presents a rough calculation of values, which can be used as an indication of the relevance (to privacy) of both attributes and attribute combinations. Increasing the complexity of obtaining data (i.e. the number of required queries from FAP) increases the accuracy of the result. Consequently, the IS_{indep} values can be calculated for the combinations not present in the collected dataset. However, this method results in higher IS and entropy values than what is obtained by the more precise IS_{dep} method, which in turn requires the highest amount of information from FAP.

We can observe the most significant difference in the IS and entropy values obtained by different methods when considering the users who have revealed six attributes in Figure 2 (b). The IS_{indep} and IS_{dep} values reach an average entropy higher than $25bits$, representing a corresponding uniqueness within a set of 22 users, while the IS_{freq} value underestimates IS and only reaches $19bits$ of entropy with a significantly lower corresponding unique user set of around 1300 users. Although there may be a number of factors contributing to the low IS_{freq} values, the most relevant one is the dependency of the frequency-based entropy estimation on the used dataset. Regardless of the large size and the unbiased sample of the full dataset that we have used for IS_{freq} calculations, a number of combinations of attributes among the profiles may still be missing and will influence the result.

4.3 On the Relevance of Disclosed Attribute Combinations

We now consider the IS values for different attribute combinations, enabling us to draw conclusions about the dominant (and less relevant) parameters contributing to privacy loss. Figure 3 shows the cumulative distributions function of the IS, for: (a) IS_{freq}, IS_{indep} and IS_{dep} with all six attributes considered; (b)–(d) IS_{freq}, IS_{indep} and IS_{dep} for selected attribute combinations that were shown to have extreme (both low and high) IS values. Similarly to the results shown in Figure 2, we can observe that revealing 6 attributes (regardless of their values) results in a high IS value for the majority of users, e.g. observing the IS_{indep} and IS_{dep} CDF values in Figure 3 (a), more than 80% of the Facebook population with six disclosed attributes has IS of more than *22 bits*. This represents users uniquely identifiable within a set size of 170.

Considering specific attribute combinations shows the importance of having a carefully considered personal privacy policy with selectively disclosed attributes. Figures 3 (b)–(d) indicate that users should be wary of concurrently disclosing the combination of *age*, *gender* and *current city*, as this reveals almost as much information as as the total of six disclosed attributes. Although the granularity of our data is significantly lower (only age is available in the PubCrawl dataset, as compared to full birth date in the dataset used in [11,23]) and we study a different community (global and online, as compared to US only and based on Census data in [11,23]), our results are in line with the previously published studies on the uniqueness of demographics [11,23], which show that the combination of *gender*, *ZIP code* and *date of birth* has a very high uniqueness. We can observe in Figure 3 (c) that around 55% of users have IS of around *25 bits* and can therefore be identified in a set of 20 users. Further to this, around 18% of users can be uniquely identified, having the IS value of their public profile at *29 bits*. This represents a significant potential threat, as the corresponding number of Facebook users is around 7.7 Million for being identifiable to within a set of 20 and 2.7 Million for unique identification.

On the other hand, revealing the *gender* and *interested in* may not be harmful from a privacy perspective for most of the Facebook users (IS is less than *5 bits* for 90% of the users). Disclosing the *relationship status* along with the *gender* and *country* of residence reveals a higher amount of information, with more than 70% of users loosing at least 11*bits* of IS.

We note that, although our results have been derived for a sample of the Facebook population, the unbiased nature of the sample (as argued in Section 2) makes them applicable to the whole Facebook population.

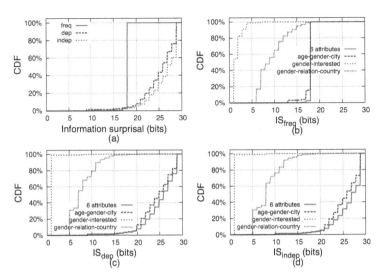

Fig. 3. Multiple attribute information surprisal distribution

4.4 Impact of Privacy Policy

This section complements the understanding of the key parameters that influence the resulting IS and entropy values of users' profiles, by studying the potential impact of users' privacy policy.

The likelihood to reveal specific attributes varies significantly amongst user profiles and there are some combinations that users may potentially prefer to hide (the dependency between probabilities to reveal pairs of attributes, shown in Table 2 partially illustrates this). One consequence of users' restrictive privacy policies is that other users revealing a rare set of attributes may be more easily identifiable, independently from the values of the attributes (i.e. regardless whether the attribute's values are rare). To verify this claim, we show in Figure 4 the information surprisal IS_{dep} as a function of the P_{dep}^{rev} (note the log scale on the x-axis).

As expected, the lower the probability with which users reveal attributes, the higher the value of IS_{dep}. However, to understand whether the increase in profile

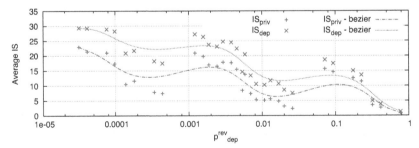

Fig. 4. Average IS as a function of P_{dep}^{rev}

uniqueness is contributed by the attributes' values themselves or by the hiding of these attributes (setting restrictive privacy policies), we also include in the figure the values of IS_{priv} denoting the information surprisal of the user's private profiles (i.e. reflecting the profile uniqueness contributed to by all the attribute values). IS_{priv} is obtained from the Facebook Ads platform statistics, for each set of attributes corresponding to a specific value of IS_{dep}. For improved clarity of the figure, we also plot the Bezier approximation of the data.

We again observe the general trend for both IS_{dep} and IS_{priv}: A decrease in P_{dep}^{rev} values corresponds to an increase in average IS_{dep} and IS_{priv} values, which illustrates that independently from the attributes values, the more a set of attributes is hidden the more unique the corresponding profiles will be. In other words, a restrictive privacy policy is also a good identifier of profiles. On the other hand, we highlight an interesting observation that can be made from Figure 4, which shows that the gap between the IS_{dep} and IS_{priv} also increases as P_{dep}^{rev} decreases. This result suggests that the more users tend to hide a combination of attributes, the more identifying this set of attributes will be for other users that do reveal it. The paradox here is that when a combination of attributes becomes rare, due to the majority of user's choice to hide it, it also becomes very identifying when revealed on other profiles.

5   Discussion

Potential Extensions. As previously mentioned, a frequency-based approach to compute profile uniqueness is dependent of the collected public profiles i.e. the captured set of combinations of attributes. It is therefore impractical, as e.g. it cannot estimate the uniqueness of a profile with a combination of attributes absent from the dataset. An alternative approach could be to adopt a smoothing-based (e.g. Good-Turing [9]) frequency estimation technique to predict the occurrences of the non-observed combinations of attributes, by relying on observed distributions of individual attributes. However, a smoothing-based method still cannot take into account the dependence between the likelihood of revealing specific attributes. In this work, we have deliberately chosen to focus on a fixed set of attributes. Our paper illustrates the extent to which the chosen attributes may identify the users revealing them. Although the results presented in this paper are only applicable to Facebook population, it is important to note that our methodology is general enough to be extended not only to other attributes but also to other online services providing similar statistics platforms, e.g. LinkedIn[14], Yelp[15]. We also did not include users' names in this study, as the application scenarios we consider focus on anonymized profiles where the identity of users is unknown.

Addressing Possible Limitations. We stress that in this work we did not investigate in depth the impact of attribute values on the uniqueness of attributes. In Section 4, we have observed the impact of some attribute values

---

[14] https://www.linkedin.com/ads
[15] http://www.yelp.com/advertise

(e.g. US in *current country*) on the IS values computed for a single attribute. Such analysis can and should be extended to other attributes and attribute combinations. In this paper we took a first step towards the analysis of profile uniqueness by examining the combinations of attributes that globally, across a selected OSN (i.e. considering a large sample of users), enable re-identification of profiles, independently from whether such re-identification would result from the rare combinations of attributes or the rarity of the attribute values.

Finally, as discussed in Section 2, our use of FAP as a statistical database for private attributes heavily relies on how these statistics are extracted by the OSN operator. Our methodology assumes that the audience statistics are only extracted from *private* profiles (which by definition include public profiles). While Facebook claims that indeed this is the case, a number of other indicators could be used to populate users' (missing) attributes. While this is possible in theory, we believe that this unlikely to happen in practice as the OSNs business model heavily depends on their credibility, and as such attribute inference, which is prone to errors, is unlikely to be adopted.

We acknowledge however that the accuracy of our profile uniqueness estimation is tightly linked to the accuracy of the statistics collected from the FAP.

6   Related Work

The study [23] was the first to show that seemingly coarse-grained information such as birth date or ZIP code, if combined, can uniquely identify their owners. Following studies such as [11] emphasize the same finding that: "few characteristics are needed to uniquely identify an individual." Our work complements these by proposing a way to measure the uniqueness of every public profile in a large Online Social Network (e.g. Facebook). Moreover, these studies differ from ours in at least two aspects. First, studied datasets are released by a third-party (e.g., government) who decides which attributes to disclose. This implies "a one rule fits all" approach, where all users are subject to the same privacy policy. Our work considers a dataset where each user has significant control over the revealed data. Second, the targeted populations are significantly different, i.e. US census data versus our world-wide and online population. Hence, our work can be viewed as a new technique to quantify user anonymity in a dynamic environment (e.g. OSNs), where both self-selected and crowd-driven privacy policies impact user anonymity. Moreover, while our approach does not explicitly address user re-identification and record linkage, it can be leveraged to assess the feasibility of such attacks. Specifically, the magnitude of the IS value of a user's profile (in the attacked dataset) can be directly related to the level of user's vulnerability to linkage. In the following, we discuss the works most closely related to ours.

Entropy has been used at various levels: to measure the fingerprint size of a web browser [8], of a host [25] or to track users across multiple services based on their usernames [21].

Privacy Leakage in OSN: Numerous works studied the information leakage resulting from OSN use. Krishnamurthy et. al. presented results for both

mobile [14] and fixed [15] OSNs. Irani et. al. [12] introduced the online social footprint, consisting of the aggregate information of OSN account owners. [6] investigated the factors that contribute to increased online social footprint, based on cross-OSN public profiles analysis. [22] investigated the evolution of user's privacy policies. A second line of research studied how to exploit publicly revealed information to infer hidden/private data using communi-
ties and friendship relations [18, 26] or profile information [5, 16]. Finally, [13]
leverages the micro-targeting platform provided by Facebook to target specific
users and infer their hidden information. After the publication of [13], several
targeting attributes were removed from the Facebook Ads platform and Facebook claims that an ad requires a minimum audience size of 20 to receive any
prints. We note that, to the best of our knowledge, none of the work related
to privacy issues in micro-targeting platforms considers them as a statistical
database.

De-anonymization: Multiple studies explored the feasibility of de-anonymizing
both statistical databases [2,3] and micro-data [4,19,20]. Different types of data
structures have been targeted, ranging from movie rating data [19] to social
network graphs [20]. All these studies share the same (attacker) goal, that is
to produce an efficient algorithm that leverages background knowledge to de-
anonymize users. Other works utilize obfuscation techniques like differential privacy to ensure privacy of publicly accessible (or released) data [7], [17]. Our
work can be seen as a possible aid to techniques which rely on obfuscation, as
it provides a measure of privacy and can potentially be utilized e.g. directly by
users to control their released data prior to obfuscation.

7   Conclusion

This paper proposes a novel method to compute the uniqueness of public profiles
independently from the dataset used for the evaluation. We exploit the Ads
platform of a major OSN, Facebook, to extract statistical knowledge about the
demographics of Facebook users and compute the corresponding IS and entropy
of user profiles. This is used as a metric to evaluate Facebook profile uniqueness
and hence the magnitude of the potential risk to cross-link a user with other
public data sources. Our findings highlight the relevance of choosing the right
combination of attributes to be released in user's public profile and the impact
of user's privacy policy on the resulting anonymity.

References

1. How microsoft and yahoo are selling politicians access to you,
   http://goo.gl/90d6j
2. Acquisti, A., Gross, R.: Predicting Social Security Numbers from Public Data.
   Proceedings of the National Academy of Sciences 106 (July 2009)
3. Blum, A., Dwork, C., McSherry, F., Nissim, K.: Practical Privacy: the SuLQ Framework. In: PODS (2005)

4. Calandrino, J., Kilzer, A., Narayanan, A., Felten, E., Shmatikov, V.: You might also like: Privacy risks of collaborative filtering. In: S&P (2011)
5. Chaabane, A., Acs, G., Kaafar, M.-A.: You Are What You Like! Information Leakage Through Users' Interests. In: NDSS (2012)
6. Chen, T., Kaafar, M.A., Boreli, R.: Is More Always Merrier? A Deep Dive Into Online Social Footprints. In: SIGCOMM WOSN (2012)
7. Dwork, C.: Differential Privacy: a Survey of Results. In: Agrawal, M., Du, D.-Z., Duan, Z., Li, A. (eds.) TAMC 2008. LNCS, vol. 4978, pp. 1–19. Springer, Heidelberg (2008)
8. Eckersley, P.: How Unique is Your Web Browser? In: Atallah, M.J., Hopper, N.J. (eds.) PETS 2010. LNCS, vol. 6205, pp. 1–18. Springer, Heidelberg (2010)
9. Gale, W.A., Sampson, G.: Good-turning Frequency Estimation without Tears. Journal of Quantitative Linguistics (1995)
10. Gjoka, M., Kurant, M., Butts, C.T., Markopoulou, A.: Walking in facebook: A case study of unbiased sampling of osns. In: INFOCOM (2010)
11. Golle, P.: Revisiting the Uniqueness of Simple Demographics in the US Population. In: WPES (2006)
12. Irani, D., Webb, S., Li, K., Pu, C.: Large Online Social Footprints–An Emerging Threat. In: SIAM CS&E (2009)
13. Korolova, A.: Privacy Violations Using Microtargeted Ads: A Case Study. In: CDMW (2010)
14. Krishnamurthy, B., Wills, C.: On the Leakage of Personally Identifiable Information via Online Social Networks. In: ACM SIGCOMM CCR (2010)
15. Krishnamurthy, B., Wills, C.E.: Privacy Leakage in Mobile Online Social Networks. In: SIGCOMM WOSN (2010)
16. Lindamood, J., Heatherly, R., Kantarcioglu, M., Thuraisingham, B.: Inferring private information using social network data. In: WWW (2009)
17. McSherry, F., Mironov, I.: Differentially Private Recommender Systems: Building Privacy into the Netflix Prize Contenders. In: KDD (2009)
18. Mislove, A., Viswanath, B., Gummadi, K.P., Druschel, P.: You are Who You Know: Inferring User Profiles in Online Social Networks. In: WSDM (2010)
19. Narayanan, A., Shmatikov, V.: Robust De-anonymization of Large Sparse Datasets. In: S&P (2008)
20. Narayanan, A., Shmatikov, V.: De-anonymizing social networks. In: S&P (2009)
21. Perito, D., Castelluccia, C., Kaafar, M.A., Manils, P.: How Unique and Traceable Are Usernames? In: Fischer-Hübner, S., Hopper, N. (eds.) PETS 2011. LNCS, vol. 6794, pp. 1–17. Springer, Heidelberg (2011)
22. Dey, R., Jelveh, Z., Ross, K.W.: Facebook Users Have Become Much More Private: A Large-Scale Study. In: WSSN (2012)
23. Sweeney, L.: Uniqueness of Simple Demographics in the U.S. Population. LIDAP-WP4 Carnegie Mellon University (2000)
24. Sweeney, L.: k-anonymity: a Model for Protecting Privacy. Int. J. Uncertain. Fuzziness Knowl.-Based Syst. (October 2002)
25. Yen, T.-F., Xie, Y., Yu, F., Yu, R.P., Abadi, M.: Host Fingerprinting and Tracking on the Web: Privacy and Security Implications. In: NDSS (2012)
26. Zheleva, E., Getoor, L.: To Join or not to Join: the Illusion of Privacy in Social Networks with Mixed Public and Private user Profiles. In: WWW (2009)

On the Acceptance of Privacy-Preserving Authentication Technology: The Curious Case of National Identity Cards

Marian Harbach[1], Sascha Fahl[1], Matthias Rieger[2], and Matthew Smith[1]

[1] Distributed Computing & Security Group, Leibniz Universität Hannover, Germany
{harbach,fahl,smith}@dcsec.uni-hannover.de
[2] Institute of Sociology, Leibniz Universität Hannover, Germany
mrieger@ish.uni-hannover.de

Abstract. Many attempts have been made to replace the ubiquitous username-and-password authentication scheme in order to improve user security, privacy and usability. However, none of the proposed methods have gained wide-spread user acceptance. In this paper, we examine the users' perceptions and concerns on using several alternative authentication methods on the Internet. We investigate the adoption of the new German national identity card, as it is the first eID-enabled card with dedicated features to enable privacy-preserving online authentication. Even though its large-scale roll-out was backed by a national government, adoption rates and acceptance are still low. We present results of three focus groups as well as interviews with service providers, showing that preserving privacy is just one of several factors relevant to the acceptance of novel authentication technologies by users as well as service providers.

Keywords: Privacy-Preserving Authentication, Usable Security, National Identity Cards, eID, Technology Acceptance, Social Factors.

1 Introduction

Username-and-password remains the prevalent mechanism for every-day online authentication. While services and usage patterns evolve, this authentication mechanism has been largely unchanged throughout the history of Information Technology. Of Alexa's top 100 websites[1], most sites offer additional features behind a username-and-password-based login or require a login to access the site at all. Users have learned to accept this form of authentication [12] and use creative schemes to tailor the system to their needs [20]. They use separate pseudonyms for different services and choose password strength according to several criteria [8,10,12] to maintain appropriate levels of privacy and security.

---

[1] cf. http://www.alexa.com/topsites/global

E. De Cristofaro and M. Wright (Eds.): PETS 2013, LNCS 7981, pp. 245–264, 2013.

Several papers (e. g. Bonneau [2], Dhamija et al. [7], Jakobsson and Dusseault [14], as well as Perito et al. [23]) and incidents[2] have shown problems with the current practice and numerous alternative online authentication schemes have been proposed to overcome these [6,3]. However, none of these schemes has found wide-spread adoption yet. In an extensive survey of proposals for improving online authentication, including password managers, graphical, cognitive, phone-based or biometric schemes, as well as paper and hardware tokens, Bonneau et al. [3] found that none of the 35 mechanisms under investigation came close to the benefits username-and-password currently offers to users. While security was generally better with the alternatives, deployability was always worse and with many usability also suffered. While hardware tokens such as smartcards could provide strong security, these mechanisms have high deployment costs for both users as well as providers and additionally require the user to carry an object around.

A trend of the past years could, however, be able to alleviate these major downsides of physical tokens. Many countries are currently in the process of rolling out or have already rolled out national identity cards with a means to access identity information electronically (electronic identity, eID). Acuity Market Intelligence projects that 85 % of identity credentials issued annually will be electronically readable by 2015 and four out of five countries will be issuing eID-capable identity cards[3]. This implies that, soon enough, a considerable portion of Internet users will be carrying a token, capable of electronic authentication, that has already been paid for.

While the USA have not yet announced plans to introduce eID documents, 24 of the 27 countries in the European Union have already deployed or plan to deploy eID cards[4]. The European Commission is actively supporting digital identities and aims to adapt legislation to increase adoption[5]. Since national eID cards are compulsory in many states, they have the potential to gain broad acceptance as an electronic means of identification. Additionally, these cards are often habitually carried by their owners and hence, similar to mobile phones, are more or less ubiquitously available. Currently, available solutions in countries such as Estonia or Belgium aim at proving real identities for public services/eGovernment as well as eCommerce and eBanking applications. This focus has however limited their applicability as a general online authentication mechanism.

In this paper, we analyze the most recently introduced eID scheme: the nPA (*Neuer Personalausweis*, new personal identity card) launched by the German government in November 2010. This official document is the first to include privacy-preserving features beyond proving one's true identity electronically.

---

[2] http://www.h-online.com/security/news/item/
Password-leaks-bigger-than-first-thought-1614516.html,
http://arstechnica.com/security/2012/08/passwords-under-assault/

[3] http://www.acuity-mi.com/GNeID_Report.php

[4] http://www.epractice.eu/en/community/eureid/view_resources/
Factsheet-on-the-electronic-Identity-at-pan-European-level—May-2012

[5] http://www.euractiv.com/infosociety/
brussels-wants-identities-eu-cit-news-512833

While the nPA can reliably verify that a person lives in a certain city or is of certain age without disclosing the actual address or age, it can also generate a provider-specific pseudonym directly on the card. It is therefore the first national ID card technically capable of substituting username and password without any threat to the user's privacy. With the nPA, the user can choose to login without disclosing identifying information or with dependable proof of his true identity.

In this paper, we aim to analyze which factors inhibit the acceptance of the nPA in order to support the development of future Internet authentication alternatives. The core contributions of this paper are as follows:

- We investigate the users' perceptions in using a new system for everyday online authentication and identify motivations for, as well as barriers to adoption.
- We present technical and social factors that influence the acceptance of alternative authentication mechanisms in general and how privacy-preserving features compare to these other factors.
- We shed light on the needs and perceptions of businesses offering such an alternative authentication mechanism for their online services.
- We provide recommendations that can support the deployment of future large-scale authentication systems.

To the best of the authors' knowledge, this paper is the first to discuss the role of national ID cards in the search for a username-and-password alternative. While we do not suggest that the nPA is the best possible solution, we believe that smartcards issued by national governments can provide a viable basis for more security and good usability in online authentication. Germany's efforts to maximize privacy in their eID scheme is an important step towards enabling wide-spread use.

2   Related Work

There is a long line of research on technology acceptance in general from the area of Information Science and Business. A recent model for security technology acceptance of Herath et al. [13] explicitly addresses IT security services. They combine the well-known and widely discussed Technology Acceptance Model (TAM) of Davis et al. for general technology acceptance [5] with Liang et al.'s Technology Threat Avoidance Theory (TTAT, [19]), which relates avoiding security threats to coping behavior and Protection Motivation Theory.

In Herath et al.'s model, a user's motivation to adopt a mechanism depends on three main factors: threat appraisal, internal coping mechanism appraisal and external coping mechanism appraisal. This means that the user needs to decide to what extent a threat applies to him or her, evaluate whether or not he or she can cope with this threat using existing – or internal – mechanisms, and whether or not another – or external – mechanism is suited to cope with this threat. In the model, the appraisal of external mechanisms mainly depends on the two main factors outlined in TAM: Ease of Use and Usefulness. Additionally, Herath et al. posit that concerns about the violation of privacy play an important role in this process. In this work, we identify the components of this model in the real-world nPA deployment, propose additional factors relevant to Internet authentication systems and provide a detailed understanding of the users' underlying decisions.

The challenges for digital identity management have been discussed in general by Dhamija and Dusseault [7] and for eID in particular by Grote et al. [11]: While, according to both these works, the eID functionality of Germany's new ID card has flaws, the scale of the roll-out and the implicit trust in a government-issued document offers an opportunity to investigate the acceptance of a real world deployment above and beyond purely academic proposals.

Sun et al. [26] found that users need more privacy control, better integration and trust in the involved parties when using OpenID. Dey and Weis [6] presented an approach to add pseudonymity to OpenID federations and Perito et al. [23] demonstrated that it can be easy to link pseudonymous and public user profiles across services to gain additional information about users. These papers argue for the need of privacy in online authentication, which the German eID scheme is able to offer to a wide audience.

Other past work has also investigated user acceptance of authentication technology: Jones et al. described users' general perceptions of authentication mechanisms [15] and Weir et al. compared the usability of two-factor authentication for eBanking applications [28]. Both papers discuss interesting individual insights into users' decisions on authentication technology, but, in contrast to this paper, do not attempt to paint a more general picture.

Furthermore, the EU projects PRIME and PrimeLife addressed many facets of digital identity management. In particular, Wästlund et al. [27] analyzed several UI metaphors to communicate privacy-enhancing features in identity management to users. This paper complements this work by investigating the role of privacy-preserving features in the light of other acceptance factors in a real-world, large-scale roll-out of a new authentication system.

3   The German eID Scheme

The information accessible on the new German ID card includes first and surnames, title, address, date of birth and document type.[6] Additionally, the card can provide functionality for residence verification, age verification and pseudonymous identification without disclosing the actual information [9]. It is the first eID-enabled document in the EU to provide such functionality while including privacy and security as major design goals.

Margraf [21] lists the requirements adhered to during the design process of the new card, including encryption of all transmitted data, explicit user consent to all data transmission, authentication of the communication partner, transmission of necessary data only, inability to monitor the card holder's activities, revocation of lost cards, the ability to provide pseudonymous authentication, and

---

[6] Currently, the only document type is the ID card itself. However, if eID functionality was integrated into other types of official documents (e.g. driver's licenses), this field would indicate which type of document the user is authenticating with.

the infeasibility of identifying the user and the card through unique properties. These requirements are met using a number of technologies (Card-Verifiable Certificates, Extended Access Control) and organizational processes. The interested reader is referred to the technical specification [4]. In the following, we present the online authentication process using the nPA from a user's perspective and will also briefly outline the requirements for a service provider.

To authenticate to a service, the user needs three things: his ID card with the corresponding PIN, a certified card reader and a certified client software to run the necessary protocols. The card reader costs between 30 Euro for a basic reader without keypad and 160 Euro for a model with display and keypad. This is also one of the major disadvantages of the scheme that we will discuss below. A free reference implementation of the software, called the *AusweisApp*, is currently available from the Ministry of the Interior. Although the need to memorize a PIN may cause problems common to password schemes, users would only need to remember one PIN instead of a larger number of passwords. Users are also used to remembering PINs through the use of banking cards and mobile phones.

When the authentication process begins, the service provider requests authentication using an eID service run by a certified third party. The eID service initiates the cryptographic protocols and establishes a secure channel between the card and the service provider. The user is then presented with information on the service he is authenticating to by the AusweisApp and can also verify which of the information on his nPA will be shared. The user enters the personal PIN code and the client software securely delivers the desired information to the service provider.

In order to use eID functionality, a service provider needs to apply for an authorization certificate at the Federal Office for Authorization Certificates. The provider's need for identifying data will be evaluated by examining her business processes. Service providers get an authorization certificate if they can demonstrate a need for the requested information in compliance with privacy regulations. Only this certificate then enables a service to read exactly the approved data items from the ID card. Currently, 85 providers hold one or more authentication certificates. It is important to note that almost any service provider would be able to get a certificate to access the pseudonymous identification function, which does not disclose any personal information to the service provider but only allows to re-identify a returning user.

In November 2011, after one year, 8 million citizens already received an nPA[7]. Our interview partners from public offices (see below) estimated based on internal statistics that in September 2012 up to 15 million German citizens were in possession of a new eID-capable personal identity card. These sources also reported that only about 20 to 30 % of card holders have their eID capabilities activated, since eID can be deactivated upon request when the user picks up the card; we discuss this further below.

---

[7] http://www.personalausweisportal.de/SharedDocs/Pressemitteilungen/DE/
2011/Jahrestag.html

4   Problem Statement

In this paper, we provide a new perspective on the question of improving online authentication and replacing username-and-password. In this line of research, the interplay of social and technological factors is often neglected. We believe this is a critical oversight which is hampering the search for new and better authentication systems. In this work, we offer new insights by examining the users' perceptions of a large-scale and secure scheme that they already have access to but are reluctant to put into use. By investigating the acceptance of a mechanism that is currently being deployed at a national scale, we have a unique opportunity to analyze what keeps users from adopting an alternative means of online authentication after a dependable, privacy-preserving and secure infrastructure was created by the government and to reveal the social as well as technological factors of their non-acceptance.

For the new German ID card and its eID functionality, Poller et al. [24] postulate one main obstacle for adoption: an imbalanced cost-benefit ratio for both businesses and end-users causing a chicken-and-egg problem. Without useful and relevant services, users shy away from investing both time and money into a new technology. Yet, without a significant user base, service providers do not implement and invest in a new technology that would only replace existing mechanisms, which currently fit their needs well. In the model of Herath et al., this means that users decide that their internal mechanism (i. e., the existing username-and-password practice) is suited to cope with the given situation, which negatively affects the appraisal of a new external mechanism.

Beyond this problem, we find that there are further factors that influence the appraisal of an external authentication mechanism, including governmental involvement, social factors and comfort or a feeling of control. In our study, we address the following questions from a user's perspective and also present the providers' views of a novel authentication technology:

1. Which technical and social factors influence authentication behavior?
2. Which deficiencies do users see in their current authentication practice?
3. How do users perceive alternative authentication mechanisms?
4. Why do users not adopt the available eID mechanism?
5. How does the official nature of the identity card influence their perceptions?
6. Which types of services can benefit from using eID?
7. Which measures might increase eID adoption?

5   The User Perspective

eID adoption has been very slow in Germany from the first day of its introduction. While many people have received a new identity card, only few services offer eID authentication. Due to the users' lack of practical experience, we chose to conduct focus groups to explore the perceptions of eID technology from the user perspective.

5.1   Method

Focus Groups are a variation of a group interview that "collects data through group interaction" [22]. Focus groups have been repeatedly used to "study perceptions, thoughts, and emotions" [1,18]. Even though the use of focus groups for HCI research has been subject to discussion [25], they can extract information where other qualitative tools fail [22]. We chose this method to collect a number of factors that might influence participants' perceptions of a rather unknown topic. Since eID mechanisms are not part of common knowledge or commonly used yet, a traditional interview might have intimidated participants. Krueger and Casey [16] suggest that interviewing participants in a homogeneous group can elicit more open and honest responses, since participants realize that others also do not know so much. Additionally, discussion and interaction between participants can raise points that would otherwise not have been addressed.

We stress that our focus groups yield purely qualitative results from which we aim to extract a set of possible factors, perceptions and influences. While group dynamics may have biased the views of individual participants, we believe that we present a superset of issues that influence the acceptance of authentication technology. Furthermore, due to the nature of focus groups, we do not analyze individual views or draw quantitative results from this analysis and will therefore not report counts for the issues raised [16]. Investigating the relative importance of each of the discovered factors will be subject to future work.

We invited 971 students from a university mailing list using a screening survey that collected demographics, technical experience and Westin's Privacy Index [17]. The invitation advertised a "group discussion on daily usage behavior on the Internet" that would last 90 to 120 minutes and offered 20 € of compensation. Students of computer science, information technology and electrical engineering did not receive the invitation in order to prevent anyone from disrupting the groups by being perceived as experts. This is an important consideration for focus groups, especially when discussing a topic where most people would readily defer to experts, since a single individual with extended knowledge can diminish the variety of responses and make participants reluctant to offer own explanations [16]. We received 76 complete responses to our screening survey. According to indicated time preferences, we randomly selected 4 groups of eight people and sent out invitations for the first three. We ran three of the four planned groups before we reached saturation (i. e. there were no more new aspects discussed in the third group).

Of the 24 people invited to the three groups, 18 attended. A demographic overview can be found in Table 1. According to their Westin index, none of our participants belonged to the privacy unconcerned category, which includes individuals that do not feel that their privacy is threatened by current practice and that the benefits of disclosing data outweighs the potential dangers. Most belonged to the pragmatist category, that would "weigh the potential pros and cons of sharing information" [17]. The remaining eight participants belonged to the so-called Privacy Fundamentalists, who are most protective of their privacy. We accept the lack of unconcerned participants for our study, considering

Table 1. Overview of demographics for focus group participants. Technical Experience is rated on a scale from (1) "I often get help from others" to (5) "I often help others". The Privacy column shows the counts for the three categories of the Westin Index: Privacy Fundamentalists/Pragmatists/Unconcerned

Group #	N (female)	Age (sd)	Tech. Exp. (sd)	Privacy
1	6 (4)	23.5 (1.4)	3.0 (1.1)	2/4/0
2	7 (3)	24.1 (4.9)	3.6 (1.3)	2/5/0
3	5 (1)	23.0 (3.2)	3.2 (0.8)	4/1/0
Overall	18 (8)	23.6 (3.4)	3.3 (1.1)	8/10/0

that privacy pragmatists and fundamentalists represent those groups that would express most concerns on using eID.

During the focus groups, one moderator and one assistant were present. The moderator actively engaged with the participants while the assistant monitored recording and took notes. We tried to create a comfortable atmosphere, using a small conference room and unobtrusive recording equipment. The moderator used informal language and first names during the entire process and encouraged direct exchanges between the participants. Name tents with first names were placed on the table to increase direct interaction.

During discussion, the moderator interfered as little as possible: he steered the conversation towards the topics of interest and encouraged participation from less active subjects. We prepared a questioning route, that gradually lead participants from their current behavior and use of authentication mechanisms towards their attitudes and perceptions of eID technology in the new German ID card. In the debriefing session, participants unanimously reported that they perceived the group as a non-threatening and interesting experience. Some participants indicated that they wished that they could participate in such groups on a regular basis to learn more about their own online security.

5.2   Results

The three sessions each lasted between 96 and 115 minutes. The audio recordings were transcribed and statements subsequently assigned to the general questions introduced above. To present the results, we report statements from all three sessions grouped by these questions. Participants are referred to as P1 to P18.

Current Authentication Behavior. We began the discussion by asking for the participants' general habits on the Internet, before focusing on their authentication practice. Most participants stated that they use two to ten passwords, assigned to "service categories". The categories having the strongest passwords were often linked to attributes such as "important", "serious" or "official".

Online banking was treated with particular care by participants: they use unique and longer passwords that they generally do not write down. Participants also reported that they may actively hide security tokens used for online banking, because, in their opinion, usernames and passwords are easily obtainable by attackers. Generally, participants reported that the consequences that might arise from a compromised account affects how they choose their passwords.

Next, we asked for password management behaviors. Those who had few passwords mostly kept them in memory, while those with a larger number often used a paper-based list. Mixing passwords and usernames or using password patterns while changing individual components was also mentioned: "I have five to six passwords, two to three usernames and I mix those and then I have to remember that. Very easy. It's good for your memory [and] good for your security" (P9).

Participants also used password managers and also synced them between devices. Interestingly, many participants did not know of password managers before the discussion. P16 indicated that he has a password manager which is secured by a fingerprint reader on his laptop, but doesn't use it because he does not care enough about security.

Deficiencies of Current Authentication Practices. When queried how secure participants feel with their current practices, participants generally said that they were confident with their schemes and that they did not see immediate problems. They offered several justifications: friends and family manage their passwords in a similar fashion and have not had problems thus far; it is too frustrating to forget a password; too many passwords get confusing or hard to manage; and fewer passwords help to keep authentication fast and effortless. P6 said: "It's not that I have to think about my password, instead it simply comes without thinking [...] I type it and then I am already logged in."

Yet, a few deficiencies of current practice came up as well. Participants mentioned that password recovery fails if the registered email address is no longer accessible. P17 reported that she does not feel safe anymore, even though she increased her password strength after being hacked. In later stages of the discussion, a number of participants seemed to realize that they might not be as safe as they thought. P3 said: "you get used to it, it works well, it's easy and you stick with it. Maybe until you have a bad experience." And P10 first stated: "I think [I'm safe]. Because, someone would tell me [if I wasn't]". However, at a later point, she said "I don't feel safe anymore with my two passwords". We suspect that some participants needed external motivation to think about their online security and did not do so before participating in the focus group. But, at the same time, some participants also offered that "when I get back home, I will be too lazy [to change anything]" (P18).

Perceptions of Alternative Authentication Mechanisms. We went on to ask about alternative authentication mechanisms, including using password managers and Facebook's OAuth (described by the moderator as the "Login with Facebook"-Button).

Password managers were perceived to be too complicated. This mirrors the fact that few participants had used or known about a password manager before. Participants also mentioned that saved passwords implied lost control: They stated that if someone had access to the password database, that person could get into all the services contained in the database, for example by "hacking" or using the computer when the password database is unlocked. P2 said: "I don't use it, because this way I still have, no matter whether or not it's actually true, the feeling that I am still in control, when I really log in and that it is not an automated process." On the other hand, other participants said that they value the comfort offered by password managers higher than avoiding possible threats.

Participants also criticized being dependent on a password manager. They were afraid that they may not be able to access accounts from other locations or that they may forget the master password and therefore loose access to all accounts. Additionally, participants felt that a cloud-sync feature is unsafe because passwords are transmitted over the Internet. They also added that passwords can be compromised when the password list is on a smartphone that gets lost.

Using Facebook's OAuth had participants afraid that their information is shared with Facebook, because they felt that "they already have enough access to many things" (P11). Participants also said that another mechanism is unnecessary since passwords work fine. They also doubted the mechanism's security, because they don't understand what happens behind the scenes. A loss of control was also mentioned, since Facebook might lock users out or go out of business.

Overall, participants expressed a general reluctance to adopt new services or technologies on the Internet, due to a feeling of insecurity and negative reports in the news. They showed no interest or motivation to gain an understanding of a new mechanism. P1 said that she would rather not use something "simply because then I can have a bit more security for myself". Others believed that they stick with their mechanisms because this is what they are used to and that they might be using other mechanisms, such as password managers, if they had been using them "from the beginning". Participants stated that they would wait for a mechanism to gain popularity, especially with their friends or family, before switching. They were also not ready to relinquish any comfort or mobility offered by their current practice.

Barriers to eID Adoption. After discussing these more or less well known password alternatives, the moderator introduced the eID functionality of the nPA and stated that this technology might be able to comfortably fulfill their authentication needs. They were told that given the necessary hardware and adoption by service providers, one would simply need to hold the ID card to a reader and enter a PIN to be securely authenticated and that it was even possible to achieve this without disclosing any personal data using the pseudonymous identity functionality. Additionally, the moderator stated that this would generally be more secure than using passwords, that the system is backed by the federal government and that service providers need to demonstrate a need for every piece of personal information before being granted access to this information on a cryptographic level. In order to keep the introduction short, the moderator used simple terms and examples. Participants had a chance to ask questions in order to gain a basic understanding of the technology. Comparing different ways of describing eID functionality was not a goal of this study, as we intended to assess the participants' perceptions of this new technology.

After answering all questions, the moderator elicited participants' attitudes towards this means of authentication. Participants saw the potential of this mechanism, even though most of them had not previously heard of all possible use cases. In each group, there was at least one person that had already received the new ID card. However, especially the pseudonymous identification functionality was not known to any of the participants.

When thinking about using their nPA for authentication, participants struggled to judge the mechanism because they did not know anyone using it, even though 10 to 15 million of German citizens have already received the nPA. Therefore, participants offered: "one would need to wait and find out whether or not it makes things easier and quicker" (P13). The following issues were raised during the discussions.

No added value/no motivation: Participants did not know of any relevant services offering authentication with the nPA, hence they saw no obvious advantages. Additionally, there was no motivation to adopt the new mechanism: "Honestly, I can't be bothered to look into [eID-based authentication], because I am happy with the way it is" (P10). Participants also didn't know of any services that cannot be used without the nPA.

Complexity: Participants stated that they would need a person they trust to tell them what it does and to convince them that it works. Those participants do not think that they can make that judgement by themselves. Participants also stated that they found the mechanism to be complicated. Participants said they would trust in expert reviews in computer magazines or similar reporting as well as positive experiences of family members, friends, or colleagues.

Control: Participants mentioned a fear that the system might behave in an unexpected way and that the user cannot react in a timely fashion: "[...] I'd rather have everything in my own hands" (P11), "I might forget to do something, to uncheck a box [...] I'm afraid of my own negligence" (P18). Participants also stated that they cannot be sure which information is actually transmitted.

Comfort: Participants suggested that fetching the card before being able to authenticate might be harder than relying on a password manager or one's memory. Participants were ready to make the extra effort if they saw an improvement for their security or if they do not have to remember passwords anymore. Additionally, the current need to have a dedicated card reader was also repeatedly mentioned as a barrier to adoption. Participants generally valued the comfort of using smartphones, tablets and laptops anywhere very highly and objected to the idea of reducing that comfort for purely security-related reasons.

Insufficient information: Participants who already had received the new ID card reported that the person at the public service office was not able or willing to convince them of the advantages of using eID functionality with their nPA. However, this is a crucial moment for the acceptance of this technology, since users are asked if they want to deactivate the functionality when the card is picked up.

Cost: Participants stated that the card readers are too expensive and offer too little added value to justify that cost at the moment.

Influence of the Official Nature of the Identity Card. Participants found that a national ID card is one of the most important documents one has and it is perceived to be "a very personal document" that might not be suitable for "playing around on the Internet" (P4). They also stated the possible contradiction between being pseudonymously authenticated while using an ID card with their photo on it. Participants said, that the card is already important enough and by using it for online authentication as well, potential trouble increases when the card is lost. They also stated that they would be reluctant to use an official identity card for every-day purposes, because, in the worst case, "the government is the one that is able to storm into your house at 5 a.m. with machine guns" (P8).

On the other hand, participants also stated that the official nature actually makes the system more trustworthy for them. One reason given as an explanation referred to the immediate uproar in the media, when a government project has problems. Participants also felt that companies, such as Google or Facebook, can get away more easily with morally doubtful practices. On the whole, participants attributed less motivation for gathering personal information to the government than to companies.

Potential eID Use. When participants where queried for which services they would more readily use eID-based authentication, they stated that they would use their ID cards on services with "an official character". This includes eGovernment services, eBanking and (health) insurance companies. Participants felt that the institutions behind these services are "more tightly bound by legal regulations" (P4) or more personal, because users know where they reside or because they have had a face-to-face encounter with someone from these institutions before. Additionally, participants would be willing to use eID with services "that already have most of [their] information anyway" (P18), such as eCommerce sites. Less "official" or less important services, such as Facebook or Skype, caused more reluctance, since these can already be used more or less anonymously if desired: "For everything that concerns my personal life and that is fun or offers entertainment, [...] I don't find [authenticating with my ID card] very useful" (P14). Participants mentioned that if they were using eID with their nPA for some services regularly, they would probably use it for all of their services.

The possibility to increase security through stronger authentication and identity assurance was acknowledged by participants. They stated that using your ID card would enable them to prove "that it is really me" (P14). However, the discussion on the utility of eID technology for different services showed that many participants, including those who had already received an nPA, had not fully understood the concepts behind eID authentication. The nPA's eID functionality was mostly reduced to how ID cards are currently used and especially the privacy-preserving pseudonymous identification functionality was quickly forgotten during the discussion. When the moderator reminded participants of that possibility and reintroduced the concept, participants would often not see an immediate advantage in the light of other issues (see above).

Measures to Make eID More Attractive. Towards the end of each session, the moderator asked for suggestions to improve the acceptance of eID features in the new identity card. Participants offered that "if, at some point, almost everyone used [eID-based authentication], then this might mean that it works [...] that it comes with a certain level of security" (P3). Participants said that testing the process and getting hands-on experience might help them to appreciate it. Participants also wished for proper and understandable information on this topic as well as having a competent person to talk to about the implications of using eID features. As noted above, participants that already had an eID-enabled card did not receive any guidance on the features and benefits of their new identity card, even after explicitly asking questions at a public service office. Participants added that banks generally explain the security measures for online banking at length and that they would appreciate such a practice for eID functionality as well.

Generally, an increased public presence and more active marketing were mentioned as possibilities to increase public awareness. Furthermore, participants postulated that services that offer benefits through using eID might make the system worthwhile. Participants felt a need for information that was not satisfied by current practice and said they would expect television, newspaper and magazine reports about a beneficial technology. They also proposed dedicated informational events, that offer opportunities to ask questions and discuss possible uses with peers.

Additional Issues. During the discussions, participants expressed that they treat the Internet as a generally insecure medium and that they therefore, for example, do not use online banking at all. Among other comments, P5 believed that password managers "surely could be hacked by someone". P9 said: "I don't believe that there will ever be perfect security on the Internet. Whether you use [an alternative mechanism] or continue using passwords [...] there are vulnerabilities everywhere." Another participant believed that there will be a way to circumvent any security system at some point in time.

We suspect that participants were not ready to invest in additional security for their Internet conduct because they don't see that this will have personal benefits in the end. Also, they might not see that security consists of several independent parts and that increasing security for one of those parts might make them safer. They do not differentiate between security risks occurring because of, for example, authentication mechanisms, lax privacy policies or missing transport security. It appears that, in several cases, this is all simply attributed to the generally unsafe Internet.

Information in Public Service Offices. Because participants stated that they were not able to obtain enough information from public service offices, we visited three of these and acted as if we were unsure of whether or not to switch to an eID-enabled ID card. During our visits, we had similar experiences as our participants: clerks were not able to answer our questions or, in one case, even refused to, saying that she was the wrong person to talk to. Yet, she was also not able to name a person to contact on this issue either. We were always referred to a brochure with a phone number inside. We tried calling that number and finally got qualified answers to the questions a layperson might have. This premium rate phone service of the Federal Ministry of the Interior can cost up to 0.42 Euro per minute.

Summary. Overall, the focus groups identified a number of problems for the acceptance of new authentication mechanisms in general and eID-based authentication in particular. The factors identified by our investigation also indicate that there are barriers to adoption beyond the chicken-and-egg-problem suggested by Poller et al. [24]. The results of the focus groups allow a more detailed understanding of the external mechanism appraisal factors presented by Herath et al. [13]: Complexity at a technical or process level and a reluctance to find out more can lead to a perceived loss of control, a lack of understanding and hence decreased motivation for adoption. Participants repeatedly stated that they do not understand technology and have no interest in it either. Hence, in order to promote privacy-preserving authentication technology to users, several other factors need to be considered before privacy benefits are appreciated. For example, our participants valued comfort and mobility highly and were not ready to relinquish any in order to gain security or privacy.

6   The Business Perspective

The focus groups confirmed the problem of a lack of relevant services that either offer an added value or demonstrate how the nPA can make daily life easier. For trans-national companies, such as Amazon, Facebook, or Google, there is obviously little reason to adopt a technology that is currently limited to a small portion of their customer base. Yet, if many governments were to agree on a global eID standard, identity cards could be used throughout the Internet. Today, there still are several national businesses that could benefit from eID technology. Banks, insurance companies and eCommerce providers would have a means to reliably establish a customer's true identity and almost any service that has a login functionality could offer an optional eID-based authentication to appear innovative or increase customer comfort, security and privacy.

According to the list of authorized services[8], 85 public offices, companies and other businesses have been certified to access eID functionality on the nPA, of which 45 actually publicly offer eID authentication in their online processes[9]. Eight of these are not related to eGovernment applications, banks or insurance companies, which traditionally need reliable identity validation. Of these eight, only two do not request any personal information and rely on the pseudonymous functionality. The remaining 40 service providers with authorization certificates would be able to offer and use eID services but chose not to. Of those, only three sought privacy-preserving functionality, such as anonymous age verification, while the rest requested the authorization certificate to reliably establish users' true identities.

---

[8] http://gsb.download.bva.bund.de/VfB/npavfb.pdf – last access: 20.09.2012
[9] http://www.ccepa.de/onlineanwendungen – last access: 20.09.2012

This indicates that, from the business perspective, a large number of service providers see eID features as a means to establish customer identities or to fulfill legal requirements. Using eID features of the nPA as a general means of authentication, especially in its pseudonymous form, is only adopted by two service providers after two years of being available. To find out more about the service provider's reluctance, we sent requests for phone interviews to selected companies.

6.1   Method

In August 2012, we sent emails to 51 service providers on the list of authorized services, leaving out infrastructure providers that mainly obtained authorization for operational or testing purposes. Additionally, we cherry-picked 26 well-known Internet services that reside in Germany and have a primarily German audience, but have not requested or received an authorization certificate yet. We asked for an interview partner that could comment on the use of eID technology in their online services. 15 providers responded, including four companies that did not appear on the authorized services list. Of the 15 respondents, two were banks, two were insurance providers, one offered free-to-play online games, one was a consulting firm that offered brochures behind a login, one a mobile phone network operator, one offered cloud-based end-user security solutions and the remaining seven were either local administrations or communal service providers for local administrations. It is important to note that eight respondents had participated in an official application testing call, run by the Ministry of the Interior prior to the nPA roll-out.

The semi-structured interviews were conducted over the phone, lasted an average of 24 minutes ($sd = 11.1$ min, ranging from 7 to 51 minutes), and were recorded with the interviewees' consent. Again, we were interested in extracting a set of factors that play a role in their decision making process and will explore the quantitative relationships in future work. The central statements of each interview were extracted into an analysis sheet by the interviewer during a subsequent replay of the recording.

6.2   Results

Our results confirm that there is little motivation for adopting eID features through non-governmental providers. Two insurance companies stated that they provide nPA-based authentication for marketing purposes and to appear customer-friendly. The two banks we spoke to stated that the functionality currently offered by the nPA does not suffice to replace the systems currently in use to authorize bank transactions, due to the lack of a qualified electronic signature (QES). While the nPA is prepared to support QES, QES certificates have not been pre-installed on the cards by the government and could also not be purchased by customers at the time of the interviews. Furthermore, strict regulations for financial transactions and bank processes require identification that cannot be provided by the nPA. German banks have also been issuing smartcards for home/online banking since 1998. The two interviewees representing banks referred to the acceptance of those smartcards and stated that, while providing considerably stronger security features, these cards were never widely adopted. When presented with an (almost) free alternative having lower security, private bank customers usually opt for the lower cost, according to the interviewees' statements.

Public administrations generally saw eGovernment as a necessary tool for the future, to streamline administrative processes and to offer convenient services for citizens. Since the new ID card was introduced with eGovernment as a central focus, its features are suitable for these applications. Yet our interview partners indicated that, even for eGovernment, several regulatory hurdles still need to be addressed in order to be able to provide more processes online, that currently still require citizens to visit offices in person. While two of the responding administrations were in the process of actively promoting the benefits of eID technology and the nPA, others were waiting for more adoption in the public or stronger internal demand before committing to the technology.

Many of the respondents stated that they saw problems for user acceptance due to expensive or bulky card readers, lengthy and complicated user authentication procedures as well as an insufficient UI in the current version of the eID software. They also saw a need for killer applications, that demonstrate the benefits and a relevance for day-to-day use. Those who offered eID-based authentication treated this mechanism as an optional offer, that a user can but does not need to use. Obtaining an authorization to use eID features did not cause any problems. As a side note, some respondents also gave accounts of trying to increase authentication security by dictating stronger password requirements. These restrictions soon needed to be reverted since customers started to complain.

The general idea of eID technology, being able to prove actual identities in the digital realm, was welcomed by all respondents. Many stated that they expect many day-to-day processes and interactions to take place on the Internet in the future and that there is a need for effective identity management. Some respondents also acknowledged that the government can effectively roll out such an infrastructure and that users will trust in such a system eventually. Others, however, were skeptical whether or not a fear of surveillance will keep users from trusting the eID features in a personal identity card, considering computer surveillance and telecommunications data retention laws being controversially discussed.

6.3 Summary

Interviews with service providers showed that card features enabling providers to offer additional functionality online are either not available yet (e. g. QES) or do not meet current legal norms. Companies see little need to replace existing mechanisms beyond legal requirements to establish a customer's true identity in some cases. This is especially true since providers indicated that their customers are happy with the current practice as well. The provider interviews also confirmed the chicken-and-egg problem. Without useful and relevant services, users will not adopt a new authentication mechanism, and without user adoption, service providers will not invest in the mechanism. For the future however, service providers indicated a need for reliable digital identity management.

7 Discussion

In our study, we found that our participants struggled to fully appreciate the benefits of the nPA's privacy-preserving features. In addition to the findings of Wästlund et al. [27], we also found that several other factors play an important role for the users' acceptance and can actually overlay the perception of privacy-preserving features. Overall, our results show that, in order to deploy novel authentication systems on a large-scale, effort particularly needs to be invested into service, marketing and guidance for users. This is true for both existing as well as for new systems. Surprisingly, after spending a very large amount of money on deploying an eID scheme, these factors were neglected by the German government and consequently the beneficial technical properties, such as the privacy-preserving nature of the card's authentication facilities, did not receive public attention.

Getting users' to accept new authentication technology is also an important precursor for adoption by businesses: the interviews showed that many companies are ready to adopt new technology in order to satisfy the customers' demands. Yet, legal hurdles and insufficient technical features can also keep providers from adopting authentication technology. Similar to the users, enhancing their customers' privacy was not a central concern when evaluating a new authentication mechanism.

In terms of Herath et al.'s acceptance model for security technology, our results show that under the given circumstances, users do not see a problem with their current authentication method (internal mechanism appraisal). Even though the new mechanism does offer beneficial properties (external mechanism appraisal) with respect to ease of use (e. g. no more need to remember passwords), usefulness (e. g. no need to remember many passwords), and privacy, other factors tip the scales in favor of the existing mechanism. Users indicated that perceived relevance, complexity and control of the mechanism as well as cost, comfort and trust in the system play an important role when judging a novel authentication technology.

7.1 Recommendations

The roll-out of the German nPA demonstrated effects of news coverage on acceptance factors in the first few weeks after a large-scale roll-out: During the introduction of the nPA, one of the first reports in the media covered how the system is vulnerable to an attack. During the focus groups, this attack vector always came up as an argument for the vulnerability of the scheme and eventually had to be clarified by the moderator, since it was only a minor issue arising due to the use of cheap card readers. To avoid this negative influence on the users' perceptions, the entire digital ecosystem of a novel authentication mechanism needs to be considered during its design.

Our results also discovered social influences for the adoption of novel authentication mechanisms: Our participants stated that they would wait until there are immediate benefits, a more wide-spread trend towards the new technology and adoption by trusted third parties, such as friends, families or experts. This goes beyond a personal appraisal of an external mechanism in Herath et al.'s model and shows that users rely on several sources to inform their decisions. Concerning the use of an eID-based online authentication solution, trust can be bipolar due to the involvement of the government. While a share of users trusts the mechanism more, others have less trust for the same reason. Future efforts should keep users' perceptions of an infrastructure or identity provider in mind.

On the technical side, novel authentication technology needs to create an effortless integration into daily workflows. While current eID systems require card readers to function, our results suggest that this additional piece of hardware is a stumbling block. Users repeatedly mentioned that the need to buy a card reader or to carry one around would keep them from adopting eID technology for daily use. We hence believe that future authentication systems need to leverage smartphone and NFC technology in order to satisfy these needs. Additionally, the complex and therefore opaque nature of the technology and processes underlying the nPA's eID functionality raised the users' concerns and is in conflict with their need for control.

Another important consequence of our findings is to establish user awareness: It is necessary to make users realize the problems of the authentication systems they currently use and to stress the security benefits of a new mechanism. While security experts know the shortcomings of passwords and benefits of novel privacy-preserving technologies, our results indicate that many users feel quite safe with their current practice of using a handful of memorized passwords. Users also showed little differentiation in terms of risks to their security on the Internet. Without knowing how certain practices can improve their security, the users will show less motivation to adopt them. Adding educational material about previous systems and current problems to information campaigns and instructing staff to provide better support is thus a simple action that can be taken to improve adoption.

8   Conclusion

In this paper, we examined users' perceptions and concerns on using alternative authentication methods on the Internet. As a concrete example, we studied why the German nPA is receiving little adoption as a privacy-preserving authentication technology, even though the technical capabilities are excellent. The take-away of this paper is that "simply" ensuring that enough users get a smartcard through a national roll-out is not enough to kick-start adoption. Non-technical factors, such as the availability of information and reviews as well as services with everyday relevance, are necessary prerequisites for the adoption of authentication mechanisms. On a technical level, our results suggest that non-intrusive technology is a central factor when designing a new authentication system. We also argue that it is necessary to find a balance between technical complexity and transparency, in order to satisfy the users' need for control. A final result of the user studies shows that users need to be made more aware of immediate problems with their current practice, since unlike "functional" technology there is a lack of intrinsic motivation to adopt new authentication technology.

References

1. Agosto, D.E., Abbas, J., Naughton, R.: Relationships and Social Rules: Teens' Social Network and Other ICT Selection Practices. JASIST 63(6), 1108–1124 (2012)
2. Bonneau, J.: The Science of Guessing: Analyzing an Anonymized Corpus of 70 Million Passwords. In: 2012 IEEE Symposium on Security and Privacy, pp. 538–552 (2012)
3. Bonneau, J., Herley, C., van Oorschot, P.C., Stajano, F.: The Quest to Replace Passwords: A Framework for Comparative Evaluation of Web Authentication Schemes. In: 2012 IEEE Symposium on Security and Privacy, pp. 553–567 (2012)
4. Bundesamt für Sicherheit in der Informationstechnik. Technical Guideline TR-03127 (2011)
5. Davis, F.D., Bagozzi, R.P., Warshaw, P.R.: User Acceptance of Computer Technology: A Comparison of Two Theoretical Models. Management Science 35(8), 982–1003 (1989)
6. Dey, A., Weis, S.: PseudoID: Enhancing Privacy in Federated Login (2010), http://www.pseudoid.net
7. Dhamija, R., Dusseault, L.: The Seven Flaws of Identity Management: Usability and Security Challenges. IEEE Security & Privacy Magazine 6, 24–29 (2008)
8. Florencio, D., Herley, C.: A Large-Scale Study of Web Password Habits. In: Proceedings of the 16th International Conference on World Wide Web. ACM (2007)
9. Fromm, J., Hoepner, P.: The New German eID Card. In: Fumy, W., Paeschke, M. (eds.) Handbook of eID Security: Concepts, Practical Experiences, Technologies, ch. 11, pp. 154–166. Publicis (2011)
10. Gaw, S., Felten, E.W.: Password Management Strategies for Online Accounts. In: Proceedings of the Second Symposium on Usable Privacy and Security. ACM (2006)
11. Grote, J.H., Keizer, D., Kenzler, D., Kenzler, P., Meinel, C., Schnjakin, M., Zoth, L.: Vom Client Zur App. Technical report, Hasso Plattner Institute (2010)
12. Hayashi, E., Hong, J.: A Diary Study of Password Usage in Daily Life. In: Proceedings of the SIGCHI Conference on Human Factors in Computing Systems. ACM (2011)
13. Herath, T., Chen, R., Wang, J., Banjara, K., Wilbur, J., Rao, H.R.: Security Services as Coping Mechanisms: An Investigation Into User Intention to Adopt an Email Authentication Service. Info Systems J. (2012)
14. Jakobsson, M., Chow, R., Molina, J.: Authentication - Are We Doing Well Enough? IEEE Security &Privacy Magazine 10(1), 19–21 (2012)
15. Jones, L.A., Antón, A.I., Earp, J.B.: Towards Understanding User Perceptions of Authentication Technologies. In: Proceedings of the ACM Workshop on Privacy in Electronic Society. ACM (2007)

16. Krueger, R.A., Casey, M.A.: Focus Groups: A Practical Guide for Applied Research, 4th edn. Sage Publications (2009)
17. Kumaraguru, P., Cranor, L.F.: Privacy indexes: A Survey of Westin's Studies. Technical Report CMU-ISRI-5-138, Carnegie Mellon University (2005)
18. Kurniawan, S., Mahmud, M., Nugroho, Y.: A Study of the Use of Mobile Phones by Older Persons. In: CHI Extended Abstracts on Human Factors in Computing Systems. ACM (2006)
19. Liang, H., Xue, Y.: Avoidance of Information Technology Threats: A Theoretical Perspective. MIS Quarterly 33(1), 71–90 (2009)
20. Malone, D., Maher, K.: Investigating the Distribution of Password Choices. In: Proceedings of the 21st International Conference on World Wide Web. ACM (2012)
21. Margraf, M.: The New German ID Card. In: Pohlmann, N., Reimer, H., Schneider, W. (eds.) ISSE 2010: Securing Electronic Business Processes (2011)
22. Morgan, D.L.: Focus Groups as Qualitative Research. Sage Publications (1996)
23. Perito, D., Castelluccia, C., Kaafar, M.A., Manils, P.: How Unique and Traceable Are Usernames? In: Fischer-Hübner, S., Hopper, N. (eds.) PETS 2011. LNCS, vol. 6794, pp. 1–17. Springer, Heidelberg (2011)
24. Poller, A., Waldmann, U., Vowé, S.: Electronic Identity Cards for User Authentication – Promise and Practice. IEEE Security & Privacy Magazine 10(1), 46–54 (2012)
25. Rosenbaum, S., Cockton, G., Coyne, K., Muller, M., Rauch, T.: Focus Groups in HCI: Wealth of Information or Waste of Resources? In: CHI Extended Abstracts on Human Factors in Computing Systems. ACM (2002)
26. Sun, S.-T., Pospisil, E., Muslukhov, I., Dindar, N., Hawkey, K., Beznosov, K.: What Makes Users Refuse Web Single Sign-On? An Empirical Investigation of OpenID. In: Proceedings of the Seventh Symposium on Usable Privacy and Security. ACM (2011)
27. Wästlund, E., Angulo, J., Fischer-Hübner, S.: Evoking Comprehensive Mental Models of Anonymous Credentials. In: Camenisch, J., Kesdogan, D. (eds.) iNetSec 2011. LNCS, vol. 7039, pp. 1–14. Springer, Heidelberg (2012)
28. Weir, C.S., Douglas, G., Carruthers, M., Jack, M.: User Perceptions of Security, Convenience and Usability for Ebanking Authentication Tokens. Computers & Security 28(1-2), 47–62 (2009)

Author Index

AlSabah, Mashael   143
Andrés, Miguel E.   82

Baldimtsi, Foteini   40
Bauer, Kevin   143
Bindschaedler, Vincent   123
Boneh, Dan   185
Bordenabe, Nicolás Emilio   82
Boreli, Roksana   225
Borisov, Nikita   205
Burleson, Wayne P.   40

Cao, Guohong   60
Chaabane, Abdelberi   225
Chatzikokolakis, Konstantinos   82
Chen, Terence   225

Elahi, Tariq   143

Fahl, Sascha   245
Fifield, David   185

Geddes, John   164
Gentry, Craig   1
Goldberg, Ian   143
Goldman, Kenny A.   1

Halevi, Shai   1
Harbach, Marian   245
Hinterwälder, Gesine   40
Hopper, Nicholas   164
Houmansadr, Amir   205
Hubaux, Jean-Pierre   123
Huguenin, Kévin   123

Jansen, Rob   164
Julta, Charanjit   1

Kaafar, Mohamed-Ali   225
Kohlweiss, Markulf   19

Learned-Miller, Erik   103
Levine, Brian Neil   103
Li, Qinghua   60
Liberatore, Marc   103
Lysyanskaya, Anna   40

Maurer, Ueli   19

Nakibly, Gabi   185

Onete, Cristina   19

Paar, Christof   40
Palamidessi, Catuscia   82

Raykova, Mariana   1
Rieger, Matthias   245

Smith, Matthew   245
Soroush, Hamed   103
Sung, Keen   103

Tackmann, Björn   19
Tournoux, Pierre Ugo   225

Venturi, Daniele   19
Vratonjic, Nevena   123

Wichs, Daniel   1

Zenger, Christian T.   40